Prentice Hall

AMERICA
HISTORY OF OUR NATION

Interactive Reading and Notetaking Study Guide

PEARSON

Boston, Massachusetts   Chandler, Arizona   Glenview, Illinois   Upper Saddle River, New Jersey

Cover image: iStockphoto.com

Pearson, Prentice Hall, and Pearson Prentice Hall
are trademarks, in the U.S. and/or other countries,
of Pearson Education, Inc., or its affiliates.

ISBN-13: 978-0-13-251694-5
ISBN-10: 0-13-251694-2
3 4 5 6 7 8 9 10 V016 13 12 11 10

Contents

Chapter 29: Challenges for a New Century (1980–Present)....... 437

How to Use This Book

The *Interactive Reading and Notetaking Study Guide* was designed to help you understand the content in your *America: History of Our Nation* textbook. It will also help you build your notetaking and historical-thinking skills. Please take the time to look at the next few pages to see how it works.

The unit opener page prepares you to read and think about the chapters in each unit. Section Summary pages provide an easy-to-read summary of each section.

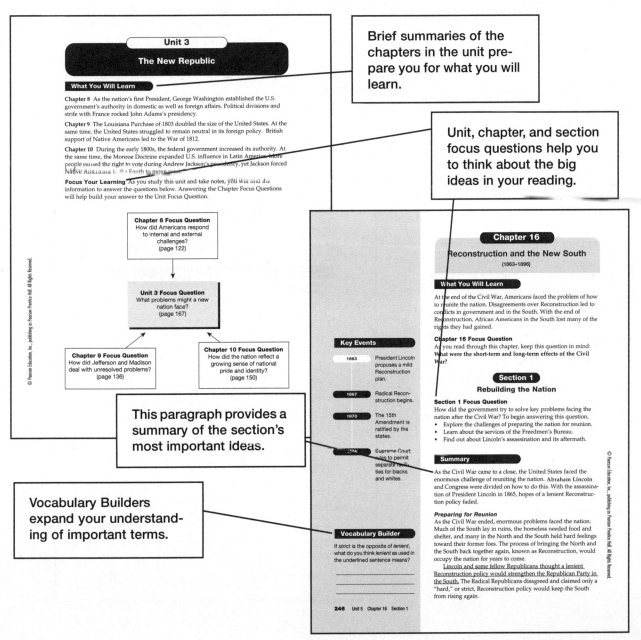

Brief summaries of the chapters in the unit prepare you for what you will learn.

Unit, chapter, and section focus questions help you to think about the big ideas in your reading.

This paragraph provides a summary of the section's most important ideas.

Vocabulary Builders expand your understanding of important terms.

Unit 3
The New Republic

What You Will Learn

Chapter 8 As the nation's first President, George Washington established the U.S. government's authority in domestic as well as foreign affairs. Political divisions and strife with France rocked John Adams's presidency.

Chapter 9 The Louisiana Purchase of 1803 doubled the size of the United States. At the same time, the United States struggled to remain neutral in its foreign policy. British support of Native Americans led to the War of 1812.

Chapter 10 During the early 1800s, the federal government increased its authority. At the same time, the Monroe Doctrine expanded U.S. influence in Latin America. More people earned the right to vote during Andrew Jackson's presidency, yet Jackson forced Native Americans in the South to move west.

Focus Your Learning As you study this unit and take notes, you will find the information to answer the questions below. Answering the Chapter Focus Questions will help build your answer to the Unit Focus Question.

Chapter 8 Focus Question
How did Americans respond to internal and external challenges?
(page 122)

Unit 3 Focus Question
What problems might a new nation face?
(page 167)

Chapter 9 Focus Question
How did Jefferson and Madison deal with unresolved problems?
(page 136)

Chapter 10 Focus Question
How did the nation reflect a growing sense of national pride and identity?
(page 150)

Chapter 16
Reconstruction and the New South
(1863–1896)

What You Will Learn

At the end of the Civil War, Americans faced the problem of how to reunite the nation. Disagreements over Reconstruction led to conflicts in government and in the South. With the end of Reconstruction, African Americans in the South lost many of the rights they had gained.

Chapter 16 Focus Question
As you read through this chapter, keep this question in mind: What were the short-term and long-term effects of the Civil War?

Section 1
Rebuilding the Nation

Section 1 Focus Question
How did the government try to solve key problems facing the nation after the Civil War? To begin answering this question,
• Explore the challenges of preparing the nation for reunion.
• Learn about the services of the Freedmen's Bureau.
• Find out about Lincoln's assassination and its aftermath.

Summary

As the Civil War came to a close, the United States faced the enormous challenge of reuniting the nation. Abraham Lincoln and Congress were divided on how to do this. With the assassination of President Lincoln in 1865, hopes of a lenient Reconstruction policy faded.

Preparing for Reunion

As the Civil War ended, enormous problems faced the nation. Much of the South lay in ruins, the homeless needed food and shelter, and many in the North and the South held hard feelings toward their former foes. The process of bringing the North and the South back together again, known as Reconstruction, would occupy the nation for years to come.
Lincoln and some fellow Republicans thought a lenient Reconstruction policy would strengthen the Republican Party in the South. The Radical Republicans disagreed and claimed only a "hard," or strict, Reconstruction policy would keep the South from rising again.

Key Events

1863 — President Lincoln proposes a mild Reconstruction plan.

1867 — Radical Reconstruction begins.

1870 — The 15th Amendment is ratified by the states.

1896 — Supreme Court rules to permit separate facilities for blacks and whites.

Vocabulary Builder

If *strict* is the opposite of *lenient*, what do you think *lenient* as used in the underlined sentence means?

_____
_____
_____

246 Unit 5 Chapter 16 Section 1

Questions and activities in the margin help you recall information from the summary. Section Notetaking Study Guides help you take notes as your read your textbook.

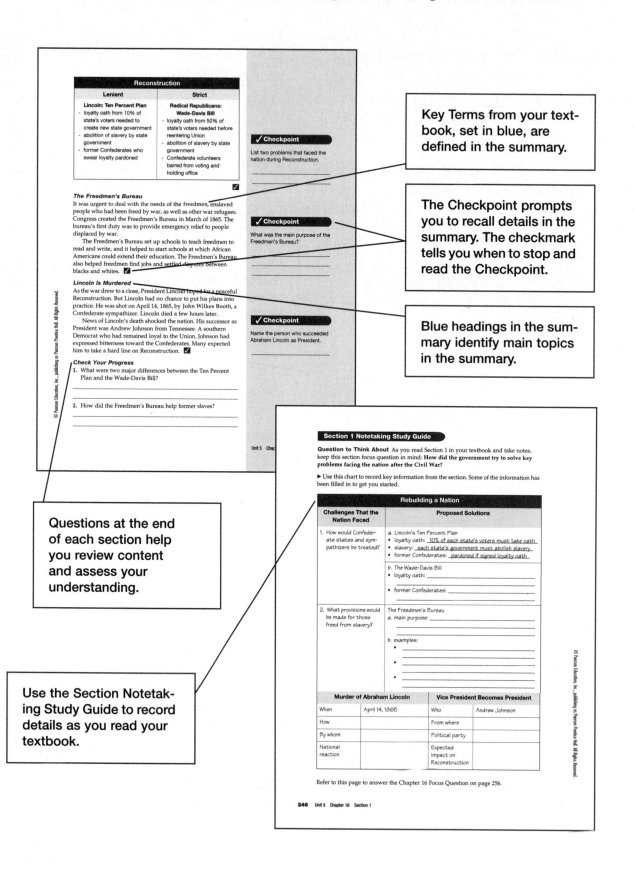

Reconstruction	
Lenient	**Strict**
Lincoln: Ten Percent Plan - loyalty oath from 10% of state's voters needed to create new state government - abolition of slavery by state government - former Confederates who swear loyalty pardoned	**Radical Republicans: Wade-Davis Bill** - loyalty oath from 50% of state's voters needed before reentering Union - abolition of slavery by state government - Confederate volunteers barred from voting and holding office

✓ Checkpoint

List two problems that faced the nation during Reconstruction.

_____

_____

☑

The Freedmen's Bureau

It was urgent to deal with the needs of the freedmen, enslaved people who had been freed by war, as well as other war refugees. Congress created the Freedmen's Bureau in March of 1865. The bureau's first duty was to provide emergency relief to people displaced by war.

The Freedmen's Bureau set up schools to teach freedmen to read and write, and it helped to start schools at which African Americans could extend their education. The Freedmen's Bureau also helped freedmen find jobs and settled disputes between blacks and whites. ☑

✓ Checkpoint

What was the main purpose of the Freedmen's Bureau?

_____

_____

Lincoln Is Murdered

As the war drew to a close, President Lincoln hoped for a peaceful Reconstruction. But Lincoln had no chance to put his plans into practice. He was shot on April 14, 1865, by John Wilkes Booth, a Confederate sympathizer. Lincoln died a few hours later.

News of Lincoln's death shocked the nation. His successor as President was Andrew Johnson from Tennessee. A southern Democrat who had remained loyal to the Union, Johnson had expressed bitterness toward the Confederates. Many expected him to take a hard line on Reconstruction. ☑

✓ Checkpoint

Name the person who succeeded Abraham Lincoln as President.

_____

_____

Check Your Progress

1. What were two major differences between the Ten Percent Plan and the Wade-Davis Bill?

_____

_____

2. How did the Freedmen's Bureau help former slaves?

_____

_____

Unit 5   Chap

Key Terms from your textbook, set in blue, are defined in the summary.

The Checkpoint prompts you to recall details in the summary. The checkmark tells you when to stop and read the Checkpoint.

Blue headings in the summary identify main topics in the summary.

Questions at the end of each section help you review content and assess your understanding.

Use the Section Notetaking Study Guide to record details as you read your textbook.

Section 1 Notetaking Study Guide

Question to Think About As you read Section 1 in your textbook and take notes, keep this section focus question in mind: **How did the government try to solve key problems facing the nation after the Civil War?**

▶ Use this chart to record key information from the section. Some of the information has been filled in to get you started.

Rebuilding a Nation	
Challenges That the Nation Faced	**Proposed Solutions**
1. How would Confederate states and sympathizers be treated?	a. Lincoln's Ten Percent Plan • loyalty oath: _10% of each state's voters must take oath_ • slavery: _each state's government must abolish slavery_ • former Confederates: _pardoned if signed loyalty oath_
	b. The Wade-Davis Bill • loyalty oath: _____ • former Confederates: _____
2. What provisions would be made for those freed from slavery?	The Freedmen's Bureau a. main purpose: _____ b. examples: • _____ • _____ • _____

Murder of Abraham Lincoln		Vice President Becomes President	
When	April 14, 1865	Who	Andrew Johnson
How		From where	
By whom		Political party	
National reaction		Expected impact on Reconstruction	

Refer to this page to answer the Chapter 16 Focus Question on page 256.

Questions help you to assess your progress. Chapter Notetaking Study Guides help you to pull together the notes you took for each section and focus on important ideas.

Chapter 16 Assessment

Directions: Circle the letter of the correct answer.

1. The case of *Plessy* v. *Ferguson* provided the legal basis for
   A poll taxes.
   B sharecropping.
   C impeachment.
   D segregation.

2. Which of the following was a result of the Ku Klux Klan's campaign of violence?
   A Andrew Johnson was impeached.
   B Rutherford B. Hayes was elected President.
   C The South became more industrialized.
   D Fewer African Americans voted.

3. Slavery and forced labor were banned by the
   A Emancipation Proclamation.
   B Freedmen's Bureau Bill.
   C Thirteenth Amendment.
   D Reconstruction Act of 1867.

4. The process of bringing the North and the South together after the Civil War became known as
   A Reconstruction.
   B Emancipation.
   C Radicalization.
   D Bureaucratization.

Directions: Follow the steps to answer this question:
What do the differences between Johnson's plan and Radical Reconstruction say about their supporters' attitudes about the South?

Step 1: Recall information: List two policies of Johnson's plan. Then list two policies of Radical Reconstruction.

Johnson's Plan	Radical Reconstruction
•	•
•	•

Step 2: Compare these policies in the chart.

How Plans Differ	What Differences Suggest

Step 3: Complete the topic ___ it follows. Then write two or three more sentences that support your topic sentence.

The details of Johnson's plan and Radical Reconstruction reveal that ___

___

___

Unit 5 Chapt___

> Questions at the end of the chapter help you review content and assess your understanding of the summary.

> Critical-thinking questions are broken into manageable steps.

> Use the Chapter Notetaking Study Guide to organize your section notes to answer the chapter focus question.

Chapter 16 Notetaking Study Guide

Now you are ready to answer the Chapter 16 Focus Question: **What were the short-term and long-term effects of the Civil War?**

► Complete the following chart to help you answer this question. Use the notes that you took for each section.

Rebuilding a Nation

As the Civil War ended, the nation faced enormous challenges:
• much of the South lay in ruins
•
•

Lincoln's Plan	Radical Republican Plan
Ten Percent Plan	Wade-Davis Bill
•	•
• 10% state voter loyalty oath	•

The first duty of the Freedmen's Bureau was to ___

Battle Over Reconstruction

Johnson's Plan	Radical Republican Goals
• Southern states ratify Thirteenth Amendment	•
	•
•	

Radical Reconstruction

• ___ imposed military rule on all southern governments that did not ratify the Fourteenth Amendment.
• During Radical Reconstruction, ___ played an important role in politics, and women were given ___
• Southern states opened ___ for the first time.
• Legislators spread ___ more evenly and made fairer ___

End of Reconstruction

As Radical Republican support died, many called for local self-government and ___

The end of Reconstruction was finalized with ___

Southern whites prevented African Americans from voting with techniques such as ___ and ___	The South's economy began to ___ due to industries based on ___

Refer to this page to answer the Unit 5 Focus Question on page 257.

256 Unit 5 Chapter 16 Notetaking Study Guide

The Pulling It Together Activity helps you to look back on your reading and focus on the unit's big ideas.

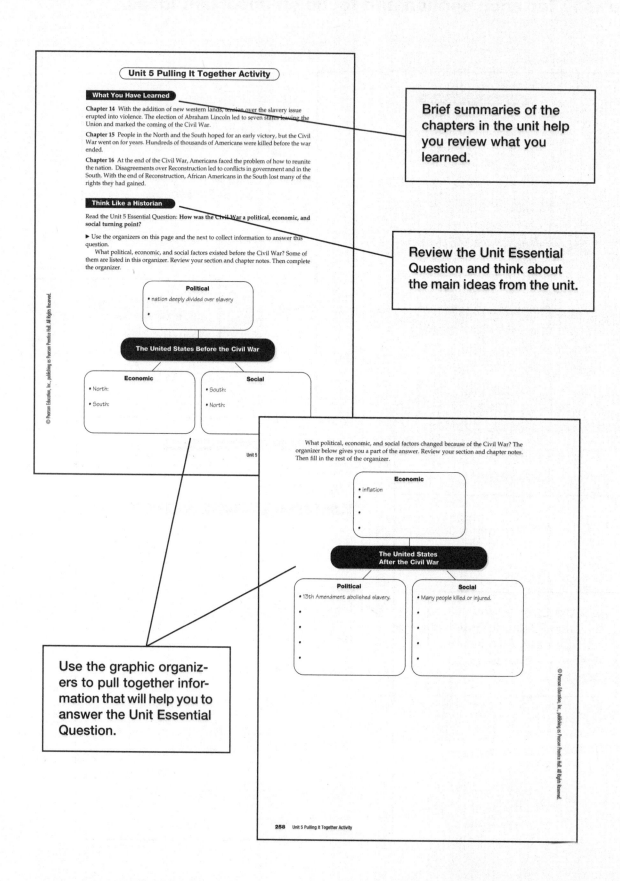

Unit 5 Pulling It Together Activity

What You Have Learned

Chapter 14 With the addition of new western lands, tension over the slavery issue erupted into violence. The election of Abraham Lincoln led to seven states leaving the Union and marked the coming of the Civil War.

Chapter 15 People in the North and the South hoped for an early victory, but the Civil War went on for years. Hundreds of thousands of Americans were killed before the war ended.

Chapter 16 At the end of the Civil War, Americans faced the problem of how to reunite the nation. Disagreements over Reconstruction led to conflicts in government and in the South. With the end of Reconstruction, African Americans in the South lost many of the rights they had gained.

Think Like a Historian

Read the Unit 5 Essential Question: **How was the Civil War a political, economic, and social turning point?**

▶ Use the organizers on this page and the next to collect information to answer this question.

What political, economic, and social factors existed before the Civil War? Some of them are listed in this organizer. Review your section and chapter notes. Then complete the organizer.

Political
- nation deeply divided over slavery
-

The United States Before the Civil War

Economic
- North:
- South:

Social
- South:
- North:

Brief summaries of the chapters in the unit help you review what you learned.

Review the Unit Essential Question and think about the main ideas from the unit.

What political, economic, and social factors changed because of the Civil War? The organizer below gives you a part of the answer. Review your section and chapter notes. Then fill in the rest of the organizer.

Economic
- inflation
-
-

The United States After the Civil War

Political
- 13th Amendment abolished slavery.
-
-
-

Social
- Many people killed or injured.
-
-
-

Use the graphic organizers to pull together information that will help you to answer the Unit Essential Question.

Unit 1

Beginnings of American History

Chapter 1 Early people spread across the Americas and built three great civilizations. As diverse cultures developed in North America, trade linked Africa, Asia, and Europe. European traditions influenced the United States.

Chapter 2 In the 1400s, European explorers experienced initial contact with Native Americans. For the next three centuries, European explorers and settlers expanded their range of influence throughout North and South America.

Chapter 3 In the 1600s, colonies were settled in North America. They included the Puritan-influenced New England Colonies, the Middle Colonies known for religious tolerance, and the Southern Colonies, which were based on slavery.

Chapter 4 While European traditions shaped England's 13 North American colonies, colonists gradually asserted their own culture. Both religion and the European Enlightenment triggered the spread of new ideas.

Focus Your Learning As you study this unit and take notes, you will find the information to answer the questions below. Answering the Chapter Essential Questions will help build your answer to the Unit Essential Question.

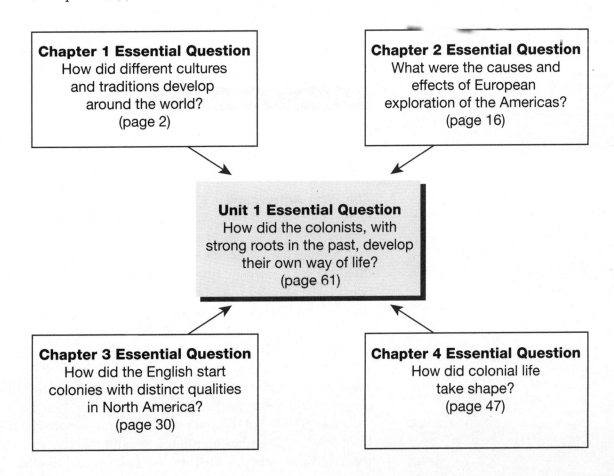

Chapter 1 Essential Question
How did different cultures and traditions develop around the world?
(page 2)

Chapter 2 Essential Question
What were the causes and effects of European exploration of the Americas?
(page 16)

Unit 1 Essential Question
How did the colonists, with strong roots in the past, develop their own way of life?
(page 61)

Chapter 3 Essential Question
How did the English start colonies with distinct qualities in North America?
(page 30)

Chapter 4 Essential Question
How did colonial life take shape?
(page 47)

Chapter 1

Roots of the American People

(Prehistory–1500)

What You Will Learn

Early people spread across the Americas and built three great civilizations—the Mayas, Aztecs, and Incas. As diverse cultures developed in North America, trade linked Africa, Asia, and Europe. European traditions would eventually influence the United States.

Chapter 1 Focus Question

As you read this chapter, keep this question in mind: **How did different cultures and traditions develop around the world?**

Section 1

The Earliest Americans

Section 1 Focus Question

How did early civilizations develop in the Americas? To begin answering this question,
* Find out how people first came to the Americas.
* Learn how farming developed.
* Distinguish among the Mayas, the Aztecs, and the Incas.

Section 1 Summary

Scientists theorize that people first came to the Americas over a land bridge from Asia. These people eventually learned to farm. The civilizations of the Mayas, the Aztecs, and the Incas arose.

The First Americans

Between 10,000 and 100,000 years ago, **glaciers,** or thick sheets of ice, covered much of the world. Ocean levels dropped, which exposed a land bridge connecting Siberia and Alaska. Today these areas are divided by a waterway called the Bering Strait. Many scientists believe that people crossed the land bridge into North America between 20,000 and 30,000 years ago. They hunted large prehistoric animals, such as the woolly mammoth. Over thousands of years, these hunting bands migrated across North and South America.

Some scientists disagree with the land-bridge theory. They think early peoples crossed the arctic seas by boat and then moved south along the Pacific coast.

As larger animals became extinct, people adapted by changing from hunting to gathering food. They still traveled from place to place, but now they searched for wild plants and smaller animals.

About 8,000 years ago, the discovery of farming completely changed life. Families could now settle in one place instead of constantly moving in search of food. Gatherers in Mexico cultivated squash, lima beans, and a variety of other plants. Farmers in dry areas developed **irrigation,** a method to water crops by channeling water from rivers or streams. They also raised livestock and traded their **surplus,** or extra, food with others. With a steady food source, the population grew. Cities arose and became centers of government and religion. ☑

Three Civilizations

The development of cities fostered **civilizations,** or advanced cultures in which people have developed science and industries. Between A.D. 250 and A.D. 900, the Mayas of Mexico and Central America built plazas lined with temples, pyramids, and palaces. They also developed arts, a system of government, and a written language. By studying the stars, the Mayas created an accurate calendar. Around A.D. 900, they mysteriously abandoned their cities. Forms of the Mayan language can still be heard throughout Central America, however.

As Mayan civilization declined, another civilization—the Aztec—was on the rise. The Aztecs built their capital city of Tenochtitlán (tay noch tee TLAHN) on a group of islands in the middle of a large lake. Stone roadways connected the large city to the mainland. Dozens of temples arose from the sacred city center. Religion <u>dominated</u> the Aztecs' lives, and they practiced human sacrifice to please their gods. After conquering half of what is today Mexico during the 1400s, the Aztecs imposed high taxes and demanded treasure and prisoners. The conquered people eventually turned against the Aztecs' harsh rule.

In the 1400s, the Incas built the world's largest empire in South America. Their rule extended along the Andes, across the Atacama desert, and into the edge of the Amazon rain forest. A vast network of roads linked Cuzco, the Inca capital, to other cities. The Incas erected buildings made of huge stones carefully fitted together, as well as canals and bridges suspended over canyons. Inca rulers wore gold and silver jewelry. ☑

Check Your Progress

1. Why was the discovery of farming so important?

_____

_____

2. List one contribution from each of the three early American civilizations.

_____

_____

_____

✓ Checkpoint

Name the waterway that now covers the ancient land bridge between Siberia and Alaska.

_____

Vocabulary Builder

The word *dominated* is a verb meaning "ruled" or "was the main feature of." Give one example of how religion dominated Aztec life.

_____

_____

✓ Checkpoint

List three early American civilizations that developed in Mexico, Central America, and South America.

_____

_____

Question to Think About As you read Section 1 in your textbook and take notes, keep this section focus question in mind: **How did early civilizations develop in the Americas?**

► Use this chart to record key information from the section. Some information has been filled in to get you started.

The Land Bridge

Why it existed: _____

What body of water covers it now: _Bering Strait_ _____

Places it linked: _____

When people crossed it: __between 20,000 and 30,000 years ago_____

Why it's important: _____

_____

How Early Civilizations Developed

1. Early people were _____, following large animals. Eventually they spread across _____ and _____.

2. As _____ became extinct, people changed from _hunting_ to _____ food.

3. About _____ years ago, gatherers in _____ began cultivating _____ and _____, among other plants.

4. Farmers developed _____, a method to channel _____ from rivers or streams. They also learned how to raise _____.

5. With a dependable food supply, the _____ grew. The Native Americans were soon producing a surplus, or _extra_ food, that could be _____ with others.

6. Some farming communities grew into _____.

Three Great Civilizations

People	Location	Accomplishments
Mayas		
Aztecs		
Incas		

Refer to this page to answer the Chapter 1 Focus Question on page 15.

Section 2

Cultures of North America

Section 2 Focus Question

How did geography influence the development of cultures in North America? To begin answering this question,

- Learn about the earliest peoples of North America.
- Note what diverse groups of Native Americans had in common.
- Explore the impact of geography on Native American cultures.

Section 2 Summary

The first cultures of North America developed between the Appalachians and the Mississippi Valley and in the Southwest. Trade and a belief in nature spirits were common traits. Yet each culture adapted its particular way of life to the environment.

First Cultures of North America

People in North America developed unique **cultures**, or ways of life. The Mound Builders began to emerge about 3,000 years ago between the Appalachian Mountains and the Mississippi Valley. They constructed large mounds to use as burial places and as the base for public buildings. One group of Mound Builders, the Mississippians, built the first North American cities, including Cahokia in Illinois. It may have held as many as 40,000 people.

The Anasazi were a very different culture located in southern Utah, Colorado, northern Arizona, and New Mexico. They made baskets, pottery, and jewelry. Their homes were cliff dwellings, which they mysteriously abandoned by 1300.

From 300 B.C. to A.D. 1450, the Hohokam people farmed in the deserts of present-day Arizona, digging canals to irrigate their crops. To create jewelry and religious items, they traded for shells with people of the Gulf of California. ✓

Ways of Life

Scholars organize Native Americans into **culture areas**, or regions in which groups of people have a similar way of life. Many culture areas share some basic traits. For example, women in many culture areas gathered edible plants while men hunted and fished. People grew crops suited to the climate, making farming tools from sticks, bones, and shells. Farming areas had higher populations than nonfarming areas.

Native Americans believed that spirits dwelled in nature, and they held a close relationship with their environment. Spiritual rituals included the Green Corn Ceremony, a tradition of the Southeast that offered renewal after the growing season. The Pueblo Indians revered benevolent spirits called kachinas. ✓

Key Events

1095 The Pope calls for the crusades to begin.

1200s The African kingdom of Mali rises.

1400s The Aztecs conquer most of Mexico.

1500s The Iroquois League is formed.

✓ Checkpoint

Name three of the first cultures of North America.

_____

_____

_____

✓ Checkpoint

List three items used as farming tools.

_____

_____

Native Americans of North America

By A.D. 1500, culture groups of North America had adapted their ways of life to their environment.

Native Americans of North America
Far North: Arctic people lived in a mostly ice-covered land. They survived on fish and birds and hunted marine mammals from **kayaks**, small boats made from skins. In the subarctic region, which was also too cold for farming, dense forests provided people with plants and animals.
Northwest: From southern Alaska to northern California, abundant game and plants allowed people to live in permanent settlements without farming. High-ranking people practiced the **potlatch**, a ceremony in which hosts gave guests gifts as a show of status.
Far West: Environments ranged from northern forests and grasslands to southern deserts. California offered mild weather and abundant food. Housing included pit houses dug into the ground, cone-shaped houses covered with bark, and houses of wooden planks.
Southwest: This region was dry, except after summer thunderstorms. Southwest groups farmed, and some hunted. People stored water for the dry season. The Hopi, Zuni, and other Pueblo people built towns with homes of **adobe**, or sun-dried brick.
Great Plains: People in the eastern Plains farmed and lived in earth lodges, or log frames covered with soil. The treeless west was unsuited to farming. People there lived in tepees or dug pits for shelter. Buffalo supplied meat, hides for tepees, and bones for tools.
Eastern Woodlands: People hunted, fished, and foraged for plants in the heavy forests. Some began farming by A.D. 1000. The Algonquian people dominated southern Canada and the Great Lakes. The Iroquois, in what is now New York, comprised five nations. Each nation had **clans**, or groups of families related to one another. Women owned all clan property and chose the clan's **sachem**, or tribal chief.
Southeast: A mild climate and steamy, hot summers supported farming. The Cherokees and Creeks built cool, dry houses of wooden frames covered with straw mats and mud. The Natchez of the Gulf Coast created a complex society with a ruler, nobles, and commoners.

Vocabulary Builder

Use the clues in the underlined sentence to explain what *comprised* means. Then explain what comprised the Iroquois.

_____

_____

✓ Checkpoint

List the seven culture areas of North America.

_____

_____

_____

_____

_____

_____

Check Your Progress

1. Why did culture groups differ in the way they built homes?

_____

_____

2. Why did Native Americans revere nature?

_____

Question to Think About As you read Section 2 in your textbook and take notes, keep this section focus question in mind: **How did geography influence the development of cultures in North America?**

▶ Use this chart to record key information from the section. Some information has been filled in to get you started.

First Cultures of North America		
Groups	**Location**	**Accomplishments**
Mound Builders	_____ _____	_____ _____
Anasazi	Southern Utah, Colorado, northern Arizona, New Mexico	_____ _____ _____
Hohokam	_____ _____	Skilled at farming, dug canals for irrigation, traded for seashells

Native Americans of North America		
Region	**Environment**	**Way of Life, Housing, Food**
Far North	Arctic: harsh, often ice-covered Subarctic: _____ _____	Arctic: Fished, hunted marine mammals Subarctic: gathered forest plants, hunted caribou, moose, bear
Northwest	Stretches from _____ to _____	_____ _____
Far West	Different geographic regions: North: _____ South: _____	_____ _____
Southwest	_____ _____	_____ _____
Great Plains	Vast region between the Mississippi River and the Rocky Mountains Eastern Plains: _____ Western Plains: _____	Eastern Plains: _____ _____ Western Plains: _____
Eastern Woodlands	_____ _____	_____ _____
Southeast	Mostly mild, but summers were _____	_____ _____

Refer to this page to answer the Chapter 1 Focus Question on page 15.

Key Events

1095	The Pope calls for the crusades to begin.
1200s	The African kingdom of Mali rises.
1400s	The Aztecs conquer most of Mexico.
1500s	The Iroquois League is formed.

Section 3 Focus Question

How did trade link Europe, Africa, and Asia? To begin answering this question,

- Read about the role played by Muslims in world trade.
- Understand how trading centers rose in East and West Africa.
- Find out how China dominated the Silk Road, an important trade route across Asia.

Section 3 Summary

The rise of trade linked people in Asia, Africa, and Europe. As trade networks developed in East and West Africa, they helped spread the religion of Islam. China dominated trade between East Asia and the Middle East.

The Muslim Link in Trade

By the 1500s, a complex trade network linked Europe, Africa, and Asia, much of it passing through the Arabian Peninsula. Ships from China and India brought spices, silks, and gems to Red Sea ports, from where they were taken overland to the Middle East.

Trade helped the rise of Islam. This religion emerged in the Arabian Peninsula in the A.D. 600s from the prophet **Muhammad.** He taught that there is one true God. Followers of Islam, called Muslims, believed that the Quran, the sacred book of Islam, contained the word of God as revealed to Muhammad. Arab armies spread Islam through conquest to North Africa and Spain. Muslim merchants also introduced the religion far into Africa's interior and to Persia and India, where millions of people converted, or changed from one religion to another.

Arab scholars made important contributions to learning and technology. They helped develop algebra and made other contributions in mathematics, medicine, and astronomy. They improved ship technology by introducing large, triangular sails that caught the wind even if it changed direction. ✔

The African Link in Trade

As early as 3100 B.C., Egyptians established trade routes throughout the eastern Mediterranean Sea and the Red Sea to bring home cedar logs, silver, and horses. They also traded for ivory, spices, copper, and cattle from south of Egypt.

Trade centers developed in East Africa about 1000 B.C. By the 1400s, Zimbabwe had become powerful from its location on the trade route between Africa's east coast and the interior. Traders paid taxes on goods passing through it. Coastal cities, such as

✓ Checkpoint

Name the religion that conquest and trade helped spread to North Africa, Spain, Persia, and India.

Kilwa, prospered as traders exchanged cloth, pottery, and other goods for gold and ivory from Africa's interior. A slave trade also developed between East Africa and Asia across the Indian Ocean.

Trade was not limited to eastern Africa, however. Desert nomads from the Middle East crossed the Sahara with camel caravans to reach West Africa. <u>Ghana, the first major trade center in West Africa, was affluent because of its location between salt mines and gold fields.</u> War and changing trade routes gradually weakened the kingdom. In the 1200s, Ghana was absorbed into the empire of Mali, ruled by **Mansa Musa.** A Muslim, Mansa Musa turned Mali's great city of Timbuktu into a center of Islamic learning. Mali declined in the 1400s under a series of weak rulers. Timbuktu was captured by the Songhai in 1468. Like Ghana and Mali, Songhai flourished from the salt, gold, and slave trades. ✔

The East Asian Link in Trade

Unified in 221 B.C., China's empire expanded across Asia, linked by highways, canals, and a postal system. As China's borders grew, so did its trade. This was made possible by advances in **navigation,** the science of locating the position and plotting the course of ships, and inventions like the magnetic compass. The compass allowed sailors to lose sight of land and still bring the ship back home.

By the 1300s, Chinese traders used sea routes extending from Japan to East Africa. The Chinese explorer **Zheng He** visited 30 nations in Asia and Africa with his fleet of giant ships. A famous trade route on land was the Silk Road. It was not really one road but a 5,000-mile series of routes stretching from Xian, in China, to Persia. Silks, spices, bronze goods, and pottery flowed west from China on this route. Merchants carried these goods across Asia to markets in the Middle East and Europe. ✔

Check Your Progress

1. What bodies of water provided trade routes between Asia, Africa, and Europe?

_____

_____

_____

2. What was the Silk Road?

_____

_____

Vocabulary Builder

In the underlined sentence, the word *affluent* means "having an abundance of material wealth." List three synonyms for *affluent*.

_____

_____

_____

✔ Checkpoint

Name the major trade centers of East and West Africa.

East Africa: _____

_____

West Africa: _____

_____

✔ Checkpoint

Name the invention that improved China's navigation.

_____

Question to Think About As you read Section 3 in your textbook and take notes, keep this section focus question in mind: **How did trade link Europe, Africa, and Asia?**

▶ Use this chart to record key information from the section. Some information has been filled in to get you started.

Trade Networks
The Muslim Link in Trade
By the 1500s, a complex trade network linked __Asia__, _____, and _____. Much of this trade passed through the _____ Peninsula in the Middle East. There, the religion of _____ emerged in the A.D. 600s through the prophet _____.   Islam spread rapidly through _____ and trade. Arab scholars made remarkable contributions to mathematics, _____, and _____. Ship technology included large, triangular_____.
The African Link in Trade
East Africa   The most powerful trade center in eastern Africa in the 1400s was _____. The coastal city of _____ exchanged cloth, _____, and manufactured goods for gold, _____, and furs from Africa's interior. The slave trade also developed between East Africa and Asia across the _____ _____.
West Africa   Trade linked the _____ and West Africa. Desert nomads guided _____ across the Sahara. _____ was the first major trade center in West Africa. The trade in _____ and _____ made West African rulers rich. Under Mansa Musa, Mali's great city of _____ became a center of learning. The third of the great West African trading empires was _____.
The East Asian Link in Trade
_____ had a higher level of technology than any other civilization of the time. The invention of the _____ allowed ships to lose sight of land and still return home safely. The explorer _____ visited _____ nations throughout Asia and Africa. The __Silk Road__ was not one _____, but_____. Goods such as _____, _____, __pottery__, and _____ flowed west from China to Middle Eastern and _____ markets.

Refer to this page to answer the Chapter 1 Focus Question on page 15.

Section 4 Focus Question

What major influences shaped European civilization? To begin answering this question,
- Consider the importance of the Judeo-Christian tradition.
- Find out how Greece and Rome shaped ideas about government and law.
- Discover the impact of the Crusades and the Renaissance on Europe.
- Learn why Europeans began to look beyond their borders.

Section 4 Summary

Judaism and Christianity shaped religious beliefs in Europe, while ancient Greece and Rome provided the basis of modern government. The Renaissance brought a rebirth of learning, which led to a desire for exploration.

The Judeo-Christian Tradition

Judaism and Christianity shaped European religious and moral beliefs. Judaism arose among the Israelites around 1700 B.C. and was the first major religion to teach **monotheism**, or the idea that there is only one God. Israelites believed that Moses brought them God's laws, including the Ten Commandments. Unlike other early religions, Judaism taught that all people, even powerful rulers, had to obey God's laws.

Christianity arose about 2,000 years ago when a Jewish teacher, **Jesus** of Nazareth, began preaching near the Sea of Galilee. Some saw him as the Messiah, the Savior chosen by God. Others saw him as a political threat and had him crucified. His followers said he rose from the dead three days later. According to Christian <u>doctrine</u>, all people have a chance for **salvation**, or everlasting life. As Christianity spread, the Romans initially viewed it as a threat and executed Christians. Later, Roman emperors accepted Christianity, and it became the dominant religion of Europe. ✓

Greek and Roman Traditions

Ancient Greek and Roman traditions shaped European political systems, and later influenced the founders of the United States. In the fifth century B.C., the Greek city-state of Athens was a **direct democracy**, a form of government in which an assembly of ordinary citizens makes decisions. Any adult male citizen could participate in the assembly, but women, slaves, and foreign-born

Key Events

1095	The Pope calls for the crusades to begin.
1200s	The African kingdom of Mali rises.
1400s	The Aztecs conquer most of Mexico.
1500s	The Iroquois League is formed.

Vocabulary Builder

The word *doctrine* means "a body of ideas, particularly in religion, taught to people as truthful or correct." What examples of Judaic doctrine are described in the bracketed paragraph?

_____

_____

✓ Checkpoint

Name two religions of the Middle East that shaped European religious and moral beliefs.

_____

_____

✓ **Checkpoint**

List three groups of people in Athens who could *not* participate in government.

_____

_____

people could not. Because Athenians believed that a democracy depended on educated citizens, boys studied many subjects.

During this time, a few small villages in central Italy grew into the city of Rome. In 509 B.C., the Romans set up a **republic,** a form of government in which people choose representatives to govern them. An elected senate and assembly made the laws. Rome's code of laws outlined citizens' rights. Everybody was equal under the law, and a person accused of a crime was considered innocent until proven guilty. ✓

New Horizons

Rome fell to invaders in A.D. 476, and Europe fragmented into small states, ushering in the 1,000-year Middle Ages. By the ninth century, kings and nobles relied on **feudalism,** in which a ruler grants parts of his lands to lords in exchange for military and financial assistance. Daily life revolved around the Catholic Church. In 1095, Pope Urban II declared a crusade, or holy war, to win control of the Holy Land from Muslims. Although the crusades failed, they resulted in introducing the Europeans to the riches and navigation technology of the advanced Muslim civilization.

✓ **Checkpoint**

Name the events associated with these dates:

476: _____

_____

1095: _____

_____

1517: _____

_____

In the 1300s, the Renaissance revived interest in ancient Greece and Rome. Art, science, and inventions flourished. Powerful nation-states arose. Spain, Portugal, France, and England shifted trade routes to the Atlantic Ocean.

In 1517 the German monk **Martin Luther** demanded that the Catholic Church reform itself. Those who joined him in protesting certain practices of the Church were called Protestants. Over time, the Protestants formed their own churches, which pushed Europe into a series of religious wars. ✓

An Age of Exploration Begins

Prince **Henry the Navigator** hoped to expand Portuguese power and spread Christianity to new lands. In the 1400s, he set up a navigation center at Sagres (SAH greesh), where sailors learned to use maps, the magnetic compass, and the astrolabe. With these skills, Portuguese sailors opened the way for exploration. ✓

✓ **Checkpoint**

Name two navigational instruments Portuguese sailors learned how to use in the 1400s.

_____

_____

Check Your Progress

1. How did Judeo-Christian traditions and Greek and Roman traditions influence Europe?

_____

_____

_____

2. How did the fall of Rome affect Europe?

_____

_____

_____

Question to Think About As you read Section 4 in your textbook and take notes, keep this section focus question in mind: **What major influences shaped European civilization?**

► Use this chart to record key information from the section. Some information has been filled in to get you started.

Ancient Traditions and Their Influence		
Place	**Religious or Political Tradition**	**Influential Idea**
Middle East	Judaism _____	_____, the idea that there is only one God
_____	_____	All people have an equal chance for _salvation_.
Greece	Direct _democracy_	An assembly of _____ makes decisions.
Rome	• _____ • _____	• People can elect _____ to govern them. • An accused person is_____ _____.

What: The Crusades
When: _____
Why It's Important:
• It put Europeans in contact with the more advanced Muslim civilization. _____

Events That Influenced Europe

What: The Renaissance
When: _____
Why It's Important:
• Scholars rediscovered _____ of ancient _____ and _____.
• Art_____, _____, and _____ flourished.

What: The Protestant Reformation
When: _____
Why It's Important:
• _____ and many others broke from the _____.
• Many _____ _____ emerged.

Refer to this page to answer the Chapter 1 Focus Question on page 15.

Directions: Circle the letter of the correct answer.

1. Where was the land bridge over which people first came to the Americas?
   - **A** between Alaska and Arizona
   - **B** between Mexico and Alaska
   - **C** between Siberia and Alaska
   - **D** between North and South America

2. Which best describes the Hohokam?
   - **A** They lived in Cahokia.
   - **B** They farmed deserts in Arizona.
   - **C** They built cliff dwellings.
   - **D** They refused to trade for shells.

3. Which was *not* a trade center in Africa?
   - **A** Xian
   - **B** Ghana
   - **C** Timbuktu
   - **D** Kilwa

4. Which event took place in 509 B.C.?
   - **A** Rome fell to invaders.
   - **B** Pope Urban II declared a crusade.
   - **C** Rome became a republic.
   - **D** The Protestant Reformation began.

Directions: Follow the steps to complete this task:

Describe how Judeo-Christian, Greek, and Roman traditions shaped European and U.S. religion and politics.

Step 1: Recall information: List details about two religions of the Middle East.

Religion	Religious Tradition	Effect on European Culture
Judaism		
Christianity		

Step 2: Compare: Briefly describe Greek and Roman political traditions.

Civilization	Political Tradition	Effect on European/U.S. Culture
Athens		
Rome		

Step 3: Complete the topic sentence that follows. Then write two or three sentences to give examples.

Judaism, Christianity, and Greek and Roman traditions affected Europe and the United States _____

_____

_____

_____

_____

_____

Chapter 1 Notetaking Study Guide

Now you are ready to answer the Chapter 1 Focus Question: **How did different cultures and traditions develop around the world?**

▶ Complete the following chart to help you answer this question. Use the notes that you took for each section.

How Early Cultures and Traditions Developed Around the World
The First Americans A _____ once connected Siberia and Alaska. Many scientists think <u>early people crossed into North America here</u> between 20,000 and 30,000 years ago.
Three Civilizations About 8,000 years ago, the discovery of _____ changed life. Three civilizations of the Americas were the _____, the _____, and the _____.
Native Americans of North America Culture groups of North America _____ to the environment, and based their shared beliefs on a close relationship with _____.
Trade Networks of Asia and Africa By the 1500s, trade linked _____, _____, and _____. Trade and conquest helped spread the religion of _____, founded by the prophet _____. In East Africa, trading centers developed, such as _____ and _____. West African trading empires included _____, _____, and _____. Goods from China flowed west along the _____.
The Judeo-Christian Tradition Judaism arose in the _____ around <u>1700s B.C.</u>, and was the first major religion to teach _____. Christianity arose about _____ years ago. Initially viewed as a _____, it became the _____ _____ of Europe.
Greek and Roman Traditions Ancient Greek and Roman traditions shaped _____ through such ideas as direct _____ and the <u>republic</u>, a form of government in which people choose _____ .
New Horizons In the _____ Ages, daily life revolved around the _____. In 1095, the _____ to the Holy Land put Europeans in contact with _____ civilization. In the 1300s, the _____ revived interest in _____. Prince _____ set up a center for exploration in Sagres, _____. Martin Luther began the _____ in 1517.

Refer to this page to answer the Unit 1 Focus Question on page 61.

What You Will Learn

In the 1400s, European explorers had their first contact with Native Americans. For the next three centuries, European explorers and settlers expanded their influence throughout North and South America.

Chapter 2 Focus Question

As you read this chapter, keep this question in mind: **What were the causes and effects of European exploration of the Americas?**

Section 1

The Age of Exploration

Section 1 Focus Question

How did the search for a water route to Asia affect both Europe and the Americas? To begin answering this question,
• Read about the first European contacts with the Americas.
• Learn about the search for water routes to Asia.
• Understand the importance of the Columbian Exchange.

Section 1 Summary

The search for a water route to Asia led to the European discovery of two continents and the exchange of resources between the Eastern and the Western Hemispheres.

First Visitors From Europe

Before **Christopher Columbus**, the only European visitors to the Americas were Vikings, a seagoing people from Scandinavia. They explored Newfoundland in 1001. Almost 500 years later, Italian-born Columbus settled in Portugal, Europe's leading seafaring nation. He hoped to <u>undertake</u> a voyage to Asia by sailing west instead of east. Portugal's king would not pay for such a trip, believing it would be too long and costly. So Columbus moved to Spain and asked for support from Queen Isabella and King Ferdinand. Six years later, they finally agreed.

In August 1492, Columbus's mostly Spanish crew of 90 set sail on small ships—the *Nina*, the *Pinta*, and the *Santa Maria*, covering 170 miles a day. On October 12, an island was sighted and Columbus claimed it for Spain. Believing he was in the Asian islands known as the Indies, Columbus called the people he saw Indians. He sailed to the island of Cuba, at first thinking it was Japan, and then to Hispaniola, where he built a settlement. He

Key Events

1492	Columbus lands in the West Indies.
1539	De Soto begins exploration of what is today the southeastern United States.
1608	The French establish a settlement at Quebec.
1626	New Netherland is settled by the Dutch.

Vocabulary Builder

To *undertake* means "to commit to doing something." Use the correct form of the word to complete these sentences:

1. The voyage that Columbus _____ was long and dangerous.

2. He had _____ the first voyage without help from Portugal.

returned to Spain in January 1493, reporting that the West Indies were rich in gold. The monarchs made him governor of all land he had claimed for Spain. In September 1493, he returned to the West Indies as commander of 17 ships with 1,500 soldiers, settlers, and priests. The Spanish wanted to colonize and rule the West Indies and convert the people to Christianity. Columbus built another settlement and enslaved Indians to dig for gold. In 1498, his third expedition reached South America, which he mistook for the Asian mainland. He tried to prove this on a fourth voyage in 1502, and died in 1506 in Spain, convinced he had reached Asia. ✓

The Continuing Search for Asia

Other explorers tried to find a western water route to Asia. Italian explorer Amerigo Vespucci sailed twice to the new lands and became convinced that they were not part of Asia. His descriptions led a German mapmaker to label the region "the land of Amerigo," later shortened to "America." In 1510, Spanish colonist **Vasco Núñez de Balboa** explored the Caribbean coast of what is now Panama. He trekked westward and became the first European to see the Pacific Ocean.

In 1519, Portuguese explorer **Ferdinand Magellan** searched the South American coast for a **strait,** a narrow passage that connects two large bodies of water, between the Atlantic and Pacific Oceans. He finally found what is now the Strait of Magellan and from there sailed into the Pacific. In the Philippine Islands, he and several others were killed. Only one ship and 18 men returned to Spain in 1522, making them the first to **circumnavigate,** or travel around, the Earth. ✓

The Columbian Exchange

The next century began the Columbian Exchange, a transfer of people, products, and ideas between the Eastern and Western Hemispheres. Some exchanges were good. Europeans brought to the new lands hogs, cows, horses, and other animals, as well as plants such as oats and wheat. The Americas introduced llamas and turkeys and crops that now account for one third of the world's food supply. Other exchanges had a negative impact, including the introduction of diseases to which Native Americans had no immunity. Smallpox, chickenpox, measles, and other diseases killed thousands of them. ✓

Check Your Progress

1. In what years did Columbus's voyages to the Americas occur?

_____

2. From the late 1400s to the early 1500s, what European explorers sailed to the new lands?

_____

_____

✓ **Checkpoint**

Name the country that supported Christopher Columbus's voyages.

_____

✓ **Checkpoint**

Name the first European to see the Pacific Ocean.

_____

✓ **Checkpoint**

List three diseases carried into the Americas from Europe.

_____

_____

_____

Section 1 Notetaking Study Guide

Question to Think About As you read Section 1 in your textbook and take notes, keep this section focus question in mind: **How did the search for a water route to Asia affect both Europe and the Americas?**

▶ Use this chart to record key information from the section. Some information has been filled in to get you started.

The Age of Exploration	
Explorer	**Accomplishments**
Leif Erikson	• A Viking who sailed from a colony on ______ in the year ______ • Spent the winter in Newfoundland, which they named ______
Christopher Columbus	• Believed he could reach Asia by ______ • Financed by ______ • Voyages: 1492: Landed on a small island, then sailed to ______ and ______ 1493: Discovered other islands, including ______ 1498: Reached the northern coast of ______, but he thought it was the Asian mainland 1502: Attempted to prove his claims in his fourth voyage
Amerigo Vespucci	• Sailed twice to the new lands • Believed that the lands were not part of ______ • A German mapmaker labeled the region ______
Vasco Núñez de Balboa	• Explored the Caribbean coast of ______ • First European to see the ______
Ferdinand Magellan	• Portuguese explorer who set out to find a(n) ______ passage in the year ______ • Spent 38 days sailing through what is today the ______ • Killed in the ______ • 18 remaining men reached ______ in 1522 • First voyage to ______ the Earth

↓

The Columbian Exchange	
What it was: ______	
Items brought from Europe to the Americas: • ______ • ______ • ______	Items brought from the Americas to Europe: • ______ • ______

Refer to this page to answer the Chapter 2 Focus Question on page 29.

© Pearson Education, Inc., publishing as Pearson Prentice Hall. All rights reserved.

Section 2

Spain's Empire in the Americas

Section 2 Focus Question

How did Spain establish an empire in the Americas? To begin answering this question,

- Discover how the Spanish defeated the empires of the Aztecs and Incas.
- Learn about Spanish explorations in areas that became part of the United States.
- Understand how Spanish society in the Americas was organized.

Section 2 Summary

The conquests of Cortés and Pizarro helped establish a Spanish empire in the Americas. Spanish explorers believed that North America had cities of gold.

Spanish Conquistadors

Spanish soldier-adventurers called **conquistadors** set out to explore and conquer the new lands. In 1519, **Hernán Cortés** sailed from Cuba to Mexico with more than 500 soldiers, where they were greeted with gifts by Native Americans. Conquered earlier by the brutal Aztecs, many Native Americans joined Cortés as he marched on Tenochtitlán. The Aztec leader Moctezuma offered gold to get Cortés to leave, but instead he was taken hostage when Cortés claimed Mexico for Spain. In June 1520, the Aztecs rebelled, forcing the Spaniards out. A year later, Cortés returned, destroyed Tenochtitlán, and built Mexico City—the capital of New Spain—in its place.

In 1531, Francisco Pizarro came to seek gold and copied Cortés's methods to subdue the Incas of Peru. In 1532, Pizarro captured the Inca ruler, Atahualpa. Despite a huge ransom paid by the Incas, Pizarro executed him. By November 1533, Pizarro had defeated the Incas and captured their capital city of Cuzco.

Several factors helped the few hundred Spanish soldiers defeat large Native American armies. The Spanish had advanced weapons of armor, muskets, and cannons. The Spaniards also rode horses, which Native Americans had never seen. In addition, the Native Americans were divided among themselves and did not present a unified force. ✔

Spanish Explorers in North America

In 1513, Juan Ponce de León sailed north from Puerto Rico to a place he called *La Florida* for its flowers. He became the first Spaniard to enter what is now the United States. In 1528, hundreds of Spaniards landed near the site of St. Petersburg, found no gold, and marched on northern Florida. When they were attacked by Native Americans, they built boats and fled. About 80 survivors,

Key Events

1492	Columbus lands in the West Indies.
1539	De Soto begins exploration of what is today the southeastern United States.
1608	The French establish a settlement at Quebec.
1626	New Netherland is settled by the Dutch.

✓ Checkpoint

Name the Aztec and Inca leaders overthrown by the Spanish conquistadors.

_____ _____

_____

✓ Checkpoint

Name four explorers who searched in vain for North American cities of gold.

_____

_____

_____

_____

Vocabulary Builder

To *administer* means "to manage public or government affairs." What noun form of this word refers to an organization or the government?

_____

✓ Checkpoint

Name the Spanish word for the land grants that allowed settlers to demand labor or taxes from Native Americans.

_____

led by Álvar Núñez Cabeza de Vaca, landed at Galveston Island on the Texas coast. The 15 who did not starve or die from disease were enslaved by Native Americans. Cabeza de Vaca, an African named Estevanico, and two others escaped years later, wandering the Southwest. They finally found their way to Mexico City in 1536. Their tales of seven great North American cities filled with gold prompted a failed quest led by Estevanico. Francisco Coronado also searched in vain for the golden cities in New Mexico, Arizona, Texas, and Kansas. Hernando de Soto searched from the Carolinas to Oklahoma. In 1542, he died in Louisiana, having found the Mississippi River but no gold. ✓

Colonizing Spanish America

At first, Spain let the conquistadors <u>administer</u> the lands they had conquered. Later, however, Spain set up a formal system to rule its new colonies. Government officials gave land to settlers to establish mines, ranches, and **plantations,** or large farms. Land grants called *encomiendas* let settlers demand labor or taxes from Native Americans. Forced to work on plantations and in gold and silver mines, many Native Americans died.

A Spanish priest, **Bartolomé de Las Casas,** tried to reform the *encomienda* system. The Spanish set up Catholic **missions,** or religious settlements, to convert Native Americans to Christianity. As the Native American death toll rose, Spanish colonists looked to Africa for new laborers. By the mid-1500s, some 2,000 enslaved Africans were shipped each year to Hispaniola alone.

A rigid social system, based on birthplace and blood, was established in the Spanish colonies. At the top were *peninsulares,* or colonists born in Spain, which included most government officials. Colonists born in America of two Spanish parents were *Creoles* and included wealthy merchants and plantation owners. People of mixed Spanish and Indian parentage, *mestizos,* could do well economically but never enter the upper levels of society. *Mulattos,* people of Spanish and African heritage, were held at the bottom of society. This class system helped Spain control its American empire for 300 years. ✓

Check Your Progress

1. Who were the conquistadors, and what were they seeking?

_____

_____

2. What were the four levels of Spanish colonial society in North America?

_____

_____

_____

_____

Question to Think About As you read Section 2 in your textbook and take notes, keep this section focus question in mind: **How did Spain establish an empire in the Americas?**

▶ Use this chart to record key information from the section. Some information has been filled in to get you started.

Spain's Empire in the Americas

Spanish Conquistadors: Soldier-adventurers called conquistadors set out to <u>explore</u> and _____ the Americas. They hoped for <u>riches</u> and _____ for themselves and _____.

Hernán Cortés	Francisco Pizarro
1. 1519: Sailed from Cuba to Mexico with more than 500 soldiers	1. Copied methods of ____<u>Cortés</u>____
2. November 8: Marched into the Aztec capital of _____	2. 1531: Landed on the coast of Peru to search for the _____
3. Native Americans joined him because _____.	3. September 1532: Led about _____ soldiers into the heart of empire
4. The Aztec leader, _____, offered Cortés gold to leave.	4. Took the Inca ruler, _____, prisoner
5. Instead, Cortés _____ _____ .	5. The Inca people paid _____ _____.
6. 1520: _____ _____	6. Pizarro instead _____ _____.
7. A year later, Cortés _____ _____.	7. By November 1533: _____ _____ _____

Why Conquistadors Defeated Native Americans:
1. The Indians' weapons _____.
2. _____, which the Native Americans had never before seen.
3. The Native Americans _____.

The Spanish Social System

Peninsulares: <u>Spanish colonists born in</u> <u>Spain</u>	• <u>Top of the social structure</u> • <u>Most were government officials</u>
Creoles: _____	Many were _____ _____.
Mestizos: _____	Could achieve economic success as _____, _____, and _____, but could not enter _____ of society.
Mulattos: _____	They were held at ____<u>bottom</u>____ of society.

Refer to this page to answer the Chapter 2 Focus Question on page 29.

Key Events

1492	Columbus lands in the West Indies.
1539	De Soto begins exploration of what is today the southeastern United States.
1608	The French establish a settlement at Quebec.
1626	New Netherland is settled by the Dutch.

Vocabulary Builder

The underlined word *magnitude* comes from the Latin term *magnum*, meaning "great size or significance." Complete these sentences using words with the same root as *magnitude*:

1. A _____ glass makes objects look bigger.

2. Spain had a vast and _____ empire.

Section 3 Focus Question

How did conflicts in Europe spur exploration in North America? To begin answering this question,

- Read about the religious and economic conflicts in Europe.
- Find out about the search for a northwest passage to Asia.

Section 3 Summary

Conflicts in Europe increased tensions on that continent, which led to struggles in the Americas. Explorers failed to locate a northwest passage through or around North America.

Conflicts in Europe

As the Protestant Reformation spread, the <u>magnitude</u> of the split between Catholics and Protestants became so great that it heightened tensions among European countries. By 1530, rulers had set up Protestant churches in Sweden, Denmark, and other European states. Protestant John Calvin's teachings and writings had great influence in France, Switzerland, Scotland, and the Netherlands. In England, King Henry VIII broke with the Catholic Church when it would not let him divorce Catherine of Aragon. Determined to remarry, Henry set up a Protestant church, the Church of England.

Wars were common. European rulers no longer trusted one another or their trade alliances. With the loss of trust in Italian and Portuguese traders, Spain supported Columbus's voyages, seeing them as a means to wealth, power, and above all, gold. Spain demanded that one fifth of all gold found in the Americas be sent to the king. This demand was supported by a system called **mercantilism**, which held that the colonies existed to make the home country wealthy and powerful. European nations needed gold to pay for their wars and strengthen their armies.

When King Henry VIII died in 1547, his son Edward ruled only briefly. Henry's daughter Mary ruled next and tried to restore the Catholic Church, but she died in 1558. This put Henry's other daughter Elizabeth I—a Protestant—on the throne. Her reign increased tension with Spain's monarch, King Phillip II, who wanted to make England Catholic again. Relations were strained further when the English raided Spanish ships carrying gold from the Americas. In 1588, Phillip assembled 130 warships, a fleet called the Spanish Armada, to force England's Queen Elizabeth from the throne. A fleet of smaller, faster English ships defeated the Armada, changing the balance of power in Europe. With Spain no longer controlling the seas, England and France were able to establish colonies in the Americas, where Europe's religious conflicts spread. ✔

Asia Continues to Beckon

After Columbus's first voyage to the Americas, Italian explorer **John Cabot** decided a northern route to Asia would be shorter. Only England was interested in supporting his voyage. Cabot left in one ship, in May 1497. His second voyage in 1498 may have reached as far south as Chesapeake Bay, but his ships vanished without a trace. Europeans realized, however, that Cabot had reached a land they had never seen. England, France, and Holland all agreed to pay for voyages to North America to find a **northwest passage,** a sea route from the Atlantic to the Pacific that passed through or around North America.

In 1524, Italian explorer Giovanni da Verrazano searched for a northwest passage for King Francis I of France. He explored the Atlantic coast from North Carolina to Newfoundland, and discovered the mouth of the Hudson River and New York Bay.

French explorer Jacques Cartier made three trips to North America for France. His search led to the St. Lawrence River, which he explored as far as present-day Montreal.

English explorer **Henry Hudson** lost support from the English after two failed voyages in the Arctic Ocean in 1607 and 1608. The Dutch supported a third voyage in 1609, which led him to New York and the river later named after him. This won English support for a voyage in 1610, but after reaching what is now Hudson Bay, icy waters halted the voyage. The crew mutinied and set Hudson, his son, and seven loyal crew members adrift. They were never heard from again. ✔

Check Your Progress

1. What happened as a result of England's victory over Spain in 1588?

_____

_____

2. What was the advantage of a northwest passage?

_____

_____

✓ **Checkpoint**

Name two reasons that European nations needed gold.

_____

_____

✓ **Checkpoint**

Name the "hoped-for" sea route from the Atlantic to the Pacific that would pass through or around North America.

_____

_____

Question to Think About As you read Section 3 in your textbook and take notes, keep this section focus question in mind: **How did conflicts in Europe spur exploration in North America?**

▶ Use this chart to record key information from the section. Some information has been filled in to get you started.

Europeans Compete in North America
Conflicts in Europe:
The split between _____ and __Protestants_____ in Europe heightened _____ and _____ tensions among European countries.
• King Henry VIII __broke with the Catholic Church___ and set up the _____.
• Teachings and writings of _____ influenced Protestant churches in France, Switzerland, _____, and the Netherlands.
• Mistrustful of Italian and Portuguese traders, Spain supported Columbus's voyages to get _____, _____, and_____.
• _____ is a system where _____ exist to make the home country wealthy.
• Queen Mary I tried to restore the _____ in England, but she died in 1558, and _____, a __Protestant___ took the throne.
• In 1588, Phillip II assembled _____ warships, a fleet known as the _____. He wanted to force _____.
Outcome:
The English _____, changing the balance of _____ in Europe. England and France were able to found colonies _____.

Attempts to Find the Northwest Passage		
Explorer	**Area of Exploration**	**How Voyage Ended**
John Cabot	_____, maybe as far south as Chesapeake Bay	His ships _____ _____ _____.
Giovanni da Verrazano	_____ _____	Discovered mouth of the _____and _____
_____	Discovered the_ St. Lawrence River_	Explored the river as far as _____
_____	Arctic Ocean, New York, Hudson Bay	Icy waters halted the voyage. The crew_____ _____.

Refer to this page to answer the Chapter 2 Focus Question on page 29.

Section 4

France and the Netherlands in North America

Section 4 Focus Question

What impact did the establishment of French and Dutch colonies in North America have on Native Americans? To begin answering this question,

- Read about the French colony that spread along the St. Lawrence River.
- Learn how the Dutch set up a colony along the Hudson River.
- Understand how the settlements influenced Native Americans.

Section 4 Summary

French settlements in North America depended on the fur trade with Native Americans. The Dutch settled along the Hudson River and also traded with Native Americans. Both colonies had a devastating effect on the native populations.

New France

By the early 1600s, England, France, and the Netherlands had supported explorations of North America. In 1603, **Samuel de Champlain** mapped the St. Lawrence River area. Champlain set up the colony's first settlement, a trading post, in Nova Scotia in 1604. Independent traders called *coureurs de bois*, French for "runners of the woods," lived among the Native Americans and went deep into the wilderness to trade for pelts. In 1608, Champlain set up Quebec on the banks of the St. Lawrence. Then he went east to explore the large lake now bearing his name. His explorations gave France a foothold in the region that lasted 150 years. New France profited from fish and furs, not precious metals like New Spain. The Spanish forced Native Americans into labor. The French, in contrast, traded with them for animal skins prized in Europe.

In the late 1600s, French colonists began farming as the European market for furs declined. The fur trade was also disrupted by the Indian wars and the arrival of 3,000 French colonists sent by King Louis XIV. In 1670, French missionary **Jacques Marquette** founded two missions along the Great Lakes in Michigan. In 1673, he and French Canadian trader Louis Joliet made their way west to the Mississippi River. This provided the French with a water route deep into North America. In 1682, explorer René Robert Cavalier, also known as La Salle, completed the river's exploration when he reached the Mississippi River mouth at the Gulf of Mexico. He claimed the entire Mississippi Valley for France, naming it Louisiana after King Louis XIV. ✓

Key Events

1492 — Columbus lands in the West Indies.

1539 — De Soto begins exploration of what is today the southeastern United States.

1608 — The French establish a settlement at Quebec.

1626 — New Netherland is settled by the Dutch.

✓ Checkpoint

Name the explorer who set up France's first colony in North America.

_____

New Netherland

Dutch land claims were based on Henry Hudson's exploration. In 1610 Dutch traders arrived in the Hudson River valley. Their trade with Native Americans was so good that the Dutch West India Company set up a permanent colony, called New Netherland. In 1624, about 300 settlers from the Netherlands settled at Fort Orange, later named Albany. In 1626, another colony and its governor, Peter Minuit, bought the island at the mouth of the Hudson River from Native Americans and named it New Amsterdam. By 1653, the island had 800 settlers. Because New Amsterdam blocked westward expansion for the settlers in the New England Colonies, the English seized the Dutch colony in 1664. They renamed it New York after the king's brother, the Duke of York. ✓

The Impact on Native Americans

Because of the rich profits made from furs, the French and Dutch valued Native Americans as trading partners. In exchange for pelts, the traders provided goods such as cloth, iron pots and tools, and guns. In addition, the French and Dutch made **alliances,** or agreements, with Indian nations. Many alliances, however, proved detrimental to Native Americans and led to warfare among the tribes. The Huron, for example, allied with the French. The Iroquois had an alliance with the Dutch. Using guns from the Dutch, the Iroquois attacked the Hurons—their longtime enemies—and devastated them.

Diseases caused by contact with Europeans also killed many Native Americans. In addition, the overtrapping of animals weakened the food chain on which Native Americans depended. As fur-bearing animals disappeared, Native Americans were no longer needed by the Europeans. Their land, however, became valuable to the colonists. ✓

Check Your Progress

1. What enabled René Robert Cavalier La Salle to claim the Mississippi River valley for the king of France?

_____

_____

2. What factors caused the decline of the fur trade in North America?

_____

_____

Section 4 Notetaking Study Guide

Question to Think About As you read Section 4 in your textbook and take notes, keep this section focus question in mind: **What impact did the establishment of French and Dutch colonies in North America have on Native Americans?**

▶ Use this chart to record key information from the section. Some information has been filled in to get you started.

France and the Netherlands in North America	
New France	**New Netherland**
Where: St. Lawrence River area _____	Where: _____
Trading posts: • _____ • _____	Traders arrived in the year _____. Trade was so profitable that New Netherland was made a permanent colony by the _____ _____.
Unlike Spain, New France profited from _____ and _____, not precious metals.	
The Spanish forced Native Americans into labor, but the French _____ _____ prized in Europe.	Other colonies: • 1624: _____ • 1626: _____ New Netherland was renamed _____ when it was seized by the _____ in 1664.
French colonists began farming as the European _____ declined.	

The Impact on Native Americans
1. In exchange for _____, the French and Dutch provided goods, such as _____ cloth _____ , _____, and _____.
2. The French and Dutch made _____, or agreements, with Native Americans, which often were detrimental to the Indian nations. The Dutch allied with the _____. The French allied with the _____.
3. _____ caused by contact with Europeans killed many Native Americans.
4. The overtrapping of animals _____ on which the Native Americans depended.
5. As _____ disappeared, the Native Americans were no longer valued. Instead, their _____ became more valuable to the colonists.

Refer to this page to answer the Chapter 2 Focus Question on page 29.

Chapter 2 Assessment

Directions: Circle the letter of the correct answer.

1. Which of the following rulers paid for the voyages of Christopher Columbus?
   - **A** the king of Portugal
   - **B** King Henry VIII of England
   - **C** Queen Isabella of Spain
   - **D** King Phillip II of Spain

2. For what did Ponce de León, Coronado, and Hernando De Soto search?
   - **A** furs for trading
   - **B** cities of gold
   - **C** the northwest passage
   - **D** the Mississippi River

3. What name describes the fleet of ships defeated by the English in 1588?
   - **A** the *Nina, Pinta,* and *Santa Maria*
   - **B** *La Florida*
   - **C** encomiendas
   - **D** the Spanish Armada

4. Which best describes the French colonies in North America?
   - **A** They profited from precious metals.
   - **B** They profited from furs.
   - **C** They profited from shipbuilding.
   - **D** They profited from the slave trade.

Directions: Follow the steps to answer this question:

Why did the Spanish explorers come to the Americas, and how successful were they?

Step 1: Recall information. In the chart, explain why Spanish explorers came to America.

The Spanish explorers, called _____, came to the Americas for two reasons: to _____ and to _____. In this way, they hoped to win _____ for themselves and _____ for Spain. European countries such as Spain required gold to _____ and _____.

Step 2: Summarize the explorers, where they explored, and their successes and failures.

Conquistador	Area of Exploration	Successes and Failures
Hernán Cortés		
		Defeated Atahualpa and the Incas, captured Cuzco
	La Florida	

Step 3: Complete the topic sentence to summarize the successes or failures of the explorers. Then write two or three more sentences that support your topic sentence.

When the Spanish explorers came to the Americas, they _____

_____

_____

_____

Now you are ready to answer the Chapter 2 Focus Question: **What were the causes and effects of European exploration of the Americas?**

▶ Complete the following chart to help you answer this question. Use the notes that you took for each section.

Europe Looks Outward	
Cause	**Effect**
1. Columbus set out to voyage to Asia.	He arrived in what are now <u>the Americas</u> .
2. Columbus and others reported tales that the new lands were rich in _____ .	
3. The Columbian exchange transferred _____, _____, and _____ between the Eastern and Western Hemispheres.	Good exchanges: Trade items such as cloth, _____ and _____ Negative exchanges: European _____, to which Native Americans had no immunity, brought _____, _____, _____, and other fatal diseases.
4. Hernán Cortés sailed to _____ ,	He subdued the _____, destroyed <u>Tenochtitlán</u>, built Mexico City, and claimed Mexico for _____ .
5. Francisco Pizarro arrived in _____ .	He executed _____ and defeated the _____ .
6. Spain set up a formal government in New Spain.	A rigid social system took hold, based on _____ and _____ . This system helped Spain control its American empire for _____ .
7. The split between_____ and _____ heightened tensions among European countries.	
8. England's smaller but faster ships defeated the _____ .	The balance of _____ changed in Europe. _____ and _____ founded colonies in the Americas.
9. French traders sought furs and animal skins to sell abroad.	_____ weakened the food chain on which Native Americans depended.
10. The fur trade declined.	_____ became more valuable to the colonists.

Refer to this page to answer the Unit 1 Focus Question on page 61.

Chapter 3

Colonies Take Root (1587–1752)

What You Will Learn

In the 1600s, England started colonies in North America that were influenced by religious beliefs. The Middle Colonies were known for religious tolerance. The Southern Colonies used slave labor.

Chapter 3 Focus Question

As you read this chapter, keep this question in mind: **How did the English start colonies with distinct qualities in North America?**

Section 1

The First English Settlements

Section 1 Focus Question

How did the English set up their first colonies? To begin answering this question,
- Read why the English sought colonies in the Americas.
- Find out why Jamestown barely survived its first year.
- Discover how Jamestown prospered.
- Understand how the Pilgrims set out to govern themselves.

Section 1 Summary

In the age of exploration, England sought colonies in the Americas. Its first permanent colony struggled for years. To practice their religion freely, Pilgrims left England and founded Plymouth. Representative government emerged, as did slavery.

England Seeks Colonies

In the 1500s, England began establishing colonies to provide new markets for its products and to obtain raw materials for its industries. In the 1580s, two colonies on Roanoke Island, off North Carolina, failed. The first, set up in 1585, was soon abandoned. The second, set up in 1587, was cut off from English ships during war with Spain until 1590, by which time the colony had vanished without a trace. ✓

Founding Jamestown

In 1607, a wealthy group formed the Virginia Company of London, hoping their American colony would yield valuable resources. King James I gave the company a **charter,** or document that grants rights, to settle much of the Atlantic coast. In 1607, colonists sailed into Chesapeake Bay and built Jamestown, England's first permanent settlement in North America. The swamps spread malaria, a disease that killed many colonists.

Key Events

1565 — Spain builds the first permanent European settlement in North America.

1607 — English start colony at Jamestown, Virginia.

1682 — William Penn founds the colony of Pennsylvania.

1732 — Georgia is founded by James Oglethorpe.

✓ Checkpoint

Explain why England established colonies.

_____

_____

Colonists seeking gold did little work to grow crops. Chief Powhatan and his people supplied some food, but by 1608, only 38 of the 100 colonists survived.

That year, new leader **John Smith** made tougher rules, including "He who works not, eats not." The colonists cut timber, put up buildings, and planted crops. In 1609, when Smith was injured and sent to England, conditions worsened. Powhatan tried to drive the colonists away by refusing to give them food. Only 60 colonists lived through the winter of 1609–1610, known as the "starving time." ✔

Jamestown Prospers

Despite hardship, the Virginia Company kept sending new colonists and leaders, and giving free land to the old colonists as an incentive to stay. The colonists prospered by growing tobacco, which was popular in Europe. Farmers began planting tobacco in 1612 and were selling all they could grow by the 1620s.

In 1619, colonists were elected to and met in Virginia's legislature—the House of Burgesses. Burgesses could pass laws and set taxes, but they shared power with Virginia's governor. This marked the start of **representative government** in North America, or government in which voters elect people to make laws for them. Also in 1619, a Dutch ship carried captive Africans to Virginia. Some slaves earned their freedom. Permanent slavery did not begin in Virginia until the late 1600s. ✔

The Plymouth Colony

In the 1500s, people wishing to separate from the Church of England were persecuted. Some Separatists settled in Holland to practice Christianity in their own way. Still unhappy, one group left for Virginia in 1620. Today we call these people the Pilgrims. A **pilgrim** is a person who takes a religious journey. In September 1620, they sailed for Virginia on the *Mayflower*, but storms along the way drove them north to Plymouth, Massachusetts. Before going ashore, 41 men signed the Mayflower Compact, the first document in which colonists claimed self-government. Half the colonists died that winter from hunger or disease. A Native American, **Squanto,** showed them how to plant corn, beans, and pumpkins. In 1621 the Pilgrims gave thanks, which is celebrated today as Thanksgiving. ✔

Check Your Progress

1. What happened to the English colony set up in 1587?

_____

_____

2. What was the name of Virginia's representative body?

_____

_____

✓ **Checkpoint**

Name the first permanent English colony in North America.

_____

_____

Vocabulary Builder

An *incentive* is "something that motivates people to act." What incentive was given to old colonists to stay in Virginia?

_____

_____

✓ **Checkpoint**

Name the crop that brought prosperity to Virginia colonists.

_____

✓ **Checkpoint**

Name the English Separatists who signed the Mayflower Compact.

_____

Question to Think About As you read Section 1 in your textbook and take notes, keep this section focus question in mind: **How did the English set up their first colonies?**

► Use this chart to record key information from the section. Some information has been filled in to get you started.

England Seeks Colonies
In the late 1500s, England began to establish colonies in North America
• to provide _____
• to get _____
The first two colonies on _____ Island _____.
• 1585: _____
• 1587: _____

Event or Situation	Why It Was Important
Founding Jamestown	
1607: _____ _____ on Chesapeake Bay.	First permanent English settlement
Many colonists spent their time _____ _____.	• Not enough _____ • By 1608, only_____
1608: _____ takes charge and draws up tough new rules.	• Most important rule:_____ _____ • Conditions _____.
1609: John Smith _____	• Conditions _____.
Winter 1609–1610: The "starving time"	• Powhatan_____ • By spring of 1610: _____
Jamestown Prospers	
1612: Colonists planted tobacco, a crop native to the Americas	• Tobacco was a source of _____. • By the 1620s, _____ _____
1619:_____ meets for the first time.	• Marked the start of representative government in North America
Summer of 1619:_____	• On board were 20 _____.
The Plymouth Colony	
1607–1609: _____ _____	• to separate _____ • to practice_____
September 1620: One group of Separatists, the _____, left _____ and landed in _____. Before going ashore, _____ _____.	• _____

Refer to this page to answer the Chapter 3 Focus Question on page 46.

Section 2

The New England Colonies

Section 2 Focus Question

How did religious beliefs and dissent influence the New England Colonies? To begin answering this question,

- Learn about the geography of the New England Colonies.
- Read about the Puritan settlement in Massachusetts.
- Understand how religious disagreements led to new colonies.
- Consider how the New England Colonies grew and changed.

Section 2 Summary

Although farming was difficult in New England, the forests and fishing grounds were rich resources. The Puritans founded a colony to practice their religion freely. Religious disputes led people to found new colonies. The growing number of colonists led to many changes in New England.

Geography of New England

New England covers the northeastern corner of the United States, with Massachusetts, Connecticut, and Rhode Island in the south, and New Hampshire, Vermont, and Maine in the north. Much of New England is hills, low mountains, and forests. The thin, rocky soil of the narrow plains made farming difficult, but just off the coast were rich fishing grounds. ☑

Puritans in Massachusetts Bay

The Puritans, a larger group than the Pilgrims, wanted to reform, not separate from, the Church of England. They were an influential group of professionals, including merchants and lawyers. In the 1620s, King Charles I forced hundreds of Puritan ministers to give up their positions. In 1630, about 900 Puritans formed the Massachusetts Bay Company and set sail for Massachusetts and New Hampshire. They were led by landowner and lawyer **John Winthrop.**

The Puritans believed their lives would be an example to others. Their main settlement was Boston, located on an excellent harbor. By 1643, about 20,000 colonists lived in the Massachusetts Bay Colony. By the mid-1630s, the colony had an elected assembly, the General Court, to which each town sent its representatives. Adult male Puritans elected the General Court and the colony's governor each year. Although they founded a colony in order to worship as they chose, the Puritans did not offer non-Puritans **toleration,** or recognition that other people have a right to different opinions. ☑

Key Events

1565 — Spain builds the first permanent European settlement in North America.

1607 — English start colony at Jamestown, Virginia.

1682 — William Penn founds the colony of Pennsylvania.

1732 — Georgia is founded by James Oglethorpe.

✓ Checkpoint

Name the present-day states that make up

- Southern New England:

  _____

  _____

- Northern New England:

  _____

  _____

✓ Checkpoint

Name the ruler who forced Puritan ministers to give up their positions.

_____

New Colonies

Religious disputes led to new colonies. **Roger Williams,** minister of a church in Salem, believed that Puritans should leave the Church of England and that colonists should pay Native Americans for land, not seize it. Forced to leave Massachusetts Bay in 1635, he moved to Rhode Island. In 1644, colonists there received a charter of self-government from the king and decided that people of all faiths could worship as they chose.

Anne Hutchinson, a Boston woman who questioned some Puritan concepts, was put on trial in 1638, expelled from Massachusetts, and founded a settlement in Rhode Island. **Thomas Hooker,** a minister, also left Massachusetts with 100 followers in 1636 and founded Hartford, Connecticut. In 1639, the Fundamental Orders of Connecticut established a new government with an elected legislature and governor. In 1662, Connecticut received a charter granting it self-government. In 1638, **John Wheelright,** who was forced out of Massachusetts for agreeing with some of Hutchinson's views, founded Exeter, New Hampshire. Massachusetts tried to control New Hampshire, but in 1680, the king made it a separate colony. ✔

Growth and Change

Puritans believed that towns and churches should govern themselves, and that people should work hard and live in stable families. Each Puritan town set up a **town meeting,** or an assembly of townspeople that decides local issues. New England families earned their living by farming, making leather and other goods, fishing, and shipbuilding. By the 1660s, 300 ships from New England were fishing off the coast or shipping goods across the Atlantic Ocean.

By the 1670s, the Native American population fell to 12,000, due to European diseases. In 1675, the chief of the Wampanoag, **Metacom** (also called King Philip), fought Puritan expansion. Some Native Americans supported him, but others helped the settlers. The fight, known as King Philip's War, killed thousands and destroyed 12 towns. In 1676, Metacom was killed. By then, a new generation born in America was focused on farming and business, not religion. ✔

Check Your Progress

1. What were Roger Williams's beliefs?

_____

_____

2. What did the Puritans believe about towns and churches?

_____

_____

✓ **Checkpoint**

List four colonists who had disagreements with some aspects of the Puritan religion.

_____

_____

_____

_____

✓ **Checkpoint**

Explain why Metacom declared war on the English.

_____

_____

Section 2 Notetaking Study Guide

Question to Think About As you read Section 2 in your textbook and take notes, keep this section focus question in mind: **How did religious beliefs and dissent influence the New England Colonies?**

▶ Use this chart to record key information from the section. Some information has been filled in to get you started.

The New England Colonies
Geography of New England:
• _____ soil made _____ difficult.
• Just off the _____ coastline are some of the _____ _____ in the world.
• The long winters and short, warm summers meant that the colonists caught _____ and _____ than colonists in Virginia.

Puritans in Massachusetts Bay	
Who They Were	**Why They Left England**
People who wanted to _____, not _____ the Church of _____	1620s: _King Charles I persecuted them_. They believed their way of life_____ _____.

Events
1630s: 900 Puritans formed the _____
• Led by _____, who was a _____
• Established _____
• Elected an assembly known as the _____
• Only _____ could vote.
• By 1634, _20,000 people lived in the Massachusetts Bay Colony_.

New Colonies
• Disagreements about religion _____.
• The Puritans did not believe in _____.
• Roger Williams: Believed Puritans should _____ and _____. Founded _____ and decided that the colony would have no _____.
• Anne Hutchinson: Questioned some Puritan teachings and was_____ _____. In 1642, she traveled to _____.
• Thomas Hooker: Disagreed with _____. Founded _____. In 1639, colonists drew up the _____.
• John Wheelright: Shared some of _____ views. Founded _____. In 1680, New Hampshire became a _____.

Refer to this page to answer the Chapter 3 Focus Question on page 46.

The Middle Colonies

Key Events

1565	Spain builds the first permanent European settlement in North America.
1607	English start colony at Jamestown, Virginia.
1682	William Penn founds the colony of Pennsylvania.
1732	Georgia is founded by James Oglethorpe.

✓ Checkpoint

List the four states that made up the Middle Colonies.

_____

_____

_____

_____

Section 3 Focus Question

How did the diverse Middle Colonies develop and thrive? To begin answering this question,

- Read about the geography of the Middle Colonies.
- Find out how New York and New Jersey shifted from Dutch to English rule.
- Find out how Pennsylvania and Delaware were founded.
- Understand how the Middle Colonies became so diverse.

Section 3 Summary

The Middle Colonies' soil and climate were conducive to farming. Quakers founded Pennsylvania and Delaware. People from many European countries settled in the Middle Colonies.

Geography of the Middle Colonies

The Middle Colonies comprised four states: New York, New Jersey, Pennsylvania, and Delaware. New York was the largest and northernmost state. The Hudson River flows south through eastern New York. It empties into the Atlantic Ocean at New York City, which is today the most populous city in the country. New Jersey, just south of New York, is mostly lowland along the Atlantic coast. Pennsylvania is the region's second-largest state. Its largest city, Philadelphia, is located on the Delaware River on lowlands in the southeast. Delaware, the smallest state, is located south of New Jersey and also lies along the Atlantic coast.

The warmer, longer growing season and fertile soil made farming easier in the Middle Colonies than in New England. Farmers grew wheat, fruits, and vegetables. ✓

New York and New Jersey

New York was originally called New Netherland and was ruled by the Dutch. By 1660, Dutch farmers in the Hudson River valley prospered, and fur traders profited from dealing with Native Americans. The Dutch also made money trading with merchants in British colonies, which violated Britain's mercantile laws. The small, ruling Dutch population felt hostility from other settlers. New Netherland blocked access between England's northern and southern colonies. In 1664, England's King Charles II granted the Dutch colonial land to his brother James, who conquered it. The colony was renamed New York, after James, the Duke of York. New Amsterdam, its capital, became New York City.

New Jersey was established in 1665, when part of southern New York was split off into a new colony. It began as a **proprietary colony,** or a colony created by a grant of land from a monarch to an individual or family. In 1702, however, it became a **royal colony**, a colony directly controlled by the English king. New York had become a royal colony in 1685. ✓

Pennsylvania and Delaware

In the 1640s and 1650s, new religious groups emerged in England, including the Quakers, whose ideas set them apart from most groups. They believed that all people are equal, have a direct link with God, and therefore do not need ministers. By the 1660s, thousands of English Quakers refused to pay taxes to support the Church of England. To provide safety from persecution, **William Penn**, a wealthy Quaker leader, used his connections with King Charles II to get a charter for a new colony in North America. In 1681, he received an area nearly as large as England. Penn viewed his colony as a "holy experiment" to see if people from different religious backgrounds could live peacefully. In 1682, he wrote his Frame of Government for Pennsylvania, which granted the colony an elected assembly and freedom of religion. He did not allow colonists to settle on land until Native Americans sold it to them.

The first European settlers in Delaware were Swedish. The Dutch briefly took control but lost it along with New York to the English. <u>Delaware settlers were averse to sending delegates to a distant Philadelphia.</u> Penn gave the area its own assembly, and in 1704, Delaware became a separate colony. ✓

Growth and Change

By the 1700s, more than 20,000 colonists lived in Pennsylvania. Farmers produced a surplus. Because of its abundant wheat crop, Pennsylvania was called America's breadbasket. Manufacturers were appearing in the Middle Colonies, producing iron, flour, and paper. Artisans in towns included shoemakers, carpenters, masons, weavers, and coopers, who made barrels to ship and store flour and other foods. Pennsylvania's **backcountry**, or the frontier region extending from Pennsylvania to Georgia, was home to Scotch-Irish, and later, Germans. They called themselves *Deutsch* for "German" and became known as the Pennsylvania Dutch. By the 1750s, non-English settlers made the Middle Colonies the most diverse part of English North America. ✓

Check Your Progress

1. Why were Quakers persecuted in England?

_____

_____

2. How did New Jersey's colonial status change in 1702?

_____

_____

✓ Checkpoint

Explain why the English wanted Dutch colonial land.

_____

_____

Vocabulary Builder

The word *averse* means "strongly opposed to or disliking something." Why were Delaware colonists averse to sending their delegates to an assembly in Philadelphia?

_____

_____

✓ Checkpoint

State how William Penn viewed his colony.

_____

✓ Checkpoint

Name five types of artisans in the Middle Colonies.

_____

_____

_____

_____

Question to Think About As you read Section 3 in your textbook and take notes, keep this section focus question in mind: **How did the diverse Middle Colonies develop and thrive?**

▶ Use this chart to record key information from the section. Some information has been filled in to get you started.

The Middle Colonies
New York
• Began as a Dutch colony named _____
• Economically successful because of _____
• Swedish, French, Portuguese, and English settlers were _____ to Dutch rule.
• Tension between England and Holland because they were rivals at _____
• New Netherland separated _____ from _____ _____.
• In 1664, _____ gave New Netherland to his brother _____.
• New Netherland became _____, and New Amsterdam became _____.
New Jersey
• Colony was established in _____ when southern New York was split off to form a new colony.
• New Jersey began as a _____ colony, but in 1702, _____ _____.
Pennsylvania
• Founder: _____
• Granted a charter from _____ in _____
• Offered religious freedom to _____
• Penn's "holy experiment": _____ _____
• In 1682, Penn's _____ granted the colony _____ and _____.
• Called America's breadbasket because _____
Diversity:
• Many settlers in the backcountry were _____.
• Germans described themselves as *Deutsch* and became known as the _____.
Delaware
• First European settlers were _____.
• Penn's charter included Delaware, but _____.
• In 1704, _____.

Refer to this page to answer the Chapter 3 Focus Question on page 46.

Section 4

The Southern Colonies

Section 4 Focus Question

What factors influenced the development of the Southern Colonies?
To begin answering this question,

- Read about the geography of the Southern Colonies.
- Learn about the early history of Virginia.
- Discover how Maryland, the Carolinas, and Georgia were founded.
- Learn about the different ways of life in the Tidewater and the backcountry.

Section 4 Summary

A farming region that required many laborers, the Southern Colonies depended on slavery. The Tidewater region and the backcountry developed two distinct ways of life.

Geography of the Southern Colonies

In the 1760s, Charles Mason and Jeremiah Dixon drew the boundary known as the Mason-Dixon line. After the American Revolution, it became the line between northern states where slavery was abolished and southern states where it persisted. Maryland, Virginia, North Carolina, South Carolina, and Georgia were south of the line. They shared the Tidewater, a flat, coastal lowland with many swamps. The warm, humid climate provided a long growing season for tobacco and rice. Both crops required many field workers, which helped spread slavery. ✔

Virginia Grows

After the 1650s, Virginia's high death rate fell, and the population grew quickly—from 10,000 in 1640 to 40,000 in 1670. Due to disease and violence, the Native American population shrank. Tobacco farmers took Native American land, causing two violent confrontations in 1622 and 1644. Although hundreds of colonists were killed, Native Americans were defeated both times, and coastal Native Americans had to accept English rule.

In the 1660s, wealthy Virginia tobacco farmers bought good farmland near the coast, leaving none for poorer colonists, who were forced to work for the owners. Without property, they could not vote. Poor colonists who moved inland to farm fought with Native Americans. The governor did not intervene, hoping to avoid war with Native Americans because he benefited from his fur trade with them.

In 1675, **Nathaniel Bacon** led 1,000 frontier settlers in attacks on Native Americans, and the governor declared Bacon and his men rebels. Bacon burned Jamestown, forcing the governor to

Key Events

1565	Spain builds the first permanent European settlement in North America.
1607	English start colony at Jamestown, Virginia.
1682	William Penn founds the colony of Pennsylvania.
1732	Georgia is founded by James Oglethorpe.

✓ Checkpoint

List the five colonies south of the Mason-Dixon line.

_____

_____

_____

_____

Vocabulary Builder

The word *intervene* comes from the Latin words *inter*, meaning "between" and *venire*, meaning "to come." What is another way to say that the governor did not intervene in this situation?

_____

_____

_____

Name the law that welcomed all Christians in Maryland.

_____

✓ Checkpoint

Name the founder of Georgia.

_____

✓ Checkpoint

State two crops that promoted slavery in the Southern Colonies.

_____

_____

flee. Bacon's Rebellion ended when Bacon became ill and died. The governor hanged 23 of his men, but he could not stop settlers from moving onto Native American land. ✓

Religious Toleration in Maryland

In 1632, George Calvert, an English Catholic, set up a colony in Maryland where Catholics could live safely from discrimination. When he died, his son Cecil Calvert, **Lord Baltimore**, oversaw the colony along with a legislative assembly. Because of tension between Protestants and Catholics, Lord Baltimore got the assembly to pass the Act of Toleration in 1649. It welcomed all Christians and gave adult male Christians the right to vote and hold office. ✓

Colonies in the Carolinas and Georgia

The colony of Carolina was chartered in 1663. The northern part developed slowly, because it lacked harbors and rivers for ships. Settlers lived on small farms and produced tobacco and lumber. The southern part grew quickly. Colonists used slave labor to grow sugar and rice in the swampy lowlands. Carolina became two colonies, North Carolina and South Carolina.

Georgia, the last of England's 13 colonies, was founded for two reasons. The English feared that Spain was expanding northward from their Florida colony. Also, wealthy Englishmen led by **James Oglethorpe** wanted a colony that would protect **debtors**, or people who owe money, from imprisonment. Oglethorpe banned slavery, but by the 1750s, it was legal. ✓

Change in the Southern Colonies

In the 1700s, the Southern Colonies developed two distinct ways of life. **Plantations,** or large farms, dominated the economy in the Tidewater region. Tobacco and rice promoted the spread of slavery, until there were more slaves than free citizens in South Carolina. The plantation system made a society of slaveholders and enslaved people, and it divided wealthy landowners from poor people who lived in the backcountry. The backcountry was cut off from the coast by poor roads. Families lived in isolation. They believed the colonial government cared only about the wealthy, not them. ✓

Check Your Progress

1. How did Virginia's population change from 1640 to 1670?

_____

_____

2. For what two reasons was Georgia founded?

_____

_____

Question to Think About As you read Section 4 in your textbook and take notes, keep this section focus question in mind: **What factors influenced the development of the Southern Colonies?**

▶ Use this chart to record key information from the section. Some information has been filled in to get you started.

The Southern Colonies

Mason-Dixon Line
- States south of the line included _____.
- Geography: ___coastal area called the Tidewater___
- Why line became important: _____

Colony	Important Events and Details
Virginia	• 1640 to 1670: The number of settlers _____. • 1607 to 1675: The number of Native Americans _____. • Wealthy farmers bought _____. • Poor colonists _____. • Bacon's Rebellion: _____ _____
Maryland	• 1632: George Calvert set up a colony where _____. • Tensions grew between _____. • 1649: Lord Baltimore helped pass the _____. • It welcomed _____ and gave _____ _____. It was an important step toward _____.
Carolinas	1663: _____ • North Carolina grew slowly because _____ _____. Settlers produced _____ and_____. • South Carolina grew __quickly__. Settlers produced _____ and _____, crops that depended on _____.
Georgia	Founded because: • England feared _____ • James Oglethorpe_____.

Change in the Southern Colonies

1700s: __The Southern Colonies developed two distinct ways of life__.

The Tidewater Region	The Backcountry
• Economy dominated by _____. • A society of _____ and _____. • Divided _____ from _____, who lived in the backcountry.	• Cut off from the coast by_____ • Women and girls _____ _____. • People believed that the colonial government _____.

Refer to this page to answer the Chapter 3 Focus Question on page 46.

Key Events

1565	Spain builds the first permanent European settlement in North America.
1607	English start colony at Jamestown, Virginia.
1682	William Penn founds the colony of Pennsylvania.
1732	Georgia is founded by James Oglethorpe.

✓ Checkpoint

Name the first permanent European settlement in the United States.

_____

_____

Section 5 Focus Question

How did the Spanish establish colonies on the borderlands? To begin answering this question,

- Read about Spain's colony in Florida.
- Discover how Spain established settlements across North America.
- Learn about life in the Spanish missions.

Section 5 Summary

Spain established a colony in Florida long before English settlers arrived in North America, and the Spanish Empire controlled much of the country in the 1600s and early 1700s. Missions were set up to convert Native Americans to Christianity and to teach them farming and crafts.

Spanish Florida

While English colonies were forming along the Atlantic coast, some Spanish colonies were already hundreds of years old. In 1565, Spanish explorers built a fort called St. Augustine to prevent France from taking over northern Florida. It was the first permanent European settlement in what is now the United States. Spanish control was threatened by English colonies spreading southward. To weaken them, the Spanish announced in 1693 that Africans who escaped to Florida would be protected and given land if they defended the colony. Hundreds of enslaved Africans did so in the 1700s. Still, by 1763, there were only three major Spanish settlements in Florida, all centered around forts in the north. ✓

Settling the Spanish Borderlands

The most important Spanish colonies were in Mexico and South America. The function of the northern **borderlands,** or lands along a frontier, was to protect Mexico from other European powers. The borderlands began east of Florida and covered much of Texas, New Mexico, Arizona, Colorado, Utah, Nevada, and California.

In 1598, Spanish explorer Juan de Oñate (WAN day ohn YAH tay) led an expedition to New Mexico to find gold, to convert Native Americans to Christianity, and to set up a permanent colony. He established Santa Fe. The Spanish used Native Americans to tend their horses, and Native Americans who ran away spread the skill of horseback riding to other Native Americans. In 1680, Native Americans in New Mexico rebelled and drove out the Spanish, who did not return for ten years.

To convert Native Americans to Christianity, Father Eusebio Francisco Kino and other Catholic missionaries built missions in Texas and Arizona. Missions are religious settlements that aim to spread a religion into a new area. The only early mission that succeeded in Texas, about 150 miles north of the Rio Grande, converted few Native Americans but attracted more colonists and became the city of San Antonio.

Spain began colonizing California in 1769. Missionary **Junípero Serra's** (hoo NEE peh roh SEHR rah) first mission later became the city of San Diego, followed by what are now San Francisco, Los Angeles, and other cities. The Spanish founded almost 20 missions in California between 1769 and 1800. Soldiers built **presidios,** or military posts, to defend the missions. They also established **pueblos,** or civilian towns. Pueblos had areas of farming and trade, and they centered around a plaza, or public square. ✔

Life in Spanish Missions

Thousands of Native American laborers in Spanish missions farmed, built churches, and learned many crafts. They were not overworked by standards of the time, working five to eight hours a day five or six days a week, and did not work on Sundays or religious holidays. However, the missionaries punished them if they did not adhere to the mission rules. Many were imprisoned, kept in shackles, or whipped. They often rebelled against the harsh treatment, and thousands of Native Americans died from the poor living conditions and European diseases. ✔

Check Your Progress

1. How did the Spanish try to weaken the English colonies in North America in 1693?

_____

_____

2. What were presidios, and what was their purpose?

_____

_____

Name two Spaniards who helped establish missions in Texas and California.

Texas: _____

California: _____

Vocabulary Builder

One meaning of the underlined word *adhere* is "to follow a rule or instructions exactly." Considering that the word *adhesive* has the same root, what is another meaning of *adhere*?

_____

✓ Checkpoint

Explain why thousands of Native Americans died in the missions.

_____

_____

Question to Think About As you read Section 5 in your textbook and take notes, keep this section focus question in mind: **How did the Spanish establish colonies on the borderlands?**

► Use this chart to record key information from the section. Some information has been filled in to get you started.

Spanish Colonies on the Borderlands
• The borderlands began in the east with_____. Farther west, they included most of _____.
St. Augustine
• Built in _____
• Why Founded: _____
• Why It's Important: _____
• In 1693: To weaken English colonies, _____ _____.
New Mexico
• Why Founded: Juan de Oñate came to New Mexico to _____ _____.
• Why It's Important: _____ became the first permanent settlement in the region.
• Oñate used Native Americans to _____. When some Native Americans ran away, they _____.
• 1680: _____

Spanish Missions
Texas and Arizona:
• _____ spread Catholicism and built missions.
• The only early mission to take root in Texas was 150 miles north of the _____ and became the city of _____.
California coast:
• Spain began colonizing California in _____.
• Missionary _____ led the effort. His first mission eventually became the city of _____. Other missions were in _____ and _____.
• Between 1769 and 1800:_____

Life in Spanish Missions	
Positive Aspects	**Negative Aspects**
• Native Americans were not <u>overworked</u>. • They worked _____ _____ and did not work on _____ _____.	• Native Americans did not have _____. • Missionaries_____ _____. • The population fell because of _____ _____.

Refer to this page to answer the Chapter 3 Focus Question on page 46.

Directions: Circle the letter of the correct answer.

1. By the 1670s, how many Native Americans remained in New England?
   - **A** 1,200
   - **B** 12,000
   - **C** 120,000
   - **D** 1,200,000

2. Which colony was founded by a Quaker?
   - **A** New York
   - **B** New Jersey
   - **C** Pennsylvania
   - **D** Maryland

3. Which of these divided southern from northern states?
   - **A** The Frame of Government
   - **B** The Great Wagon Road
   - **C** The Act of Toleration
   - **D** The Mason-Dixon Line

4. Which was *not* part of the Spanish borderlands?
   - **A** Georgia
   - **B** Texas
   - **C** Arizona
   - **D** California

Directions: Follow the steps to answer this question:

How did the ability to produce food affect the development of the English colonies?

Step 1: Recall information: In the chart, briefly describe colonists' ability to produce food in the first permanent English settlements in North America.

Jamestown	• • •
Plymouth	• •

Step 2: Provide more details. How did geography affect farming in the English colonies?

New England	• •
Middle Colonies	• •
Southern Colonies	• •

Step 3: Complete the topic sentence that follows. Then write one or two more sentences, giving two examples that support your topic sentence.

The ability of English colonists to sustain themselves in North America depended on such factors as _____

_____

_____

_____

Chapter 3 Notetaking Study Guide

Now you are ready to answer the Chapter 3 Focus Question: **How did the English start colonies with distinct qualities in North America?**

▶ Complete the following chart to help you answer this question. Use the notes that you took for each section.

English Colonies in North America
England established 13 colonies in North America. New England Colonies: _____ Middle Colonies: _____ Southern Colonies: _____
English colonists sought **economic** opportunity: • _England wanted to establish colonies to provide new markets for their goods and get raw materials_ • Because of the thin, rocky soil and long, jagged coastlines, _____. • Because of its abundant wheat, _____. • The _____ system of the _____ Colonies helped spread _____.
English colonists showed their **power**: • In 1664, King Charles II granted _____. The colony of _____ became _____. • Even after Bacon's Rebellion collapsed, _____ • As well as offering debtors protection from imprisonment, Georgia was founded to _____.
English colonists exercised freedom of **religion**: • 1620: English Separatists, known today as the _____, landed at _____. • _____ who wanted to reform the Church of England established settlements in what are now_____ and New Hampshire. • Disagreements about religion led to the founding of other colonies, including _____ settlement in Rhode Island, _____ settlement in Connecticut, and _____ settlement in New Hampshire. • _____, who refused to pay taxes to the Church of England, settled in _____ and _____. • George Calvert founded _____ so_____.
English colonists claimed the right to freedom of **government**: • 1619: Virginia's _____ marked the start of_____ _____ in North America. • 1620: _____ was the first document in which American colonists claimed_____. • The Puritans believed towns and churches should _____.

Refer to this page to answer the Unit 1 Focus Question on page 61.

Chapter 4

Life in the Colonies (1650–1750)

What You Will Learn

Government and daily life in the American colonies were shaped by English tradition and ideas. By the mid-1700s, however, the colonies had developed traditions and ideas of their own.

Chapter 4 Focus Question

As you read this chapter, keep this question in mind: **How did colonial life take shape?**

Section 1

Governing the Colonies

Section 1 Focus Question

How did English ideas about government and trade affect the colonies? To begin answering this question,

- Learn about key elements of the English political tradition.
- Understand how colonies passed laws and who could vote.
- Read about a case that established freedom of the press.
- Find out how the Navigation Acts affected trade.

Section 1 Summary

English ideas about government, individual rights, and trade deeply affected colonial life.

The English Parliamentary Tradition

In 1215, King John signed the Magna Carta, the first document to limit the English monarch's power and protect the rights of nobles and other citizens. It also formed the basis for Parliament, a two-house **legislature,** or group of people who have the power to make laws. Parliament included two groups: the hereditary nobles of the House of Lords and the elected members of the House of Commons. The monarch needed the consent of Parliament to raise taxes— Parliament's greatest power. Conflict between King Charles I and Parliament led to the English Civil War in the 1640s. Charles I was executed by Parliamentary forces. The monarchy was restored in 1660, yet Parliament retained its rights.

Parliament gained more power in 1688 when it removed King James I from the throne and replaced him with his daughter Mary and her husband William. After this so-called Glorious Revolution, the new monarchs signed the English Bill of Rights. A **bill of rights** is a written list of freedoms that a government promises to protect, including the right to a trial by jury. ✓

Key Events

1730s — The Great Awakening sweeps through the colonies.

1735 — The Zenger case marks a step toward freedom of the press.

1750 — Georgia becomes the last of the colonies to permit slavery.

✓ Checkpoint

State Parliament's greatest power.

_____

_____

The American colonists expected to receive many of the same rights that Englishmen possessed under Parliamentary law. They set up legislatures, including the House of Burgesses in Jamestown and the General Court in Massachusetts. However, the British government gave William Penn full ownership of Pennsylvania. Penn and his council had the power to make laws. In 1701, colonists in Pennsylvania forced Penn to change the legal system so that only the General Assembly could make laws. By 1760, every colony had a legislature, although they frequently clashed with the colonial governors.

More white males could vote in the American colonies than in England. However, many groups could not vote, including women, Native Americans, and Africans. ✓

Freedom of the Press

The Zenger trial of 1735 helped to establish **freedom of the press,** or the right of journalists to publish the truth without restriction or penalty. Publisher John Peter Zenger was arrested for printing articles that criticized the governor of New York. Zenger was accused of **libel,** the publishing of statements that damage a person's reputation. The jury found Zenger not guilty, however, because the articles were based on fact. ✓

Regulating Trade

Under the theory of mercantilism, colonies existed to serve the economic needs of their parent country. In 1651, the English Parliament passed the first of several Navigation Acts to support mercantilism. The laws required that any shipments bound for the colonies had to stop in England first. Any colonial shipments to England had to travel in British-owned ships. Colonies could sell tobacco, sugar, and other key products only to England. These laws benefited the colonies in many ways by providing a secure market. Yet many colonists resented the laws, which they felt limited the colonists' opportunities to make money by not being able to sell goods to foreign markets. ✓

Check Your Progress

1. What was the significance of the Magna Carta?

_____

_____

2. Why did some colonists resent the Navigation Acts?

_____

_____

✓ Checkpoint

List three groups of people who could not vote in the American colonies.

_____

_____

_____

✓ Checkpoint

Name the publisher whose case helped establish freedom of the press.

_____

✓ Checkpoint

Explain why Parliament passed the Navigation Acts.

_____

_____

Question to Think About As you read Section 1 in your textbook and take notes, keep this section focus question in mind: **How did English ideas about government and trade affect the colonies?**

▶ Use this chart to record key information from the section. Some information has been filled in to get you started.

The English Parliamentary Tradition

In __1215__, English nobles forced King John to sign the _____.
This was the first document to place restrictions on _____
and limited the monarch's right to _____.
It also protected the right to own __private property__ and guaranteed the right to
_____.
In _____, William and Mary signed the _____
that upheld these rights: _____
_____.

Colonial Self-Government

In the Jamestown colony, laws were made by the_____.
In Massachusetts, laws were made by the _____.
The British government gave full ownership of _____ to William Penn.
However, the colonists forced Penn to agree that only the _____
_____.
By _____, every British colony in America had some form of_____.

Freedom of the Press

John Peter Zenger was put on trial because_____.
He was charged with _____. The jury found that Zenger was_____.
This case helped to establish the principle of freedom of the press, which ensures that
_____
_____.

Regulating Trade

Three laws of the Navigation Acts:
• Ships from Europe to English colonies had to _____
_____.
• Imports to England from the colonies had to_____
_____.
• The colonies could sell _____
_____.
The Navigation Acts benefited colonies because _____
_____. However, many colonists resented the
Navigation Acts because _____
_____.

Refer to this page to answer the Chapter 4 Focus Question on page 60.

Key Events

1730s	The Great Awakening sweeps through the colonies.
1735	The Zenger case marks a step toward freedom of the press.
1750	Georgia becomes the last of the colonies to permit slavery.

✓ Checkpoint

Explain why extended families were useful on colonial farms.

_____

_____

Vocabulary Builder

The word *assess* is the verb form of the related noun, *assessment.* You might know that an assessment is a test. Use this fact and clues in the underlined sentence to define the word *assess.*

_____

_____

Section 2 Focus Question

What were the characteristics of colonial society? To begin answering this question,

- Understand family structure in colonial times.
- Read about the different roles held by men, women, and children.
- Learn about the main social classes in colonial society.

Section 2 Summary

Although colonists had many differences, they were united by a common culture and faced many of the same daily challenges.

The Family in Colonial Times

Many colonists lived with their **extended families,** groups that include parents, children and other family members, such as grandparents, aunts, uncles, and cousins. Most colonists lived on farms, where large families were advantageous because there was so much work to be done. Farms were usually isolated, so each family had to be able to survive independently.

Farmhouses were not very comfortable, mostly made of wood and with few rooms. During cold winters, families might sleep near the only source of heat in the home, the fireplace.

There were few cities and towns in the colonies. Single people found it easier to support themselves in towns than on farms. In Puritan New England, however, single men and women were expected to live with a family as a servant or boarder. ✓

Men, Women, and Children

In colonial society, men, women, and children had clearly defined roles. Men controlled the family income and property, and they represented their family in public life. <u>Women were expected to marry men chosen by their parents, who would first assess a man's property, religion, and interests</u>. A woman's property and income became her husband's when she married. In addition to childcare, women were expected to take care of household responsibilities such as cooking, cleaning, and spinning yarn for cloth. Women also milked cows, tended chickens, and preserved food. If the family was wealthy, a wife might have help from a servant. Women only rarely had a role in public life. They could not hold office or vote.

Until the age of seven, children could spend their time playing. Toys, such as cornhusk dolls, were usually homemade. By the age of seven, however, children were expected to work, helping with household and farm work, while poor children might become servants for other families. Older children had even greater responsibilities. Boys worked in the fields, and girls labored beside their mothers. Some boys became **apprentices,** or someone who learns a trade by working for a person in that trade for a certain period of time. ✓

Social Classes

Many colonists came to America with the hope of owning land and building a better life. In England, land meant wealth, but most of the land was already owned by the upper classes. Social class in Europe was rigid, and those born poor had little opportunity to improve their status. In the colonies, however, land was available. There was also greater social equality in colonial America, although class distinctions still existed.

Colonial Class Distinctions
The **gentry** was the upper class of colonial society and included merchants, owners of large farms, royal officials, and lawyers. The gentry had great power and could often live in luxury.
The **middle class,** neither very rich nor very poor, included the great majority of colonists. These were the small planters, independent farmers, and artisans. Middle-class men could vote, and some held office. Most of the middle class were white, although a small percentage were of African descent. Unlike in England, the poor could move upward socially and enter the middle class.
Indentured servants were people who signed a contract to work in the colonies for anywhere from 4 to 10 years. The contract holder paid for a servant's ocean passage to America. Indentured servants had few rights while in service, but once the contract expired, the servant was freed. A few became landowners or artisans. Others returned home or lived in poverty.
Free African Americans were not a large part of the colonial population. They could own property (including slaves), but most could not vote or sit on juries.

✓

Check Your Progress

1. Describe the roles that women had in colonial society.

_____

_____

2. How could people move up in class in colonial society?

_____

_____

✓ **Checkpoint**

Name one way in which life changed for colonial children at the age of seven.

_____

_____

✓ **Checkpoint**

List two differences between the middle class and the gentry.

_____

_____

_____

_____

Question to Think About As you read Section 2 in your textbook and take notes, keep this section focus question in mind: **What were the characteristics of colonial society?**

▶ Use this chart to record key information from the section. Some information has been filled in to get you started.

Colonial Society	
I. The Family in Colonial Times Most colonists lived on _farms_. Homes were far apart, so families needed to be _____. It was easier for _____ to support themselves in towns than on farms. **II. Men, Women, and Children** The key roles that men had: • _fulfill home duties_____ • _____ • _____ The key roles that women had: • _childcare_____ • Domestic responsibilities: _____ • Outdoor responsibilities: _____ _____ The key roles that children had: • Until about the age of seven, children _____. • By the age of seven, children_____ _____. • An apprentice was_____ _____.	**III. Social Classes** Social class in England was very rigid. People could not easily _move from a lower class to a higher class_____. **Classes in Colonial America** **The Gentry** The gentry were the _____ class of colonial society. People in this class included _____ _____. **The Middle Class** This class included the great _majority_ of colonists. People in this class included _____ _____. The poor could become part of this class by _____. **Indentured Servants** An indentured servant signed a _____ agreeing to_____ in exchange for_____. When the contract was over, the signer was _____. **Free African Americans** Free African Americans could own _____. They could not _____ or_____.

Refer to this page to answer the Chapter 4 Focus Question on page 60.

Slavery in the Colonies

Section 3 Focus Question

How did slavery develop in the colonies and affect colonial life?
To begin answering this question,

- Learn how the slave trade brought captive Africans to the colonies.
- Understand why slavery developed and how it was maintained.
- Read about African cultural traditions in America.

Key Events

1730s	The Great Awakening sweeps through the colonies.
1735	The Zenger case marks a step toward freedom of the press.
1750	Georgia becomes the last of the colonies to permit slavery.

Section 3 Summary

Captive Africans were brought to the colonies and enslaved on farms and plantations as a source of steady labor.

The Atlantic Slave Trade

Between the 1500s and the 1800s, more than 10 million Africans were enslaved and brought to the Americas. The first Africans were brought to the Americas by the Spanish and the Portuguese. In time, the British, Dutch, and French also entered the slave trade. Slave traders in Africa bought captives from the interior. Many captives died during the long journey to the coast.

Enslaved Africans were traded for guns and other goods. They then traveled the Middle Passage, a voyage across the Atlantic Ocean that was so brutal that from 15 to 20 percent of the captives died or committed suicide on route In the Americas, the captives were sold at auction. The vast majority worked on plantations in New Spain, Brazil, or the Caribbean.

Slave traders developed a routine known as the **triangular trade**, a three-way trade between the colonies, the West Indies (islands of the Caribbean), and Africa:

- Ships from New England carried fish, lumber, and other goods to the West Indies. They returned with sugar and molasses, a syrup used to make rum.
- Ships from New England carried rum, guns, and other goods to West Africa, where they were traded for enslaved Africans.
- Ships from West Africa carried the slaves to the West Indies, where they were sold. With the profits, traders bought more molasses.

The triangular trade often disobeyed the Navigation Acts, which required colonists to buy goods only from English colonies. ✓

Slavery in the Colonies

Unlike in some earlier societies, the system of slavery that developed in the Americas was harsh and permanent. The plantation system contributed to the rise of slavery in the colonies. Planters used thousands of enslaved Africans to grow and harvest tobacco and

✓ Checkpoint

List the three regions connected by the triangular trade.

_____

_____

_____

Be alert for words with more than one meaning. The word *episodes* can refer to programs in a TV series. Define the word as it is used in the underlined sentence.

_____

_____

✓ Checkpoint

Explain why the plantation system encouraged the growth of slavery.

_____

_____

_____

✓ Checkpoint

Name three African cultural traditions maintained in America.

_____

_____

_____

rice. Slaves were preferable to indentured servants for several reasons. Indentured servants were temporary, and their number decreased as conditions improved in England. Africans could be enslaved for life.

Laws were passed to make slavery permanent. A 1639 Maryland law prevented slaves from becoming free by declaring that baptism did not lead to freedom. A 1663 Virginia court decision declared that the child of a slave was also a slave. Early attempts to stop slavery, such as a 1652 Rhode Island antislavery law, were not successful. When Georgia lifted its ban on slavery in the 1750s, slavery became legal in all of the colonies.

Although not every African in America was a slave, slavery was restricted to people of African descent. Because of this, slavery in America was linked to **racism**, the belief that one race is superior or inferior to another.

The first serious slave revolt took place in Gloucester, Virginia, in 1663, although the uprising failed. <u>Fearing similar episodes, colonists wrote **slave codes**, or strict laws that restricted the rights and activities of slaves.</u> Enslaved people could not meet in large numbers, own weapons, or leave a plantation without permission. It became illegal to teach enslaved people to read or write. Masters who killed slaves could not be tried for murder. Revolts continued to occur until slavery ended in 1865. ✓

African Cultural Influences

About 10 percent of enslaved Africans lived north of Maryland, where they worked as blacksmiths, house servants, or farm workers. On isolated rice plantations in South Carolina, enslaved Africans saw few white settlers. They maintained many of the customs of West Africa, such as speaking Gullah, a dialect that blended English and several African languages. Although other Africans in the South were less isolated, they still maintained many African customs. African craft styles were continued in America, and African drum rhythms became part of American music. ✓

Check Your Progress

1. What work was done by most enslaved Africans?

_____

_____

2. What racist ideas did the slave codes reinforce?

_____

_____

Question to Think About As you read Section 3 in your textbook and take notes, keep this section focus question in mind: **How did slavery develop in the colonies and affect colonial life?**

▶ Use this chart to record key information from the section. Some information has been filled in to get you started.

The Atlantic Slave Trade

- The first enslaved Africans were brought to the Americas by the __Spanish__ and _____. Later, the _____, _____, and _____ also entered the slave trade.
- Most slaves were captured in _____ and then sold to traders along the _____ coast.
- The Middle Passage was _____. Between _____ and _____ percent of captives died during this journey.

Three Parts of the Triangular Trade

1. Ships from New England carried _____ to __the West Indies__. They returned with _____ _____.	2. Ships from New England carried _____ to _____. There, merchants traded these goods for _____ _____.	3. Ships sailed from _____ to the _____, where they sold _____ and bought __molasses__.

Slavery in the Colonies

The plantation system helped slavery take root in America because _____ _____.
Early attempts to stop slavery were ____ not successful and did not last long ____.
In 1663 in Gloucester, Virginia, _____, but failed.
In 1739 an enslaved African named Jemmy_____.
Slave codes were written to _____.

African Cultural Influences

_____ percent of enslaved Africans lived north of Maryland.
Slaves on rice plantations in South Carolina kept many customs of West Africa because _____.
Gullah is _____.
Other examples of West African culture in the Americas:
- crafts such as _____
- rhythms of _____ and musical instruments such as _____
- _____

Refer to this page to answer the Chapter 4 Focus Question on page 60.

Section 4

The Spread of New Ideas

Section 4 Focus Question

How did ideas about religion and government influence colonial life? To begin answering this question,

- Learn about colonial schools.
- Find out about three early American writers.
- Discover the impact of the Great Awakening.
- Read about Enlightenment ideas that influenced America.

Section 4 Summary

Puritan ideas influenced education in the colonies, and American literature began to be written. The religious movement called the Great Awakening and the intellectual ideas of the Enlightenment influenced American thought.

The Importance of Education

Puritans in New England combined education with religion. They passed laws requiring towns to provide schools. While **public schools** are supported by taxes, Puritan schools were supported by both public and private money. Colonial schools taught religion as well as reading, writing, and arithmetic. Most schools were in the north, where people lived more closely together. In the South, members of the gentry hired private tutors, while children of poorer families often received no education.

Only some schools admitted girls. **Dame schools** were opened by women to teach girls and boys to read. Enslaved Africans were not admitted to schools, although some Quaker and Anglican missionaries taught slaves to read.

After elementary school, some boys went to grammar school. The first American colleges were founded mainly to educate men for the ministry. ✓

Roots of American Literature

The first American literature was sermons and histories. Poetry developed slowly, beginning with America's first published poet, **Anne Bradstreet.** Published in 1650 after her death, Bradstreet's poems described the joys and hardships of life in Puritan New England. **Phyllis Wheatley** was an enslaved African in Boston whose first poem was published in the 1760s when she was about 14. She wrote in an academic style that was popular in Europe.

Benjamin Franklin started writing the *Pennsylvania Gazette* when he was 17. His most popular work, *Poor Richard's Almanack*, was published yearly from 1733 to 1753. He was also a scientist,

---

Key Events

1730s	The Great Awakening sweeps through the colonies.
1735	The Zenger case marks a step toward freedom of the press.
1750	Georgia becomes the last of the colonies to permit slavery.

✓ Checkpoint

List four subjects that were taught in colonial schools.

_____

_____

_____

_____

Vocabulary Builder

An *academy* is a school. Use this clue and the underlined sentence to explain what an academic writing style might be like.

_____

_____

businessman, inventor, and diplomat who became one of the founders of the United States. ☑

The Great Awakening

Religion was always a part of colonial life, but by the 1700s, rules on religion had become less strict in many of the colonies. This trend led to the Great Awakening, a strong Christian movement that swept through the colonies in the 1730s and 1740s. **Jonathan Edwards** was a Massachusetts preacher who called on people to commit themselves to God. Other preachers spread the movement on sermon tours, and the Great Awakening led to the rise of many new churches and sects. Methodists and Baptists grew quickly. Presbyterian, Dutch Reformed, and Congregationalist churches split into two groups: those who followed the Great Awakening and those who did not. The growth of new churches led to more tolerance of various religions and reinforced democratic ideas. ☑

The Enlightenment

The Enlightenment was an intellectual movement that began in Europe in the late 1600s. Enlightenment thinkers believed that all problems could be solved by human reason. They looked for "natural laws" that governed politics, society, and economics. Englishman John Locke contributed some of the movement's key ideas, including the belief that people have **natural rights,** or rights that belong to every human from birth and cannot be taken away. Locke argued that government exists to protect the rights of people, and that if a monarch violates those rights, the people have a right to overthrow the monarch. His ideas shaped the founding of the United States.

Frenchman Baron de Montesquieu also influenced American ideas. He believed that the powers of government should be clearly defined and limited. He also favored **separation of powers,** or a division of the power of government into separate branches, to protect against any one group from gaining too much power. He suggested dividing a government into three branches: a legislative branch to make laws, an executive branch to enforce laws, and a judicial branch to make judgments based on law. ☑

Check Your Progress

1. What was the focus of the Great Awakening?

_____

_____

2. What were two ideas held by Enlightenment thinkers?

_____

_____

✓ Checkpoint

Describe the topic of Anne Bradstreet's poems.

_____

_____

✓ Checkpoint

Identify the trend to which the Great Awakening reacted.

_____

_____

✓ Checkpoint

Explain the concept of natural rights.

_____

_____

Question to Think About As you read Section 4 in your textbook and take notes, keep this section focus question in mind: **How did ideas about religion and government influence colonial life?**

▶ Use this chart to record key information from the section. Some information has been filled in to get you started.

The Importance of Education
Massachusetts' laws requiring schools were the beginning of __public__ schools in America. Colonial elementary schools taught _____, _____, _____, and _____. Dame schools were_____.

Roots of American Literature	
Poetry	• Anne Bradstreet was America's first __published poet__. Her poetry described _____. • Phyllis Wheatley was _____ _____.
Ben Franklin	• At age 17, Benjamin Franklin started the newspaper_____. • _____ was his most popular work.

The Great Awakening	
Cause	**Effect**
Religion played a key role in the 13 colonies, but by the 1700s <u>rules on religion had become less strict.</u> →	The Great Awakening was a reaction against this trend. It was _____ _____.
The Great Awakening led to the rise of _____. →	As a result, _____ _____.

The Enlightenment	
John Locke	• Defined natural rights:_____ • Justified the overthrow of a monarch if _____ _____.
Montesquieu	• Separation of powers: <u>division of government into separate branches</u> Government should be divided into three branches:, _____, and _____.

Refer to this page to answer the Chapter 4 Focus Question on page 60.

Chapter 4 Assessment

Directions: Circle the letter of the correct answer.

1. What was one key idea behind the Navigation Acts?
   - **A** Religious freedom must be protected.
   - **B** Colonists must trade with England only.
   - **C** The slave trade is profitable.
   - **D** People have natural rights.

2. Where did most colonists live?
   - **A** in small towns
   - **B** in Massachusetts
   - **C** in large cities
   - **D** on farms

3. What part of colonial culture does the Gullah dialect reflect?
   - **A** African cultural influences
   - **B** the gentry
   - **C** indentured servants
   - **D** the middle class

4. What was the goal of the Great Awakening?
   - **A** economic growth
   - **B** end slavery
   - **C** religious commitment
   - **D** separation of powers

Directions: Follow the steps to answer this question:

What was the main reason that slavery took root in the colonies?

Step 1: Recall information: Note how three factors below affected the growth of slavery.

Factors Leading to Slavery
Plantation System: _____
Indentured Servants:_____
Racism: _____

Step 2: Evaluate: Rank the three factors from most to least important. Give two reasons why you chose the element you ranked as most important.

_____ Plantation System _____ Indentured Servants _____ Racism

- Reason 1: _____
- Reason 2: _____

Step 3: Complete the topic sentence that follows. Then write two or three more sentences that support your topic sentence.

The main reason that slavery took root in the colonies was _____

_____

_____

_____

Chapter 4 Notetaking Study Guide

Now you are ready to answer the Chapter 4 Focus Question: **How did colonial life take shape?**

▶ Complete the following chart to help you answer this question.

Ideas That Shaped the Colonies	
Rights	• As English subjects, colonists believed that they had political _rights_ . • In America, _____ had the right to vote. Colonial _____ made laws. • The Zenger Trial helped establish the _____. • Enlightenment thinkers believed that _____ _____.
Education	Colonies developed public schools to teach religion and _____, _____, and _____. The first college in the colonies was _____, which opened in the year _____.
Religion	The Great Awakening was a _____ movement that_____ _____.
Racism	Racism in the colonies encouraged the development of_____.
Laws That Shaped the Colonies	
Navigation Acts	First passed in _____, these laws were designed to _____ _____.
Slave Codes	These laws were passed in order to _____ _____.
Economic Systems That Shaped the Colonies	
Plantations	The plantation system led to slavery because plantations needed _____.
Triangular Trade	This three-way trade between _____, _____, and _____ resulted in _____.
Roles That Shaped the Colonies	
Family Roles	Men: _____ Women: _____ Children: _____
Social Classes	The major social classes in the colonies were _____ _____.

Refer to this page to answer the Unit 1 Focus Question on page 61.

Unit 1 Pulling It Together Activity

What You Have Learned

Chapter 1 Early people spread across the Americas as different cultures were developing in Africa, Asia, and Europe. European traditions that influenced the United States included Judaism, Christianity, and Greek democracy.

Chapter 2 During the 1400s, European explorers came into contact with Native Americans. From the 1500s to the 1700s, European nations competed to explore and build settlements in the Americas.

Chapter 3 The English established colonies in North America. The religious beliefs of Puritans influenced the New England Colonies, the Middle Colonies became known for religious tolerance, and the Southern Colonies developed plantations based on slavery.

Chapter 4 Although life in the English colonies was influenced by European ideas, the colonies developed their own distinct ideas and traditions. As slavery became a part of American life, the European Enlightenment influenced scientific and political thought.

Think Like a Historian

Read the Unit 1 Essential Question: **How did the colonists, with strong roots in the past, develop their own way of life?**

▶ Use the organizers on this page and the next to collect information to answer this question.

How did colonists develop their own way of life? Some details are listed in the chart below and on the next page. Review your section and chapter notes. Then complete the organizer.

How Colonists Developed Their Own Way of Life	
Government	**Religion**
Colonial legislatures: • • Colonial documents: • •	Religions that came to the colonies: • • • • Colonies that offered religious tolerance: • •

How Colonists Developed Their Own Way of Life (*Continued*)	
New Colonies	**Economic Developments in:**
• New England Colonies:	• New England Colonies:
• Middle Colonies:	• Middle Colonies:
• Southern Colonies:	• Southern Colonies:

Look at the other part of the Unit 1 Essential Question: **How was the colonists' way of life rooted in the past?** The organizer below gives you a part of the answer. Review your section and chapter notes. Then fill in the rest of the organizer.

How the Colonists' Way of Life Was Rooted in England's Past	
England's Political Traditions	**England's Religion**
• Monarchy	•
•	• Persecution of
•	
•	
England's Economic Control	
• Mercantilism: Colonies expected to	
• Navigation Acts:	
•	
•	

Unit 2

Forming A New Nation

Chapter 5 The American colonists, although united with Britain throughout the French and Indian War, grew rebellious over Britain's effort to control them. As tensions increased, the spirit of rebellion turned into a call for independence and war.

Chapter 6 In 1776, the colonists officially announced their Declaration of Independence. A difficult war followed. The American Revolution ended in 1783 with the signing of a peace treaty declaring American independence from British rule. The United States was finally its own nation.

Chapter 7 The new United States set up its first national government. Weaknesses in the Articles of Confederation, however, led to the drafting of a new constitution for the nation. After much debate, the states approved the Constitution, but many insisted that a bill of rights be added.

Citizenship Handbook To be an active citizen, it is important to understand the ideas behind the U.S. Constitution.

Focus Your Learning As you study this unit and take notes, you will find the information to answer the questions below. Answering the Chapter Essential Questions will help build your answer to the Unit Essential Question.

Chapter 5 Focus Question
How did the relationship between Britain and the colonies fall apart?
(page 64)

Chapter 6 Focus Question
How did the American colonists gain their independence?
(page 78)

Unit 2 Focus Question
How did the colonists break away from Britain and create a republican form of government?
(page 119)

Chapter 7 Focus Question
What were major successes and failures of the government under the Articles of Confederation?
(page 92)

What You Will Learn

Britain and the American colonists win the French and Indian War. When Britain tries to exert greater control over the colonies, tensions mount and finally erupt into a war of revolution.

Chapter 5 Focus Question

As you read this chapter, keep this question in mind: **How did the relationship between Britain and the colonies fall apart?**

Section 1

Trouble on the Frontier

Section 1 Focus Question

How did the British gain French territory in North America? To begin answering this question,

- Understand how territorial conflicts caused war between Britain and France.
- Find out why British generals suffered so many early defeats.
- Learn about the Battle of Quebec and how the Treaty of Paris increased British territory.

Section 1 Summary

Britain and France fought over North American territory. After several defeats, the British rallied to win the key battle of Quebec. The French surrendered their American territories to Britain and Spain.

Competing Empires

France and Britain controlled large areas of North America by the mid-1700s. In 1753, the French began building forts to back their claim to the Ohio River valley. The Virginia Colony disputed France's claim. The governor of Virginia sent soldiers, led by young **George Washington**, to build a fort where the Ohio River forms. But the French were already building Fort Duquesne (du KANE) at the spot. A large French army forced Washington and his men to return to Virginia.

At the request of the British government, colonial leaders met in Albany, New York. They discussed the war looming with France and a possible **alliance** with the Iroquois. An alliance is an agreement made between two countries to help each other. The Iroquois, believing the French had the stronger military advantage, chose not to ally with the British. At the meeting, Benjamin Franklin pre-

---

Key Events

1754	French and Indian War begins.
1765	Stamp Act is passed.
1775	Fighting at Lexington and Concord marks the beginning of the American Revolution.

Vocabulary Builder

Reread the underlined sentence. If an *alliance* is an agreement between two nations to help each other, what does it mean to *ally* with someone?

_____

_____

sented his Albany Plan of Union. Under this plan, colonial assemblies would elect a council that had authority over western settlements, as well as the power to organize armies and collect taxes to pay war expenses. The Albany Congress agreed to the plan, but the colonial assemblies, fearful of losing control of their taxes and armies, rejected it. ✓

Early British Defeats

In 1755, the British government sent General Edward Braddock to push the French from the Ohio River valley. Braddock was not familiar with the fighting tactics of Native Americans in the wilderness. As Braddock's British troops and Virginia militia neared Fort Duquesne, the French and their Native American allies launched a crushing ambush. Braddock and more than half his men were killed. During this same year, the British colonials were also defeated at Fort Niagara and suffered heavy losses near Lake George.

In May 1756, Britain declared war on France—the official beginning of the Seven Years' War. Shortly after, the French captured two more British forts. ✓

The British Turn the Tide

When William Pitt became Britain's prime minister in 1757, he appointed superior generals whose talents were equal to the French challenge. This change of military command paid off. In 1758, Britain captured the fort at Louisbourg and then Fort Duquesne. These two victories, followed by others, finally convinced the Iroquois to ally with the British. With growing confidence in their military strength, Britain prepared to attack the city of Quebec, the capital of New France.

The Battle of Quebec took place in September 1759. General James Wolfe led the British. The French were led by General Montcalm. The British won a key victory. Without Quebec, France could not defend the rest of its territories. In 1763, the two countries signed the Treaty of Paris. France **ceded,** or surrendered, almost all of its North American possessions to Britain and Spain. ✓

Check Your Progress

1. What were the provisions of the Albany Plan of Union?

_____

_____

2. What two military changes helped the British win?

_____

_____

✓ **Checkpoint**

State the cause of the initial clash between the British and the French.

_____

_____

✓ **Checkpoint**

Explain why Braddock's well-trained troops suffered defeat at Fort Duquesne.

_____

_____

✓ **Checkpoint**

Name two victories that convinced the Iroquois to ally with the British.

_____

_____

Section 1 Notetaking Study Guide

Question to Think About As you read Section 1 in your textbook and take notes, keep this section focus question in mind: **How did the British gain French territory in North America?**

▶ Use this chart to record key information from the section. Some information has been filled in to get you started.

Competing Empires

The French and Indian War begins
- By the 1750s, the British and French were in conflict over the ____Ohio River valley____.
- To protect Britain's claim to the valley, _____ built Fort Necessity south of France's Fort ____Duquesne____.
- A large French army forced Washington to _____.

The Albany Congress
- During a meeting in Albany, New York, colonial leaders discussed how to win the war and forming an alliance with the _____, who refused to ally with the British.
- _____ drew up the Albany Plan of Union.
- Provisions of the Plan:
    1. A council would have authority over _____ and relations with _____.
    2. The council could organize __armies__ and collect _____.
- Colonial assemblies _____ the plan.

Early British Defeats

- British General _____ was defeated at Fort Duquesne when he ignored warnings about the dangers of ambushes.
- In May 1756, Britain declared war on France, the official beginning of the _____ _____.
- French General Montcalm captured _____ on Lake Ontario and _____ on Lake George.

The British Turn the Tide

- British Prime Minister _____ sent top generals to command the British.
- In the fall of 1758, the British took _____.
- In 1759, the British captured _____, the capital of New France. The other major French city, _____, fell in 1760.

Terms of the Treaty of Paris, 1763
- Britain's new territories: _____
- Spain's new territories: _____

Refer to this page to answer the Chapter 5 Focus Question on page 77.

Section 2

The Colonists Resist Tighter Control

Section 2 Focus Question

How did the French and Indian War draw the colonists closer together but increase friction with Britain? To begin answering this question,

- Find out why Britain prevented colonists from settling beyond the Appalachian Mountains.
- Learn why Britain tried to increase the colonists' taxes.
- Find out how the colonists reacted to the Stamp Act.
- Understand why the Townshend Acts provoked protest.

Section 2 Summary

To pay its war debts, Britain levied new taxes and controls on the American colonists. Each new act caused greater disunity between the British government and the colonies.

Conflict With Native Americans

By 1763, Britain controlled most of North America east of the Mississippi River. <u>Native Americans within this region feared the encroachment of British settlers onto their lands.</u> In May 1763, the Ottawa leader, Pontiac, attacked British forts and settlements. Many settlers were killed, and Britain retaliated. By August 1763, Pontiac's forces were defeated. Pontiac fought for another year, but by the fall of 1764, the war was over.

To avoid more conflicts, Britain issued the Proclamation of 1763. It banned colonial settlements west of the Appalachian Mountains. Many colonists felt the ban violated their right to live where they pleased. The ban was largely ignored. ✔

British Rule Leads to Conflict

The colonists were proud of their contribution to winning the French and Indian War. Although most colonists felt a degree of independence from Britain, they were still loyal British subjects. That loyalty began to erode when Britain, now deeply in debt from the French and Indian War, began to impose new taxes.

In 1764, Parliament passed the Sugar Act, which put a **duty**, or import tax, on several products, including molasses. Colonial merchants protested. A year later, Parliament tried to save money with the Quartering Act, requiring colonists to provide housing and provisions to British troops stationed in the colonies. The colonists angrily complained that the Quartering Act violated their rights. ✔

© Pearson Education, Inc., publishing as Pearson Prentice Hall. All rights reserved.

Key Events

1754	French and Indian War begins.
1765	Stamp Act is passed.
1775	Fighting at Lexington and Concord marks the beginning of the American Revolution.

Vocabulary Builder

Reread the underlined sentence. To *encroach* means "to intrude gradually." Why did Native Americans fear the encroachment of settlers?

_____

_____

✓ Checkpoint

Explain why Britain banned the colonists from settling west of the Appalachian Mountains.

_____

_____

✓ Checkpoint

Describe what the Quartering Act required colonists to do.

_____

_____

The Stamp Act

In 1765, Parliament passed the Stamp Act. This required colonists to buy special tax stamps to put on products, newspapers, and legal documents. In protest, some colonies passed a resolution declaring that only the colonial governments had the right to tax the colonists. Merchants in major cities **boycotted**, or refused to buy, British goods.

Finally, colonial delegates sent a **petition**, a written request to the government, demanding an end to the Sugar Act and the Stamp Act. Parliament repealed the Stamp Act, but it passed the Declaratory Act, which said that Parliament had full authority over the colonies. ✓

Protests Spread

In 1767, Parliament passed the Townshend Acts, which declared that only products imported *into* the colonies would be taxed. To enforce these taxes, as well as to find smuggled goods, customs officers used **writs of assistance.** These legal documents allowed customs officers to make searches without saying what they were looking for.

Colonists boycotted British goods to protest this violation of their rights. Merchants in Britain suffered from the boycott. They pressured Parliament to repeal the Townshend duties, which it did—except for the tax on tea.

Then, on March 5, 1770, a small group of soldiers in Boston fired into an angry crowd, killing five citizens. After this incident, which became known as the Boston Massacre, **Samuel Adams** established a Committee of Correspondence in Massachusetts. Soon other colonies set up committees. They wrote letters and pamphlets to keep colonists informed of British actions. This helped to unite the colonies. ✓

Check Your Progress

1. Why did Britain impose the Sugar Act and Quartering Act?

_____

_____

2. How did the Committee of Correspondence help to unite the colonists?

_____

_____

✓ Checkpoint

State how colonial merchants protested the Stamp Act.

_____

_____

✓ Checkpoint

Name the informational organization set up by Samuel Adams.

_____

_____

Question to Think About As you read Section 2 in your textbook and take notes, keep this section focus question in mind: **How did the French and Indian War draw the colonists closer together but increase friction with Britain?**

▶ Use this chart to record key information from the section. Some information has been filled in to get you started.

The Colonists Unite to Resist British Control	
1754–1763	Colonists fought alongside the British to win __the French and Indian War__, expecting gratitude for their service. But the war put Britain deeply in __debt__.
1763	Britain issued the _____, banning settlement west of the Appalachian Mountains. The British hoped to avoid more wars with Native Americans, but the colonists largely _____ the ban.
1764	Colonists protested __the Sugar Act__, which put a _____ on several products, including molasses, and called for harsh punishment of _____.
1765	Colonists protested the _____, which required them to provide homes and food for British soldiers. Colonists also protested the _____, which put a tax on items such as newspapers and legal documents. Colonial governments declared that only they could levy taxes. Patrick Henry made an emotional speech that bordered on _____. Colonial merchants _____ British goods.
1766	Parliament repealed the _____, but passed the _____, which claimed that Parliament had total authority over the colonies.
1767	The _____ set up a system to enforce new import duties. Colonists protested court orders called _____, which were used to search for illegal goods. Once again, the colonists boycotted.
1770	Parliament repealed all the Townshend duties, except the one on _____. That tax was left in force to demonstrate _____ _____. On March 5, the _____ occurred, in which five Boston citizens were killed and six were injured. The colonies set up _____ to keep colonists informed of British actions.

Refer to this page to answer the Chapter 5 Focus Question on page 77.

From Protest to Rebellion

Section 3 Focus Question

How did British tax policies move the colonists closer to rebellion? To begin answering this question,

- Understand why the colonists resented the Tea Act.
- Learn how Britain responded to the Boston Tea Party.
- Read about events that led to the battle that began the Revolution.

Section 3 Summary

The colonists' protests over British policies continued to escalate until the British sent in troops to control the situation. This caused a confrontation that started the American Revolution.

A Dispute Over Tea

Although most of the Townshend duties had been repealed, the tax on tea remained. Then in 1773, Parliament passed the Tea Act. It gave the British East India Company a **monopoly** on British tea. This meant that the company had total control over all tea sold in the colonies. Although the Tea Act actually lowered the price of tea, it also kept colonial merchants from selling Dutch tea at competitive prices.

The colonists resented the tea tax and the way it limited competitive commerce. To protest the Tea Act, the Sons of Liberty prevented the unloading of tea from the East India Company at many of the colonial ports. However, in Boston, Governor Thomas Hutchinson decided not to allow the tea ships to leave port until they were unloaded.

On the night of December 16, 1773, a large group of men disguised as Native Americans boarded the tea ship waiting in Boston harbor. The ship's cargo of tea, worth thousands of dollars, was tossed into Boston harbor. This event became known as the Boston Tea Party. ✓

The Intolerable Acts

In response to the Boston Tea Party, the enraged British government passed harsh laws that the colonists called the Intolerable Acts. The laws closed the port of Boston, increased the powers of the royal governor, decreased the power of colonial self-government, and strengthened the Quartering Act. Parliament also passed the Quebec Act. This set up new Canadian boundaries that blocked colonists from moving west.

As citizens in all the colonies sent food and supplies to help Boston through the embargo, the Committee of Correspondence held a meeting to discuss what to do next. This meeting, known

Key Events

1754	French and Indian War begins.
1765	Stamp Act is passed.
1775	Fighting at Lexington and Concord marks the beginning of the American Revolution.

✓ Checkpoint

Explain why colonial merchants resented the Tea Act.

_____

_____

Vocabulary Builder

An *embargo* is an order to close a seaport to block import and export trade. What smaller word within *embargo* means "to block"?

_____

as the First Continental Congress, took place in Philadelphia in 1774. Delegates from all the colonies except Georgia participated. The Congress demanded that Parliament **repeal,** or officially end, the Intolerable Acts. It also declared that the colonists had a right to tax and govern themselves. The Congress made it a priority to begin training militias, and the delegates called for a new boycott against British goods. Finally, the Congress voted to meet again in May 1775 if their demands weren't met. ✔

The Shot Heard Round the World

Britain rejected the demands of the First Continental Congress. It decided to restore its authority in the colonies by force. Anticipating this move, the colonists formed new militia units called **minutemen.** These were citizen soldiers who could be ready to fight in a minute.

In April, the governor of Massachusetts sent for troops to seize the colonists' weapons stored at Concord, Massachusetts, and capture important colonial leaders. On April 18, 1775, Paul Revere and William Dawes rode all night to warn the minutemen that the British were on the march. The British soldiers and the minutemen had their first confrontation in the town of Lexington, Massachusetts. A shot now known as "the shot heard round the world" was fired, setting off gunfire between the soldiers and the minutemen. In nearby Concord, another battle was taking place. The American Revolution had begun. ✔

Check Your Progress

1. What event prompted the British to pass the Intolerable Acts?

_____

_____

2. What did the First Continental Congress accomplish?

_____

_____

✓ **Checkpoint**

List the provisions of the Intolerable Acts.

_____

_____

_____

_____

✓ **Checkpoint**

Name the location of the "shot heard round the world."

_____

Question to Think About As you read Section 3 in your textbook and take notes, keep this section focus question in mind: **How did British tax policies move the colonists closer to rebellion?**

▶ Use this chart to record key information from the section. Some information has been filled in to get you started.

Escalating Toward Rebellion	
Tea Act	What it did: • It lowered the _price of tea_, but kept _the tea tax_. • It gave the East India Tea Company _a British tea monopoly_. • It prevented colonial merchants from _____. Colonial reaction: • They stopped East India ships from _____. • They dumped _____.
The Intolerable Acts	What prompted their enactment: • They were Britain's response to _____. What they did: • _____ • _____ • _____ • _____ • _____ The Quebec Act • Took away _____ • Blocked _____
First Continental Congress	What it was: • a meeting in _____ in September and October of _____ to decide what to do next What it did: • _____ • _____ • _____ • _____ Britain's reaction Britain chose to use _____.
Battles of Concord and Lexington	On the night of April 18, 1776, _____ and William Dawes rode to warn the _____ that the British were on their way. The first shot was fired at _____. By the time the British retreated to Boston, almost _____ British soldiers had been killed or wounded.

Refer to this page to answer the Chapter 5 Focus Question on page 77.

Section 4

The War Begins

Section 4 Focus Question

How did the American Revolution begin? To begin answering this question,

- Learn what happened when the Second Continental Congress started to act like a government and began to prepare for war.
- Understand why the Battle of Bunker Hill was such an important conflict for the colonists.

Section 4 Summary

The Second Continental Congress prepared for war with Britain, while Parliament sent a large army to end the revolt. Early battles between the British and the colonists indicated that the colonists could and would fight for their freedom.

The Second Continental Congress

In May 1775, the Second Continental Congress met in Philadelphia. The delegates were divided about what to do. <u>Some wanted to declare independence from Britain, while others wanted more diplomatic action</u>. Nearly all, however, realized that they had to prepare for war. They formed the Continental army, made George Washington the commander, and printed paper money to pay for war expenses.

Like the delegates, the American people themselves were split in their loyalties. Farmers, workers, and many merchants who were affected by the new tax laws were willing to fight for independence. They were called Patriots. Those who owned property and held government positions had more to lose if America lost a war with Britain. These colonists, called Loyalists, remained loyal to the British monarchy in order to keep their lands and positions. Also siding with the British were many enslaved African Americans who hoped to win their freedom, and most Native Americans who feared losing their lands if the colonists won the war. Thousands of Loyalists fought for Britain, and most of them left the colonies during or after the war.

As the Second Continental Congress began, Patriot Ethan Allen and his Green Mountain Boys captured Fort Ticonderoga, a British garrison near Lake Champlain. This victory gave the Continental army control over the main water route between Canada and the Hudson River valley. It also provided the colonists with much-needed weapons, especially cannons.

In July 1775, the Second Continental Congress sent two petitions to the King. The first one, called the Olive Branch Petition after an ancient symbol of peace, stated that the colonists were the King's

Key Events

1754	French and Indian War begins.
1765	Stamp Act is passed.
1775	Fighting at Lexington and Concord marks the beginning of the American Revolution.

Vocabulary Builder

Someone who is *diplomatic* handles people or issues with great sensitivity and skill. What title is given to government workers who interact with foreign officials? Why is it important to handle such interactions with sensitivity and skill?

_____

_____

_____

Name the opposing sides of Americans during the Revolutionary War.

_____

_____

✓ **Checkpoint**

Explain what finally drove the British from Boston.

_____

_____

loyal subjects. The second stated that the colonists were ready to fight for their freedom. The British Parliament ignored the Olive Branch Petition and voted to send 20,000 soldiers to the colonies to end the revolt. ✓

Early Battles

By June 1775, there were 6,500 British troops camped in Boston, while about 10,000 Americans surrounded the city. Nearly 1,600 of the colonial militia were atop Breed's Hill, which overlooked the city and the harbor. Nearby were more Americans on Bunker Hill. These colonial troops were farmers and workers, not trained soldiers. British General William Howe decided to attack straight up the hill. His first and second attacks failed, and many of his men were killed. His third attack succeeded, but only because the Americans ran out of ammunition. Although the British won this battle, known as the Battle of Bunker Hill, it proved that the Americans could successfully fight professional British soldiers.

In July 1775, George Washington took charge of the army surrounding Boston. He had the cannons seized earlier at Fort Ticonderoga moved to high ground overlooking Boston, thus making it impossible for the British to defend the city. On March 17, 1776, the British withdrew from Boston. Although the Americans won this battle, Britain still held most of the advantages. Its navy **blockaded,** or shut off, American ports. The British also strengthened their ranks with hired **mercenaries,** soldiers who serve another country for money.

While Washington trained one army outside Boston, two other armies attempted to invade Canada and take Quebec. One was led by Richard Montgomery; the other by Benedict Arnold. Due to severe winter weather, sickness, and hunger, the attack failed. The Americans withdrew, leaving Canada to the British. ✓

Check Your Progress

1. What three things did the Second Continental Congress do to prepare for war?

_____

_____

2. Why was the Battle of Bunker Hill so important to the Americans?

_____

_____

Section 4 Notetaking Study Guide

Question to Think About As you read Section 4 in your textbook and take notes, keep this section focus question in mind: **How did the American Revolution begin?**

▶ Use this chart to record key information from the section. Some information has been filled in to get you started.

Preparing for War

Second Continental Congress
Date: May 1775
New delegates: <u>Thomas Jefferson</u>, _____, and _____
Steps taken:
   • _____
   • _____
   • _____

Colonists Divided
   • Colonists who wanted independence were called _____ .
   • Colonists who were loyal to the British Crown were called_____ .

Fort Ticonderoga On May 10, 1775, _____ and 83 men, called the _____ _____ captured Fort Ticonderoga. The men seized weapons, including _____, which were later moved to Boston.

Petitions to Britain
These two resolutions showed the uncertainty among the colonists:
   • The <u>Olive Branch Petition</u> stated that_____
   _____ .
   • The Declaration of the Causes and Necessities of Taking Up Arms stated that the
   <u>colonists were ready to die for freedom</u> .

Early Battles
Bunker Hill The British won the Battle of Bunker Hill after the third _____ because the American militia ran out of _____. This battle proved that the Americans could _____ .
Canada In December 1775, one army led by _____ and another led by _____ invaded Canada and attacked the city of _____. The attack failed.

Refer to this page to answer the Chapter 5 Focus Question on page 77.

Directions: Circle the letter of the correct answer.

1. Over which area did Britain and France go to war?
   A   the city of Quebec   C   land east of the Appalachians
   B   the Ohio River valley   D   Spanish Florida

2. Why did Britain increase the colonists' taxes?
   A   to exert control over the colonies   C   to pay for war debts
   B   to pay for the costs of imports   D   to purchase Louisiana

3. What did the colonists resent most about the Tea Act?
   A   It raised the price of tea.
   B   It gave Britain a tea monopoly.
   C   It strengthened the law against smuggling.
   D   It limited the amount of tea for sale.

4. What was one advantage of the capture of Fort Ticonderoga?
   A   It provided cannons for the rebellion.
   B   It proved the Americans could fight against overwhelming odds.
   C   It became a strategic fortress for the colonists.
   D   It convinced the Iroquois to ally with the Americans.

Directions: Follow the steps to answer this question:

How united were the colonists against Britain?

Step 1: Recall information: Identify the colonists who supported independence from Britain and those who did not.

Who Supported America's Independence?	Who Did Not Support America's Independence?

Step 2: Compare and contrast: Briefly describe the differences between the two sides.

Those Who Supported American Independence	Those Who Did Not Support American Independence

Step 3: Draw conclusions: Complete the topic sentence that follows. Then write two or three more sentences that support your topic.

The colonies' conflict with Britain also caused a conflict between _____

_____

_____

_____

Chapter 5 Notetaking Study Guide

Now you are ready to answer the Chapter 5 Focus Question: **How did the relationship between Britain and the colonies fall apart?**

► Complete the charts to help you answer this question. Use the notes that you took for each section.

The Path to Revolution

Result of the French and Indian War

- Although the Treaty of Paris gave Britain more North American territory, Britain banned settlement west of the _____. Britain hoped this would _____.
- Because the French and Indian War left Britain in debt, Parliament increased the colonists' _____ to raise money, and expected the colonists to house and feed _____ to save money.
- Expecting gratitude for their role in winning the war, the colonists became outraged. The colonists organized _____ against British goods.

⬇

Cause and Effects of the Tea Act

- Colonists protested the Tea Act by _____
- The British retaliated by _____.
- The First Continental Congress called for _____.
- The "shot heard round the world" occurred in _____.

⬇

Preparing for War

- The Second Continental Congress established the _____ with _____ as its commander.
- Ethan Allen and his men captured Fort _____.
- The Second Continental Congress sent Britain a declaration stating <u>that they were willing to die fighting for freedom.</u> _____

⬇

Results of Early Battles

- The Americans <u>lost</u> the Battle of Bunker Hill because they ran out of _____.
- The British finally left Boston, but their navy was able to _____ American ports, and their army was strengthened because they hired _____.
- After an American attack on Quebec failed, Canada was left for the _____.

Refer to this page to answer the Unit 2 Focus Question on page 119.

What You Will Learn

In 1776, the colonies proclaimed their separation from Britain in the Declaration of Independence. Then they fought a difficult war for their freedom. The American Revolution ended in 1783 with the signing of a peace treaty declaring American independence from British rule.

Chapter 6 Focus Question

As you read this chapter, keep this question in mind: **How did the American colonists gain their independence?**

Section 1
A Nation Declares Independence

Section 1 Focus Question

Why did many colonists favor declaring independence? To begin answering this question,

- Find out how the call for independence gained support.
- Learn how the Declaration of Independence explained the colonists' reasons for breaking away from British rule.
- Read about the final steps the colonists took to declare their freedom from Britain.

Section 1 Summary

The first half of the year 1776 was marked by a major change in the colonists' thinking about their relationship with Britain. These months were also filled with actions by Patriots and delegates to the Continental Congress that led to a united and formal statement of independence.

A Call for Independence

At the beginning of 1776, few colonists were inclined to support a struggle for independence. Even in the Continental Congress, only one third of the delegates supported independence. The publication of **Thomas Paine**'s *Common Sense,* however, marked the beginning of a shift in people's thinking. In May 1776, **Richard Henry Lee** presented to Congress a **resolution,** or formal statement of opinion, from his home state of Virginia on the right of the colonies to be free. Before voting on Lee's resolution, the Congress assigned a committee to write a formal statement listing reasons why the colonies should separate from Britain. The delegates chose Thomas Jefferson to draft the document. ✔️

Key Events

1776	The Continental Congress issues the Declaration of Independence.
1777	The American victory at Saratoga marks the turning point in the war.
1781	British troops surrender to the Americans at the Battle of Yorktown.

✓ Checkpoint

Name the publication that shifted the colonists toward independence.

_____

The Declaration of Independence

Jefferson's brilliance as a writer is evident in the Declaration of Independence. <u>The document has a logical flow through an introduction and three distinct sections</u>.

> **Preamble:** This introduction explains why the document is being written.

> *General Ideas About Society and Government:* This section states the colonists' basic beliefs:
> * All people have natural rights.
> * Government should protect those rights.
> * When government fails to protect people's rights, the people should abolish the government.

> List of **Grievances:** This section states the formal complaints against King George III of England. He is accused of failing to protect the colonists' rights. Beyond that, the King is accused of actually violating their rights.

> *Conclusion:* This section puts together the colonists' beliefs and grievances to show that the only course left to the colonists is to dissolve all political ties with Britain. An ending pledge demonstrates the seriousness of the colonists' declaration of independence.

✓

Impact of the Declaration

Congress met in July 1776 to decide whether to adopt Lee's resolution and approve the Declaration of Independence. On July 4, 1776, the approval was announced. The Declaration was signed by the delegates on August 2. From that time forward, the Patriots were fighting to become an independent nation.

Check Your Progress

1. What two things happened to bring the colonists and the Congress closer to a formal call for independence?

_____

_____

2. What did the signing of the Declaration of Independence mean for the colonists?

_____

_____

Vocabulary Builder

If the noun *logic* means "careful thought," what does the adjective *logical* mean? Write a definition from context clues in the underlined sentence.

_____

_____

✓ Checkpoint

State the purpose of the Preamble.

_____

_____

✓ Checkpoint

Describe the event that occurred on August 2, 1776.

_____

_____

Question to Think About As you read Section 1 in your textbook and take notes, keep this section focus question in mind: **Why did many colonists favor declaring independence?**

► Use these charts to record key information from the section. Also refer to the Declaration of Independence on pages 174–178 of your textbook. Some information has been filled in to get you started.

A Call for Independence		
Date	**Event**	**Results**
January 1776	Publication of *Common Sense*_____ Description: a pamphlet by_____ explaining _____ _____	• People inspired by words • 500,000 copies distributed • _____
May 1776	Introduction of Virginia resolution to Congress Description: _____ _____	• _____ • _____ _____

The Declaration of Independence	
Sections	**Important Points to Remember**
Preamble	States why the document was written: to explain the need for independence
Declaration of Natural Rights	• _____ • _____ • _____
List of Grievances	• _____ • _____ • _____ _____
Resolution of Independence	• _____ • _____ • _____
Declaration written by: _____ Date approved: _____ Date signed: _____ Immediate result: _____ Lasting result: _____	

Refer to this page to answer the Chapter 6 Focus Question on page 91.

Section 2 Focus Question

How were the early years of the war a critical time? To begin answering this question,

- Read about the first military setbacks for the Continental army.
- Learn how the Continental soldiers' low spirits were raised.
- Find out why the Battle of Saratoga was a turning point of the war.
- Understand how Europeans helped Americans in their fight for freedom.
- Learn about the Continental army's struggles at Valley Forge.

Section 2 Summary

The early years of the war included significant losses as well as victories for the Continental army. Help came in surprising ways to cause the tide to turn in favor of the Americans.

Retreat From New York

By mid-1776, the war shifted from Boston and New England to the Middle States. In New York, the Continental army did not fare well against the British. Led by Sir William Howe, 34,000 British troops and 10,000 sailors attacked the much smaller and less experienced American forces on Long Island. Washington and his soldiers were forced to retreat from Long Island to New York City, then north to White Plains, and eventually west and south through New Jersey. **Nathan Hale** was an American hero who emerged as a legend from these difficult times. He volunteered to spy on the British at Long Island, but he was caught behind British lines and hanged. His famous last words were, "I only regret that I have but one life to lose for my country." ✔

Surprises for the British

By December 1776, the Continental army had retreated all the way into Pennsylvania. The soldiers' spirits plunged as they failed to achieve any victories. Some soldiers even began to desert the army. Thomas Paine wrote *The Crisis* to inspire soldiers to remain committed to the cause of freedom.

On Christmas night, Washington led his soldiers across the Delaware River for a surprise attack on Trenton from two sides. The defeated troops were Hessian **mercenaries,** or soldiers who are paid to fight for a country other than their own. Another American attack near Princeton boosted morale throughout the army. ✔

Key Events

1776	The Continental Congress issues the Declaration of Independence.
1777	The American victory at Saratoga marks the turning point in the war.
1781	British troops surrender to the Americans at the Battle of Yorktown.

✓ Checkpoint

List two reasons the Continental army had to keep retreating from General Howe's attacks.

_____

_____

✓ Checkpoint

Explain why Thomas Paine wrote *The Crisis.*

_____

_____

✓ Checkpoint

List three improvements Baron von Steuben made to American recruits.

_____

_____

_____

✓ Checkpoint

Name four things that soldiers at Valley Forge desperately needed.

_____

_____

Saratoga: A Turning Point

British General John Burgoyne developed a plan that he thought would quickly defeat the Americans. He designed a three-pronged attack to cut off New England from the other states. King George III, however, issued orders that interfered with this plan, and American troops rushed to block British movements. By September 1777, American General Horatio Gates had 6,000 men ready to fight. On October 17, 1777, they forced Burgoyne and his troops to surrender in Saratoga, New York. This victory secured the New England states for the Americans, lifted the Patriots' spirits, and showed Europe that the Continental army might be able to win the war. ✓

Help From Overseas

In 1778, France became the first foreign country to sign a treaty with the United States. France and two of its allies, Spain and the Netherlands, then joined the war against Britain. This caused the British to focus their war efforts on several fronts besides North America, which helped the American cause.

Individual Europeans also aided the Americans in their quest for independence. **Marquis de Lafayette,** a French noble, became a good friend of Washington's as they led troops together. Casimir Pulaski from Poland trained the Patriot **cavalry,** or units of troops on horseback. **Baron Friedrich von Steuben,** a masterful German commander, was especially helpful in teaching American recruits how to march, aim, and attack with bayonets. ✓

Valley Forge

Through the bitter winter of 1777–1778, Washington and his troops suffered terribly at Valley Forge, Pennsylvania. The army was undersupplied, with shortages in food, clothing, and medicine. Drafty huts could not keep out the chill. About one fourth of the soldiers were sick at any given time. Nevertheless, the soldiers gathered their strength and sharpened their skills for the battles to come. ✓

Check Your Progress

1. What were the effects of the Battle of Saratoga?

_____

_____

2. How did European countries and individuals help the Americans?

_____

_____

Section 2 Notetaking Study Guide

Question to Think About As you read Section 2 in your textbook and take notes, keep this section focus question in mind: **How were the early years of the war a critical time?**

► Use these charts to record key information from the section.

Important Battles and Places			
Where	**When**	**What Happened**	**Why Important**
New York State		American forces had to keep retreating .	
Trenton			
Saratoga			
Valley Forge	Winter of 1777–1778		The army gathered its strength for the coming battles .

Important People	
Who	**What They Did and Why It Was Important**
Sir William Howe	• _____ • led British during the worst days of the war for the Patriots
Nathan Hale	• _____ • showed the highest level of commitment to freedom
Thomas Paine	• _____ • _____
George Washington	• _____ • great military leader and an inspiring hero
John Burgoyne	• British general who planned to cut off New England • _____
Horatio Gates	• _____ • _____
Marquis de Lafayette	• _____ • helped Washington win key battles
Thaddeus Kosciusko	• _____
Casimir Pulaski	• _____
Baron von Steuben	• _____ • _____

Refer to this page to answer the Chapter 6 Focus Question on page 91.

Key Events

1776 The Continental Congress issues the Declaration of Independence.

1777 The American victory at Saratoga marks the turning point in the war.

1781 British troops surrender to the Americans at the Battle of Yorktown.

✓ Checkpoint

Explain why Washington decided to accept African American soldiers.

_____

_____

✓ Checkpoint

Name one thing Congress did to try to pay for the costs of the war.

_____

_____

Section 3 Focus Question

How did the effects of the war widen? To begin answering this question,

- Learn why African Americans joined both sides of the war effort.
- Read about the role of American women in wartime, and financial difficulties created by the war.
- Find out how the war reached into the western frontier.
- Understand the importance of skirmishes at sea.

Section 3 Summary

Although the American Revolution was mostly centered in the colonies and fought by free men, all peoples and areas of the country were affected by the war.

African Americans in the War

Both free and enslaved African Americans were soldiers from the beginning of the war. The British offered freedom to all enslaved people who would serve on their side. Americans at first blocked African Americans from service in the army. Washington changed this policy after seeing how many African Americans joined the British cause. By the end of the war, some 7,000 African Americans had joined the American armed forces. Most southern states still kept African Americans out of state armies for fear of slave revolts, but several northern states made moves to end slavery during the Revolutionary War. ✓

The War at Home

Difficult times during the war were not limited to the battlefields. **Civilians,** or people not in the military, also had to deal with problems such as food shortages, enemy attacks, and increased responsibilities in areas in which they previously had little involvement. Women especially experienced huge changes in daily life. Along with these changes came many new opportunities as women took on the roles traditionally held by their husbands, fathers, and brothers.

Hardships also occurred because of the monetary costs of fighting a war. Soldiers had to be paid and supplied. Without the power to tax, Congress had to beg the states for money. Congress began to print money, known as **continentals.** As they printed more and more currency, it eventually became practically worthless. ✓

Fighting in the West

As the war pushed into the western frontier, most Native Americans sided with the British. The Native Americans feared that an American victory would result in continuing takeovers of their lands. In 1778, **George Rogers Clark** was sent by Virginia to try to capture British forts west of the Appalachian Mountains. During that year and the next, Clark and his forces took three important posts in the Ohio Valley area from the British and their Native American allies.

Spain also helped the Americans to maintain control in the west. **Bernardo de Gálvez**, the governor of Louisiana, provided money and weapons for Clark's efforts. He offered American ships safe harbor in New Orleans. From 1779 to 1781, Gálvez played a key role in capturing British forts on the Mississippi River and the Gulf of Mexico. Wealthy Spanish women in Cuba, known as "Havana's Ladies," also joined together to give millions of dollars to the Americans at a time when money was desperately needed. ☑

The War at Sea

The American navy was tiny in comparison to the mighty British fleet. Britain blockaded American ports throughout the war. However, Americans became skilled at hit-and-run attacks. One famous American sea victory came under the command of **John Paul Jones**, who refused to give up the fight. His ship, the Bonhomme Richard, defeated the British warship Serapis off the coast of England in a ferocious 1779 battle. The American navy was also assisted by hundreds of **privateers.** These armed civilian ships were not part of any navy, but they were allowed by their governments to attack enemy ships. After successful attacks, privateers claimed all goods aboard the enemy ships. ☑

Check Your Progress

1. What positive change happened for American women during the Revolution?

_____

_____

2. What role did George Rogers Clark play in the battle on the western frontier?

_____

_____

✓ Checkpoint

Describe how Spain and Cuba helped the American war effort.

_____

_____

_____

_____

✓ Checkpoint

Name the person whose heroic naval efforts are still remembered today.

_____

Section 3 Notetaking Study Guide

Question to Think About As you read Section 3 in your textbook and take notes, keep this section focus question in mind: **How did the effects of the war widen?**

▶ Use these cause-and-effect diagrams to record key information from the section. Some information has been filled in to get you started.

African Americans in the War		
The British offered enslaved African Americans freedom in exchange for fighting on their side.	<u>Many African Americans join the British effort.</u>	Washington decides _____ _____ _____.

The War at Home		
Many men enlist in the army. Women take over traditional male roles.	• Women on farms _____ _____. • Women in towns _____ _____ _____. • Women in military camps _____ _____.	<u>Women have new confidence and opportunities open to them.</u>
Congress has little money to pay for war.	• States _____ _____. • Congress _____ _____.	Printed money _____ _____.

Fighting in the West	
Most Native Americans choose to join the British side.	George Rogers Clark is sent _____ _____. He captures _____.
Spain joins the American side.	Bernardo de Gálvez _____ _____. Havana's Ladies _____.

The War at Sea	
Huge British navy blockades American ports.	• <u>Small American navy uses hit-and-run attacks</u> . • Famous navel battle between American ship _____ and the British warship _____ • Captain _____ refuses to give up. • American navy has help from some 800 _____.

Refer to this page to answer the Chapter 6 Focus Question on page 91.

Section 4

Winning Independence

Section 4 Focus Question

How did the Americans win the war and make peace? To begin answering this question,

- Read about the battles in the southern states and the final victory by the Americans in Virginia.
- Learn about the terms for peace in the Treaty of Paris.
- Find out the main reasons why Americans won the war.
- Understand the lasting effects of the American Revolution.

Section 4 Summary

Although the British purposefully shifted their battle plans to southern states in what they viewed to be a sure way to achieve victory, the strategy did not work. American troops took bold actions that resulted in a final American victory, leading at last to peace and independence from Britain.

Fighting Moves South

Beginning late in 1778, the British focused their efforts on the South. Seizing key cities, the British marched north under Commander **Charles Cornwallis,** moving from Florida all the way into North Carolina.

To slow the British advance, the Americans fought using **guerrilla** tactics, working in small groups to perform surprise hit-and-run attacks against the British. **Francis Marion,** also called the Swamp Fox, was the most famous leader of these efforts. Meanwhile, Loyalist bands burned, plundered, and massacred men, women, and children throughout the South. In addition, a high-ranking American named Benedict Arnold, perhaps the most infamous **traitor** in American history, switched his allegiance to the British and led other Loyalists in successful attacks.

Things seemed very grim for the Patriots as these actions unfolded. Nevertheless, by the fall of 1780, American fortunes began to improve. Key victories in South Carolina and strong leadership by General **Nathanael Greene** resulted in the Americans beginning to push the British out of the Deep South. At this point, Cornwallis made a <u>strategic</u> blunder. He moved his troops to the Yorktown peninsula in Virginia, planning to get help from the British fleet. However, French ships soon pushed out the British navy, and Washington's American and French troops surrounded Cornwallis on land. Trapped on all sides, Cornwallis was forced to surrender. This American victory was the last major battle of the war. ✓

Key Events

1776 The Continental Congress issues the Declaration of Independence.

1777 The American victory at Saratoga marks the turning point in the war.

1781 British troops surrender to the Americans at the Battle of Yorktown.

Vocabulary Builder

The underlined word *strategic* is a form of the word *strategy*, which refers to moving troops into the best position for fighting.

✓ Checkpoint

Describe the key strategic blunder made by the British near the end of the war.

_____

_____

_____

_____

List four factors that helped the
Americans win the Revolutionary
War.

_____

_____

_____

_____

List two important ideas for which
Americans fought.

_____

_____

Making Peace With Britain

Following the surrender at Yorktown, the British Parliament decided it was time to make peace. The process began in Paris in 1782 and eventually resulted in the Treaty of Paris. Under the terms of the treaty, Britain recognized the United States as independent. Borders were established for the new country— Canada to the north, the Atlantic Ocean on the east, Florida to the south, and the Mississippi River on the west. On April 15, 1783, Congress approved the treaty, officially ending the war. General Washington bade farewell to his officers and returned to his plantation life. ✓

Why Did the Americans Win?

Four things worked in favor of the Americans during the Revolutionary War. First, the Americans knew the geography of the country and had local supply lines. Second, patriotism kept the troops fighting with fervor. Third, help from allies was an indispensable part of American success. French military and naval assistance as well as money and privateers from Spain and the Netherlands were crucial. Finally, the Americans had great leaders. George Washington's courage and knowledge made him the nation's most admired hero. ✓

Impact of the Revolution

After winning the war, the United States was finally an independent nation with 13 states. The American ideals of equality and liberty were ideas that appealed to the rest of the world, too. Over the next few decades, independence movements in France and Latin America modeled many of their efforts after the successful American Revolution. ✓

Check Your Progress

1. Describe the British plan of attack and its successes during late 1778 and early 1779.

_____

_____

2. What important effect did the American Revolution have on the rest of the world?

_____

_____

Question to Think About As you read Section 4 in your textbook and take notes, keep this section focus question in mind: **How did the Americans win the war and make peace?**

▶ Use these charts to record key information from the section. Some information has been filled in to get you started.

The End of the War
The British march north under Cornwallis and important cities are captured: In Georgia: _Savannah___ In South Carolina: _____ Loyalists also play a part:_____ _____
The Americans Fight Back 1. Guerrilla attacks What they were: _____ Important leader: _____ 2. Frontier fighters When: _____ Where: _____ What happened: _____ 3. Nathanael Greene's Plan: _____ What resulted: _____
Weakened, the British go to Virginia. Where: _____ Why: _Cornwallis expected help from the British fleet_____ What happened: _____

The Peace Process
Peace Talks Where: _____ When: _____ Terms of the Treaty of Paris: Britain agreed _____ The United States agreed _____ Congress approved treaty on _____

Why the Americans Won
1. 2. 3. 4.

Refer to this page to answer the Chapter 6 Focus Question on page 91.

Chapter 6 Assessment

Directions: Circle the letter of the correct answer.

1. How did the Declaration of Independence end?
   - **A** with a list of grievances against King George III
   - **B** with an overview of colonial beliefs
   - **C** with a solemn pledge by Congress to uphold the ideas stated
   - **D** with a definition of independence

2. Which battle was an early turning point in the war?
   - **A** Valley Forge
   - **B** Saratoga
   - **C** Savannah
   - **D** Cahokia

3. For what is John Paul Jones remembered?
   - **A** showing heroism during a sea battle
   - **B** turning into an American traitor
   - **C** serving as an American spy
   - **D** securing frontier forts

Directions: Follow the steps to answer this question:

How can we see evidence of the power of the written word during the American Revolution?

Step 1: Recall information: List all the important pieces of writing you have read about that were part of American history from 1776 to 1783.

-
-
-
-
-

Step 2: Description: For each piece of writing, describe why it was written. Explain the powerful effect it produced.

Writing	Why It Was Written	Effect

Step 3: Complete the topic sentence that follows. Then write two or three more sentences that support your topic sentence.

During the American Revolution, the written word was used _____

_____

_____

_____

Chapter 6 Notetaking Study Guide

Now you are ready to answer the Chapter 6 Focus Question: **How did the American colonists gain their independence?**

▶ Fill in the chart to help you answer this question. Use the notes you took for each section.

The American Revolution
The colonists gathered support for independence. In 1776, two Patriots took actions that made people more interested in independence: Thomas Paine _published Common Sense_____ . Richard Henry Lee _____ .
The colonists declared their freedom. In 1776, the Continental Congress decided to_____ . The delegates chose _____ for this job. The result was _the Declaration of Independence____ . It included these sections:

	Section	Purpose
1.		
2.		
3.		
4.		

The colonists fought and won the war for freedom. Major battles were fought from 1776 to 1781. Early battles were centered in _the Middle States___ . A turning point for the Americans occurred in _____ at_____ . Following this victory, Americans received help from _____, _____, and _____. Foreigners such as Frenchman_____ and German _____ were vital to the war effort. When the British focused on the South, Americans fought back with _____ tactics and frontier fighters such as Francis Marion, known as _____ , and _____, the commander of the Continental army in the South. The final American victory came in _____ at _____ .
The British agreed that the colonists were free and independent. Peace talks began in __1782_____ in _Paris___ . According to the Treaty of Paris: • • • Congress approved the treaty on _____ .

Refer to this page to answer the Unit 2 Focus Question on page 119.

Chapter 7

Creating the Constitution (1776–1790)

What You Will Learn

Weaknesses in the Articles of Confederation led to the drafting of a new constitution for the nation. After much debate, the states approved the Constitution, but many insisted that a bill of rights be added.

Chapter 7 Focus Question

As you read this chapter, keep this question in mind: **How did the U.S. Constitution overcome the weaknesses of the Articles of Confederation and provide for the organization of the new government?**

Section 1

Governing a New Nation

Section 1 Focus Question

What were major successes and failures of the government under the Articles of Confederation? To begin answering this question,
- Learn about the new state constitutions.
- Learn about the Articles of Confederation.
- Find out about laws for settling new lands in the west.
- Understand the problems of the Articles of Confederation.

Section 1 Summary

Americans created new state and national governments based on the principles of the American Revolution. Problems under the Articles of Confederation led to calls for a stronger national government.

Government by the States

Many of the former colonies wrote new state constitutions. A **constitution** is a document stating the rules under which government will operate. Most states minimized the power of state governors because colonial governors had abused their power. Instead, most power was given to the state legislature, the lawmaking body elected by the people.

The new state constitutions allowed more people to vote. In most states, white men 21 years or older could vote if they owned some property, but women and African Americans were not allowed to vote. Virginia was the first state to have a bill of rights, which is a list of essential freedoms that the government is required to respect. ✔

Key Events

1776 Many new American states write constitutions.

1787 Constitutional Convention creates a new plan of government.

1791 After three fourths of states approve it, the Bill of Rights goes into effect.

✓ Checkpoint

List one characteristic of the new state governments.

_____

_____

_____

The Articles of Confederation

The Continental Congress created the Articles of Confederation in 1777. This plan created a new national government for the United States with restricted powers.

The national government had a single branch, a one-house legislature called Congress, which had the power to pass laws, deal with foreign nations and Native Americans, make war and peace, coin or borrow money, and run a post office. Congress was not given the power to collect taxes or to interfere with trade between the states. All states were equal, and most power remained in the hands of the states. ✓

Settling the Western Lands

The Land Ordinance of 1785 created a way for national lands to be sold to the public. It divided public western lands into square townships of six miles on each side. This would result in a grid of squares. Within each township there would also be a grid, one mile on each side. Each township had one section that was set aside to support schools. This reflected the belief of the nation's leaders that democracy depended on education.

A law called the Northwest Ordinance of 1787 applied to the territory north of the Ohio River. It guaranteed basic rights to settlers, outlawed slavery, and established a process for creating new states in the territory. Eventually, five states would be settled in the Northwest Territory. ✓

Growing Problems

Under the Articles of Confederation, the United States won its independence, negotiated a peace treaty with Britain, and created rules for settling new territories. There were also problems: trade rivalries and taxation between states hurt the economy, the national government was too weak to stop public unrest, and it had little money because it could not collect taxes.

During the mid-1780s, economic hard times in Massachusetts caused many farmers to lose their land because they could not pay their taxes. In Shays' Rebellion, a group of Massachusetts farmers rose up against the state in protest. The rebellion failed, but it led to calls for a stronger national government. ✓

Check Your Progress

1. Why were the state and national governments' powers limited?

_____

_____

2. List two problems with the national government under the Articles of Confederation.

_____

_____

_____

✓ Checkpoint

List two powers of the national government created by the Articles of Confederation.

_____

_____

✓ Checkpoint

Name two laws that related to the settling of western lands.

_____

_____

✓ Checkpoint

List two successes of the national government created by the Articles of Confederation.

_____

_____

_____

Question to Think About As you read Section 1 in your textbook and take notes, keep this section focus question in mind: **What were major successes and failures of the government under the Articles of Confederation?**

► Use these charts to record key information from the section. Some of the information has been filled in to get you started.

Government by the States

Problems the Colonists had with Colonial Government		**Main Characteristics of the State Governments**
Colonial governors: Most colonists were unhappy with the governors appointed by the British Crown.	Changed in new constitutions →	**State governors:** had _____ power
Parliament: Parliament, which was part of the __central__ government, exerted power over the elected _____ legislatures.		**Voting:** _____ people were allowed to vote
		Individual rights: protected in several states' _____ of _____

National Government Under the Articles of Confederation

Main Characteristics

- No _____executive_____ or _____ branch of government
- One legislative branch, called _____, with each state having one vote
- _____ out of 13 states had to approve laws
- Legislative power limited to:
  - •
  - •
  - •
  - •
  - •

Strengths

- Won _____ from Britain and negotiated peace treaty
- The _____ and the _____ established rules for settling new lands and creating new states.

Weaknesses

- No authority to regulate _____ or collect _____
- Could not protect land from foreign occupation
- Could not stop public unrest as shown in _____

Refer to this page to answer the Chapter 7 Focus Question on page 102.

The Constitutional Convention

Section 2 Focus Question

What role did compromise play in the creation of the U.S. Constitution? To begin answering this question,

- Learn how the Constitutional Convention began.
- Read about the proposals in the Virginia Plan.
- Find out about the terms of the Great Compromise.
- Learn how slavery issues influenced the Constitution.
- Discover the source of the new Constitution's authority.

Section 2 Summary

By its end, the Constitutional Convention of 1787 had replaced the Articles of Confederation. The new U.S. Constitution created a stronger, more complex national government based on the authority of the people, not the states.

The Constitutional Convention Begins

The Constitutional Convention met in Philadelphia in 1787. At the start, the delegates agreed to hold discussions in secret so that there would be less public pressure. The convention's initial purpose was to revise the Articles of Confederation, but soon its members agreed that revising the Articles was not enough. The 55 delegates, representing 12 states, included respected leaders of the Revolution. George Washington was quickly voted president of the convention. ✔

The Virginia Plan

From the start, an entirely new framework of government was proposed. **James Madison** wrote the Virginia Plan, which called for a strong central government with three branches instead of one. The **judicial branch** would consist of a system of courts to settle disputes involving national issues, and an executive branch would carry out the laws. It was agreed that the executive branch would have one chief executive, called the President.

Congress would remain the legislative branch. However, the Virginia Plan sought to change Congress. It added a second house and made it so each state would be represented in the two houses based on its population. The more people a state had, the more seats it would have in each house. This idea drew support from big states like Virginia, Pennsylvania, and Massachusetts. ✔

The Great Compromise

States with small populations opposed the changes in the legislative branch and offered their own plan called the New Jersey Plan. It called for a single house of Congress where all the states would have equal representation.

Key Events

1776	Many new American states write constitutions.
1787	Constitutional Convention creates a new plan of government.
1791	After three fourths of states approve it, the Bill of Rights goes into effect.

✓ Checkpoint

Name the location of the Constitutional Convention of 1787.

_____

_____

✓ Checkpoint

List the three branches of government proposed in the Virginia Plan.

_____

_____

_____

✓ **Checkpoint**

List the two houses of Congress that the Great Compromise proposed.

_____

_____

✓ **Checkpoint**

Name two main issues about slavery that divided the northern and southern states during the Constitutional Convention.

_____

_____

_____

_____

✓ **Checkpoint**

Name the author of the Preamble to the U.S. Constitution.

_____

The Great Compromise settled the disagreement between the large and small states. A **compromise** is an agreement in which each side gives up part of what it wants. To please the large states, the House of Representatives was developed. Each state's representation in the House would be based on population, and its members would serve two-year terms. In the Senate, which was formed to please the small states, each state would have two senators serving six-year terms.

The Great Compromise was a vital step in creating a new Constitution. Now, small-state delegates were willing to support a strong central government. ✓

Debates Over Slavery

Slavery also divided the convention. The southern states, where there were more slaves, wanted slaves to count toward representation in the House. Northerners argued that slaves, who were not allowed to vote, should not be counted. It was agreed that each slave would count as three fifths of a person. This was called the Three-Fifths Compromise.

The Three-Fifths Compromise was a gain for the South, which got more seats in the House. Northern delegates reluctantly agreed in order to keep the South in the Union.

A second dispute arose when northern delegates called for a total ban on the buying and selling of slaves. A compromise was reached whereby the import of slaves from other countries could be banned in 20 years, while there would be no restrictions on the slave trade within the United States. ✓

A New Constitution

After many more weeks of debate, the delegates agreed on all the terms. A "Committee of Style" wrote the Constitution's final wording. **Gouverneur Morris** was largely responsible for writing the Preamble, or introduction. The Preamble highlights a difference between the Constitution and the Articles of Confederation. The Articles were a pact between separate states. By opening with "We the People of the United States," the Constitution made it clear that its authority came from the people, not the states. ✓

Check Your Progress

1. What was the initial purpose of the Constitutional Convention of 1787?

_____

_____

2. What was important about the first words of the Preamble to the new U.S. Constitution?

_____

_____

Question to Think About As you read Section 2 in your textbook and take notes, keep this section focus question in mind: **What role did compromise play in the creation of the U.S. Constitution?**

▶ Use these organizers to record key information from the section. Some of the information has been filled in to get you started.

The Constitutional Convention

Issue: How to encourage debate during the convention without public pressure

Solution: Convention delegates voted to hold discussions in secret.

↓

Issue: How to create a stronger national government with more powers than under the Articles of Confederation

Solution Provided by the Virginia Plan: Create a government with _____ branches, and separate _____ into two houses. James Madison authored the plan.

↓

Issue: How many people should lead the executive branch

Solution Reached After a Vote: _____

↓

Issue: How to elect representatives to the two houses of the legislative branch

Solution Proposed by the Virginia Plan: Elect representatives to both houses according to _____.
Solution Proposed by the New Jersey Plan: Give each state _____ vote(s), regardless of its population.
Solution Reached by the Great Compromise: House of _____ would be based on _____, and states would be represented equally in the _____. _____ suggested The Great Compromise.

↓

Issue: How to show that the Constitution derived its authority from the people

Solution: Add a preamble that says, "We the _____..." Gouverneur Morris wrote the Preamble.

Refer to this page to answer the Chapter 7 Focus Question on page 102.

Debating the Constitution

Section 3 Focus Question

How did those in favor of the Constitution achieve its ratification? To begin answering this question,

- Read about the arguments for and against the Constitution.
- Learn about the debate over ratification of the Constitution.
- Find out why the Bill of Rights was added to the Constitution.

Section 3 Summary

After the 1787 Convention, the Constitution was sent to the states for approval. Its opponents and supporters debated energetically, and after the Bill of Rights was added, all the states approved the Constitution.

Federalists Versus Antifederalists

The Federalists wanted a strong federal, or national, government. Three important Federalist leaders, **Alexander Hamilton, John Jay,** and James Madison, wrote a series of 85 newspaper essays called the *Federalist Papers* in support of the Constitution.

At the heart of the Federalist position was the need for a stronger central government. The Federalists argued that in order for the Union to last, the national government had to have powers denied it under the Articles of Confederation, including the power to enforce laws.

The opponents of the Constitution were known as Antifederalists. Many Antifederalists, such as **George Mason** and Patrick Henry, agreed that the Articles of Confederation were not strong enough. However, they felt that the Constitutional Convention had gone too far.

	Antifederalist Arguments Against the Constitution
1	The Constitution weakened the state governments by giving too much power to the national government. Antifederalists feared that a too strong central government would wipe out state power and individual freedom.
2	The Constitution also did not include a bill of rights to protect basic freedoms.
3	The President could become like a king by being repeatedly reelected.

✓

Key Events

1776 Many new American states write constitutions.

1787 Constitutional Convention creates a new plan of government.

1791 After three fourths of states approve it, the Bill of Rights goes into effect.

Vocabulary Builder

Federal means "formed by a union of states, in which each gives up power to a central authority." How does this relate to the goal of the Federalists?

_____

_____

_____

✓ Checkpoint

Name the Federalists' main argument in favor of the Constitution.

_____

_____

The Ratification Debate

The Constitution was submitted to the states, and each state called a convention to decide whether to ratify, or approve, the Constitution. At least nine states had to ratify the Constitution, or it would not go into effect. Delaware acted first. Its convention approved the Constitution in December 1787. Pennsylvania, New Jersey, Georgia, and Connecticut followed close behind.

The Federalists' strong efforts in Massachusetts led to approval in that state despite opposition in rural areas from which Shays' Rebellion had drawn its strength. By then, Maryland and South Carolina had ratified, which made a total of eight state ratifications. Then in June 1788, New Hampshire became the ninth state to ratify the Constitution, meaning it could now go into effect. The other states eventually approved the Constitution, with Rhode Island being the last of the original 13 states to do so in May 1790. ✓

The Bill of Rights

After nine states had ratified the Constitution, Congress took steps to prepare for a presidential election. George Washington was elected the first President, with John Adams as Vice President.

During the debate on the Constitution, many states had insisted that a bill of rights be added. This became one of the first tasks of the new Congress that met in March 1789

In 1789, Congress passed a series of amendments, or changes to a document. By December 1791, three fourths of the states had ratified 10 amendments. These amendments are known as the Bill of Rights.

The Bill of Rights protects citizens against governmental abuses of power. The First Amendment protects freedom of religion, speech, and the press. Recalling the importance of colonial militias, the Second Amendment deals with the right to bear arms. The Third Amendment bars Congress from forcing citizens to keep troops in their homes, as Britain had done. The Fourth Amendment protects citizens from unreasonable searches of their homes or seizure of their property. The Fifth through Eighth Amendments mainly protect those accused of crimes. The last two amendments restricted the powers of the national government to those granted in the Constitution. ✓

Check Your Progress

1. Why did the Antifederalists object to the Constitution?

_____

_____

2. What role does the Bill of Rights play?

_____

_____

✓ Checkpoint

Name the first and last states to ratify the Constitution.

First: _____

Last: _____

✓ Checkpoint

List three freedoms the First Amendment protects.

_____

_____

_____

Question to Think About As you read Section 3 in your textbook and take notes, keep this section focus question in mind: **How did those in favor of the Constitution achieve its ratification?**

▶ Use these charts to record key information from the section. Some of the information has been filled in to get you started.

Federalists Versus Antifederalists

Federalists
Leaders: 1. John Jay, 2. _____, 3. _____
Position on the new Constitution: _____
Main argument for position: need for a _____ central government

Antifederalists
Leaders: 1. Patrick Henry, 2. _____
Position on the new Constitution: _____
  Arguments for position:
  1. _____
  2. _____
3. The President could become like a king by being repeatedly reelected.

The Ratification Debate

- Approval needed from _____ states before the Constitution could go into effect.
- Importance of Massachusetts: Antifederalists hoped it would reject the Constitution because opposition was strong where Shays' Rebellion had occurred. It was approved after a major campaign by the Federalists.
- Importance of Virginia: Virginia was _____ and _____. If it rejected the Constitution, _____ and other states might do so, too.

The Bill of Rights

Many states believed that a bill of rights was essential to protect basic _____liberties_____ and to protect against abuses by the _____.
- First Amendment: guarantees freedom of _____, _____, and _____.
- Second Amendment: deals with the right to _____.
- Third Amendment: bars Congress from _____.
- Fourth Amendment: protects citizens from _____ or _____.
- Fifth through Eighth Amendments: protect citizens who are _____ _____.
- Ninth and Tenth Amendments: limit the powers of the _____ to those granted in the _____.

Refer to this page to answer the Chapter 7 Focus Question on page 102.

Chapter 7 Assessment

Directions: Circle the letter of the correct answer.

1. Who had the most political power under the Articles of Confederation?
   - **A** the state governments
   - **B** the President
   - **C** the Continental Congress
   - **D** the Supreme Court

2. What was a result of the Great Compromise during the Constitutional Convention?
   - **A** the immediate end of the slave trade
   - **B** adding the Bill of Rights to the Constitution
   - **C** the organization of a national government with only one branch
   - **D** the creation of a legislative branch with two houses

3. One reason that some of the Antifederalists opposed the Constitution was
   - **A** they believed they had a better plan for the national government.
   - **B** they believed it gave too much power to the states.
   - **C** they believed the Constitution should include a bill of rights.
   - **D** they believed slavery should be allowed north of the Ohio River.

Directions: Follow the steps to answer this question:

What do the successes and failures of the government under the Articles of Confederation tell you about it?

Step 1: Recall information. List two successes and two failures of the government under the Articles of Confederation.

Successes	Failures
1. 2.	1. 2.

Step 2: Compare: What do the successes of the government tell you about it? What do the failures of the government tell you about it?

What the Successes Tell You	What the Failures Tell You

Step 3: Complete the topic sentence that follows. Then write two or three more sentences that discuss the strengths and weaknesses of the Articles of Confederation.

Under the Articles of Confederation, the United States _____

_____

_____

_____

_____

_____

_____

_____

Chapter 7 Notetaking Study Guide

Now you are ready to answer the Chapter 7 Focus Question: **How did the U.S. Constitution overcome the weaknesses of the Articles of Confederation and provide for the organization of the new government?**

▶ Complete the following charts to help you answer this question. Use the notes that you took for each section.

Articles of Confederation	
Form of government	• single branch: a one-house legislature called Congress • each state had _____ vote(s) • _____ states had to agree before a law could go into effect
Limited government	• limited _____ government; most power held by the _____ • _____ could not enforce laws

Constitutional Convention of 1787	

Virginia Plan	• strong central government
	• three branches of government:
	  •
	  •
	  •
	• legislature divided into _____ houses
	• representation based on _____
	• Small states objected to the plan because the more _____ a state had, the more _____ it would have.

New Jersey Plan	• _____ house(s) in Congress • _____ representation for each state • expanded powers of Congress to _____ and _____

The Great Compromise	Two houses of Congress
	• lower house: _____
	  • representation based on _____
	• upper house: _____
	  • each state had _____ seats

The Three-Fifths Compromise	• Southerners said that enslaved people should be counted in calculating how many _____ a state should have in Congress. Northerners objected because enslaved people were not allowed to _____. • As a compromise each enslaved person was counted as three fifths of a _____ .

Refer to this page to answer the Unit 2 Focus Question on page 119.

Constitution Notetaking Study Guide

Question to Think About As you read the Constitution in your textbook and take notes, keep this question in mind: **How do the amendments affect life in the United States today?**

► Use the charts on this page and the next to record key information about amendments to the U.S. Constitution. Some of the information has been filled in to get you started.

AMENDMENTS 11–18 TO THE U.S. CONSTITUTION				
Amendment	**Year Ratified**	**Subject**	**Does the amendment allow…**	**Yes or No**
Eleventh	1795	suits against states	a citizen of one state to sue the government of another state in federal court?	no
Twelfth			electors to cast one ballot for President and Vice President?	
Thirteenth			slavery to exist in the United States?	
Fourteenth			states to make laws that limit the rights of citizens?	
Fifteenth			the federal government or states to limit the right to vote based on race?	
Sixteenth			Congress to tax people on their income?	
Seventeenth			state legislatures to choose senators?	
Eighteenth			people to make, sell, or transport alcohol?	

► Complete this chart to record information about the last nine amendments to the U.S. Constitution.

AMENDMENTS 19–27 TO THE U.S. CONSTITUTION				
Amendment	**Year Ratified**	**Subject(s)**	**Does the amendment allow...**	**Yes or No**
Nineteenth	1920	women's suffrage	women to vote in state and federal elections?	yes
Twentieth			the Vice-President-elect to become President if the President-elect dies before taking office?	
Twenty-first			people to make, sell, or transport alcohol?	
Twenty-second			a person to serve as President for more than two terms?	
Twenty-third			the people living in the District of Columbia to vote for President?	
Twenty-fourth			U.S. citizens to be required to pay a tax before voting in federal elections?	
Twenty-fifth			the Vice President to take over the duties of President if the President declares that he or she is unable to carry them out?	
Twenty-sixth			citizens eighteen or older to vote?	
Twenty-seventh			members of Congress to receive right away a pay increase they voted for themselves?	

Refer to these charts to answer the Unit 2 Focus Question on page 119.

Citizenship Handbook

What You Will Learn

The U.S. Constitution is the supreme law of the United States. It determines the structure of the federal government. Government also operates at the state and local levels.

Citizenship Handbook Focus Question

As you read this handbook, keep this question in mind: **How did the Constitution create a strong government with roots in history that allowed for change and met the needs of the people?**

Summary 1

Summary 1 Focus Questions
- What were the ideas behind the Constitution?
- What is the structure of the Constitution?
- What are the principles underlying the U.S. Constitution?

Summary

In drafting the Constitution, the Framers used ideas and principles from a variety of historical documents and important thinkers of Europe.

Ideas Behind the Constitution

The delegates to the Constitutional Convention were influenced by past experiments with democracy and natural rights. American leaders looked to the ancient Roman Republic as a model. A **republic** is a government in which citizens rule themselves through elected representatives.

The following principles from the Magna Carta and the English Bill of Rights influenced the U.S. Constitution:
- Citizens have rights, which the government must protect.
- Even the head of the government must obey the law.
- Taxes cannot be raised without the consent of the people.
- Elections should be held frequently.
- People accused of crimes have the right to trial by jury and the right of **habeas corpus,** meaning no person may be held in prison without being charged with a specific crime.
- People have the right to **private property,** or property owned by an individual.

Enlightenment thinkers John Locke and Baron de Montesquieu were also key influences. Locke declared that every person has a natural right to life, liberty, and property. Montesquieu

Vocabulary Builder

Republic comes from two Latin words: *res*, which means "interest" and *publicus*, which means "public." How does a republic represent the public interest?

_____

_____

_____

_____

✓ Checkpoint

Name two documents from British history that influenced the U.S. Constitution.

_____

_____

Vocabulary Builder

Preamble comes from Latin roots meaning "walking in front of."

✓ Checkpoint

List two issues dealt with in Article 4 of the Constitution.

_____

_____

_____

_____

✓ Checkpoint

List three of the basic principles embodied in the Constitution.

_____

_____

_____

suggested the concept of separation of powers. **Separation of powers** states that the powers of government must be clearly defined and divided into legislative, executive, and judicial branches.

The Pilgrims drafted the first document of self-government in North America, the Mayflower Compact. Each of the 13 colonies' charters identified the power and limits of government by the king of England. In writing the Constitution, the Framers sought to prevent the abuses listed by Thomas Jefferson against George III in the Declaration of Independence. ✓

Structure of the Constitution

The Preamble, or opening statement, of the Constitution outlines the goals of the document. Seven sections called the articles make up the main body of the Constitution. The first three articles describe the branches of government: legislative, executive, and judicial. Article 4 requires states to honor one another's laws and sets up a system for admitting new states. Article 5 provides a process for amending the Constitution. Article 6 declares the Constitution as the "supreme law of the land." Article 7 sets up the procedure for the states to ratify the Constitution. In more than 200 years, only 27 changes have been made to the Constitution. ✓

Principles of the Constitution

The Constitution rests on seven basic principles.

- **Popular sovereignty** asserts that the people are the main source of the government's authority.
- **Limited government** means the government only has powers given to it by the Constitution.
- Separation of powers divides the federal government into three branches. Each branch has its own duties.
- **Checks and balances** is a system by which each branch of government has the power to limit the actions of the other two. Like the separation of powers, this is designed to prevent the abuse of power.
- **Federalism** is the division of power between the federal government and the states.
- Republicanism provides for a government in which people elect representatives to carry out their will.
- The principle of individual rights means the Constitution protects rights such as freedom of speech and the right to trial by jury. ✓

Check Your Progress

1. What was Montesquieu's idea of the separation of powers?

_____

_____

2. What is described in the first three articles of the Constitution?

_____

Constitution Notetaking Study Guide

Keep in mind the Summary 1 Focus Questions as you read about the Constitution in your textbook and take notes.

▶ Use these charts to help you record key Constitution facts. Some information has been filled in to get you started.

Ideas Behind the Constitution

Ideas from Rome and England

The Example of Rome: The government of early Rome was a ___republic___ in which citizens ruled through _____. However, this form of government collapsed and was replaced with a _____.

Documents from England: The _____ and the English _____ placed limits on the power of rulers and protected the _____ of citizens.

Ideas from the Enlightenment

John Locke:
1.
2.
3. People have a right to rebel if a ruler violates the people's natural rights.

Baron de Montesquieu:
Goal of separation of powers: _____

Articles of the Constitution

Article	Subject of the Article
Article 1	
Article 2	establishes the powers of and limits on the President
Article 3	
Article 4	
Article 5	
Article 6	
Article 7	

Seven Principles of the Constitution

Principle	Meaning
Popular Sovereignty	
Limited Government	
Separation of Powers	
Checks and Balances	
Federalism	
Republicanism	
Individual Rights	

Refer to this page to answer the Citizenship Handbook Focus Question on page 118.

Summary 2 Focus Question
What are the powers of each branch of government?

Summary

The federal government consists of three branches, each of which has its own unique powers and responsibilities.

How the Federal Government Works: The Legislative Branch
Article 1 of the Constitution sets up the Congress to make the nation's laws. Congress consists of two bodies: the Senate and the House of Representatives.

The Senate is based on equal representation and includes two senators from each state. Senators serve six-year terms. The Vice President serves as the president of the Senate.

The House of Representatives is the larger of the two bodies. Representation in the House is based on a state's population. People elect their representatives for two-year terms. The leader of the House, called the Speaker, regulates debates and <u>agendas</u> in the House.

Congress's most important power is the power to make the nation's laws. A law starts as a **bill**, or proposal, which can be introduced in either the House or the Senate. Congress can also collect taxes, coin money, establish post offices, fix standard weights and measures, and declare war.

Much of the work in Congress is done through committees. Each committee deals with a specific topic, such as defense, education, or science. ✔

How the Federal Government Works: The Executive Branch
Article 2 of the Constitution sets up the executive branch to carry out laws and to run the affairs of the national government. The President is the head of the executive branch, which also includes the Vice President and the Cabinet. The people in the many departments and agencies are also part of the executive branch. The Framers of the Constitution intended Congress to be the most powerful branch of government. Therefore, while the Constitution is very specific about the powers of the legislature, it offers few details about the powers of the President. Beginning with George Washington, Presidents have taken the actions they thought were necessary to meet the nation's changing needs. Today, the President can veto bills, propose laws, grant pardons, appoint high officials, negotiate treaties, and serve as commander in chief of the armed forces.

The President serves a four-year term and cannot serve more than two terms. The President is elected through a system called

Vocabulary Builder

Read the bracketed text. Based on context clues, write a definition of *agenda*.

_____

_____

✓ Checkpoint

Name the two bodies of the legislative branch.

_____

_____

the electoral college. Americans do not directly elect the President; rather, they vote for a group of electors. The number of electors depends on each state's number of senators and representatives. In most states, the presidential candidate with the majority of popular votes receives all of that state's electoral votes. The candidate who receives the most electoral votes becomes President. ✓

✓ Checkpoint

Name the system by which the President is elected.

_____

How the Federal Government Works: The Judicial Branch

The Constitution also establishes a Supreme Court and authorizes Congress to establish other courts that are needed. The system of federal courts was set up under the Judiciary Act of 1789.

Most federal cases begin in district courts, where evidence is presented and a judge or a jury decides the facts of a case. If a party disagrees with the decision of the judge or jury, it may appeal. An **appeal** asks that the decision be reviewed by a higher court. A judge in an appellate court, or court of appeals, reviews the decision to determine if the lower court interpreted and applied the law correctly.

Court cases can be filed under federal or state jurisdiction. A **jurisdiction** is the power to hear and decide cases. Most cases are tried under state jurisdiction because they involve state laws. A case may be placed under federal jurisdiction if:

- The United States is either suing another party or being sued by another party
- The case is based on the Constitution or on a federal law.
- The case involves disputes between different states.

The Supreme Court is at the top of the judicial branch, and it consists of a chief justice and eight associate justices. The President nominates the judges, and Congress must approve the appointments. The Supreme Court is the final court of appeals. Decisions rest on a majority of at least five of the justices.

There is no court of appeal beyond the Supreme Court. However, the Supreme Court may sometimes reverse its own past decisions.

The most important power of the Supreme Court is the power to decide what the Constitution means. The Court can declare whether acts of the President or laws passed by Congress are unconstitutional. **Unconstitutional** means that an act or law is not allowed by the Constitution. ✓

✓ Checkpoint

List the two things that the Supreme Court can declare unconstitutional.

_____

_____

Check Your Progress

1. What and who makes up the executive branch?

_____

_____

2. Describe the process by which a justice is added to the Supreme Court.

_____

_____

Branches of Government Notetaking Study Guide

Keep in mind the Summary 2 Focus Question as you read about the structure of the U.S. government in your textbook and take notes.

▶ Use these charts to help you record key facts about the branches of government. Some information has been filled in to get you started.

The Legislative Branch

The Senate
Number of members for each state:
 two per state
Length of term: _____
President of the Senate:
_____

House of Representatives
Number of members for each state:
 based on population
Current number of members: _____
Representatives elected by: _____
_____
Length of term: _____

Powers of Congress:
1. make nation's laws , 2. collect _____, 3. coin _____, 4. establish post offices ,
5. fix standard _____ and _____, 6. declare _____

The Executive Branch

Duties: Carry out the _____ and run the affairs of _____
Head executive: _____
Other members: Vice President, Cabinet, _____, _____
Length of President's term: _____, but no more than two terms
System by which President is elected: _____

The Judicial Branch

Lower Courts
1. In district courts, _____ is presented during trials, and a _____ or a _____ decides the facts of the case.
2. A party that disagrees with a decision may _____ to a higher court.
3. Appellate court judges review the decisions of district courts to _____
_____.
4. Jurisdiction is _____.

The Supreme Court
Court consists of: _____
Justices appointed by:_____
Appointments must be approved by: _____
Length of Justices' service: _____
Main job: _____
Number of cases heard per year: _____
Most important power: _____
What the court can declare as unconstitutional: _____
_____.

Refer to this page to answer the Citizenship Handbook Focus Question on page 118.

Summary 3

Summary 3 Focus Question
How can the Constitution be amended to meet changing needs?

Summary

The Founders created a Constitution that allowed for change. The first ten changes made to the Constitution concerned the rights of the American people.

Amending the Constitution

Some of the Framers were dissatisfied with the Constitution because the final document did not address the rights of the American people. The Framers fixed the <u>omission</u> by adding the Bill of Rights, the first ten amendments to the Constitution. Such an addition was possible because the Constitution included Article 5, which laid out the method of amending the Constitution. **Amending** is another word for changing the Constitution.

The Constitution can be changed in one of four ways. There are two ways of proposing an amendment. First, Congress can propose an amendment. Second, state legislatures can call for a national convention to propose an amendment.

An amendment can be ratified or approved through the actions of the state legislatures, or it can be ratified through the actions of state conventions. Conventions are special meetings that are called to address a specific issue.

The first ten amendments, also known as the Bill of Rights, are the part of the Constitution that addresses the freedoms guaranteed to all citizens.

The Bill of Rights	
Amendment	**Subject Addressed**
First	freedom of religion, speech, and the press; right of petition and assembly
Second	right to bear arms
Third	government cannot force people to quarter troops in their homes
Fourth	protects against unreasonable search and seizure
Fifth	rights of people accused of crimes
Sixth	right to trial by jury in criminal cases
Seventh	right to trial by jury in civil cases
Eighth	forbids excessive bail and cruel or unusual punishment
Ninth	people's rights are not limited to those listed in the Constitution
Tenth	states or people have all powers not denied or given to federal government by the Constitution

✓

Vocabulary Builder

Omission is a noun meaning "something left out." Based on this definition, what do you think the verb *omit* means?

_____

_____

✓ Checkpoint

What are the first ten amendments called?

_____

The colonial experience inspired the First Amendment to the Constitution. Pilgrims, Puritans, Quakers, and Catholics had all come to North America in the 1600s because they wanted to practice their religion freely. However, some religious leaders, such as Thomas Hooker, Roger Williams, and Anne Hutchinson, were driven out of their New England towns after disputes with their community leaders over religious issues. The Constitution's Framers sought to end such church-versus-state disputes by drafting the First Amendment. Thus, the First Amendment affirms freedom of religion as a basic right. Americans are free to follow any religion or no religion at all. It is their choice.

The freedom-of-religion part of the First Amendment had been inspired by the Virginia Statute on Religious Freedom, which was written by Thomas Jefferson. Jefferson later spoke of a "wall of separation between Church and State." However, not everyone agrees on how religion and government should be separated. Some people believe that the First Amendment means that religion should play no role in government. Others argue that the Amendment merely says that Congress cannot establish an official, state-supported church or make laws that interfere with freedom of worship.

The First Amendment also protects the right of Americans to speak without fear of punishment. In addition, the amendment protects the press from government censorship. **Censorship** is the power to review, change, or prevent the publication of news. Undemocratic governments often shut down newspapers and jail people who criticize the government. These governments must silence <u>dissent</u> to stay in power.

The founders remembered that King George III and Parliament had ignored colonists' petitions protesting the Stamp Act. Such experiences had a powerful effect on the leaders who wrote the Bill of Rights. The First Amendment thus guarantees the right of Americans to assemble in peaceful protest and protects Americans' right to petition the government for a change in policy. ✔

Check Your Progress

1. Explain the two ways by which an amendment to the U.S. Constitution can be ratified.

   _____

   _____

2. What colonial experience led American leaders to specifically protect the right of citizens to follow any religion or no religion?

   _____

   _____

   _____

Vocabulary Builder

If *consent* is the opposite of *dissent*, what does *dissent* mean?

_____

_____

✓ Checkpoint

List the five freedoms covered by the First Amendment.

_____

_____

_____

_____

_____

Keep in mind the Summary 3 Focus Question as you read about changing the Constitution in your textbook and take notes.

▶ Use these charts to help you record key facts. Some information has been filled in to get you started.

Amendment Process	
Proposing Amendments 1. 2. State legislatures call for a national convention to formally propose an amendment.	Ratifying Amendments 1. 2.

The Bill of Rights	
Amendment	**Rights and Protections**
First Amendment	• Protects freedom of _religion_, freedom of _____, and freedom of the _____ • Also protects the right of petition and peaceful _____
Second Amendment	Right to _____
Third Amendment	Protects against the _____ of _____ in people's homes
Fourth Amendment	Protects against unreasonable _____ and _____
Fifth Amendment	Protects the rights of people accused of _____
Sixth Amendment	Right to a _____ by _____ in criminal cases
Seventh Amendment	Right to a _____ by _____ in _____ cases
Eighth Amendment	Forbids _____ and cruel or unusual _____
Ninth Amendment	People's _____ are not limited to _____
Tenth Amendment	States or people have all _____ not denied or _____ by the Constitution

Refer to this page to answer the Citizenship Handbook Focus Question on page 118.

Summary 4 Focus Questions
- What are the powers of state and local governments?
- What are the rights and responsibilities of citizens?

Summary

Not only do state and local governments have many important responsibilities, but individual citizens have many important responsibilities as well.

State and Local Government

Under the principle of federalism, the Constitution divides powers between the federal government and the governments of the states. In general, the federal government deals with national issues. The states concern themselves with local needs.

State governments resemble the federal government in many ways. Each state has its own constitution that can be amended, and it has the same three branches of government. Each state has a legislature, a governor who serves as the chief executive, and a judiciary. There are some differences between federal and state governments. Nebraska, for instance, is the only state in the Union with a one-house legislature.

The Constitution lays out many of the powers given to the states. State governments have the power to create corporate law, regulate trade within the state, maintain public schools, and establish local governments. States also make laws about marriage and divorce, conduct elections, and provide for public safety. States and the federal government also share some powers. They both provide for the public welfare, administer criminal justice, charter banks, raise taxes, and borrow money.

The Constitution identifies the powers of the federal and state government, but it says nothing about local government, which consists of smaller units such as counties, cities, and towns.

Like federal and state governments, local governments have budgets. Local budgets are generally spent on education. Cities, towns, and school districts hire teachers, buy books, and maintain school buildings. Although local governments control the school system, they are required by law to meet the state's education standards.

Local governments play a more direct role in people's everyday lives than federal or state governments do. For instance, local governments hire people who interact with citizens on a regular basis. These include firefighters, police officers, and garbage collectors. Local governments also maintain local roads and hospitals, provide public services, run libraries, oversee parks and recreational facilities, and inspect the safety of buildings. ✔

✓ Checkpoint

Name three units of local government.

_____

_____

_____

Rights and Responsibilities of Citizenship

A **citizen** is someone who is entitled to all the rights and privileges of a nation. To be a citizen of the United States, a person must be born in the United States, have a parent who is a United States citizen, be naturalized, or be 18 years old or younger when his or her parents are naturalized. **Naturalization** is the official legal process of becoming a citizen. To be naturalized, a person must live in the United States for at least five years. The person must then apply for citizenship, take a citizenship exam, undergo interviews, and finally take the citizenship oath before a judge. In this oath, the person swears to "support and defend the Constitution and laws of the United States."

A naturalized citizen enjoys every right of a natural-born citizen except one. Only natural-born citizens may serve as President or Vice President.

Many of American citizens' rights are spelled out in the Bill of Rights. But the Ninth Amendment states that citizens' rights are not limited to those specifically listed in the Constitution. Over the years, federal and state laws have identified rights that were not mentioned in the Constitution. For example, the Constitution does not mention education. But today, laws in every state guarantee that children have the right to an education.

The law holds citizens to certain responsibilities. For example, every citizen must obey the law and pay taxes—or face legal punishment. Good citizens meet other responsibilities as well. These are not required by law, but they are important. These responsibilities include learning about important issues and voting in federal, state, and local elections.

Some people participate in the political process through interest groups. An **interest group** is an organization that represents the concerns of a particular group. These groups work to influence lawmakers. Examples of interest groups are the National Rifle Association and the Sierra Club.

Young people, too, can get involved in the political process. For example, students in one community in California organized to get assistance paying for public transportation. Using their First Amendment rights, they collected signatures on petitions and held peaceful public rallies. Finally, local transportation officials came up with a plan to solve the problem. ✔

Check Your Progress

1. Which level or levels of government are responsible for education?

   _____

2. Which amendment states that citizens have rights not mentioned in the Constitution?

   _____

Vocabulary Builder

Political comes from the Greek word *polis*, meaning "city." The word *police* shares the same root.

✓ Checkpoint

Name two examples of interest groups.

_____

_____

Keep in mind the Summary 4 Focus Questions as you read about the powers of state and local governments and the responsibilities of citizens in your textbook and take notes.

▶ Use these charts to help you record key facts. Some information has been filled in to get you started.

State Government

Each state has its own _constitution_. State governments made up of: • executive (headed by _____) • •	Powers of State Government: • create corporate law • • • • • •

Local Government

Includes _county_, _____ and _____
Most of local budgets are spent on _____.

Local governments hire _____, _____, and
_____.

Local governments maintain _____ and _____ and provide public services.

Citizenship

• A _____ is entitled to all the rights and privileges of a particular nation.
• To be a citizen of the United States, a person must be one of the following:
  1.
  2.
  3.
• _____ is the official legal process of becoming a citizen. Steps in process:
  1.
  2.
  3.
  4.
  5.
• Some responsibilities of citizens are required by _____.
• Other responsibilities are not required by law. These include serving the _community_, staying well informed, _____ in elections, and helping to create a just _____.

Refer to this page to answer the Citizenship Handbook Focus Question on page 118.

Citizenship Handbook Assessment

Directions: Circle the letter of the correct answer.

1. The electoral college is the system used to determine who becomes
   A chief justice.   C President.
   B representative.   D senator.

2. In what way are state governments like the federal government?
   A Both levels of government are divided into three branches.
   B Both levels of government maintain schools.
   C All states have two-house legislatures, as does the federal government.
   D Both levels of government have the power to coin money.

3. Which of the following principles of the U.S. Constitution introduces the idea that government authority comes from the people?
   A limited government   C checks and balances
   B republicanism   D popular sovereignty

Directions: Follow the steps to answer this question:

How does the structure of the federal government reflect the Framers' belief that power should rest in the hands of citizens?

Step 1: Recall details about each branch of the federal government.

	Branch		
	Executive	**Legislative**	**Judicial**
Highest office or level		Congress	
How officeholders are selected	nationwide election through electoral college system		

Step 2: Compare: In which of the three branches are the top officeholders most directly selected by voters?

_____

Step 3: Complete the topic sentence that follows. Then write two or three more sentences that support your topic sentences.

The Framers of the Constitution felt that power should rest in the hands of the citizens because _____

_____

_____

_____

Citizenship Handbook Notetaking Study Guide

Now you are ready to answer the Citizenship Handbook Focus Question: **How did the Constitution create a strong government with roots in history that allowed for change and met the needs of the people?**

► Complete the following chart to help you answer this question. Use the notes that you took for each section.

The Foundation of Strong Government
Ideas Behind the Constitution
American leaders looked to Rome as an example of a _____, or government in which citizens rule themselves through elected _____.
The _____ and the English _____ placed limits on the ruler and protected the rights of citizens.
The ideas of the European Enlightenment thinkers _____ and _____ were very influential.

Structure of the Constitution

The _____ , or opening statement, of the Constitution outlines six main goals.	The first three Articles describe the branches of government: _____ , _____ and _____ .

The Constitution rests on seven basic principles: _popular sovereignty_ , _____ , _____ , _____ , _____ , _federalism_ , and _____ .

Amendments to the Constitution

An amendment can be ratified or approved by three fourths of _____ or _____.

The first ten amendments are known as _____.

They address _____.

The _____ states that Americans are entitled to many rights, not just those spelled out in the Constitution.

State and Local Government

Like the federal government, each state has a _____ and three _____.

Some of the many duties of state government include regulating _____ within the state, making laws about _____ and divorce, conducting _____, and providing for public _____.

_____ government plays the most direct role in people's lives.

Refer to this page to answer the Unit 2 Focus Question on page 119.

Unit 2 Pulling It Together Activity

What You Have Learned

Chapter 5 The American colonists, although united with Britain thoughout the French and Indian War, grew rebellious over Britain's effort to control them. As tensions increased, the spirit of rebellion turned into a call for independence and war.

Chapter 6 In 1776, the colonists officially announced their Declaration of Independence. A difficult war followed. The American Revolution ended in 1783 with the signing of a peace treaty declaring American independence from British rule. The United States was finally its own nation.

Chapter 7 Delegates from each state met in Philadelphia in 1787 to revise the Articles of Confederation. The delegates decided that the nation needed a stronger federal government.

Citizenship Handbook To be an active citizen, it is important to understand the ideas behind the U.S. Constitution.

Think Like a Historian

Read the Unit 2 Essential Question: **What are the roles and responsibilities of governments and citizens?**

▶ Use the organizers on this page and the next to collect information to answer this question.

What are the responsibilities of citizens? Some of them are listed in this organizer. Review your section and chapter notes. Then complete the organizer.

Rights and Responsibilities of Citizens

From the Bill of Rights
- freedom of religion, speech, and the press
- trial by jury and equal treatment before the law
-
-

Civic Responsibilities
- voting
-
-

Look at the other part of the Unit Essential Question. It asks about responsibilities of government. The organizer below gives you a part of the answer. Review your section and chapter notes. Then fill in the rest of the organizer.

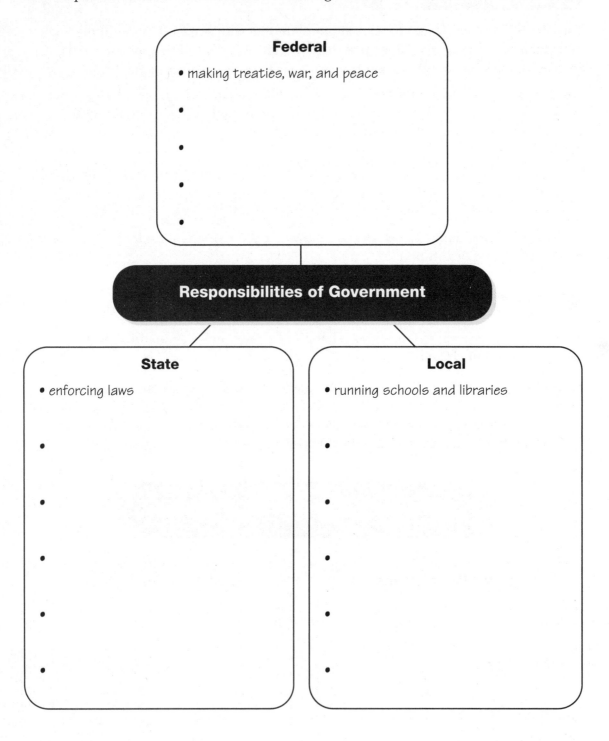

Federal

• making treaties, war, and peace

•

•

•

•

Responsibilities of Government

State

• enforcing laws

•

•

•

•

•

Local

• running schools and libraries

•

•

•

•

•

The New Republic

What You Will Learn

Chapter 8 As the nation's first President, George Washington established the U.S. government's authority in domestic as well as foreign affairs. Political divisions and strife with France rocked John Adams's presidency.

Chapter 9 The Louisiana Purchase of 1803 doubled the size of the United States. At the same time, the United States struggled to remain neutral in its foreign policy. British support of Native Americans led to the War of 1812.

Chapter 10 During the early 1800s, the federal government increased its authority. At the same time, the Monroe Doctrine expanded U.S. influence in Latin America. More people earned the right to vote during Andrew Jackson's presidency, yet Jackson forced Native Americans in the South to move west.

Focus Your Learning As you study this unit and take notes, you will find the information to answer the questions below. Answering the Chapter Essential Questions will help build your answer to the Unit Essential Question.

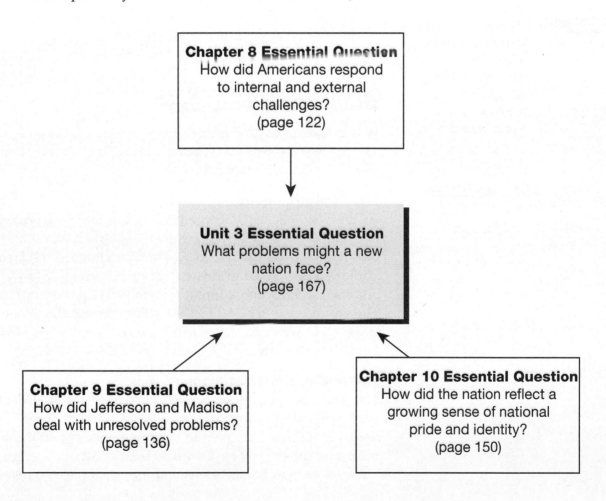

Chapter 8 Essential Question
How did Americans respond to internal and external challenges?
(page 122)

Unit 3 Essential Question
What problems might a new nation face?
(page 167)

Chapter 9 Essential Question
How did Jefferson and Madison deal with unresolved problems?
(page 136)

Chapter 10 Essential Question
How did the nation reflect a growing sense of national pride and identity?
(page 150)

What You Will Learn

The new federal government dealt with challenges at home and abroad. During John Adams's presidency, disagreements increased between the parties.

Chapter 8 Focus Question

As you read this chapter, keep this question in mind: **How did Americans respond to internal and external challenges?**

Section 1
Washington Takes Office

Section 1 Focus Question

How did President Washington set the course for the new nation? To begin answering this question,
- Learn about the first President, George Washington.
- Understand the nation's first economic crisis.
- Read about Hamilton's financial plan.
- Find out about the Whiskey Rebellion.

Section 1 Summary

Washington organized the executive branch, and Hamilton worked to end the nation's financial crisis. The Whiskey Rebellion tested the new government.

The First President

As the first President, George Washington set many **precedents,** or examples to be followed by others in the future. He created new federal departments. Alexander Hamilton led the Treasury, Thomas Jefferson led the State Department, Henry Knox was Secretary of War, and Edmund Randolph was Attorney General. The group came to be called the Cabinet. In addition, the Judiciary Act of 1789 established a federal court system headed by the Supreme Court. ✓

The Nation's First Economic Crisis

The American Revolution had left the nation deeply in debt. The debt was mainly in the form of bonds. A **bond** is a certificate issued by a government for an amount of money that the government promises to pay back with interest. Most of the original buyers sold their bonds to **speculators,** or people who invest in a

Key Events

1789	Washington organizes new government departments and appoints heads.
1795	Senate approves Jay's Treaty with Britain.
1798	"XYZ Affair" becomes public and sours relations with France. Congress passes the Alien and Sedition acts.

✓ Checkpoint

List the members of President Washington's cabinet.

_____

_____

_____

_____

risky venture in the hope of making a large profit. Because speculators bought the bonds for less than they were worth, it did not seem fair to pay them in full, especially since the original bondholders had lost money. The government also questioned whether or not it should pay back state debts. ✔

Hamilton's Financial Plan

It fell to Alexander Hamilton, the new secretary of the treasury, to come up with a plan to solve the financial crisis. The first part of his plan was for the government to pay back all federal and state debts. However, many southern states did not want the federal government to pay state debts because they had paid theirs on their own. The South eventually agreed to this part of Hamilton's plan, and in return, the government would build its capital in the South.

The second part of the plan was to charter a national bank for depositing government funds. Members of Washington's cabinet fought over whether the government had the right to do this. Jefferson argued that a national bank was **unconstitutional**— contrary to what is permitted by the Constitution. He called for a "strict" interpretation, or reading, of the Constitution. According to this view, the government's power was limited to what the Constitution specifically says. Hamilton, on the other hand, called for a "loose" interpretation. He believed that the Constitution gave Congress the power to do things not directly permitted, as long as they were "necessary and proper." A national bank was created, but constitutional interpretation continues to provoke disagreement.

Southerners also opposed the last part of Hamilton's plan, a national **tariff**, or a tax on imported goods. The tariff benefited northern industries because it protected them from lower priced foreign goods. Since southerners had little industry, the tariff only hurt them by raising prices. Congress did not pass the tariff. ✔

The Whiskey Rebellion

Congress imposed a tax on all whiskey made and sold in the country, but many farmers who made whiskey opposed this tax. Some Pennsylvania farmers started a violent protest. Washington sent federal troops to Pennsylvania, showing that armed rebellion would not be accepted. ✔

Check Your Progress

1. What two crises occurred during the early part of President George Washington's administration?

_____

_____

2. What were the three parts to Hamilton's financial plan?

_____

_____

✔ Checkpoint

After the American Revolution, the nation's debt was mostly in what form?

_____

Vocabulary Builder

Provoke comes from the Latin verb *provocare*, which means "to call out." What is being "called out" in the underlined sentence?

✔ Checkpoint

Name the two types of constitutional interpretation used during the debate about the national bank.

_____

_____

✔ Checkpoint

What caused the Whiskey Rebellion?

_____

Question to Think About As you read Section 1 in your textbook, keep this question in mind: **How did President Washington set the course for the new nation?**

▶ Use this chart to record key information from the section.

Washington Takes Office

The first job of the President and Congress: <u>to put a working government in place</u>

Executive Branch

- Congress passed laws to set up three executive departments: _____
  _____
- The President appointed a <u>secretary</u> to head each department. He also appointed an _____ to advise him on legal matters.
- This group of people became known as the _____.

Judicial Branch

- The Constitution called for a <u>judiciary</u>, or a court system.
- The _____ provided for a Supreme Court of 6 justices, ____ circuit courts, and 13 _____ courts.
- Main job of federal courts: _____
  _____
  _____

Hamilton's Financial Plan

The American Revolution had left the national government and states deeply in <u>debt</u>, which was mainly in the form of _____.

Part 1: Paying the Debt

- Hamilton wanted the United States to honor its _____.
- Many <u>southerners</u> opposed the plan to repay _____ debts.
- The agreement: _____
  _____
  _____
  _____
  _____

Part 2: _____

- The debate over the bank focused on the powers of the _____ under the _____.
- Some had a _____ interpretation of the Constitution. Others had a _____ interpretation.
- The bank was _____.

Part 3: High Tariff

- Hamilton wanted a high tariff to _____ for the federal government and to protect U.S. manufacturers from _____.
- Southerners argued the tariff would help the _____ but _____ the South.
- Congress _____ it.

The Whiskey Rebellion

- To raise money, Congress _____ all whiskey made and sold in the United States.
- It led to a _____ that tested the _____ of the new government.
- Washington sent the _____ as a sign that armed revolt was unacceptable.

Refer to this page to answer the Chapter 8 Focus Question on page 135.

Section 2

The Birth of Political Parties

Section 2 Focus Question

How did two political parties emerge? To begin answering this question,

- Learn why political parties emerged.
- Read about the differences between Republicans and Federalists.
- Find out about the election of 1796.

Section 2 Summary

The Framers did not expect political parties to develop. But differences over issues led to the creation of parties. After the 1796 election, tensions increased between the parties.

Political Parties Emerge

The Framers of the Constitution did not expect political parties to form in the United States. Rather, they thought that government leaders would rise above personal or local interests and work together for the sake of the whole nation. They proved to be wrong.

In those days, people spoke of *factions* rather than *political parties*. A **faction** was an organized political group, and the word was not complimentary. **James Madison** thought factions were selfish groups that ignored the well-being of the whole nation. In the *Federalist Papers*, he wrote that an effective national government would prevent the growth of factions. President Washington feared the effects of factions and tried to discourage their growth. Despite his efforts, by the early 1790s, political parties began to form. ✔

Republicans Against Federalists

The two parties that formed were called the Republicans and the Federalists. The Republicans developed out of Democratic-Republican clubs that accused the federal government of growing too strong. They wanted to keep most power at the state or local level. The Federalists took their name from the people who had supported the adoption of the Constitution. They believed that the United States needed a strong federal government to hold the country together.

At the time that both parties were organizing, the Federalists had an advantage. This was because President Washington usually supported **Alexander Hamilton** and his policies rather than **Thomas Jefferson** and his policies. Finally, in 1793, Jefferson resigned as secretary of state because he was unhappy with the federal government's support of Federalist policies.

Key Events

1789 — Washington organizes new government departments and appoints heads.

1795 — Senate approves Jay's Treaty with Britain.

1798 — "XYZ Affair" becomes public and sours relations with France. Congress passes the Alien and Sedition acts.

✓ Checkpoint

Name the term that people used instead of the term *political parties*.

_____

Republicans	Federalists
• **Main Supporters:** southern planters and northern artisans and farmers • **Main Leaders:** Thomas Jefferson and James Madison • Supported strong state government • Opposed a national bank • Opposed a tariff on imported goods • Supported France because it had recently overthrown its king • Strictly interpreted the Constitution	• **Main Supporters:** merchants, other property owners, and workers in trade and manu- facturing • **Main Leader:** Alexander Hamilton • Supported a strong national government • Supported a national bank • Supported a tariff on imported goods • Were pro-British • Loosely interpreted the Constitution

✓ **Checkpoint**

List the main supporters of the Republicans and Federalists.

Republicans: _____

_____

Federalists: _____

_____

_____

Vocabulary Builder

A *precedent* is an action or deci- sion that is used as an example for a later one.

✓ **Checkpoint**

Name the person elected president in 1796.

_____

The Election of 1796

George Washington announced he would not run for a third term as President. His action set an important <u>precedent</u>. Not until Franklin Roosevelt ran for and won a third term in 1940 would any President seek more than two terms. In 1951, the Twenty- second Amendment limited the President to two terms.

Today, the President and Vice President run together on the same ticket. However, at the time of the 1796 election, the President and the Vice President were not elected as a ticket. The candidate with the most votes became President, and the candi- date who came in second place was elected Vice President. In the 1796 election, a Federalist, **John Adams,** became President, but a Republican candidate, Thomas Jefferson, was elected Vice Presi- dent. Not surprisingly, this led to serious tensions during the next four years. ✓

Check Your Progress

1. Why did the Framers of the Constitution not expect political parties?

_____

_____

_____

2. What were the two political parties' positions on the power of the national government?

_____

_____

_____

Question to Think About As you read Section 2 in your textbook and take notes, keep this question in mind: **How did two political parties emerge?**

▶ Use these charts to record key information from the section. Some information has been filled in to get you started.

The Birth of Political Parties
At first, political parties did not exist because people felt a leader should represent _____.   President ___Washington___ tried to discourage the growth of political parties, which were originally called _____.

The Two Parties		
	Federalists	**Republicans**
Origin	Took name from early supporters of the Constitution	Democratic-Republican clubs
Leaders	•	• James Madison •
Supporters	• merchants • •	• •
Position on state vs. federal power	•	•
Positions on other issues	Favored: • • • • close ties with _____	Favored: • • close ties with _____ Opposed: • •
Presidential candidate in 1796	•	•

Results of the 1796 Election
President: _____   Vice President: _____

Refer to this page to answer the Chapter 8 Focus Question on page 135.

Section 3

Troubles at Home and Abroad

Key Events

1789 Washington organizes new government departments and appoints heads.

1795 Senate approves Jay's Treaty with Britain.

1798 "XYZ Affair" becomes public and sours relations with France. Congress passes the Alien and Sedition acts.

Section 3 Focus Question

How did the actions of Britain and France affect the United States? To begin answering this question,

- Find out about conflicts in the Northwest Territory.
- Learn about the French Revolution and how Americans reacted to it.
- Note President Washington's accomplishments and advice.

Section 3 Summary

President Washington faced conflict with Native Americans and foreign threats to American shipping. He advised Americans to avoid political divisions and involvement in European affairs.

Conflicts in the Northwest Territory

The Northwest Territory was the land north and west of the Ohio River to the Mississippi River. The United States acquired the territory from Britain as part of the terms of the Treaty of Paris that ended the American Revolution.

Under the treaty, Britain had pledged to withdraw its forts from the region within "a reasonable time." Ten years later, however, the forts were still there. The British were also supplying Native American groups in the region with guns and ammunition. The British hoped that this would limit American settlement in the Northwest Territory.

Many American leaders believed that the country's future depended on settling its western lands, and during the 1780s, many American settlers migrated into the Northwest Territory. Native Americans, worried about holding onto their lands, joined together to oppose American settlement.

By 1790, the federal government had bought much of the Native Americans' lands south of the Ohio River. However, Native Americans in the Northwest Territory refused to sell and attacked settlers. In 1790, Washington sent troops to the Northwest Territory. Three battles occurred between American troops and Native Americans led by Little Turtle of the Miami Nation and Blue Jacket of the Shawnees. The Native Americans won the first two battles. The second battle was the worst defeat U.S. troops ever suffered in a battle with Native Americans.

In 1794, Washington sent General **Anthony Wayne** to lead the troops. He defeated the Native Americans at the Battle of Fallen Timbers. That battle broke the Native American hold on the Northwest. In the 1795 Treaty of Greenville, Native Americans surrendered most of their lands in the part of the Northwest Territory that is now Ohio. ✓

✓ Checkpoint

Name the battle and the treaty that ended conflict between settlers and Native Americans in the Northwest Territory.

_____

_____

The French Revolution

When the French Revolution began in 1789, Americans supported the effort of the French people to overthrow their king. By 1793, however, growing violence in France was becoming controversial in the United States, and it led Federalists to oppose the revolution. Republicans continued to support it, arguing that some violence could be expected in a fight for freedom.

By 1793, Britain and France were at war. Republicans supported France, and Federalists supported Britain. <u>President Washington issued a proclamation that said the United States would remain **neutral**, not favoring either side of the dispute.</u> However, the United States would trade with both sides. Neither France nor Britain agreed with the U.S. position. Both countries started seizing American ships, fearing that trade with the United States would benefit the enemy. Britain made matters worse by the **impressment** of sailors on American ships, which meant seizing the sailors and forcing them to serve in the British navy.

Washington sent **John Jay** to negotiate a treaty with Britain. In 1795 Jay returned with a treaty. The United States agreed to pay debts owed to British merchants. Britain agreed to pay for the ships it had seized and to withdraw its troops from the Northwest Territory. But it refused to stop impressing sailors. It also refused to recognize a U.S. right to trade with France.

Republicans opposed Jay's Treaty, arguing that it gave away too much and got too little. But the Federalist-controlled Senate approved it to keep peace with Britain. ✔

Washington Retires From Public Life

Washington published his Farewell Address at the end of his second term. He advised Americans to avoid political divisions at home. He feared that violent divisions might tear the nation apart. Washington also emphasized his belief that the United States must stay out of European affairs. Washington's main accomplishments were establishing a federal government, ending the country's economic crisis, forcing the British to leave the Northwest Territory, and keeping the country out of war. ✔

Check Your Progress

1. What role did Britain play in conflicts in the Northwest Territory?

_____

_____

_____

2. How did public support in the United States for the French Revolution change over time?

_____

_____

_____

Reread the underlined sentence. If to proclaim something means to announce it, what is a *proclamation*?

_____

✓ Checkpoint

What led the Federalists to oppose the French Revolution?

_____

_____

✓ Checkpoint

List the two things that Washington recommended in his Farewell Address.

_____

_____

Section 3 Notetaking Study Guide

Question to Think About As you read Section 3 in your textbook and take notes, keep this question in mind: **How did the actions of Britain and France affect the United States?**

▶ Use this chart to record key information from the section. Some information has been filled in to get you started.

I. Conflicts in the Northwest Territory	
Conflict with Britain	• A decade after the _____, British troops still occupied _forts_ in the Northwest Territory. • The British were also supplying Native Americans with _____ and _____ to help limit American _____.
Conflict with Native Americans	• Americans tried to _____ Native Americans to sell their lands in the Northwest Territory. • Native Americans sold some land but _____ to sell other lands. • After an American victory at the _____, the leaders of defeated Native American nations gave up most of their land in the 1795 _____.

II. The French Revolution

• At first, Americans _____ the revolutionaries.
• Reasons the French Revolution became controversial
  1. Violence peaked in a period called the _____. _____ denounced the violence, but _____ said some violence should be expected.
  2. Both _Britain_ and _____ , which were at war, began stopping American ships and _____ their cargoes. The British made matters worse by the _____ of the ships' sailors.
• Terms of Jay's Treaty
What the Americans agreed to: _____
What the British agreed to: _____
_____
What the British did not agree to: _____
_____

III. Washington Retires	
Farewell Address Advice	• •
Washington's Accomplishments	• established federal government • • •

Refer to this page to answer the Chapter 8 Focus Question on page 135.

130 Unit 3 Chapter 8 Section 3

The Presidency of John Adams

Section 4 Focus Question

How did problems with France intensify the split between the
Federalists and Republicans? To begin answering this question,

- Find out about America's troubles with France.
- Discover the impact of the Alien and Sedition acts.
- Learn about the idea of states' rights.

Section 4 Summary

Events in Europe intensified the split between Federalists and
Republicans. Tensions increased further with the passage of the
Alien and Sedition acts.

Troubles With France

The decision of the United States to remain neutral during the war
between France and Britain angered France because it had been
an ally during the American Revolution. Also, the signing of Jay's
Treaty with Britain made it appear as if the United States favored
Britain over France. As a result, France refused to meet with an
American diplomat and continued to seize American ships.

In 1797, Adams sent three diplomats to France. Agents of the
French foreign minister demanded a bribe from the American
diplomats, but the Americans refused to pay one. Many Americans, especially Federalists, were outraged when they learned of
the so-called XYZ Affair. (XYZ refers to the three French agents
whose real names were kept secret.)

The XYZ Affair led to an undeclared naval war with France.
Adams and the Congress increased the size of the army and
rebuilt the navy. In addition, Adams created a new department of
the navy.

Adams, who opposed war, sent another group of diplomats to
France. In 1800, a treaty was signed. France agreed to stop seizing
American ships, and the United States avoided a full-scale war
with France. The treaty angered many of Adams's fellow Federalists who wanted war with France. ☑

The Alien and Sedition Acts

The undeclared war with France increased distrust between the
Federalists and Republicans. Federalists feared that European
immigrants would spread dangerous ideas inspired by the French
Revolution to America. They also feared that the new immigrants
would favor the pro-French Republican Party when they became
citizens.

The Federalist-controlled Congress decided to pass several
laws. They had two main goals. First, they wanted to slow the

Key Events

1789	Washington organizes new government departments and appoints heads.
1795	Senate approves Jay's Treaty with Britain.
1798	"XYZ Affair" becomes public and sours relations with France. Congress passes the Alien and Sedition acts.

✓ Checkpoint

To what did the XYZ Affair lead?

_____

process of becoming a citizen. Second, they wanted to stop immigrants and Republicans from spreading ideas that threatened Federalist control of the federal government.

The Alien Act increased the length of time from 5 to 14 years that it took for an **alien**, or outsider or someone from another country, to become a citizen. It also allowed the President to jail or deport aliens he considered dangerous.

The Sedition Act targeted Republicans. **Sedition** is an activity aimed at overthrowing a government. The act made saying or writing anything insulting or false about the government a crime punishable by jail or a fine. The Sedition Act placed the harshest limits on free speech in America's history. During 1798 and 1799, ten people were convicted under the act. Most were Republican editors and printers. ✔

States' Rights

Republicans denounced the Alien and Sedition acts. They declared that the Sedition Act violated free speech protections under the First Amendment of the Constitution. However, it had not yet been clearly established that the Supreme Court had the power to strike down a law as unconstitutional. To overturn this law, therefore, the Republicans worked through state legislatures.

James Madison and Thomas Jefferson wrote resolutions for the Virginia and Kentucky legislatures, respectively. They stated that the Alien and Sedition acts were unconstitutional and that states had the right to declare federal laws unconstitutional.

The Virginia and Kentucky resolutions had little short-term impact. No other states supported them. By 1802 the Alien and Sedition acts had expired, and Congress restored the waiting period for citizenship to five years.

The resolutions were far more important over the long run because they established the principles of states' rights and nullification. **States' rights** is the idea that the union binding "these United States" is an agreement between the states and that they therefore can overrule federal law. Nullification is the related idea that states have the power to **nullify,** or deprive of legal force, a federal law. The ideas increased in importance when the southern states began defending slavery. ✔

Check Your Progress

1. What was John Adams's response to problems with France after the XYZ Affair?

_____

_____

2. What two principles did the Virginia and Kentucky resolutions help to establish?

_____

_____

✓ **Checkpoint**

Name the act that targeted Republicans.

_____

Vocabulary Builder

The word *resolution* has different meanings depending on its context. Which definition is most like that in the bracketed text?

A. A statement of a group's opinion

B. The solving of a problem

✓ **Checkpoint**

Name the two men who wrote resolutions for Virginia and Kentucky.

_____

_____

Question to Think About As you read Section 4 in your textbook and take notes, keep this question in mind: **How did problems with France intensify the split between the Federalists and Republicans?**

▶ Use this chart to record key information from the section. Some information has been filled in to get you started.

The Presidency of John Adams

Troubles With France

- France was angry that the United States remained _____ in the war between France and Britain. The French also felt that __Jay's Treaty__ favored Britain.
- France _____ an American diplomat and continued to seize _____ .
- XYZ Affair
  - French officials demanded a _____ from three American _____ .
  - Many Americans, especially _____ , were outraged.
- American anger over the XYZ Affair led to an _____ . Adams increased the size of the _____ and established a _____ .
- In 1800, France and the United States signed a treaty. France agreed to _____ , and the United States _____ _____ .
- The treaty angered many _____ , which _____ President Adams's political power.

The Alien and Sedition Acts

- Reasons Federalists opposed European immigration
  -
  -
- The Alien Act increased the time it took for an alien to _____ _____ . It also allowed the President to __jail__ or _____ an alien he considered dangerous.
- The Sedition Act made it a crime to _____ about the government. This was a limit on _____ .

States' Rights

- The legislatures of _____ and _____ passed resolutions stating that the Alien and Sedition acts were unconstitutional and that states had the right to _____ .
- The long-term effect was to establish the principles of states' rights and _____ , or the idea that states have the power to deprive a federal law of legal force.

Refer to this page to answer the Chapter 8 Focus Question on page 135.

Chapter 8 Assessment

Directions: Circle the letter of the correct answer.

1. Which was a crisis faced by President George Washington?
   - **A** Shays' Rebellion
   - **B** repaying war debt
   - **C** fighting a war with France
   - **D** Boston Tea Party

2. Which best describes the Republican Party?
   - **A** It supported Britain over France.
   - **B** Its leader was Alexander Hamilton.
   - **C** It opposed a national bank.
   - **D** Its supporters were merchants.

3. Which did George Washington support in his Farewell Address?
   - **A** avoiding political divisions at home
   - **B** adding a bill of rights to the Constitution
   - **C** supporting the French Revolution
   - **D** passing the Alien and Sedition acts

4. Which was a result of the Virginia and Kentucky resolutions?
   - **A** idea of nullification
   - **B** freedom of religion
   - **C** individual rights
   - **D** Three-fifths Compromise

Directions: Follow the steps to answer this question:

How did the advice Washington gave in his Farewell Address reflect or not reflect his accomplishments as President?

Step 1: Recall information: In the chart, list Washington's advice and accomplishments.

Washington's Advice	Washington's Accomplishments
1.	1.
	2.
2.	3.
	4.

Step 2: Identify similarities and differences between his advice and accomplishments.

_____

_____

_____

Step 3: Complete the topic sentence that follows. Then write two or three sentences explaining how Washington's accomplishments did or did not reflect his advice.

Washington's accomplishments as President _____

_____

_____

_____

Chapter 8 Notetaking Study Guide

Now you are ready to answer the Chapter 8 Focus Question: **How did Americans respond to internal and external challenges?**

▶ Complete the following chart to help you answer this question. Use the notes that you took for each section.

Challenges Facing the New Government	
Internal Challenges	**External Challenges**
Organizing the Government • Congress passed laws to set up three departments in the executive branch: _____, _____, and _____ • Judicial branch: _Judiciary Act of 1789_	**The French Revolution** • Federalist reaction: _denounced the violence of the revolution_ • Republican reaction: _____ _____
The Nation's First Economic Crisis • Problem: _____ • Solution: Alexander Hamilton proposed a _____ plan. Congress agreed to 1. _____ 2. _____	**France and Britain at War** • U.S. position: _____ • Effect of position: _____ _____ _____
The Whiskey Rebellion • To raise money, Congress imposed a _____ that led to a revolt. • Washington sent in the militia, which confirmed _____.	**Troubles with Britain** Jay's Treaty: • Americans agreed to: _____ _____ • British agreed to: _____ _____
Political Disagreements • Two parties formed: _____, _____.	• British did not agree to: _____ _____ _____
Conflicts in the Northwest Territory • Reasons U.S. upset with Britain: _____ _____ _____ • Source of conflict with Native Americans: _____ _____ _____ Terms of the Treaty of Greenville: _____ _____	**Troubles with France** • Jay's Treaty and XYZ Affair led to an _____ • U.S. agreement with France: _____ _____
	Alien and Sedition Acts Increasing tensions with France prompted the Federalist-led government to pass laws that made it harder to gain _____ and restricted _____.

Refer to this page to answer the Unit 3 Focus Question on page 167.

The Era of Thomas Jefferson (1800–1815)

What You Will Learn

During Thomas Jefferson's presidency, the United States acquired a vast expanse of western territory. Conflicts with the British and Native Americans soon led to the War of 1812.

Chapter 9 Focus Question

As you read this chapter, keep this question in mind: **How did Jefferson and Madison deal with unresolved problems?**

Section 1

Jefferson Takes Office

Section 1 Focus Question

How did Jefferson chart a new course for the government? To begin answering this question,
- Learn about the Republican victory in the election of 1800.
- Find out about Jefferson's new course for government.
- Learn about judicial review.

Section 1 Summary

After a bitter campaign, Thomas Jefferson took office as President. Jefferson tried to reduce the power of the federal government over states and citizens. Meanwhile, judicial review increased the Supreme Court's power.

Republicans Take Charge

The presidential campaign of 1800 was a bitter contest between the Federalists and the Republicans. The Federalists threatened a civil war if Jefferson won the election. **Thomas Jefferson,** the Republican candidate, received 73 electoral votes, defeating John Adams, the Federalist candidate. According to the Constitution, the person who received the next highest total of electoral votes would become Vice President. However, **Aaron Burr,** Jefferson's running mate, also received 73 votes. It was up to the House of Representatives to break the tie. After six days of deadlock, the House chose Jefferson. To avoid this situation in the future, the Twelfth Amendment to the Constitution established separate votes for President and Vice President.

Beginning with his inauguration, Jefferson established simpler customs that he believed were appropriate for a republic. For

Key Events

1803 The United States purchases Louisiana from France.

1811 Americans defeat Native Americans at Battle of Tippecanoe.

1812 United States declares war on Britain.

example, he walked to his inauguration rather than ride in a carriage. Equally important, Jefferson used his inaugural address to bring the country together. ✔

Jefferson Charts a New Course

The new President saw his election as a chance to introduce new ideas. He thought of it as the "Revolution of 1800." Jefferson's first goal was to reduce the federal government's power over states and citizens. He believed in an idea known as **laissez faire**, which means that the government should not interfere with the economy.

Jefferson's Main Policy Changes
• Reduced the number of people in government • Cut military spending • Eliminated federal taxes in the country, except tariffs • Released those jailed under the Sedition Act

Jefferson did not reverse all Federalist policies, however. For example, he believed that the nation should keep repaying its debt, and he did not fire most Federalist officeholders. ✔

The Supreme Court and Judicial Review

During his last hours in office, Adams appointed several judges. The Republicans argued that the appointments were an attempt to maintain Federalist power. When Jefferson took office, he ordered James Madison, his secretary of state, to stop work on the appointments. William Marbury, one of Adams's appointees, sued Madison to receive his commission. In his lawsuit, Marbury cited the Judiciary Act of 1789, which gave the Supreme Court the power to review cases brought against a federal official.

The outcome of the case, called *Marbury* v. *Madison,* changed the relationship of the three branches of government. In an opinion written by Chief Justice **John Marshall,** the Court declared the Judiciary Act was unconstitutional. Marshall stated that the Court's powers came from the Constitution. Therefore, Congress did not have the right to give the Court power in the Judiciary Act. This ruling established **judicial review,** or the authority of the Supreme Court to strike down unconstitutional laws. ✔

Check Your Progress

1. How did the election of 1800 affect future elections?

_____

_____

2. What power does judicial review give the Supreme Court?

_____

_____

✓ Checkpoint

Name the body that decided the election of 1800.

_____

✓ Checkpoint

List a Federalist policy that Jefferson kept.

_____

Vocabulary Builder

Reread the bracketed paragraph. The text says Marbury was one of Adams's appointees. Using context clues in the paragraph, write a definition of *appointee* on the lines below.

_____

_____

✓ Checkpoint

Name the justice who wrote the Supreme Court's decision in *Marbury* v. *Madison.*

_____

Section 1 Notetaking Study Guide

Question to Think About As you read Section 1 in your textbook and take notes, keep this section focus question in mind: **How did Jefferson chart a new course for the government?**

▶ Use these charts to record key information from the section. Some information has been filled in to get you started.

The Election of 1800

- **The presidential candidates**
  1. Federalist: <u>John Adams</u>
  2. Republican: <u>Thomas Jefferson</u>

- The tie between _____ and _____ occurred because
  _____
  _____

- Deadlock resolved by _____

- Amendment passed as a result of the tie: _____

- Amendment established _____
  _____

Jefferson Charts a New Course

- Jefferson's first goal as president: _____

- The reforms Jefferson made to meet his goal:
  -
  -
  -
  -

- Federalist policies Jefferson did not reverse:
  -
  -

The Supreme Court and Judicial Review

- In _____ v. _____, the Supreme Court ruled the
  _____ unconstitutional because
  _____

- This decision established _____, or the authority of
  the Supreme Court to strike down _____ laws.

Refer to this page to answer the Chapter 9 Focus Question on page 149.

The Louisiana Purchase

Section 2 Focus Question

What was the importance of the purchase and exploration of the Louisiana Territory? To begin answering this question,

- Learn about the nation's westward expansion.
- Find out about the Louisiana Purchase.
- Learn about Lewis and Clark's western expedition.

Section 2 Summary

Westward expansion sped up after the United States won its independence. The Louisiana Purchase almost doubled the size of the United States, and the Lewis and Clark expedition provided Americans with new knowledge of the West.

The Nation Looks West

By 1800, more than one million settlers lived between the Appalachian Mountains and the Mississippi River. Most settlers were farmers. Because there were few roads to the West, they shipped their crops down the Mississippi to the port at New Orleans. From there, the goods were shipped to markets in the East.

Spain, which controlled the Mississippi and New Orleans, had several times threatened to close the port to American ships. To prevent this from happening, the United States negotiated the Pinckney Treaty with Spain in 1795, which guaranteed Americans the right to ship goods down the Mississippi to New Orleans.

In 1801, Jefferson discovered that Spain had secretly transferred New Orleans and the rest of its Louisiana territory to France. Jefferson feared that Napoleon Bonaparte, the French leader, intended to expand France's control in America. ✓

Buying Louisiana

In 1802, before the transfer of Louisiana to France took place, Spain withdrew the right of Americans to ship their goods through New Orleans. Westerners demanded that Jefferson go to war to win back their rights.

Instead Jefferson sent James Monroe to Paris to offer to buy the city of New Orleans and a territory to the east called West Florida from the French. Monroe was assisted by Robert Livingston, the American minister in Paris.

Around this time, a revolution had driven the French from their Caribbean colony of Haiti. Without this base, France would have trouble defending Louisiana in a war. At the same time, tensions between France and Britain were rising, and war loomed. Napoleon needed money to support the war effort. As a result, France offered to sell not only New Orleans, but the entire

Key Events

1803	The United States purchases Louisiana from France.
1811	Americans defeat Native Americans at Battle of Tippecanoe.
1812	United States declares war on Britain.

✓ Checkpoint

Describe the route by which Western farm products traveled to markets in the East.

_____

_____

_____

_____

List the four boundaries of Louisiana Territory.

_____

_____

_____

_____

Vocabulary Builder

An early definition of *expedition* was "helping forward or accomplishing." How can this definition still explain the word *expedition*?

_____

_____

_____

✓ **Checkpoint**

Name the Native American woman who served as a translator for Lewis and Clark.

_____

Louisiana Territory to the United States. The territory stretched from the Gulf of Mexico to Canada and from the Mississippi River to the Rocky Mountains.

Jefferson was delighted with the deal, which almost doubled the size of the country and gave the United States control of the Mississippi. However, the Constitution did not give the President the power to buy land from a foreign country. In the end, Jefferson decided that the power the Constitution gave the President to make treaties allowed him to buy Louisiana. The Senate approved the treaty, and Congress quickly voted to pay for the land. ✓

Lewis and Clark Explore the West

Even before the United States had bought Louisiana, Jefferson called on Congress to finance a western **expedition**, or long and carefully organized journey. Army officers **Meriwether Lewis** and **William Clark** were to lead the expedition.

Lewis and Clark's mission had three goals. First, they were to report on the geography, plants, animals, and other natural features of the region. Second, they were to make contact with Native Americans. Third, they were to find out if a waterway connected the Mississippi River to the Pacific Ocean.

Lewis and Clark left St. Louis in the spring of 1804 with about 40 men. In October, a Native American woman named Sacagawea joined the expedition as a translator. The following August, they reached the Continental Divide. A **continental divide** is the place on a continent that separates river systems flowing in opposite directions. On the western side of the Rockies, they reached the Columbia River, which carried them to the Pacific Ocean. They spent the winter at the point where the Columbia River meets the Pacific before beginning their half-year-long return journey in March 1806. With them, they brought a new awareness of a rich and beautiful part of the continent.

Zebulon Pike led another expedition through the southern part of the Louisiana Territory from 1805 to 1807. His return route took him into Spanish New Mexico, where he and his men were arrested as spies. After several months, they were released. As the Spanish had feared, Pike's reports about the Spanish borderlands created great American interest in the region. ✓

Check Your Progress

1. Why was the Louisiana Purchase important?

_____

_____

2. What was one purpose of the Lewis and Clark expedition?

_____

_____

Question to Think About As you read Section 2 in your textbook and take notes, keep this section focus question in mind: **What was the importance of the purchase and exploration of the Louisiana Territory?**

▶ Use these charts to record key information from the section. Some information has been filled in to get you started.

Westward Expansion
Importance of access to the Mississippi River: *few roads; farmers depended on the river to move their farm products to the East*
Importance of Pinckney's Treaty:
Jefferson's fear about the transfer of Louisiana to France:

Buying Louisiana
Jefferson's proposed deal:
Situation in France at the time: • •
France's offer:
Jefferson's dilemma:
Resolution to the dilemma:

Exploring the West
Reasons for Lewis and Clark's expedition: • • •
• Route to Pacific: • Result:
• Route of Pike's Expedition: • Result:

Refer to this page to answer the Chapter 9 Focus Question on page 149.

A Time of Conflict

Section 3 Focus Question

How did Jefferson respond to threats to the security of the nation? To begin answering this question,

- Learn about the defeat of the Barbary States.
- Find out about the threats to American neutrality.
- Read about the trade embargo Jefferson imposed.
- Explore the efforts of Tecumseh and the Prophet to preserve Native American lands and ways of life.

Section 3 Summary

Jefferson faced numerous threats to the nation's security and economy, including piracy, seizure of American ships by Britain and France, and unrest among Native Americans.

Defeating the Barbary States

Trade with Europe was critical to the U.S. economy. After the American Revolution, pirates began attacking American ships in the Mediterranean Sea. The pirates came from four North African countries known as the Barbary States. They were Morocco, Algiers, Tunisia, and Tripoli. European nations paid the Barbary States **tribute**, or money paid by one country to another in return for protection. In exchange, pirates left their ships alone.

For a time, the United States also paid tribute. But Jefferson put an end to that practice and sent warships to the Mediterranean to protect American merchant ships. At first these military patrols went badly. For example, the warship *Philadelphia* ran aground near the Tripoli coast, and its crew was captured. However, the next year, a small force of American marines marched 600 miles across the Sahara to capture Tripoli. This victory inspired confidence in the ability of the United States to deal forcefully with threats from foreign powers. ✔

American Neutrality Is Challenged

By 1803 Britain and France were once again at war. The United States, which remained neutral, continued trading with both countries. Britain and France began seizing American ships carrying trade goods to the other country. This was an attempt to weaken each other by cutting off the other's foreign trade. In addition, Britain impressed, or forced, thousands of American sailors to serve in the British navy. ✔

Jefferson Responds With an Embargo

Jefferson tried to force Britain and France to respect American neutrality by issuing an **embargo**. This is a government order that forbids foreign trade. In 1807 Congress passed the Embargo Act.

Key Events

1803 The United States purchases Louisiana from France.

1811 Americans defeat Native Americans at Battle of Tippecanoe.

1812 United States declares war on Britain.

✓ Checkpoint

List the four Barbary States.

_____

_____

_____

_____

✓ Checkpoint

Name the countries that challenged the United States' neutrality.

_____

_____

The embargo applied to American ships sailing to any foreign port. Jefferson predicted that France and Britain would soon stop attacking American ships.

However, Jefferson did not foresee the result of the embargo. The big loser proved to be the American economy. Declining exports caused crop prices to fall and tens of thousands of Americans to lose their jobs. The embargo was especially unpopular in New England, where merchants depended heavily on foreign trade. To evade the embargo, thousands of Americans turned to **smuggling,** or the act of illegally importing or exporting goods.

Congress finally repealed the Embargo Act in 1809. It then passed a law that reopened trade with all countries except Britain and France. The law stated that trade with Britain and France would resume when they started respecting America's trading rights as a neutral nation. ✓

Tecumseh and the Prophet

After the Battle of Fallen Timbers, tens of thousands of settlers moved westward. Ohio became a state in 1803, and settlers moved into Indiana Territory and beyond.

The tide of settlement had a terrible impact on Native Americans. Westward expansion exposed Native Americans to disease, threatened their hunting grounds, and drove away game. The Native American population declined, as did the power of their traditional leaders.

Two Shawnee brothers, **Tecumseh** and Tenskwatawa, or the Prophet, began urging Native American resistance. They called on Native Americans to preserve their traditional ways.

American officials were concerned by Tecumseh's activities. While Tecumseh was gone, **William Henry Harrison,** the governor of the Indiana Territory, led an attack on Shawnee villages on the Tippecanoe River. Harrison's troops defeated the Native Americans. The Battle of Tippecanoe marked the high point of Native American resistance to settlement. Still, Tecumseh and his warriors continued their struggle for several more years. ✓

Check Your Progress

1. What were the main threats to American trade?

_____

_____

2. How did westward expansion affect Native Americans?

_____

_____

✓ **Checkpoint**

List two effects of the Embargo Act on the United States' economy.

_____

_____

✓ **Checkpoint**

Name the two Native American leaders who fought back against American settlement in the West.

_____

_____

Question to Think About As you read Section 3 in your textbook and take notes, keep this section focus question in mind: **How did Jefferson respond to threats to the security of the nation?**

▶ Use this organizer to record key information from the section. Some information has been filled in to get you started.

Barbary Pirates

- Why they were a threat: _stole property and enslaved sailors_
- Some nations responded by _____
- How Jefferson responded: _____
  _____

Challenges Faced by the United States

American Neutrality Challenged

- Causes: War between Britain and France leads to restrictions on U.S. trade
- Actions taken by Britain and France:
  _____
  _____
  _____
  _____
- U.S. response: _____
  _____
  _____
- Results of embargo:
  • _____
  _____
  • _____
  • _____
  _____
- Congress repealed Embargo Act in 1809.

Native American Unrest

- Cause of unrest: _rapid westward settlement_
- Effects on Native Americans
  • exposed to deadly diseases
  • _____
  • _____
  • _____
  • _____
- Tecumseh and Tenskwatawa urged Native Americans to:
  • _____
  • _____
- U.S. response to unrest:_____
  _____
  _____
  _____
  _____
  _____

Refer to this page to answer the Chapter 9 Focus Question on page 149.

Section 4
The War of 1812

Section 4 Focus Question
What were the causes and effects of the War of 1812? To begin answering this question,

- Find out why the United States moved toward war with Britain.
- Learn about the early days of the war.
- Read about the war in the West and South.
- Learn about the final battles of the war.

Section 4 Summary

The War of 1812 started badly for the United States. However, America's eventual victory increased American nationalism.

The Move Toward War
When James Madison became President in 1809, Americans were angry with the British for supplying arms to Native Americans and impressing American sailors. To most Americans, the country's honor was at stake. They felt a new sense of **nationalism**, or pride in one's country.

In 1810, Henry Clay of Kentucky and John C. Calhoun of South Carolina became leaders in the House of Representatives. The two men and their supporters were called **war hawks** because they were eager for war with Britain. Opposition to war was strongest in New England, where many believed war would harm American trade.

Relations with Britain worsened in the spring of 1812 when the British told the United States they would continue impressing sailors. Meanwhile, Native Americans in the Northwest began new attacks on frontier settlements. In June, Congress declared war on Britain. ✔

Early Days of the War
Britain was still at war in Europe at the time, but it was not willing to meet American demands in order to avoid war. When the war began, Americans were confident they would win. However, because of military cuts under Jefferson, the United States military was not prepared for war.

At the beginning of the war, Britain set up a blockade of the American coast. A **blockade** is the action of shutting a port or road to prevent people or supplies from coming into an area or leaving it. By the end of the war, the British were able to close off all American ports.

One early naval success for the United States was the USS *Constitution*'s defeat of the British warship the *Guerrière*. ✔

Key Events

1803 — The United States purchases Louisiana from France.

1811 — Americans defeat Native Americans at Battle of Tippecanoe.

1812 — United States declares war on Britain.

✓ Checkpoint
Name the region in the United States where opposition to the war with Britain was strongest.

_____

_____

✓ Checkpoint
Name an action the British took at the beginning of the war.

_____

_____

Vocabulary Builder

The word *negotiate* comes from the Latin word for "to carry on business." What do you think the word *negotiating* means in the context of the underlined sentence?

_____

_____

✓ Checkpoint

Name the battle that occurred after the peace treaty was signed.

_____

The War in the West and South

In the West, the Americans and British fought for control of the Great Lakes and the Mississippi River. The British captured American General William Hull's troops after they tried to invade Canada. American forces under **Oliver Hazard Perry,** however, scored an important victory against the British on Lake Erie. William Henry Harrison and his troops defeated the British at the Battle of the Thames. In the South, Creek warriors attacked several American settlements. **Andrew Jackson** led American troops to victory against the Creeks in the Battle of Horseshoe Bend. ✔

Final Battles

After the British defeated Napoleon in 1814, they sent more troops to fight against the United States. In August, British troops attacked Washington, D.C., burning several government buildings, including the White House. The British moved on to Baltimore, where they attacked Fort McHenry. British warships bombarded the fort throughout the night of September 13, 1814. At dawn, however, the Americans still held the fort. An American, Francis Scott Key, witnessed the battle and wrote the poem, "The Star-Spangled Banner." Set to music, it later became the national anthem of the United States.

Britain began to tire of the war, so the two sides began negotiating a peace treaty. On Christmas Eve 1814, the United States and Britain signed the Treaty of Ghent, ending the war. It took several weeks for the news to reach the United States, and during this time, the two sides fought one last battle. In January 1815, American forces under General Andrew Jackson defeated the British at the Battle of New Orleans.

Meanwhile, opponents of the war met in Hartford, Connecticut, in December 1814. Some delegates suggested that New England **secede,** or withdraw, from the United States. However, the convention quickly ended when news of the treaty arrived.

To some Americans, the War of 1812 was the "Second War of Independence." Once and for all, the United States had secured its independence from Britain, and European nations would now have to treat the young republic with respect. ✔

Check Your Progress

1. What British actions led to the War of 1812?

_____

_____

2. Why was the United States unprepared for war?

_____

_____

Question to Think About As you read Section 4 in your textbook and take notes, keep this question in mind: **What were the causes and effects of the War of 1812?**

▶ Use these charts to record key information. Some information has been filled in to get you started.

The Move Toward War
The President during the War of 1812 was <u>James Madison</u>.
The two main reasons Americans wanted to go to war with Britain were _____ and _____.
Supporters of the war were called _____.
New Englanders opposed the war because _____.

Early Days of the War
The war did not come at a good time for Britain because _____ _____.
Near the start of the war, the British Navy _____.
The U.S. warship that won an early battle was the _____.

The War in the West and South
U.S. General William Hull invaded _____, and then _____ . Then British General Isaac Brock _____.
The U.S. naval commander _____ won an important battle on Lake Erie. U.S. General William Henry Harrison won the Battle of _____ where _____ was killed.
_____ defeated the Creeks in the Battle of _____.

Final Battles
In 1814, the British could send more troops to fight the war in the United States because _____.
During an attack on the nation's _____ in 1814, British troops burned _____.
During the British attack on _____ in Baltimore, Francis Scott Key wrote the words to _____.
The Treaty of _____ ended the War of 1812.
Before news of the war's end reached the U.S., _____ led the U.S. to victory in the Battle of _____.
Federalists met at the _____ where some suggested New England _____ from the U.S.

Refer to this page to answer the Chapter 9 Focus Question on page 149.

Chapter 9 Assessment

Directions: Circle the letter of the correct answer.

1. Which was a goal of President Thomas Jefferson?
   A   declare war on Britain
   B   add a Bill of Rights to the Constitution
   C   reduce the size of the federal government
   D   reduce the powers of state governments

2. Who was the Treaty of Ghent between?
   A   Thomas Jefferson and James Madison
   B   William Marbury and John Marshall
   C   the United States and France
   D   the United States and Britain

3. What was an effect of the Embargo Act?
   A   increased unemployment in America
   B   higher prices for American crops
   C   war between Britain and France
   D   war with Native Americans

Directions: Follow the steps to answer this question:

How might the United States be different if the Louisiana Purchase had not occurred?

Step 1: Recall information: In the chart, list three benefits of the Louisiana Purchase for the United States.

Benefits of the Louisiana Purchase in 1803
• • •

Step 2: Now imagine what two ways the United States would be different today if it had been denied those benefits.

Differences in the United States Without Those Benefits
• •

Step 3: Complete the topic sentence that follows. Then write two or three more sentences that support your topic sentence.

Without the Louisiana Purchase, the United States _____

_____

_____

_____

_____

Chapter 9 Notetaking Study Guide

Now you are ready to answer the Chapter 9 Focus Question: **How did Jefferson and Madison deal with unresolved problems?**

▶ Complete the following organizer to help you answer this question. Use the notes that you took for each section.

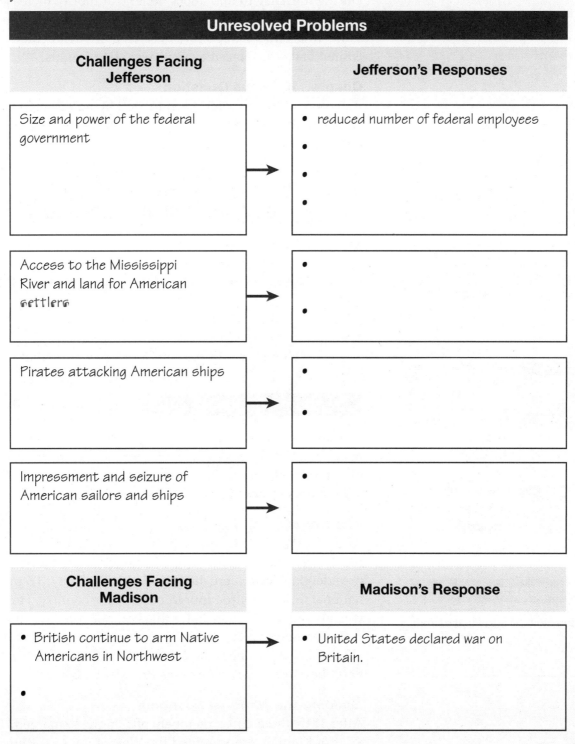

Unresolved Problems

Challenges Facing Jefferson	Jefferson's Responses
Size and power of the federal government	• reduced number of federal employees • • •
Access to the Mississippi River and land for American settlers	• •
Pirates attacking American ships	• •
Impressment and seizure of American sailors and ships	•

Challenges Facing Madison	Madison's Response
• British continue to arm Native Americans in Northwest •	• United States declared war on Britain.

Refer to this page to answer the Unit 3 Focus Question on page 167.

What You Will Learn

During the early to mid-1800s, federal authority increased, and the status of the United States among other nations grew. At the same time, American politics became more democratic. The United States also faced a crisis over states' rights.

Chapter 10 Focus Question

As you read this chapter, keep the following question in mind: **How did the nation reflect a growing sense of national pride and identity?**

Section 1

Building a National Identity

Section 1 Focus Question

How was the power of the federal government strengthened during the Era of Good Feelings? To begin answering this question,

- Find out about the Era of Good Feelings.
- Explore the building of the national economy.
- Learn about three important Supreme Court rulings.

Section 1 Summary

Following the War of 1812, the United States experienced a rise in national unity. This sense of unity was tested by disagreements over tariffs. However, key Supreme Court rulings aided the federal government in steadily increasing its power.

The Era of Good Feelings

After the War of 1812, the Republicans controlled the government. Republican James Monroe's huge victory in the 1816 presidential election crushed the Federalist Party. To promote national unity, Monroe toured parts of the country. He was warmly greeted even in states that had not voted for him in 1816. A Boston newspaper called the new spirit of national unity the "Era of Good Feelings," and the name has since been used to describe Monroe's two terms as President. ✔

Building the National Economy

After 1815, three gifted members of Congress emerged. **Henry Clay** of Kentucky represented the West. **John C. Calhoun** of South Carolina spoke for southern interests. **Daniel Webster** of Massachusetts was a leading politician for the Northeast.

Key Events

1816	Congress passes Tariff of 1816.
1823	Monroe Doctrine is issued.
1828	Andrew Jackson elected President.
1837	Panic of 1837 brings economic collapse.

✓ Checkpoint

Name the political party that gained power after the War of 1812.

_____

The economy was one topic of debate for these men. When the first Bank of the United States closed in 1811, the U.S. economy suffered. In 1816, Congress approved a new **charter**—a legal document giving certain rights to a person or company—for a second Bank of the United States. This federal bank stabilized the money supply and helped business, but it did not solve all the nation's economic problems. After the War of 1812, British companies began to sell manufactured goods below market price in America, a practice known as **dumping**. This drove many New England companies out of business. Congress responded by passing the Tariff of 1816, which taxed foreign goods like cloth, iron, leather goods, and paper. Congress passed even higher tariffs in 1818 and 1824. Such protective tariffs were popular in the North, where they protected local factories. But in the South, people resented the high tariffs that made goods more expensive.

Henry Clay defended high tariffs in a plan he called the American System. He said the money from tariffs could pay to build infrastructure, such as bridges, canals, and roads. Clay argued that this would help all regions. Southerners rejected the American System and continued to oppose the tariffs. ✓

Three Important Supreme Court Rulings

Between 1819 and 1824, the Supreme Court issued three major rulings that affected the economy and the power of the federal government. In *Dartmouth College v. Woodward* (1819), the Court protected private contracts. A **contract** is an agreement between two or more parties that can be enforced by law. This ruling promoted **capitalism,** an economic system in which private businesses compete in a free market. In *McCulloch* v. *Maryland* (1819), the Court ruled that a state cannot pass a law that violates a federal law. In addition, the Court said states had no power to interfere with federal institutions. This protected the second Bank of the United States from being taxed by the state of Maryland. In *Gibbons* v. *Ogden* (1824), the Court blocked New York State from giving a steamboat company the sole right to carry passengers on the Hudson River. Because the trip involved trade between two or more states, it was considered **interstate commerce**. Only Congress can regulate such trade. The *McCulloch* v. *Maryland* and *Gibbons* v. *Ogden* rulings both increased the power of the federal government when dealing with the states. ✓

Check Your Progress

1. Why did Congress pass protective tariffs?

_____

_____

2. How did the Supreme Court's rulings increase the power of the federal government?

_____

_____

Unit 3   Chapter 10   Section 1   **151**

Vocabulary Builder

The word *infrastructure* means "foundation" or "basic framework." How do structures like roads and bridges serve as a foundation or framework for the nation?

_____

_____

✓ Checkpoint

Name three key members of Congress and the regions they represented.

Member: _____
Region: _____
Member: _____
Region: _____
Member: _____
Region: _____

✓ Checkpoint

Name the Supreme Court ruling that said states cannot pass laws that violate federal laws.

_____

Question to Think About As you read Section 1 in your textbook and take notes, keep this section focus question in mind: **How was the power of the federal government strengthened during the Era of Good Feelings?**

▶ Use these charts to record key information from the section.

Important Political Figures During the Era of Good Feelings	
Henry Clay	Congressman from _____ who represented _____ interests; proposed the _____
John C. Calhoun	Congressman from _____ who represented _____ interests; emphasized _____
	Congressman from _____ who represented _northern_ interests; supported _____

Important Economic Issues		
Topic	**Why It Was Needed**	**What It Did**
Second _Bank of United States_	_____ made too many loans and issued too much money.	Loaned money and controlled the_____
Tariff of 1816	_____ manufacturers were _____, which hurt American businesses.	_____ on foreign goods, pleasing _____ and upsetting _____

Key Supreme Court Cases	
Case	**Supreme Court Ruling**
_____ v. _____ (_____)	**Question:** Can _Maryland_ tax a state branch of the _____? **Decision:** States cannot _____ federal institutions or violate _____.
_____ v. Woodward (1819)	**Question:** Can New Hampshire change the charter of _____? **Decision:** The charter was a _private contract_ protected by the _____.
Gibbons v. Ogden (1824)	**Question:** Can _____ grant a steamship company a _____ on the Hudson River ferry? **Decision:** The ferry trip involved _____, which only _____ can _____.

Refer to this page to answer the Chapter 10 Focus Question on page 166.

Section 2

Dealing With Other Nations

Section 2 Focus Question

How did U.S. foreign affairs reflect new national confidence? To begin answering this question,

- Learn about U.S. relations with Spain.
- Find out how Spanish colonies won independence.
- Learn about the Monroe Doctrine.
- Examine U.S. relations with Canada.

Section 2 Summary

After the War of 1812, the United States settled border disputes with Spain and Britain involving Florida and Canada. Many Latin American colonies declared independence. The Monroe Doctrine aimed to prevent European powers from interfering with these nations or other U.S. interests in the Americas.

Relations With Spain

The Spanish territory of Florida was a source of conflict between the United States and Spain. The Spanish could not stop enslaved African Americans who had escaped from plantations in Georgia and Alabama from crossing into Florida. Many of these former slaves joined the Seminole Nation. The Seminoles in turn often crossed the border to raid American settlements. In 1817, the U.S. government sent Andrew Jackson to recapture escaped slaves. Jackson destroyed Seminole villages and then captured two Spanish towns. Spain realized that it could not defend Florida from the United States, so it decided to give up the territory. Spain **ceded**, or gave up, Florida to the United States in the Adams-Onís Treaty of 1819. ✓

Spanish Colonies Win Independence

Spain's control of its other American colonies was also fading. The people of Latin America were inspired by the American and French revolutions to seek independence. In 1810, **Father Miguel Hidalgo** (ee DAHL goh) led an unsuccessful rebellion against Spanish rule in Mexico. But in 1820, there was another revolution, forcing Spain to grant Mexico independence in 1821. Mexico overthrew its emperor and became a republic in 1823.

In South America, **Simón Bolívar** (see MOHN boh LEE vahr) led several struggles for independence. Known as the Liberator, Bolívar defeated the Spanish in 1819 and formed the Republic of Great Colombia. This included what are now Colombia, Ecuador, Panama, and Venezuela. The people of Central America soon followed by declaring their independence from Spain in 1821. They formed the United Provinces of Central America two years later. By 1825, most of Latin America had thrown off European rule. ✓

Key Events

1816	Congress passes Tariff of 1816.
1823	Monroe Doctrine is issued.
1828	Andrew Jackson elected President.
1837	Panic of 1837 brings economic collapse.

✓ Checkpoint

Name the reason Spain was willing to cede Florida to the United States.

_____

_____

Vocabulary Builder

To *liberate* means "to set free." Why do you think Simón Bolívar was called the Liberator?

_____

_____

_____

✓ Checkpoint

Name two events that inspired Latin American independence movements.

_____

_____

The Monroe Doctrine

In 1822, the United States recognized the independence of Mexico and six other former colonies in Latin America. But European powers like France and Russia wanted to help Spain regain its colonies. Great Britain and the United States opposed this idea. In 1823, Britain suggested that America and Britain act jointly. They would announce that they would protect the freedom of Latin America. President **James Monroe** approved, but Secretary of State **John Quincy Adams** argued that the United States would look like Britain's junior partner if the two cooperated.

In a message to Congress in 1823, the President stated what is now called the Monroe Doctrine. The United States would not allow European nations to create American colonies or to interfere with the free nations of Latin America. Any attempt to do so would be considered "dangerous to our peace and safety." In truth, the United States was not strong enough to block European action. Only the British navy could do that. As U.S. power grew, however, the Monroe Doctrine boosted the influence of the United States in the region. ✓

Relations With Canada

Britain faced its own challenges in Canada. In 1791, this British colony was divided into Upper and Lower Canada. After each part rebelled in 1837, Britain rejoined the colony in 1841 under the Act of Union. This act gave the Canadian people greater **self-government**—the right of people to rule themselves independently. Britain, however, still had ultimate control.

Canadian relations with the United States were strained. Tensions were particularly high during the War of 1812 when U.S. forces tried to invade Canada. However, relations improved as Britain and the United States settled several border disputes involving Canada from 1818 to 1846. Eventually, the United States and Canada established excellent relations. These relations remain strong even today. ✓

Check Your Progress

1. What are two reasons the United States was upset about relations with Spanish Florida?

   _____

   _____

   _____

2. Why did Secretary of State Adams not want the United States to work with Great Britain on the Monroe Doctrine?

   _____

   _____

✓ **Checkpoint**

Name the region covered by the Monroe Doctrine.

_____

✓ **Checkpoint**

Name the act that reunited Canada in 1841.

_____

Question to Think About As you read Section 2 in your textbook and take notes, keep this section focus question in mind: **How did U.S. foreign affairs reflect new national confidence?**

► Use these organizers to record key information from the section. Some information has been filled in to get you started.

Latin American Independence		
Region	**Country/countries to gain independence**	**When**
North America	Mexico : First a _____, then a _____	•
	People in this region declared their independence from Spain and formed the _____.	• 1821 •
South America	_____ made up of today's nations of Colombia, Ecuador, Panama, and Venezuela Brazil announced its independence from _____.	• •

U.S.-Foreign Relations

Relations With Spain →

Sources of U.S. Conflict With Spain:
- Escaped slaves _____.
- Seminoles in Florida raided _____.
- The United States seized _____.
- Spain ceded _____ to the United States in _____.

Relations With Canada →

- How Canada was divided before 1841: Upper and Lower Canada
- What the Act of Union was: _____
- Importance of the Act of Union: _____
- Why tensions were high during the War of 1812: _____

Monroe Doctrine →

- What it stated: _____
- When issued: _____
- Factors that led up to its statement: _____

Refer to this page to answer the Chapter 10 Focus Question on page 166.

Key Events

1816 — Congress passes Tariff of 1816.

1823 — Monroe Doctrine is issued.

1828 — Andrew Jackson elected President.

1837 — Panic of 1837 brings economic collapse.

✓ Checkpoint

List two reasons Jackson was deeply loved by millions of Americans.

_____

_____

Section 3 Focus Question

How did the people gain more power during the Age of Jackson? To begin answering this question,

- Find out about the conflict between Adams and Jackson.
- Learn about a new era in politics.
- Discover how Jackson became President.

Section 3 Summary

The period from the mid-1820s to the end of the 1830s is called the Age of Jackson, after President Andrew Jackson. Jackson had a huge impact on American politics. His administration allowed everyday Americans to play a greater role in government.

Adams and Jackson in Conflict

Born in a log cabin, **Andrew Jackson** began his life with very little. However, Jackson's toughness and determination helped him become wealthy. Jackson stood for the idea that ordinary people should participate, or take part, in American political life. As a general and later as President, Andrew Jackson was deeply loved by millions of ordinary Americans who respected his humble beginnings and firm leadership.

In the presidential election of 1824, Jackson won the most popular and electoral votes, but not a majority. According to the Constitution, the House of Representatives would have to decide the election. Candidate and Speaker of the House Henry Clay told his supporters to vote for John Quincy Adams. When Adams was elected and made Clay his secretary of state, Jackson was outraged. His supporters claimed that Clay and Adams had made a "corrupt bargain." These rumors burdened Adams as President. He had ambitious plans for the nation, but he lacked the political skill to push his programs through Congress. Adams never won Americans' trust, and as a result, he served only one term. ✓

A New Era in Politics

Jackson's defeat was the beginning of a new era in politics. By 1824, **suffrage**—the right to vote—had been granted to almost all adult white males, not just those who owned property. However, suffrage was still restricted. Women and enslaved African Americans could not participate in government. States also were changing how they chose presidential electors. Previously, state legislatures chose them. Now, that right went to the voters. In 1824, the voters in 18 out of 24 states chose their electors.

Greater voting rights were part of a larger spread of democratic ideas. Jackson and his supporters believed that ordinary people should vote and hold public office. Jackson did not trust government and banks, which he felt favored the rich. Jackson and his supporters strongly opposed special privileges for those of high social status.

During the 1824 election, the Republican Party split. Jackson's supporters called themselves Democrats. Supporters of Adams called themselves National Republicans. After his defeat in 1824, Jackson won the 1828 presidential election over Adams. Later he won the 1832 election over National Republican candidate Henry Clay.

In 1836, the new Whig Party replaced the Republicans. The Democrats and Whigs would be the two major parties in U.S. politics until 1852. The new parties adopted a new way of choosing their presidential candidates. The two parties began to hold **nominating conventions,** or large meetings of party delegates who choose party candidates. Previously, a party's members of Congress held a **caucus**—a meeting of members of a political party. ✓

Jackson Becomes President

Three times as many people voted in the election of 1828 as had voted in 1824. Most of these new voters supported Jackson, who easily defeated Adams. The election revealed growing sectional and class divisions among American voters. Jackson did best in the West and South and had strong support from farmers, small business people, and workers nationwide. Adams was most popular in his home region of New England.

Jackson's supporters called the election a victory for the "common man." Some supporters called Jackson the "People's President." Tens of thousands of ordinary people came to the Capitol to attend Jackson's inauguration. Once in office, Jackson replaced some government officials with his own supporters. Although this was not a new practice, Jackson openly defended what he was doing. He claimed that bringing in new people furthered democracy. This practice of rewarding government jobs to supporters of a party that wins an election became known as the **spoils system.** ✓

Check Your Progress

1. What was different about the voting rights enjoyed by citizens in 1824 compared to earlier elections?

_____

_____

_____

_____

2. How did political parties change the way they chose candidates after 1836?

_____

_____

✓ Checkpoint

Name two political parties that formed during the Age of Jackson.

_____

_____

Vocabulary Builder

There is an old military saying, "to the victors belong the spoils." *Spoil* is another word for loot or prize. Why do you think the name *spoils system* was given to Jackson's practice of putting his supporters in office?

_____

_____

✓ Checkpoint

How many more people voted in the 1828 election than in the 1824 election?

_____

Question to Think About As you read Section 3 in your textbook and take notes, keep this section focus question in mind: **How did people gain more power during the Age of Jackson?**

▶ Use these charts to record key information from the section. Some information has been filled in to get you started.

| Important Events During the Age of Jackson ||
Year	Event
1824	**Presidential Election** • Who ran: _____ • Who won the electoral vote: <u>Jackson</u> • Problem with results: _____ • How election was decided: <u> by a vote in the House of Representatives </u> • Who was ultimately elected: _____
1824–1828	**John Quincy Adams's Presidency** • Burdened by charges of a _____ • Had _____ plans but accomplished _____ • Lacked the <u> political </u> skills to push his programs through _____
1828	**Presidential Election** • Who ran: _____ • Who won: _____ • Revealed growing _____ and _____ divisions
1832	**Presidential Election** • Who ran: _____ • Who won: _____

| Key Political Changes During the Age of Jackson |||
What Changed	How It Changed	What It Replaced
Suffrage	Almost all adult white males were allowed to vote and hold office.	Most states had required men to own property before they could vote.
Choosing the electoral college		
Choosing political candidates		
Ideas about who should participate in political life		Only those with money and power should vote and run for office.

Refer to this page to answer the Chapter 10 Focus Question on page 166.

Section 4

Indian Removal

Section 4 Focus Question

Why did Jackson use force to remove Indians from the Southeast?
To begin answering this question,

- Learn about the Native Americans of the Southeast.
- Explore the conflict over land.
- Follow the Trail of Tears.

Section 4 Summary

As the population of white settlers in the Southeast grew, conflicts arose with Native Americans in the region. President Andrew Jackson decided to forcibly remove thousands of Native Americans and relocate them to the West.

Native Americans of the Southeast

In 1828, more than 100,000 Native Americans lived east of the Mississippi River. These nations included the Cherokee, Chickasaw, Choctaw, and Creek. The groups lived in various parts of Alabama, Mississippi, Georgia, North Carolina, and Tennessee. The Seminoles, who lived in Florida, had an unusual origin. They were a combination of Creeks who had moved into Florida in the late 1700s, Florida Native Americans, and escaped African American slaves. Many of the southeastern Native Americans were farmers or lived in towns.

The Cherokees in particular adopted some white customs. Many Cherokees became Christians. They also had businesses, small industries, schools, and even a newspaper written in English and Cherokee. The alphabet for the Cherokee language was created by a leader named **Sequoyah** (sih KWOY uh). In 1827, the Cherokee set up a government based on a written constitution. They claimed status as a separate nation. ✓

Conflict Over Land

To many government leaders and white farmers, Native Americans stood in the way of westward expansion. Furthermore, Native Americans lived on fertile land. White farmers wanted that land for growing cotton.

Policies to move Native Americans from their lands dated from the presidency of Thomas Jefferson. Jefferson thought that the only way to prevent conflict and protect Native American culture was to send the Native Americans west. After the War of 1812, the federal government signed treaties with several Native American groups in the Old Northwest. Groups agreed to give up their land and move west of the Mississippi River. The pressure to move increased on the Native Americans who remained in the Southeast.

Key Events

1816	Congress passes Tariff of 1816.
1823	Monroe Doctrine is issued.
1828	Andrew Jackson elected President.
1837	Panic of 1837 brings economic collapse.

✓ Checkpoint

List two white customs adopted by the Cherokees.

_____

_____

Vocabulary Builder

The "Old Northwest" is the name for land around the Great Lakes that was once the northwestern part of the United States. Why do you think we do not call the Southeast the "Old Southeast"?

_____

_____

In 1825 and 1827, the state of Georgia passed a law that forced the Creeks to give up most of their land. Then in 1828, Georgia tried to get the Cherokees to leave the state, but they refused to move, choosing instead to sue the state of Georgia. Two cases eventually made their way to the Supreme Court. The first case, *Cherokee Nation* v. *Georgia*, reached the Supreme Court in 1831. The decision in this suit went against the Cherokees. However, in the second case, *Worcester* v. *Georgia* (1832), the Court declared that Georgia's laws "can have no force" within Cherokee land. In his ruling, John Marshall pointed to treaties that the United States had signed guaranteeing certain territory to Native Americans. These treaties meant Georgia could not take away Cherokee territory. President Andrew Jackson, who wanted to move Native Americans to the West, refused to support the Court's decision. Instead, Jackson chose to enforce the Indian Removal Act of 1830. This law gave him the power to offer Native Americans land west of the Mississippi for their land in the East. ✓

On the Trail of Tears

Believing they had no choice, most Native American leaders signed treaties agreeing to move westward to Indian Territory. Today, most of that area is in the state of Oklahoma. The Choctaws signed the first treaty in 1830, and they moved between 1831 and 1833. However, the federal government did not give the Choctaw enough food and supplies for the long trip. As a result, many people died in the cold winter weather. The Cherokees held out a few years longer. Finally, President Martin Van Buren forced the Cherokees to move in the winter of 1838–1839 while being guarded by 7,000 soldiers. Once again, there were not enough supplies. Some 4,000 of the 15,000 Cherokees who began the journey died along the route that became known as the Trail of Tears.

The Seminoles refused to move, choosing instead to fight a war against removal. In the 1840s, most Seminoles were eventually removed to Indian Territory. In their new homes, Native Americans struggled to rebuild their lives under very difficult conditions. ✓

Check Your Progress

1. What did the Supreme Court rule in *Worcester* v. *Georgia*?

_____

_____

_____

2. What happened to most of the Native American groups in the Southeast?

_____

_____

✓ Checkpoint

Name the law that allowed President Jackson to move Native American groups to the West.

_____

✓ Checkpoint

What was the Trail of Tears?

_____

_____

_____

Question to Think About As you read Section 4 in your textbook and take notes, keep this section focus question in mind: **Why did Jackson use force to remove Indians from the Southeast?**

▶ Use these organizers to record key information from the section. Some information has been filled in to get you started.

Time Line of Indian Removal	
Date	**Events**
After 1812	Indian groups in the Old Northwest give up their land and move to Indian Territory.
1825, 1827	Georgia passes law that forces the Creeks to give up their land.
1827	The Cherokees form an independent government with a _____ _____.
1828	The Cherokees refuse Georgia's order to leave, suing the state instead.
1832	The Supreme Court rules in _Worcester_ v. _Georgia_ that _____ _____.
1831 1833	The U.S. government forces the Choctaws to leave the Southeast and settle in _____.
1838– 1839	The U.S. government forces the Cherokees to leave the Southeast for Indian Territory. Thousands die on the journey known as _____ _____.
1840s	Many of the _____ are forced to leave after fighting U.S. forces to resist removal to Indian Territory.

Cause and Effect: Indian Removal

Cause: Conflict Over Land

- Why government wanted Native American land: _____ _____

- Why white settlers wanted Native American land: _____ _____ _____

- Native American groups living in the Southeast:
  1.
  2.
  3.
  4.
  5.

→

Effect: Indian Removal

- Policies to move Native Americans from their land dated from the time of Thomas Jefferson
- What the Indian Removal Act of 1830 did: _____ _____

- Believing they had no choice, most Native Americans signed treaties agreeing to _____ _____

- What happened on the Trail of Tears: _____ _____

Refer to this page to answer the Chapter 10 Focus Question on page 166.

Key Events

1816	Congress passes Tariff of 1816.
1823	Monroe Doctrine is issued.
1828	Andrew Jackson elected President.
1837	Panic of 1837 brings economic collapse.

✓ Checkpoint

Name the two men who opposed each other over the Bank charter.

_____

_____

✓ Checkpoint

Name the Constitutional amendment that reserves certain powers to the states and people.

_____

Section 5 Focus Question

How did old issues take a new shape in the conflict over a national bank and tariffs? To begin answering this question,

- Learn about the disagreement over the Bank of the United States.
- Explore the viewpoints towards states' rights.
- Examine the nullification crisis.
- Find out about the end of the Jackson Era.

Section 5 Summary

Jackson faced two major political conflicts during his presidency. One involved the second Bank of the United States. The other dealt with the thorny issue of states' rights.

The Bank War

The second Bank of the United States earned strong support from business people. The Bank loaned money to many businesses and was a safe place for the federal government to keep its money. The money it issued formed a stable currency. But Andrew Jackson and many other Americans believed that the Bank favored the rich and hurt everyday people. For example, the Bank sometimes limited the amount of money that state banks could lend. In the South and West, the Bank was blamed for the economic crisis of 1819, which cost many people their farms.

In 1832, Nicholas Biddle, the Bank's president, got Congress to renew the Bank's charter. Jackson vetoed this bill, promising to defeat Biddle. Most voters stood behind Jackson, who won the election by a large margin. As a result, the Bank ceased to exist when its charter ran out in 1836. ☑

The Question of States' Rights

Since the founding of the United States, Americans had debated how to divide power between the federal government and the states. The Constitution gives the federal government many significant powers, but at the same time, the Tenth Amendment states that powers not specifically given to the federal government are reserved to the states or to the people. Over the years, the issue of balancing federal and state power had come up repeatedly. During Jackson's presidency, arguments over this issue caused a serious crisis. ☑

The Nullification Crisis

The issue of states' rights was raised again in 1828 when Congress passed a new tariff on manufactured goods. This tariff helped northern businesses but hurt southerners, who were forced to pay more for goods. Southerners felt the law was unfair, and to many, the tariff issue was part of a larger problem. If the federal government could enforce what southerners considered an unjust law, could it also use its power to ban slavery? Vice President John C. Calhoun argued that the states had the right of **nullification**—an action by a state that cancels a federal law to which the state objects.

Vocabulary Builder

To *nullify* means "to make of no value." To nullify a law means to take away its power. How was nullification supposed to protect states' rights?

_____

_____

_____

Arguments For Nullification	Arguments Against Nullification
• The Union was formed by an agreement between the states. • States kept the right to nullify federal laws that the people of the state considered unfair.	• The Union had been formed by the American people, not the states. • The supreme power in the land lay with the American people, not the states.

When Congress passed another high tariff in 1832, South Carolina voted to nullify the tariffs. State leaders also threatened to secede, or leave the Union. Jackson asked Congress to allow the federal government to collect its tariff by force if necessary. But he also supported a compromise bill that would lower the tariffs. In 1832, Congress passed both laws. South Carolina accepted the new tariff, ending the crisis. ✓

The End of the Jackson Era

Martin Van Buren, Jackson's Vice President, won the presidency in 1836. Just as he took office, the U.S. economy faced the Panic of 1837. British mills began buying less cotton, which caused cotton prices to fall. Cotton growers could not repay their bank loans, which caused hundreds of banks to fail. Van Buren's presidency was ruined.

In 1840, the Whig candidate, **William Henry Harrison,** easily beat Van Buren. The Whigs had learned how to reach ordinary voters by using parades and other forms of entertainment in their campaign. The Age of Jackson had ended. ✓

Check Your Progress

1. What did supporters and opponents of the second Bank believe?

_____

_____

_____

2. What caused the nullification crisis?

_____

_____

_____

✓ Checkpoint

Name the act of Congress that South Carolina was trying to nullify.

_____

_____

✓ Checkpoint

Name the crisis that ruined Van Buren's presidency.

_____

_____

Question to Think About As you read Section 5 in your textbook and take notes, keep this section focus question in mind: **How did old issues take a new shape in the conflict over a national bank and tariffs?**

▶ Use these charts to record key information from the section.

The Bank War
The second Bank of the United States held the _____ government's money and lent money to _____ banks. It also issued ___paper money___, which helped create a _____ currency.
Many people blamed the Bank for the _____.
In 1832, Jackson _____ the bill to renew the Bank's charter. He won the 1832 election while _____ the Bank, which closed when its charter ran out in _____.

States' Rights and the Nullification Crisis
Americans had always debated about the balance between the powers of the _____ and _____ governments. The Constitution gave the federal government _____. The Tenth Amendment _____ federal power by stating that _____.
Congress passed a law in 1828 raising tariffs. It helped ___northern manufacturers___, but _____ felt the law was unfair.
_____ argued that states had the right of nullification, which means they could _____. This theory was based on the idea that Union was formed from a voluntary agreement between _____.
The clearest argument against nullification came from _____. He argued that the Union was formed by _____, not the states.
After Congress passed another tariff in 1832, _____ voted to nullify the tariffs. It threatened to _____ if the federal government interfered. Federal threats to _____ as well as a lowering of the _____ led _____ to vote to _____.

The End of the Jackson Era
Jackson's choice to succeed him was _____, who won the presidential election of ___1836___. However, soon afterward, an economic collapse, called the _____, occurred. As a result of the hard times that followed, Van Buren did not _____.

Refer to this page to answer the Chapter 10 Focus Question on page 166.

Chapter 10 Assessment

Directions: Circle the letter of the correct answer.

1. Which of the following cases established the principle that a state cannot pass a law that breaks a federal law?

   A *Marbury* v. *Madison*   C *Gibbons* v. *Ogden*
   B *McCulloch* v. *Maryland*   D *Dartmouth College* v. *Woodward*

2. What did the Monroe Doctrine declare?

   A The United States would consider any European interference in Latin America to be a threat to American peace and security.
   B The United States and Spain would protect new Latin American nations.
   C The United States would support European nations that wanted to regain their colonies in Latin America.
   D The United States would not get involved in Latin American affairs.

3. What is the name given to the journey to Indian Territory made by the Cherokees in the winter of 1838–39?

   A The Great Migration   C The Trail of Tears
   B The Long Walk   D The Overland Trail

Directions: Follow the steps to answer this question:

What was the basis of the disagreement over nullification?

Step 1: Recall information: Briefly describe what those who supported nullification believed. Then briefly describe what those who opposed it believed.

Beliefs of Supporters of Nullification	Beliefs of Opponents of Nullification

Step 2: Compare information: What justification did each side give for its position?

Arguments For Nullification	Arguments Against Nullification

Step 3: Draw conclusions: Complete the topic sentence that follows. Then write two or three more sentences that support your topic sentence.

Supporters and opponents of nullification disagreed about _____

_____

_____

_____

_____

Chapter 10 Notetaking Study Guide

Now you are ready to answer the Chapter 10 Focus Question: **How did the nation reflect a growing sense of national pride and identity?**

▶ Fill in the following chart to help you answer this question. Use the notes that you took for each section.

Building a National Identity

U.S.–Foreign Relations

- The Monroe Doctrine stated that _____ _____.
- How relations with Canada changed after the War of 1812: _____

Federal Government Versus States' Rights

Key Supreme Court cases that strengthened the power of the federal government:
1. _____
2. _____
3. _____
- South Carolina said that states had the right to _____.

Indian Removal

- Why there was a conflict over land between white settlers and Native Americans: _____ _____

- Native Americans were forced _____.
- The Cherokees called their journey _____.

Democratic Reforms in the Age of Jackson

- States dropped property requirements for voting.
- Presidential electors were chosen by _____, not by _____.
- Candidates for office were chosen by _____ instead of caucuses.

A National Economy

- The second Bank of the United States
  - made loans to businesses.
  - was a safe place for the _____ to keep its money.
  - issued _____ that formed a stable _____.
- However, many Americans opposed the bank because _____ _____.

Refer to this page to answer the Unit 3 Focus Question on page 167.

Unit 3 Pulling It Together Activity

What You Have Learned

Chapter 8 As the nation's first President, George Washington established the U.S. government's authority in domestic as well as foreign affairs. Political divisions and strife with France rocked John Adams's presidency.

Chapter 9 The Louisiana Purchase of 1803 doubled the size of the United States. At the same time, the United States struggled to remain neutral in its foreign policy. British support of Native Americans led to the War of 1812.

Chapter 10 During the early 1800s, the federal government increased its authority. At the same time, the Monroe Doctrine expanded U.S. influence in Latin America.

Think Like a Historian

Read the Unit 3 Essential Question: **What problems might a new nation face?**

▶ Use the organizers on this page and the next to collect information to answer this question.

What types of national problems did the new nation face? Some of them are listed in this organizer. Review your section and chapter notes. Then complete the organizer.

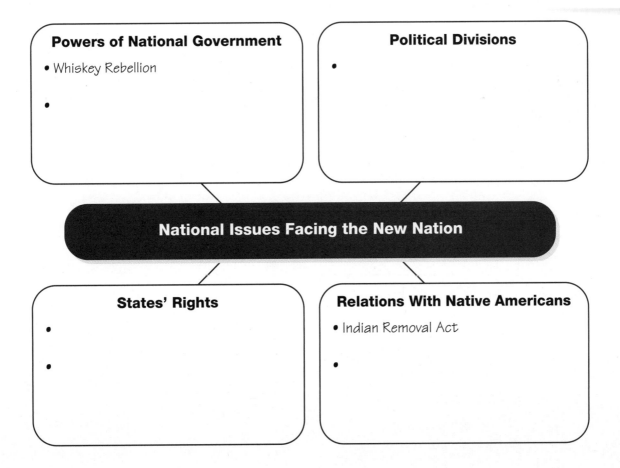

Powers of National Government

- Whiskey Rebellion

-

Political Divisions

-

National Issues Facing the New Nation

States' Rights

-

-

Relations With Native Americans

- Indian Removal Act

-

What types of international problems did the new nation face? The organizer below gives you a part of the answer. Review your section and chapter notes. Then fill in the rest of the organizer.

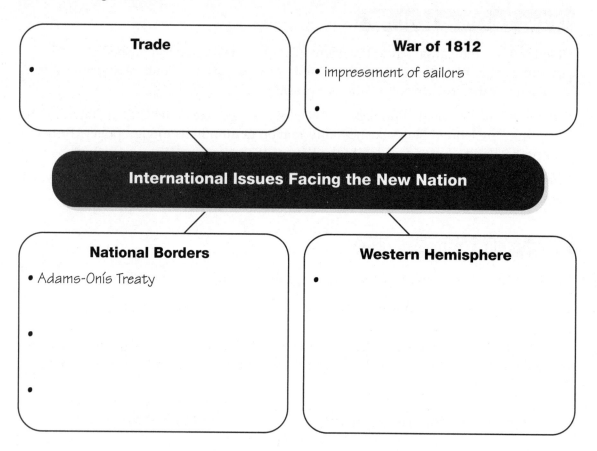

Trade
•

War of 1812
• impressment of sailors
•

International Issues Facing the New Nation

National Borders
• Adams-Onís Treaty
•
•

Western Hemisphere
•

The Nation Expands and Changes

What You Will Learn

Chapter 11 The North industrialized and urbanized rapidly in the early to mid-1800s. The South became highly dependent on cotton and the slave labor needed to cultivate it. Tensions between North and South spread to the western territories.

Chapter 12 By the mid-1800s, Americans were seeking reform in education and abolition. Some sought equality for women. Artists and writers also began to develop a distinct style.

Chapter 13 In the mid-1800s, many Americans wanted the nation to expand westward to the Pacific Ocean. American settlers overcame hardships in making this happen.

Focus Your Learning As you study this unit and take notes, you will find the information to answer the questions below. Answering the Chapter Essential Questions will help build your answer to the Unit Essential Question.

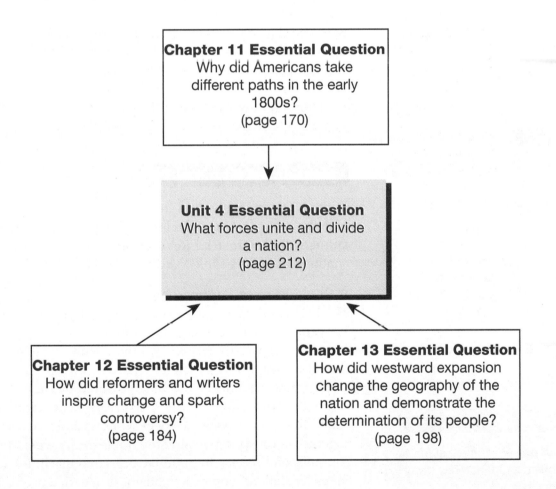

Chapter 11 Essential Question
Why did Americans take different paths in the early 1800s?
(page 170)

Unit 4 Essential Question
What forces unite and divide a nation?
(page 212)

Chapter 12 Essential Question
How did reformers and writers inspire change and spark controversy?
(page 184)

Chapter 13 Essential Question
How did westward expansion change the geography of the nation and demonstrate the determination of its people?
(page 198)

North and South Take Different Paths
(1800–1845)

What You Will Learn

The North industrialized and urbanized rapidly in the early to mid-1800s. The South became highly dependent on cotton and the slave labor needed to cultivate it. Tensions between North and South spread to the western territories.

Chapter 11 Focus Question

As you read through this chapter, keep this question in mind: **Why did Americans take different paths in the early 1800s?**

Section 1
The Industrial Revolution

Section 1 Focus Question

How did the new technology of the Industrial Revolution change the way Americans lived? To begin answering this question,
- Study the revolution in technology.
- See how this revolution came to the United States.
- Find out how American industry grew.
- Learn how the revolution took hold.

Section 1 Summary

In the 1700s, machines and new sources of power such as water and steam began to replace labor once performed by people and animals. This **Industrial Revolution**, as it was called, greatly changed the way people lived and worked.

A Revolution in Technology

The Industrial Revolution began in Britain in the textile industry. For centuries, workers had spun thread and woven cloth in their own homes. In the 1760s, the spinning jenny speeded up the thread-making process. Then Richard Arkwright invented the water frame, a spinning machine powered by running water rather than by human energy. This created a new way of working called the **factory system,** where workers and machines come together in one place outside the home. Mill owners turned to capitalists for money to build factories and machines. **Capitalists** invest capital, or money, in a business to earn a profit. The use of steam power in the 1790s allowed factories to be built away from rivers. ✔

Key Events

1794 Eli Whitney patents the cotton gin.

1808 Importation of enslaved people is banned.

1820 The Missouri Compromise highlights disagreements between North and South over slavery.

1830 Peter Cooper builds the steam locomotive.

✓ Checkpoint

Name the power source that made it possible to build factories away from running water.

The American Industrial Revolution

Britain tried to guard its secrets of industrial success. Skilled workers were forbidden to leave the country. In 1789, a young apprentice in one of Arkwright's factories named Samuel Slater immigrated to America. Working from his memory of Arkwright's factories, Slater built new spinning machines for American merchant Moses Brown. Slater's mill became a great success. ✓

American Industry Grows

The success of Slater's mill marked the beginning of American industrialization. Industrialization began in the Northeast. U.S. industry did not grow significantly until the War of 1812. Without British imports, Americans had to depend on their own industries. **Francis Cabot Lowell** built a mill that combined spinning and weaving in a single factory. This idea led to the growth of a mill town called Lowell. The workforce was made up of young women known as "Lowell girls," who lived in boarding houses. ✓

The Revolution Takes Hold

Another key innovation in American industry was the invention of **interchangeable parts**—identical pieces that could be quickly put together by unskilled workers. Traditional craftsmen had built machines by hand. No two parts were the same, making machinery slow to build and hard to repair. Eli Whitney came up with the idea for interchangeable parts in the 1790s. The idea led to **mass production**—the rapid manufacture of large numbers of identical objects. As a result, many goods became cheaper, and American industry continued to grow.

Many factories, mines, and mills employed children as young as 7 or 8. These children had little chance for an education and worked in difficult conditions. Working conditions for adults were no better. Many spent the 12- or 14-hour workday in poorly lit factories with little fresh air. The machines were often dangerous and injuries were common. There were no payments for disabled workers. By 1844, workers were demanding shorter days. Conditions gradually improved, but the eight-hour workday was far in the future. ✓

Check Your Progress

1. How did the Industrial Revolution change working life?

_____

_____

_____

2. How do interchangeable parts make mass production possible?

_____

_____

_____

✓ Checkpoint

Name the person who brought new spinning technologies from Britain to the United States.

_____

✓ Checkpoint

What were workers in the Lowell mills called?

_____

Vocabulary Builder

How would replacing the word *exactly* with the word *mostly* change the meaning of the following sentence? "Interchangeable parts were exactly alike." Would this make interchangeable parts more or less useful?

_____

✓ Checkpoint

Name a reason that factory work was unhealthy and dangerous.

_____

_____

Question to Think About As you read Section 1 in your textbook and take notes, keep this section focus question in mind: **How did the new technology of the Industrial Revolution change the way Americans lived?**

▶ Use these charts to record key information from the section. Some information has been filled in to get you started.

The Industrial Revolution
In the Industrial Revolution, ____machines____ took the place of many hand tools. Much of the power once provided by _____ and _____ began to be replaced, first by _____ and then by _____.
For centuries, workers had _____ in their _____ on spinning wheels. In the 1760s, the _____ speeded up the thread-making process.
This system of working was replaced by the _____, which brought workers and _____ together in one place.
In 1764, _____ invented the _____, a spinning machine powered by _____ rather than human energy. Textile mills began to be built on _____.
In 1790, _____ built the first steam-powered _____ _____. Factories no longer had to be built on _____.
_____ built the first water-frame-style spinning machine in the United States.
In the 1790s, inventor _____ devised a system of _____ _____, identical pieces that could be assembled quickly by _____.
During the ____War of 1812____, the British navy blockaded U.S. ports. This caused _____ to grow significantly.
Francis Cabot Lowell and his partners built a mill that was organized a new way. It combined _____ and _____ in one building. Later, the town of Lowell, Massachusetts, was built. Factories there employed _____ from nearby farms.

Typical Factory Working Conditions
Length of workday: _12–14 hours_ Factory conditions: _____ Safety conditions: _____ Treatment of disabled workers: _____

Refer to this page to answer the Chapter 11 Focus Question on page 183.

The North Transformed

Section 2 Focus Question

How did urbanization, technology, and social change affect the North? To begin answering this question,

- Learn about northern cities.
- Explore the growth of northern industry.
- Find out about the transportation revolution.
- Learn about a new wave of immigrants.
- Examine the lives of African Americans in the North.

Section 2 Summary

New inventions and breakthroughs in transportation helped industry expand in the United States. Much of this industry was located in the North, where it encouraged the growth of cities.

Northern Cities

In the 1800s, the Industrial Revolution led to **urbanization,** or the growth of cities due to movement of people from rural areas to cities. As capitalists built more factories, agricultural workers were attracted to the new types of work available in the cities. As cities in the East became crowded, newly arrived immigrants headed westward. Growing cities faced many problems. Poor sewers, a lack of clean drinking water, and filthy city streets encouraged the spread of disease. Citywide fires were another major concern. Most city buildings were made of wood. Cities relied on volunteer firefighters who had little training or equipment. ✔

The Growth of Northern Industry

American inventors helped industry grow. In 1844, **Samuel F.B. Morse** tested the **telegraph,** an invention that used electrical signals to send messages very quickly over long distances. The telegraph revolutionized communication. In the Midwest, Cyrus McCormick built a mechanical reaper that cut wheat much faster than could be done by hand. Such machines allowed more wheat to be grown and harvested using fewer workers. This made it easier for farmers to settle the prairies of the Midwest. Other inventions revolutionized the way goods were made. The invention of the sewing machine made the production of clothing more efficient. Introduced in 1846 by Elias Howe and improved by Isaac Singer, sewing machines could make clothes faster and cheaper than ever before.

By 1860, New England and the Middle Atlantic states were producing most of the nation's manufactured goods. Ninety percent of business investment was concentrated in the North. ✔

Key Events

1794	Eli Whitney patents the cotton gin.
1808	Importation of enslaved people is banned.
1820	The Missouri Compromise highlights disagreements between North and South over slavery.
1830	Peter Cooper builds the steam locomotive.

✓ Checkpoint

List three factors that led to the spread of disease in cities.

_____

_____

_____

✓ Checkpoint

Name two key American inventors and their inventions.

Inventor: _____

Invention: _____

Inventor: _____

Invention: _____

A Transportation Revolution

Improvements in transportation also spurred the growth of industry. Better transport allowed factories to make use of raw materials from farther away, and manufactured goods could be delivered to distant markets. American Robert Fulton built the first practical steamboat, the *Clermont*, in 1807. But in 1850, a new type of American-built ship appeared, the clipper ship. Long and slender, with tall masts, clipper ships were the fastest vessels on the ocean. But the Yankee clippers, as they were called, were eventually replaced by faster oceangoing steamships.

Of all the forms of transportation, railroads did the most to tie together raw materials, manufacturers, and markets. In 1830, Peter Cooper built the first American-made steam locomotive. By 1840, there were 3,000 miles of railroad track in the United States. ✓

A New Wave of Immigrants

In the 1840s, millions of immigrants came to the United States, mainly from western Europe. In 1845, disease wiped out the potato crop in Ireland. Because the potato was the staple food for most of the population, Ireland suffered from a **famine,** or widespread starvation. Huge numbers of Irish came to America, most of them former farm laborers. Many took jobs laying railroad track, or as household workers. Many Germans also came to the United States, fleeing failed revolutions in Germany. Unlike the Irish, German immigrants came from many levels of society. Most moved to the Midwest.

Some Americans worried about the growing foreign population. These were **nativists,** or people who wanted to preserve the country for white, American-born Protestants. ✓

African Americans in the North

African Americans in the North also faced **discrimination,** or the denial of equal rights or equal treatment to certain groups of people. Though free, African Americans were often not allowed to vote or to work in factories and skilled trades. Public schools and churches were often segregated. So African Americans formed their own churches. They also started their own newspapers and magazines. ✓

Check Your Progress

1. Name the invention that revolutionized communication.

2. How did better transportation help industry?

✓ Checkpoint

List three major breakthroughs in transportation.

✓ Checkpoint

Name the countries from which most immigrants to the United States came in the 1840s.

✓ Checkpoint

Define discrimination.

Question to Think About As you read Section 2 in your textbook and take notes, keep this section focus question in mind: **How did urbanization, technology, and social change affect the North?**

▶ Use these charts to record key information from the section. Some information has been filled in to get you started.

Key Inventions			
Invention	**Inventor(s)**	**When**	**What It Did**
Sewing machine	Elias Howe and Isaac Singer	1846	Made sewing clothes faster and cheaper
			Harvested more wheat with fewer workers
			Made river travel faster and cheaper
	Peter Cooper		
		1844	
Clipper ship	No single inventor		

Changes in Population			
	What Happened?	**Why Did It Happen?**	**Results**
Cities	Cities began growing rapidly, especially in the Northeast.	Factories moved to cities, followed by people moving from rural areas for factory jobs.	Cities faced the spread of disease and the threat of fire.
Immigration	Millions of immigrants from _____, particularly Ireland and Germany, came to the U.S. in the 1840s.	The Irish came to escape _____.	Nativists: _____ _____
		The Germans came to escape _____.	Know-Nothings:_____ _____
African Americans in the North	African Americans formed their own schools, churches, and publications.	_____ _____ _____ _____ _____	African Americans continued to face _____. They were often denied the right to _____. They were not allowed to work in factories or in _____.

Refer to this page to answer the Chapter 11 Focus Question on page 183.

Section 3
The Plantation South

Section 3 Focus Question

How did cotton affect the social and economic life of the South?
To begin answering this question,

- Find out about the "Cotton Kingdom."
- Examine the life of African Americans in the South.

Section 3 Summary

Cotton production expanded in the South to supply the textile industry. Whether free or enslaved, African Americans in the South faced many hardships.

The Cotton Kingdom

As the textile industry in the North grew, the demand for cotton rose. Eli Whitney's invention of the **cotton gin** in 1793 allowed the South to meet this demand. The cotton gin used a spiked wooden cylinder to remove seeds from cotton fibers.

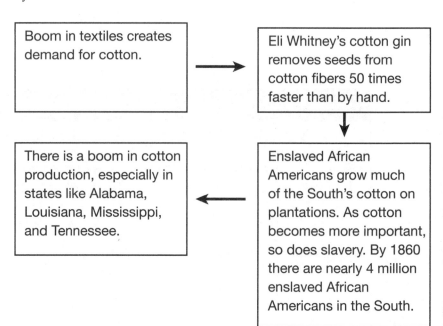

Cotton became the greatest source of wealth for the United States. The southern "Cotton Kingdom" society was dominated by slaveholding owners of large plantations. Most southern whites accepted the system of slavery. Supporters of slavery said that the system was more humane than the free labor system of the North. But critics pointed out that factory workers could quit a job if conditions became too harsh. Also, critics said, people held in slavery often suffered physical or other abuse from white owners. By the 1830s, some northerners were urging that slavery be banned. ✓

1794 — Eli Whitney patents the cotton gin.

1808 — Importation of enslaved people is banned.

1820 — The Missouri Compromise highlights disagreements between North and South over slavery.

1830 — Peter Cooper builds the steam locomotive.

Vocabulary Builder

Gin is early English slang for "engine" or machine. What do you think the term *cotton gin* refers to?

_____

_____

✓ Checkpoint

Why did the invention of the cotton gin lead to a boom in cotton production?

_____

_____

_____

African Americans in the South

About six percent of African Americans in the South were free. Many had purchased their freedom. But laws denied them even basic rights. By law they were excluded from most jobs. They could not vote, serve on juries, testify against whites in court, or attend public schools. Free African Americans were even discouraged from traveling. They also risked being kidnapped and sold into slavery. Many free African Americans still made valuable contributions to southern life.

However, enslaved African Americans faced greater trials. They had no rights at all. Laws called **slave codes** controlled every aspect of their lives. A Kentucky court ruled in 1828 that "...a slave by our code is not treated as a person but as a ...thing...." Most enslaved African Americans did heavy farm labor, but many became skilled workers. Some worked in households. Wherever they worked, they faced the possibility of violent punishment for many offenses.

Enslaved African Americans had only one protection against mistreatment: Owners looked on them as valuable property that they needed to keep healthy and productive. Families of enslaved African Americans were often broken apart when slave owners sold one or more of their family members.

After 1808, it was illegal to import enslaved Africans to the United States. Yet African Americans kept many African customs alive, including styles of music and dance. Many looked to the Bible for hope. African Americans composed **spirituals** — religious folk songs that blended biblical themes with the realities of slavery.

African Americans found ways to resist slavery. Some worked slowly, broke equipment, and even fled to seek freedom in the North. Some led rebellions. **Nat Turner** led the most famous slave uprising in 1831. He and his companions killed some 60 whites. In reprisal, many innocent African Americans were executed. ✓

Check Your Progress

1. How were cotton and slavery connected?

_____

_____

_____

2. In what ways did free African Americans in the South have their rights taken away?

_____

_____

_____

✓ Checkpoint

List three ways African Americans resisted slavery.

_____

_____

_____

Question to Think About As you read Section 3 in your textbook and take notes, keep this section focus question in mind: **How did cotton affect the social and economic life of the South?**

▶ Use these charts to record key information from the section. Some information has been filled in to get you started.

The Southern Economy	
Cotton gin	**What it was:** a machine invented by _____ in 1793 that speeded the processing of cotton **Impact on Economy:** • made cotton growing more _____ • increased the use and value of _____ • led to huge growth in _____ • made cotton the greatest _____ in the United States
Slave labor	**Argument for slave labor:**
	Arguments against slave labor: • •

African American Life in the South	
What	**Effect on African American Life**
Restrictions placed on free African Americans' rights	Could hold only _____ They were not allowed to: _____, _____, _____, _____ They were discouraged from _____.
Hardships faced on plantations	Enslaved African Americans • received _____ • had to perform _____ • families were often _____
Types of work enslaved African Americans performed	• • •
African American culture	Preserved African _____, _____, and _____ Composed _____
Ways of resisting slavery	• • • •

Refer to this page to answer the Chapter 11 Focus Question on page 183.

Section 4

The Challenges of Growth

Section 4 Focus Question

How did Americans move west and how did this intensify the debate over slavery? To begin answering this question,

- Follow along as Americans move west.
- Learn about roads and turnpikes.
- Find out about canals.
- Examine the extension of slavery.

Section 4 Summary

As the U.S. population grew, more people moved west to find new land. A transportation system of new roads and canals kept the country connected. Increasing differences between North and South became apparent when Missouri asked to join the Union as a slave state.

Moving West

By the 1750s, the Scotch-Irish and Germans of Pennsylvania began settling the backcountry between the Atlantic Coast and the Appalachian Mountains. In 1775, pioneer **Daniel Boone** helped create the Wilderness Road, a new route to the West. By the early 1800s, the flow of immigrants to the West had become a flood. As western populations grew, many areas applied to become states. Between 1792 and 1819, eight states joined the Union: Kentucky (1792), Tennessee (1796), Ohio (1803), Louisiana (1812), Indiana (1816), Mississippi (1817), Illinois (1818), and Alabama (1819). ✓

Roads and Turnpikes

Traveling west was not easy. Roads were unpaved, rough, and easily washed out by rain. The nation needed better roads. Farmers and merchants had to have a way to move their goods to market quickly and cheaply. Private companies began building **turnpikes,** or toll roads. One example was the Lancaster Turnpike in Pennsylvania, the nation's first long-distance stone road. In marshy areas, builders constructed **corduroy roads** out of sawed-off logs laid side by side. These roads were bumpy and dangerous to horses. The first road built with federal money was the National Road. Begun in 1811 in Cumberland, Maryland, the road eventually stretched hundreds of miles, reaching Vandalia, Illinois, by 1850. ✓

Canals

Roads were still a slow and costly way to ship goods between East and West. The fastest, cheapest way to ship goods was by water. The solution was to build **canals**—channels that are dug across

Key Events

1794	Eli Whitney patents the cotton gin.
1808	Importation of enslaved people is banned.
1820	The Missouri Compromise highlights disagreements between North and South over slavery.
1830	Peter Cooper builds the steam locomotive.

✓ Checkpoint

Name two states admitted to the Union in the 1790s.

_____

_____

✓ Checkpoint

Name the first road built with federal money.

_____

✓ Checkpoint

Name the two places connected by the Erie Canal.
_____

land and filled with water. Canals allow boats to reach more places. In 1808, Governor DeWitt Clinton of New York suggested that a canal be built to connect the Hudson River and Lake Erie. Building the canal was challenging for engineers and workers. Locks had to be built to raise or lower boats in the canal. Within two years of its opening in 1825, the canal had paid for itself. Produce from the Midwest came across Lake Erie, passed through the Erie Canal, and was carried down the Hudson River to New York City. New York City soon became the richest city in the nation. The success of the Erie Canal sparked a surge of canal building. ✔

The Extension of Slavery

In 1819, the nation consisted of 11 "slave states" and 11 "free states." Since 1817, Missouri had been seeking admission as a slave state. Adding another slave state would upset the balance in the Senate, where each state had two votes. Adding two more senators from a slave state would make the South more powerful than the North. Representative James Tallmadge of New York proposed that Missouri be admitted as a slave state. Once admitted, however, no more slaves could be brought into the state. The bill failed in the Senate. Then Maine applied to join the Union as a free state. The admission of both a free state and a slave state would maintain the balance in the Senate. In 1820, Senator **Henry Clay** persuaded Congress to adopt the Missouri Compromise. This permitted Maine to be admitted to the Union as a free state and Missouri to be admitted as a slave state. In addition, the Compromise provided that the Louisiana Territory north of the southern border of Missouri would be free of slavery. It also gave southern slave owners a clear right to pursue escaped fugitives into "free" regions and return them to slavery.

The Missouri Compromise revealed how much sectional rivalries divided the states of the Union. The Compromise seemed to balance the interests of the North and the South. However, the South was not happy that Congress was becoming involved in the issue of slavery. The North was not happy that Congress had admitted another slave state into the Union. The bitterness of feelings about slavery posed a serious threat to national unity. ✔

✓ Checkpoint

Name the two states admitted to the Union under the Missouri Compromise.
_____

_____

Check Your Progress

1. Why were canals and better roads needed?

_____

_____

2. What was the Missouri Compromise?

_____

_____

_____

_____

Question to Think About As you read Section 4 in your textbook and take notes, keep this section focus question in mind: **How did Americans move west and how did this intensify the debate over slavery?**

▶ Use these organizers to record key information from the section. Some information has been filled in to get you started.

Roads and Canals		
Term	**What it was**	**Why it was important**
turnpike	A type of privately built toll road	Provided a much-needed way to move people and goods over land
	A road made of sawed-off logs	
		Allowed boats to reach more places
Project	**What it was and when it started**	**Why it was important**
	Road running from Cumberland, Maryland, to Vandalia, Illinois; 1811	
Erie Canal		• started a ___canal building boom___ • allowed goods to be shipped more _____ and cheaply between _____ and Midwest • helped make _____ the richest city in the nation

The Missouri Compromise
In 1820, Senator _Henry Clay_____ persuaded Congress to approve the Missouri Compromise. Its provisions: 1. _____ was admitted as a free state. 2. _____ was admitted as a slave state. 3. _____ north of Missouri's southern border was free of slavery. 4. Southern slave owners gained the right to pursue_____ into free regions.

Refer to this page to answer the Chapter 11 Focus Question on page 183.

Chapter 11 Assessment

Directions: Circle the letter of the correct answer.

1. The rapid manufacture of large numbers of identical objects is called
   - **A** the Industrial Revolution.
   - **B** mass production.
   - **C** the factory system.
   - **D** the Lowell system.

2. Which of the following inventors made a major contribution to the Transportation Revolution?
   - **A** Richard Arkwright
   - **B** Francis Cabot Lowell
   - **C** Cyrus McCormick
   - **D** Robert Fulton

3. Which of the following inventions transformed the southern economy?
   - **A** the cotton gin
   - **B** the telegraph
   - **C** the clipper ship
   - **D** the mechanical reaper

4. The Missouri Compromise involved a debate over what issue?
   - **A** the right of way for western railroads
   - **B** the borders of the new Indian Territory
   - **C** the westward expansion of slavery
   - **D** the admission of California into the Union

Directions: Follow the steps to complete this task: **Compare the economy of the North with the economy of the South.**

Step 1: Recall information: List one characteristic of the northern economy and one characteristic of the southern economy.

Section	Economy
North	
South	

Step 2: Compare and contrast: Record how the characteristics of the economies are alike and how they are different.

	How They Are Alike	How They Are Different
Economies		

Step 3: Complete the topic sentence that follows. Then write two or three more sentences that support your topic sentence.

The economies of the North and South _____

_____

_____

_____

_____

Chapter 11 Notetaking Study Guide

Now you are ready to answer the Chapter 11 Focus Question: **Why did Americans take different paths in the early 1800s?**

▶ Fill in the following charts to help you answer this question. Use the notes that you took for each section.

The North and South Take Different Paths	
The North	**The South**

Economy
• Depended on industry
• Some important inventions of Industrial Revolution:
  1. spinning jenny
  2.
  3.
• The factory system is the _____ _____.
• Labor conditions were poor.
• _____ labor was often used.
	Economy
	• Depended on slavery
	• Eli Whitney's invention of the _____ increased the South's dependency on slavery.
	• Cotton plantations were important because cotton became America's greatest _____.

Society • Urbanization: the growth of cities due to movement from rural to urban areas. • Urban problems included _____ and poor _____. • New advances in transportation included _____, _____, and _____. These allowed goods to be shipped to distant markets. • Immigration provided _____ for industry and caused a rapid growth in _____.	**Society** • Society was dominated by _____. • Slave codes gave slaves no _____ and allowed every aspect of their lives to be _____. • Free African Americans were not allowed to _____ in elections or serve on _____. Their children could not attend _____, and they were discouraged from _____.

Growing Sectional Differences

In 1820, Senator Henry Clay proposed ___the Missouri Compromise___.
• What this proposal involved: _____
 	
• How this revealed sectional tensions:
  1. Southerners were not happy because _____
 	
  2. Northerners were not happy because _____

Refer to this page to answer the Unit 4 Focus Question on page 212.

Chapter 12

An Age of Reform (1820–1860)

What You Will Learn

By the mid-1800s, Americans were seeking reform in education and slavery. Some sought equality for women. Artists and writers also began to develop a distinct style.

Chapter 12 Focus Question

As you read through this chapter, keep this question in mind: **How did reformers and writers inspire change and spark controversy?**

Section 1

Improving Society

Section 1 Focus Question

How did key people bring about reform in education and society? To begin answering this question,
- Learn about the roots of the reforming spirit.
- Find out about temperance and prison reform.
- Explore education reform.

Section 1 Summary

The expansion of democracy during the presidency of Andrew Jackson and the Second Great Awakening led many to organize efforts to reform American society.

The Reforming Spirit

In the 1830s, many Americans became interested in **social reform,** or organized attempts to improve conditions of life. Social reform had its roots in both politics and religion. The expansion of democracy during the Age of Jackson helped encourage reform. As the political system became more fair, more people began to support causes such as rights for women and the end of slavery.

Religious ideas were another factor encouraging reform. In the early 1800s, some ministers began questioning traditional views, a movement known as the Second Great Awakening. Leaders of the movement questioned **predestination,** the idea that God decided the fate of a person's soul even before birth. They argued that people's own actions determined their salvation, an idea called the "doctrine of free will." In 1826, the minister **Charles Finney** held the first of many **revivals,** or huge outdoor religious meetings, to convert sinners and urge people to reform.

1831 William Lloyd Garrison starts antislavery newspaper.

1848 Women's rights convention is held in Seneca Falls, New York.

1850s American writers publish *The Scarlet Letter, Moby-Dick, Walden,* and *Leaves of Grass.*

The Second Great Awakening promoted improvement of self and society.

The idea of creating a more perfect society led some to experiment with building utopian, or ideal, communities. In 1825, Robert Owen founded a utopian community called New Harmony in Indiana. Residents were supposed to produce enough food and other goods to make the community self-sufficient. However, like most utopian communities, New Harmony did not last very long. ✔

Social Reformers at Work

While utopian reformers attempted to create perfect communities apart from the larger community, others tried to change the existing society. The **temperance movement** was an organized effort to end alcohol abuse and the problems created by it. This would be difficult since alcohol was widely used in the United States. Many women were drawn to this movement. Most citizens favored temperance, or moderation in drinking. But other people supported **prohibition,** or a total ban on the sale and consumption of alcohol. Those who supported prohibition were able to get nine states to pass laws banning the sale of alcohol.

Some reformers sought to improve the prison system. **Dorothea Dix,** a schoolteacher, took up this cause. She supported the building of new, more sanitary, and more humane prisons. She also urged the government to create separate institutions, called asylums, for people with mental illnesses. ✔

Education Reform

Education was another area reformers hoped to change. The Puritans of Massachusetts established the first **public schools,** or free schools supported by taxes, in 1642. Many reformers believed public schools created better-informed voters, and could help immigrants assimilate, or become part of, American culture.

The leader of education reform was **Horace Mann.** With his encouragement, colleges were created to train teachers, the salaries of teachers were raised, and the school year was lengthened. These improvements did little for African Americans. However, in 1855, Massachusetts became the first state to admit African Americans to public schools. ✔

Check Your Progress

1. What religious movement contributed to reform?

_____

2. What is the difference between temperance and prohibition?

_____

_____

✓ **Checkpoint**

Name the person who held the first revival meetings.

_____

✓ **Checkpoint**

Name the schoolteacher who took up the cause of prison reform.

_____

✓ **Checkpoint**

Name the main leader of the movement for education reform.

_____

Question to Think About As you read Section 1 in your textbook and take notes, keep this section focus question in mind: **How did key people bring about reform in education and society?**

▶ Complete this chart to record key information from the section.

Improving Society
The Reforming Spirit of Jacksonian Democracy
Some people worked to make the political system fairer. They supported causes such as legal rights for _____ and the end of _____.
How the Second Great Awakening encouraged reform: • Doctrine of free will: _____ • Charles Finney: _____ • If people had the power to improve themselves, they could _____.
Utopian Communities • Definition: <u>communities that tried to create perfect societies</u> _____ • Robert Owen: _____ • Results: _____
Social Reformers at Work
Temperance Movement • Definition: an organized effort to _____ • Many women supported this movement because _____ _____. • Some reformers supported prohibition, which is _____ _____.
Movement to Reform Prisons • Dorothea Dix worked to support the building of _____ _____. • Dix urged the government to create _____asylums_____ for _____.
Education Reform • Public schools were supported as a way to create more informed _____ and help new _____. • Horace Mann: reformer from Massachusetts who _____ _____ • Reformers of African American education _____. • First state to admit African Americans to public schools: _____ • Ashmun Institute: _____

Refer to this page to answer the Chapter 12 Focus Question on page 197.

The Fight Against Slavery

Section 2 Focus Question

How did abolitionists try to end slavery? To begin answering this question,

- Learn about the roots of the antislavery movement.
- Discover why there was growing opposition to slavery.
- Find out about the Underground Railroad.
- Explore why some opposed the abolition of slavery.

Section 2 Summary

The reform movement of the 1800s led to growing calls to end slavery. However, other Americans continued to defend slavery.

Roots of the Antislavery Movement

Many leaders of the early republic, such as Alexander Hamilton and Benjamin Franklin, opposed slavery. They believed that slavery violated the principle that "all men are created equal." In 1780, Pennsylvania became the first state to pass a law gradually ending slavery. By 1804, every northern state had either ended or pledged to end slavery.

In 1817, the American Colonization Society began an effort to gradually free and then send slaves back to Liberia, a colony in Africa. The colonization movement was unsuccessful. The majority of enslaved people had been born in America and did not want to return to Africa. By 1830, only about 1,400 African Americans had migrated to Liberia. ✓

Growing Opposition to Slavery

<u>Antislavery feeling increased during the Second Great Awakening when preachers like Charles Finney began to condemn slavery.</u> By the mid-1800s, more Americans had become **abolitionists**, reformers who wanted to abolish slavery. Instead of gradual emancipation, they supported a complete and immediate end to slavery. **William Lloyd Garrison** was an important abolitionist leader who founded an abolitionist newspaper, the *Liberator,* in 1831. He supported giving all African Americans full political rights. Garrison also cofounded the New England Anti-Slavery Society.

African Americans in the North also joined the abolitionist movement. In 1829, David Walker wrote his *Appeal: to the Coloured Citizens of the World*, which called on slaves to rebel to gain their freedom. Perhaps the most powerful speaker for abolitionism was **Frederick Douglass.** He was a former slave who had escaped to freedom. Douglass often spoke to large crowds and published an antislavery newspaper, the *North Star.*

Key Events

1831   William Lloyd Garrison starts antislavery newspaper.

1848   Women's rights convention is held in Seneca Falls, New York.

1850s   American writers publish *The Scarlet Letter, Moby-Dick, Walden,* and *Leaves of Grass.*

✓ Checkpoint

Name the first state to pass a law gradually ending slavery.

_____

Vocabulary Builder

What word in the underlined sentence could be replaced by the word *oppose?*

_____

✓ **Checkpoint**

Name the organization William Lloyd Garrison cofounded.

_____

Abolitionists won the support of a few powerful people. Former President John Quincy Adams, now a member of Congress, supported abolition. He read antislavery petitions in the House of Representatives and introduced a constitutional amendment to ban slavery in new states.

Later, Adams spoke to the Supreme Court for nine hours to help captive Africans aboard the slave ship *Amistad* regain their freedom. ☑

The Underground Railroad

Some abolitionists helped people escape from slavery using a system known as the Underground Railroad. In spite of its name, the system was neither underground nor a railroad. It was a network of people—both black and white and both northerners and southerners—who secretly helped slaves reach freedom. Known as "conductors," these people helped runaway slaves move between "stations," which were usually abolitionists' homes. They could also be churches or caves.

✓ **Checkpoint**

Name the escaped slave who led over 300 slaves to freedom on the Underground Railroad.

_____

One Quaker, Levi Coffin, helped 3,000 slaves escape. Escaped slave **Harriet Tubman** escorted over 300 slaves to freedom. Each year, hundreds of slaves moved along the Underground Railroad to freedom in the North or in Canada. In total, perhaps as many as 50,000 may have gained their freedom in this way. ☑

Opposing Abolition

Abolitionists faced obstacles in the North and the South. Northern textile mill owners and merchants relied on cotton produced by slave labor. Northern workers feared that freed slaves might take their jobs. Some northerners reacted violently towards abolitionists. In 1835, a mob dragged William Lloyd Garrison through the streets of Boston with a rope around his neck.

✓ **Checkpoint**

Why did some northern factory owners oppose abolitionism?

_____

_____

Southerners had long defended slavery as a positive force. As support for abolition grew, they went on the offensive. Southerners won passage of a "gag rule" in Congress that blocked discussion of antislavery petitions. ☑

Check Your Progress

1. Describe Frederick Douglass' roles in abolitionism.

_____

_____

2. What was the Underground Railroad?

_____

_____

Question to Think About As you read Section 2 in your textbook and take notes, keep this section focus question in mind: **How did abolitionists try to end slavery?**

▶ Complete this chart to record key information from the section.

The Fight Against Slavery
Roots of the Antislavery Movement
• 1780: <u>Pennsylvania</u> became the first state to pass a law gradually ending slavery. • Ohio was the first state to _____. • By 1804, _____ had ended or pledged to end slavery. • The American Colonization Society _____,   but it was _____.
Growing Opposition to Slavery
Abolitionists • definition: _____
William Lloyd Garrison • important abolitionist leader who founded the newspaper _____ in 1831 • supported giving all African Americans _____ • cofounded the _____
David Walker • wrote _____ in 1829, a pamphlet that called on   enslaved people to _____
Frederick Douglass • an escaped _____ and powerful _____ • published the North Star, an _____
John Quincy Adams • As a member of Congress, he read _____. • spoke to the Supreme Court for _____
The Underground Railroad
• definition: _____ • "conductors": <u>people who helped runaway slaves move between "stations"</u> • "stations": usually _____ • Harriet Tubman: nicknamed _____, escorted _____
Opposition to Abolition
In the North: • Northern textile mill owners and merchants relied on cotton produced by   _____. • Northern workers feared that _____.
In the South: • defended slavery as a _____ • Southerners in Congress won passage of a "gag rule," which blocked discussion of   _____.

Refer to this page to answer the Chapter 12 Focus Question on page 197.

Key Events

1831 — William Lloyd Garrison starts antislavery newspaper.

1848 — Women's rights convention is held in Seneca Falls, New York.

1850s — American writers publish *The Scarlet Letter*, *Moby-Dick*, *Walden*, and *Leaves of Grass*.

✓ Checkpoint

List three things women could not do in 1820.

_____

_____

_____

Vocabulary Builder

Exclude in the underlined sentence means to "keep out" or "reject." What would be an antonym of *exclude*?

_____

✓ Checkpoint

Name the document that demanded full equality for women in all areas of life.

_____

Section 3 Focus Question

How did the women's suffrage movement begin? To begin answering this question,

- Learn about the beginnings of the women's rights movement.
- Read about the Seneca Falls Convention.
- Find out about new opportunities for women.

Section 3 Summary

Women reformers organized the women's rights movement, which led to new civil and legal rights and new educational and career opportunities for women.

The Struggle Begins

In 1820, women had limited civil and legal rights. They could not vote or serve on juries, attend college, or enter professions like medicine or law. They also had limited educational opportunities. Married women could not even own property or keep their own wages. Women were expected to remain in the private world of the home.

Women who were active in abolition and other reform movements began to demand rights as equal citizens. Among these women was Sojourner Truth. **Sojourner Truth** was an illiterate former slave who spoke on behalf of both African Americans and women. **Lucretia Mott**, a Quaker, was also an abolitionist. Mott had organization skills and public speaking experience that most women of her day did not. ✓

Seneca Falls Convention

In 1840, Mott traveled to London to attend an antislavery convention. There, she met another abolitionist, **Elizabeth Cady Stanton**. They were infuriated to learn that women were excluded from taking an active role in the proceedings. They organized a convention for women's rights held in Seneca Falls, New York, in 1848. Over 300 men and women attended, among them, Frederick Douglass.

Stanton wrote a Declaration of Sentiments based on the Declaration of Independence. It declared that all men and women are created equal and listed injustices against women. The declaration demanded full equality for women in all areas of life. Stanton's argument was the beginning of the battle for **women's suffrage**, or the right of women to vote. Other delegates, including Lucretia Mott, feared that demanding suffrage might harm other causes because it was so controversial. Still, the convention narrowly voted to support the demand for women's suffrage. ✓

New Opportunities for Women

The Seneca Falls Convention was the birthplace of the women's rights movement. The **women's rights movement** was the organized effort to improve the political, legal, and economic status of women in American society. Stanton and **Susan B. Anthony** worked closely together. As an unmarried woman, Anthony, a former schoolteacher, abolitionist, and temperance supporter, was able to travel to promote their cause. Stanton, who was raising a family, often wrote speeches from home. Together, Stanton and Anthony founded the National Woman Suffrage Association in 1869. They also convinced New York to pass a law protecting women's property rights. Many other states followed, some even revising their laws to allow married women to keep their wages.

Even before Seneca Falls, reformers worked to provide educational opportunities for girls. American schools emphasized education for boys. Girls seldom studied advanced subjects like math and science. The women's rights movement focused much attention on education. In 1821, Emma Willard founded the Troy Female Seminary in New York, which served as a model for girls' schools everywhere. Other women also started schools. In 1837, Mary Lyon founded the first college for women, Mount Holyoke Female Seminary.

American society came to accept that girls could be educated, and women could be teachers. More and more schools began hiring women who had been trained at one of the new academies or colleges for women. Some women tried to enter other professions as well. Margaret Fuller, a journalist, scholar, and literary critic, wrote about the need for women's rights in the book *Women in the Nineteenth Century*. Other women entered scientific fields. Elizabeth Blackwell was the first woman to graduate from a medical school. Astronomer Maria Mitchell was the first professor hired at Vassar College and the first woman elected to the American Academy of Arts and Sciences. ☑

Check Your Progress

1. Why did many reformers, including Lucretia Mott, oppose the demand for women's suffrage?

_____

_____

2. What other movement were both Sojourner Truth and Lucretia Mott involved in before they began to demand rights for women?

_____

_____

✓ Checkpoint

Name the first college for women in the United States.

_____

Question to Think About As you read Section 3 in your textbook and take notes, keep this section focus question in mind: **How did the women's suffrage movement begin?**

▶ Complete this chart to record key information from the section.

Women's Rights Movement
Roots of the Movement
Important leaders • Sojourner Truth: <u>former slave who spoke on behalf of African Americans and women</u> • Lucretia Mott: _____ • Elizabeth Cady Stanton: _____
Seneca Falls Convention
How it came about: Lucretia Mott and Elizabeth Cady Stanton were not allowed to take an active role in an _____ convention. In response, they organized a _____ in Seneca Falls, New York, in 1848.
Declaration of Sentiments • the beginning of the battle for _____ • It demanded _____.
Suffrage • definition: _____
New Opportunities for Women
The Seneca Falls Convention launched the women's rights movement. • Stanton and Susan B. Anthony founded _____ in 1869. • In 1860, Stanton and Anthony convinced New York to pass a law _____.
Education • Emma Willard: founded _____, which served as _____ • Mary Lyon: founded _____, the first _____
Careers • Margaret Fuller: wrote _____, which was about <u>the need for women's rights</u> • Elizabeth Blackwell: the first _____ • Maria Mitchell: the first _____ and the first _____

Refer to this page to answer the Chapter 12 Focus Question on page 197.

American Literature and Arts

Section 4 Focus Question

How did American literature and arts have an impact on American life? To begin answering this question,

- Discover how a distinctly American culture developed.
- Find out about the flowering of American literature.
- Learn about new American styles of art and music.

Section 4 Summary

In the 1800s, America developed its own unique culture. This included new ideas and changes in literature, art, and music.

An American Culture Develops

Before 1800, American writers and artists modeled their work on European styles. Most American artists trained in Europe. By the mid-1800s, Americans had begun to develop their own styles that reflected the optimism of the reform era.

Writer Washington Irving based many of his stories, such as "The Legend of Sleepy Hollow" and "Rip Van Winkle," on the Dutch history of early New York. James Fenimore Cooper wrote about a character named Natty Bumppo, a frontiersman who kept moving westward.

By the early 1800s, a new artistic movement called Romanticism took shape in Europe. It was a style of writing and painting that placed value on nature, the emotions, or strong feelings, and the imagination. Americans developed their own form of Romanticism, called **transcendentalism.** Its goal was to explore the relationship between man and nature through emotions rather than through reason.

Transcendentalists tried to live simply, and sought an understanding of beauty, goodness, and truth. The writings and lectures of **Ralph Waldo Emerson** reflected transcendentalism. Emerson stressed **individualism,** or the unique importance of the individual. He influenced **Henry David Thoreau,** another important writer and thinker. In his 1854 book *Walden*, Thoreau urged people to live simply. He also encouraged **civil disobedience,** the idea that people should disobey unjust laws if their consciences demand it. ✓

Flowering of American Literature

Herman Melville and **Nathaniel Hawthorne** changed the optimistic tone of American literature by introducing psychological themes and extreme emotions. Melville's novel, *Moby-Dick* (1851), was the story of an obsessed ship captain who destroyed himself, his ship, and his crew in pursuit of a whale. Hawthorne's stories

Key Events

1831	William Lloyd Garrison starts antislavery newspaper.
1848	Women's rights convention is held in Seneca Falls, New York.
1850s	American writers publish *The Scarlet Letter, Moby-Dick, Walden,* and *Leaves of Grass.*

Vocabulary Builder

If the word *optimum* means "best" and the suffix *-ism* means "belief," what do you think *optimism* in the underlined sentence means?

_____

_____

✓ Checkpoint

List two important United States transcendentalists.

_____

_____

used historical themes to explore the dark side of the mind. **Louisa May Alcott** wrote about a heroine as a believable, imperfect person, rather than as a shining ideal.

Poets helped create a new national voice. Henry Wadsworth Longfellow based poems on American history. He wrote "Paul Revere's Ride." His long poem *The Song of Hiawatha*, was one of the first works to honor Native Americans.

Walt Whitman published *Leaves of Grass* in 1855. Whitman wrote about familiar subjects but his book of poems shocked many readers because he did not follow the accepted set of rules. Most important, Whitman is seen as the poet who best expresses the democratic American spirit. His poetry celebrated the common man. In his poem, "Song of Myself," Whitman reaches out to all people.

Other poets used their poetry for social protest and social reform. John Greenleaf Whittier was a Quaker from Massachusetts. Frances Watkins Harper was an African American woman from Maryland. Both Whittier and Harper wrote poems that described and condemned the evils of slavery. ☑

Art and Music

After 1820, artists also began to create a unique American style. They focused on the landscapes around them or the daily lives of Americans. Painter Thomas Cole was part of the Hudson River school, which was inspired by Romanticism. Artists in this school sought to stir emotion by reproducing the beauty and power of nature. Other painters, such as George Caleb Bingham, painted scenes of everyday life. George Catlin captured the ways and dignity of Native Americans.

American music also began to develop its own identity. A wide variety of new songs emerged, such as "Yankee Doodle." Other popular songs were work songs sung by men who worked on ships or the railroad. The era's most popular songwriter was Stephen Foster. Many of his tunes, such as "Camptown Races," are still familiar today. ☑

Check Your Progress

1. What aspect of the reform era was reflected in American literature and art?

2. How did Herman Melville and Nathaniel Hawthorne change the tone of American literature?

✓ **Checkpoint**

Name the first writer to create realistic heroines.

✓ **Checkpoint**

Name the school of painting inspired by Romanticism.

Question to Think About As you read Section 4 in your textbook and take notes, keep this section focus question in mind: **How did American literature and arts have an impact on American life?**

▶ Complete this chart to record key information from the section.

American Literature and Arts
Development of an American Culture
• Before 1800, American writers and artists modeled their work on _____.   • By the mid-1800s, American __writers__ and _____ developed styles that reflected American __optimism__ and _____.
Early Writers   • Washington Irving based many of his stories on the _____ _____; he wrote "The Legend of Sleepy Hollow" and "Rip Van Winkle."   • James Fenimore Cooper wrote about _____.

• Romanticism: a European _____ that placed value on _____
 	
 • Transcendentalism: goal was to explore _____ _____
 	
     • Ralph Waldo Emerson stressed _____.
     • Henry David Thoreau urged people to _____ and encouraged civil disobedience.

Flowering of American Literature
Herman Melville and Nathaniel Hawthorne changed the tone of American literature by _____.
Louisa May Alcott: first to write about a heroine as a _____
Poetry   • Henry Wadsworth Longfellow based his poems on _____.   • Walt Whitman rejected _____ and expressed the _____.   • John Greenleaf Whittier and Frances Watkins Harper wrote poems that described and condemned _____.
Art
Hudson River school: The school's artists sought to reproduce _____. George Caleb Bingham's paintings showed _____. George Catlin's paintings showed _____.
Music
A new American style of song emerged, including _____ chanted by sailors and laborers, and _____ developed among African Americans.

Refer to this page to answer the Chapter 12 Focus Question on page 197.

Chapter 12 Assessment

Directions: Circle the letter of the correct answer.

1. Who was an important leader of education reform?
   - **A** Lucretia Mott
   - **B** Harriet Tubman
   - **C** William Lloyd Garrison
   - **D** Horace Mann

2. What document declared that all men and women are created equal and listed injustices against women?
   - **A** the U.S. Constitution
   - **B** the Declaration of Sentiments
   - **C** the Declaration of Independence
   - **D** *Moby-Dick*

3. Whose writings changed the tone of American literature by introducing psychological themes and extreme emotions?
   - **A** Charles Finney
   - **B** Henry David Thoreau
   - **C** Herman Melville
   - **D** Louisa May Alcott

Directions: Follow the steps to answer this question:

How did religious ideas encourage an era of social reform?

Step 1: Recall information: Define *social reform* and identify its roots.

Social Reform		
Concept	**Definition**	**Rooted In**
Social Reform		

Step 2: Explain the new religious movement and how it was spread.

Second Great Awakening	How It Was Spread

Step 3: Complete the topic sentence that follows. Then write two or three more sentences that support your topic sentence.

Religious ideas helped spark an era of social reform by _____

_____

_____

_____

_____

Chapter 12 Notetaking Study Guide

Now you are ready to answer the Chapter 12 Focus Question: **How did reformers and writers inspire change and spark controversy?**

▶ Complete the following chart to help you answer this question.

American Reforms and Ideas

Society and Education

Social reform: organized attempts to improve conditions of life
- Two factors encouraging reform:
  1. _____
  2. _____
- The temperance movement was
  _____
  _____
  _____.

Prison reform
- Dorothea Dix convinced state legislatures to build _____
  and create _____.

Education reform
- _____ called for
  colleges to train teachers and higher
  teacher salaries.
- _____ was
  the first state to admit African
  Americans to public schools.

Slavery

Abolitionists: reformers who wanted to abolish slavery
- William Lloyd Garrison cofounded the
  Liberator, an _____
  _____.
- Frederick Douglass: an escaped slave
  and powerful speaker

The Underground Railroad
- "Conductors" helped slaves move
  between "stations."
- _____,
  an escaped slave, escorted over 300
  slaves to freedom.

Opposing Abolition
- Northerners relied on cotton
  produced by slaves.
- The "gag rule" blocked _____
  _____.

Women's Rights

Women's rights movement
- Women began to demand equal rights
  as citizens.
- Elizabeth Cady Stanton wrote
  _____.

The Seneca Falls Convention
- birthplace of _____
- 1869: Stanton and Susan B. Anthony
  founded the _____.

New Opportunities
- Women started schools for girls and
  women.
- career "firsts" in _medicine_____,
  _____, _____

Culture

Ideas
- Transcendentalism was a form of
  _____, a
  European artistic movement.
- The writings of _____
  and _____ reflected
  transcendentalism.
- Louisa May Alcott was the first to
  depict a woman as _____
  _____
  _____.
- American artists began to focus on
  landscapes around them or
  _____
  _____.

Refer to this page to answer the Unit 4 Focus Question on page 212.

Chapter 13

Westward Expansion (1820–1860)

What You Will Learn

In the mid-1800s, many Americans wanted the nation to expand westward to the Pacific Ocean. American settlers overcame hardships in making this happen.

Chapter 13 Focus Question

As you read this chapter, keep this question in mind: **How did westward expansion change the geography of the nation and demonstrate the determination of its people?**

Section 1

The West

Section 1 Focus Question

What cultures and ideas influenced the development of the West? To begin answering this question,
- Explore what "the West" was.
- Learn about the Mexican settlements.
- Understand the concept of Manifest Destiny.

Section 1 Summary

The lands that made up the West were constantly shifting. They included lands under Mexican control. Americans believed they were destined to take possession of the West.

What Was "The West"?

As the nation grew, the lands that made up "the West" changed. When the United States first became a nation, the West meant the land between the Appalachian Mountains and the Mississippi River. By the 1820s, this land was almost completely settled. The West moved again, to the lands beyond the Mississippi.

The vast Great Plains lay between the Mississippi and the Rocky Mountains. But this land was overlooked by settlers, who believed it could never be farmed because it would be too hard to clear the thickly rooted grasses that covered it. Settlers looked past the Great Plains to the Northwest and Southwest.

The Northwest had fertile lands stretching from the Rocky Mountains to the Pacific Ocean. This region was claimed by the United States, Great Britain, Russia, and Spain.

The Southwest included present-day California, Utah, Nevada, Arizona, New Mexico, Texas, and half of Colorado.

Key Events

1821 William Becknell opens the Santa Fe Trail.

1836 Texas declares independence from Mexico.

1849 California gold rush begins.

Ruled first by Spain, then by Mexico, this vast area was home to a culture that was very different from the one that existed in the United States. ☑

Mexican Settlements

Like England and France, Spain followed a policy of mercantilism in its colonies. It was illegal for settlers in New Spain to trade with other countries.

Over time, many Spanish settlers had children. These children were called creoles. In addition, Spanish settlers, Native Americans, and Africans would sometimes intermarry, and the children of these couples were called mestizos. By the 1800s, the combination of these ethnic groups had produced a Southwestern culture that was very different from the cultures that had previously existed in this part of the world.

Spanish missionaries tried to convert the local Native Americans to Catholicism. Many Native Americans were forced to live and work at <u>missions</u>. In the end, thousands of Native Americans died from overwork or disease.

Over the years, Spanish settlers mixed with Native Americans to create a blended culture. The region followed Spanish law and religion and used the Spanish language. Its foods and building materials were Native American.

In 1821, Mexico won its independence from Spain. The Mexican government opened up the region to trade with foreign countries, including the United States. It also removed the missions from church control and gave their lands in large **land grants,** or government gifts of land, to Mexican settlers. Many of these grants were made to **rancheros,** or owners of ranches. Much of this land belonged to Native Americans, who responded by raiding ranches. However, they were soon crushed, and their population in the Southwest was drastically reduced. ☑

Manifest Destiny

Many Americans were interested in westward **expansion,** or extending the nation beyond its existing borders. Under Jefferson, the Louisiana Purchase had doubled the size of the nation. But just forty years later, Americans were looking even farther west. A newspaper editor coined the phrase "manifest destiny" in 1845. The phrase described the belief that the United States was destined, or meant, to stretch from coast to coast. ☑

Check Your Progress

1. Why weren't the Great Plains settled quickly?

_____

_____

2. What phrase described American feelings about westward expansion?

_____

✓ Checkpoint

List three areas that made up the West after the 1820s.

_____

_____

_____

Vocabulary Builder

Reread the bracketed paragraph. Based on context clues in the paragraph, what do you think the word *missions* means?

_____

_____

_____

✓ Checkpoint

Name two changes that Mexico made when it took control of the Southwest.

_____

_____

_____

✓ Checkpoint

Name the term that described the idea that the United States should stretch from coast to coast.

_____

Question to Think About As you read Section 1 in your textbook and take notes, keep this section focus question in mind: **What cultures and ideas influenced the development of the West?**

▶ Use this chart to record key information from the section. Some information has been filled in to get you started.

Westward Expansion

The Great Plains

Where: <u>between the Mississippi River</u> <u>and the Rocky Mountains</u>
Problem with land: _____

_____

For many settlers, the Great Plains was: _____

_____

The Northwest

Where: _____

Included present-day states of

_____

Claimed by: _____

_____

Settlers attracted to _____

_____

Manifest Destiny

From the beginning, Americans were interested in westward expansion.
The Louisiana Purchase, which <u>doubled</u> the territory of the nation, helped with this goal. Forty years later, the idea of Manifest Destiny became popular. It meant _____

_____.

Mexican Settlement

The Southwest included the present-day states of: _____

_____

_____

Spanish Missions
• Purpose: _____

_____

• Effect of missions on Indians: _____

_____

Blended culture
• Spanish influence: _____

_____

• Native American influence: _____

_____

• Creoles were _____

_____.

• Mestizos were _____

_____.

Trade under Spanish rule: _____

_____

Trade under Mexican rule: _____

_____

Under Spanish rule, land grants were given mostly to _____.
Under Mexican rule, <u>missions</u> were removed from _____ control. Their lands were given as land grants to _____.
Much of this land belonged to _____

_____, who responded by _____.
But soon _____ and their population _____.

Refer to this page to answer the Chapter 13 Focus Question on page 211.

Section 2

Trails to the West

Section 2 Focus Question

Why did people go west, and what challenges did they face? To begin answering this question,

- Learn how traders led the way into the West.
- Explore the Oregon Trail.
- Learn about life in the West.

Section 2 Summary

People went west for different reasons. Whether to find gold, become a trader, work as a missionary, or farm, people who went west suffered many hardships.

Traders Lead the Way

Trade drove the first western crossings. Traders were looking for new markets in which to sell their goods. In the process, they blazed important trails for those who followed.

After Mexico won independence, it allowed trade with the United States. In 1821, Captain **William Becknell** led a wagon train filled with merchandise from Independence, Missouri, to Santa Fe, New Mexico. It was a difficult journey, but Becknell's group reached Santa Fe. The Santa Fe Trail soon became a busy international trade route.

John Jacob Astor, a German fur merchant, sent the first American fur-trading expedition to Oregon. In 1808, he established the American Fur Company at Fort Astor, now Astoria, Oregon. Astor's expedition consisted of two groups. One group sailed around South America and up the Pacific coast, and the other group traveled across the continent. On the way, the second group found the South Pass through the Rocky Mountains, which became an important trade route that helped open up the Northwest for the missionaries and settlers who followed.

The fur trade made Astor the richest man in the country. **Mountain men,** or fur trappers of the Northwest, supplied him with furs. For most of the year, they lived isolated lives, but once a year they gathered for a **rendezvous** (RAHN day voo), or a meeting where they would trade furs for supplies.

Beaver fur was in great demand in the East. However, by the 1830s, the supply of beavers was nearly exhausted, so most of the trappers moved back east to become farmers, merchants, or even bankers. Others stayed as guides for the wagon trains that brought thousands of settlers west in the 1840s. ✔

The Oregon Trail

The first white easterners to build permanent homes in Oregon were missionaries, who began to travel west in the 1830s to bring

Key Events

1821	William Becknell opens the Santa Fe Trail.
1836	Texas declares independence from Mexico.
1849	California gold rush begins.

Vocabulary Builder

The word *isolated* comes from the Latin word *insula*, which means "island." Think about the position of an island relative to the mainland. What do you think the word *isolated* means as it is used in the text?

_____

_____

✓ Checkpoint

List three people or groups who developed trade in the West.

_____

_____

_____

their religion to the Indians. The missionaries' glowing reports of Oregon led more easterners to make the journey west. Farmers sought the free and fertile land, the mild climate, and the plentiful rainfall in river valleys. Settlers from all over the country began to come down with "Oregon Fever."

Most settlers followed the Oregon Trail, a route that stretched over 2,000 miles from Missouri to Oregon. Travelers left in the spring and had five months to make their journey. If they were caught in the Rocky Mountains during the winter, their chances of survival were slim.

Pioneers on the Oregon Trail banded together in wagon trains for mutual protection. During the day, teams of horses or oxen would pull the long trains of covered wagons, which were filled with the settlers' food and possessions. Meanwhile, the pioneers would walk, often for 15 hours a day. At night, the wagons were drawn up in a circle to keep the cattle from wandering off. The trip was a great hardship and dangerous. As mile followed mile, people would begin to discard personal items to lighten their wagons. In addition, disease and accident killed one out of every ten travelers, and clean, safe water was hard to find. Still, over 50,000 people reached Oregon between 1840 and 1860. ✔

Life in the West

Settlers in the West had few possessions and little money. They worked hard to clear land, plant crops, and build shelters. Disease, accidents, and such natural disasters as storms and floods were a constant threat.

Women in the West worked just as hard as men did. Because their labor was so necessary for a family's survival, women had a higher status in the West. In 1869, Wyoming Territory became the first area of the United States to grant women the vote.

Native Americans in Oregon lived in an uneasy peace with the white settlers. While Native Americans in southern Oregon usually got along with whites, in the north, Native Americans were angered by the presence of strangers on their land. When gold was discovered in northern Oregon in the 1850s, a large number of white and Chinese miners arrived in the area. In 1855, war broke out briefly between the Native Americans and miners. After the U.S. government intervened, the tribes were forced to accept peace treaties. ✔

Check Your Progress

1. What first drove people to find safe trails to the West?

_____

_____

2. Why did western women have a higher status?

_____

_____

✓ **Checkpoint**

List two groups of people who went to Oregon.

_____

_____

✓ **Checkpoint**

List three dangers that settlers in Oregon faced.

_____

_____

_____

Question to Think About As you read Section 2 in your textbook, keep this section focus question in mind: **Why did people go west, and what challenges did they face?**

▶ Use these charts to record key information from the section.

Traders Lead the Way
The Santa Fe Trail
• In 1821, _____ led a wagon train from _____ to _____.
• Hardships experienced along the way: _____
• Importance: established a route for _____ trade with _____ that stretched about _____ miles
The Oregon Fur Trade
• ___John Jacob Astor_____ sent the first American fur-trading expedition to Oregon and established the _____ Fur Company in 1808.
• Trappers who supplied furs were called_____.
• What happened to the fur trade in the 1830s: _____ _____

The Oregon Trail
Missionaries Travel West to Oregon in the 1830s
• Purpose of missionaries: _____
• Famous missionary couple: _____
• How missionaries spurred settlement of the West: _____ _____
On the Trail
• Trail stretched more than _____ miles from _____ to _____
• Travelers left in _____ and had to reach Oregon in 5 months. If they did not make it in time, they risked _____.
• Between 1840 and 1860, more than _____ people reached Oregon.

Life in the West
Pioneer Life
• Settlers had only _____ to clear the land, _____, and ___build shelters___.
• Threats included _____, _____, and _____.
Women in the West
• Reason women's status was raised in the West: _____ _____
• In 1869, _____ was the first area to grant women the right to _____.
Native Americans and Settlers
• Relationship between the two groups: _____
• In the 1850s, _____ brought large numbers of _____ to _____ Oregon. In 1855, _____ broke out there briefly.

Refer to this page to answer the Chapter 13 Focus Question on page 211.

Conflict With Mexico

Section 3 Focus Question
What were the causes and effects of the Texas War for Independence and the Mexican-American War? To begin answering this question,
- Find out how Texas won independence.
- Learn how Texas and Oregon were annexed by the United States.
- Discover the causes of the Mexican-American War.
- Explore how the United States achieved Manifest Destiny.

Section 3 Summary

In negotiations with Britain, the United States acquired Oregon, but U.S. expansion in the Southwest came at the cost of war with Mexico.

Texas Wins Independence
In 1820, the Spanish gave Moses Austin a land grant to establish a small colony in Texas. After Moses Austin died, his son, **Stephen Austin,** led a group of some 300 settlers there. After Mexico won its independence from Spain and took possession of Texas, Texans came into conflict with the Mexican government. Mexico had outlawed slavery, but settlers brought slaves in. Texans wanted a democratic government.

In 1833, General Antonio López de Santa Anna became president of Mexico. He overturned Mexico's democratic constitution and started a **dictatorship,** or one-person rule, that clamped down on Texas. Stephen Austin convinced Texans to declare independence from Mexico. The Republic of Texas was created in 1836.

When **Sam Houston,** commander of Texan forces, finally defeated Santa Anna, he became president of the Republic of Texas. Texans hoped the United States would **annex,** or add on, their republic to the Union. ✓

Annexing Texas and Oregon
Annexation became a major political issue because Texas would come in as a slave state. How could the balance of slave and free states be maintained? President **James K. Polk** solved this problem by negotiating a treaty to acquire Oregon from Britain. In 1845, Texas was admitted as a slave state. Oregon was annexed as a free territory.

But trouble was looming. Mexico had never recognized Texas independence. Now Mexico claimed that the southern border of Texas was the Nueces River, not the Rio Grande. Polk pressured Mexico to accept the Rio Grande border.

Key Events

1821 — William Becknell opens the Santa Fe Trail.

1836 — Texas declares independence from Mexico.

1849 — California gold rush begins.

✓ Checkpoint

Name the three men who played major roles in the war over Texas.

_____

_____

_____

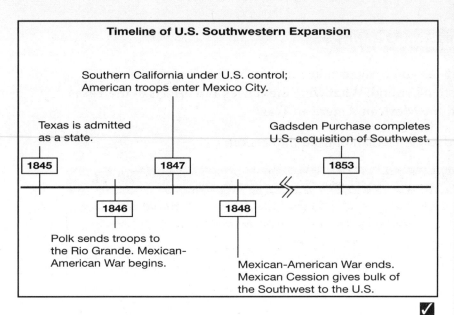

Timeline of U.S. Southwestern Expansion

Southern California under U.S. control;
American troops enter Mexico City.

Texas is admitted
as a state.

Gadsden Purchase completes
U.S. acquisition of Southwest.

1845 **1847** **1853**

1846 **1848**

Polk sends troops to
the Rio Grande. Mexican-
American War begins.

Mexican-American War ends.
Mexican Cession gives bulk of
the Southwest to the U.S.

The Mexican-American War

Mexico would not accept the Rio Grande border. It also refused to **cede**, or give up, California and New Mexico to the United States when President Polk offered to purchase them. So Polk sent General Zachary Taylor to the Rio Grande border. The Mexican government saw this as an act of war and attacked. Polk then urged Congress to declare war. He sent Stephen Kearny to capture Santa Fe. **John C. Frémont**, an explorer, led a rebellion against Mexican rule in California. By early 1847, all of southern California was under U.S. control.

General Taylor invaded Mexico and defeated Santa Anna at the Battle of Buena Vista. General Winfield Scott marched to Mexico City. Santa Anna fled the city, and Mexico was under U.S. occupation.

Achieving Manifest Destiny

The United States and Mexico signed the Treaty of Guadalupe-Hidalgo in 1848. Mexico recognized Texas as a U.S. state. Then in the Mexican Cession, it gave present-day California, Nevada, and Utah, as well as parts of Wyoming, Colorado, Arizona, and New Mexico to the United States for $18 million.

In the Gadsden Purchase of 1853, the United States paid Mexico $10 million for a narrow strip of present-day Arizona and New Mexico. The United States had fulfilled what it saw as its destiny to occupy the West.

Check Your Progress

1. What did Texans want from the Mexican government?

2. What action started the Mexican-American War?

✓ Checkpoint

List the two rivers that were claimed as Texas's southern border.

_____

_____

✓ Checkpoint

Name four Americans who led the United States in the Mexican-American War.

_____

_____

_____

_____

✓ Checkpoint

List the two things that gave the United States the entire Southwest.

_____

_____

Question to Think About As you read Section 3 in your textbook and take notes, keep this section focus question in mind: **What were the causes and effects of the Texas War for Independence and the Mexican-American War?**

▶ Use these charts to record key information from the section.

Events Leading to Texas's Independence
American settlers in Texas came into conflict with the Mexican government because they were _____slaveholders_____, even though the Mexican government had abolished _____. In 1830, Mexico banned further _____.
After Santa Anna established a(n) _____, Texans declared independence. Mexican troops laid siege to _____, a mission in San Antonio. Although the Texans were defeated, this event inspired _____. Later, the Texans defeated Santa Anna's army at _____.
_____ became president of the new Republic of Texas. He hoped that the United States would _____ Texas. However, public opinion in the United States was divided because _____.

Annexing Texas and Oregon
James K. Polk negotiated a treaty with _____Britain_____ to divide Oregon, which became the states of _____, _____, and _____.
Tensions with Mexico increased because Mexico had never _____. Also, the United States claimed that the southern Texas border was the _____, while Mexico claimed it was the _____.

The Mexican-American War
When war broke out between Mexico and the United States, it was most popular among _____ and _____, who wanted _____. Many _____, however, opposed the war because they thought it was an attempt to _____.
Stephen Kearny led troops that captured _____ and later_____.
_____ won a victory at the Battle of Buena Vista. An American army under _____ captured Veracruz and then marched on to _____.
The Treaty of _____ formally ended the war. Under the treaty, Mexico recognized _____ and ceded a vast territory known as _____ to the United States. This territory included present-day _____.
In the _____ of 1853, the United States paid Mexico $10 million for a narrow strip of present-day _____.

Refer to this page to answer the Chapter 13 Focus Question on page 211.

A Rush to the West

Section 4 Focus Question

How did Mormon settlement and the gold rush lead to changes in the West? To begin answering this question,

- Learn about Mormon settlement in Utah.
- Find out about the California gold rush.
- Explore California's changing population.

Section 4 Summary

While Mormons migrated to Utah in search of religious freedom, fortune seekers flocked to California in search of gold.

Mormons Settle Utah

In 1830, **Joseph Smith,** a New York farmer, founded the Church of Jesus Christ of Latter-day Saints. His followers were called the Mormons. The church grew quickly, but its teachings placed its followers in conflict with their neighbors. For example, Smith favored **polygamy,** or the practice of having more than one wife at a time.

Hostile communities forced the Mormons to move from New York to Ohio to Missouri to Illinois, where Joseph Smith was murdered. In 1847, **Brigham Young,** the new Mormon leader, led the group to the valley of the Great Salt Lake in Utah. Over the next few years, some 15,000 Mormons made the trek to Utah.

As a result of the Mexican Cession, Utah became part of the United States in 1848, and the U.S. government created the Utah Territory. The Mormons immediately came into conflict with the federal government over three issues. The first issue was the election process, which was controlled by the Mormon Church. As a result, non-Mormons had no say in the government. Another was the fact that the church supported Mormon-owned businesses, so non-Mormons had difficulty doing business in the territory. Third, polygamy was illegal in the rest of the country. In time, Congress passed a law that took control of elections away from the Mormon Church, and church leaders agreed to ban polygamy and to stop favoring Mormon-owned businesses. ✓

The California Gold Rush

After the Mexican Cession, easterners began migrating to California. At the time, there were about 10,000 Californios, or Mexican Californians, living in the territory.

A flood of other settlers came to California when gold was discovered in 1848 at Sutter's Mill near Sacramento. <u>News of the discovery spread quickly, and the prospect of finding gold drew about 80,000 fortune seekers</u>. These people who came to California in search of gold were known as the **"forty-niners."** In just two

Key Events

1821	William Becknell opens the Santa Fe Trail.
1836	Texas declares independence from Mexico.
1849	California gold rush begins.

✓ Checkpoint

List three issues that were a source of conflict between the Mormons and the U.S. government.

_____

_____

_____

Vocabulary Builder

Reread the underlined sentence. Which of the following words could replace *prospect*, as it is used in the sentence?

a. hope
b. guarantee
c. mining claim

years, California's population zoomed from 14,000 to 100,000. Prospectors, or gold seekers, searched throughout the Sacramento Valley for gold.

Since much of California was desert, disputes over water rights were common. **Water rights** are the legal rights to use the water in a river, stream, or other body. Often, such disputes erupted in violence.

Mining towns sprang up overnight and emptied just as quickly when news spread of a gold strike somewhere else. These towns attracted miners and people hoping to make money from miners. Since California was not yet a state, federal law did not apply within mining towns. Often **vigilantes,** or self-appointed law enforcers, punished people for crimes, although such vigilantes had no legal right to do so.

Other migrations in U.S. history included men and women, young and old. The forty-niners, however, were mainly young men. Still, some women did come to California, which offered women profitable work.

Few forty-niners struck it rich, and after the gold rush ended, many people continued to search for gold throughout the West. Others settled in the West for good. ✔

California's Changing Population

The gold rush brought enormous ethnic diversity to California. People came from Europe, Asia, Australia, and South America. After news of the gold rush reached China, about 45,000 Chinese men went to California. They faced prejudice and were generally hired only for menial labor.

Although some southerners brought slaves with them during the gold rush, slavery did not take root in California. Other miners objected to anyone profiting from mining who did not participate in the hard labor of finding gold.

The gold rush brought tragedy for Native Americans in California. Miners swarmed onto Indian lands, and vigilante gangs killed many Indians. About 100,000 Indians, nearly two thirds of California's Native American population, died during the gold rush period.

By 1850, only 15 percent of Californians were Mexican. Laws were passed that discriminated against Californios, and many lost their land as a result. ✔

Check Your Progress

1. Why did the Mormons migrate to Utah?

_____

_____

2. How did California's population change after gold was discovered in the state?

_____

_____

✔ **Checkpoint**

Name one way the gold rush was different from other migrations in U.S. history.

_____

_____

_____

✔ **Checkpoint**

Describe one reason why slavery did not take root in California.

_____

_____

_____

Question to Think About As you read Section 4 in your textbook, keep this question in mind: **How did Mormon settlement and the gold rush lead to changes in the West?**

▶ Use these charts to record key information from the section.

Mormons Move West

Seeking Refuge
The Mormon Church was founded by <u>Joseph Smith</u> in 1830. Hostility forced the Mormons to move from _____ to _____, and then to _____. After_____ was murdered, _____ led the Mormons to the valley of Utah's _____.

Conflict With the Government
Utah became part of the United States in _____. The Mormons almost immediately came into conflict with the U.S. government over three issues:
1. Problem: _____
   Solution: <u>1.Congress took away control of elections from the Mormon Church</u>.
2. Problem: _____
   Solution: _____.
3. Problem: Polygamy, which is _____,
   was illegal in the United States.
   Solution: _____.
Finally, in _____, Utah became a state.

The California Gold Rush

Gold Is Discovered
In January _____, gold was discovered at Sutter's Mill near _____. Fortune seekers, called _____, came to California in search of gold. In just two years, the population of settlers in California zoomed from _____ to _____.

Miners and Mining Towns
Mining towns supplied miners with _____, _____, and _____.
Since California was not yet a state, <u>federal law</u> did not apply within mining towns, so _____, or _____, punished people for crimes.

California's Changing Population
During the gold rush, people from _____, _____, _____, and _____ came to California. Chinese workers faced _____ and were usually hired only for _____. Some southerners brought their slaves to California, but slavery did not take root because _____ _____. California's Native American population declined by about _____ thirds during the gold rush. They were killed by _____ gangs who wanted their land. By 1850, only _____ percent of Californians were _____.

Refer to this page to answer the Chapter 13 Focus Question on page 211.

Directions: Circle the letter of the correct answer.

1. The largest region of the West was
   A the Southwest.   C the Great Plains.
   B the Northwest.   D the Pacific Coast.

2. Most early travelers to the West were
   A missionaries.   C traders.
   B farmers.   D merchants.

3. Which of the following was a result of the Mexican-American War?
   A the Mexican Cession   C the annexation of Florida
   B the annexation of Texas   D the Gadsden Purchase

4. Which of the following was a result of the gold rush in California?
   A Many people became rich from mining.
   B Slavery became widespread in the territory.
   C California's population became more diverse.
   D Native Americans were forced to move to Indian Territory.

Directions: Follow the steps to answer this question:

How did the Mexican-American War help achieve Manifest Destiny?

Step 1: Define Manifest Destiny.

_____

_____

_____

Step 2: Recall information: Describe the results of the Mexican-American War.

Results of the Mexican-American War
•
•

Step 3: Complete the topic sentence that follows. Then write two or three more sentences that support your topic sentence.

The effect of the Mexican-American War helped achieve Manifest Destiny by _____

_____

_____

_____

_____

_____

Chapter 13 Notetaking Study Guide

Now you are ready to answer the Chapter 13 Focus Question: **How did westward expansion change the geography of the nation and demonstrate the determination of its people?**

► Complete the following chart to help you answer this question. Use the notes that you took for each section.

Westward Expansion Changes the Nation's Geography

The West

- **What was the West?** By the 1820s, lands west of the Mississippi
  - **Northwest:** Land that stretched from _____ the Rockies _____ to the _____; in the early 1800s was claimed by _____ _____
  - **Southwest:** Lands in the southwest that included present-day California, Utah, Nevada, Arizona, New Mexico, Texas, and half of Colorado; ruled first by Spain, then by Mexico
- **What was Manifest Destiny?** _____

Trails to the West

- **The Santa Fe Trail:** overland trade route that carried merchandise from Independence, Missouri, to Santa Fe, New Mexico
- **The Oregon Trail:** _____
- **Life in the West**
  - **For women:** _____
  - **For Native Americans and settlers:** _____ _____

Texas and the Mexican-American War

- **Texans rebel against Mexico because** of religious differences, conflicts over slavery, and a lack of democracy _____.
- **Annexation of Texas was controversial in the United States because** _____ _____
- **The solution that led to the annexation of Texas was that** _____ _____
- **Causes of the Mexican War:** _____ _____
- **Results of the Mexican War:** The nation's geography greatly changed after the United States acquired a vast territory under the Mexican Cession.

A Rush to the West

- **Who were the Mormons?** a religious group founded by Joseph Smith in 1830
- **Why did they migrate to Utah?** to escape conflict with _____
- **Discovery in 1848 that brought a flood of settlers to California:** _____

Refer to this page to answer the Unit 4 Focus Question on page 212.

Unit 4 Pulling It Together Activity

Chapter 11 The North industrialized and urbanized rapidly in the early to mid-1800s. The South became highly dependent on cotton and the slave labor needed to cultivate it. Tensions between North and South spread to the western territories.

Chapter 12 By the mid-1800s, Americans were seeking reform in education and abolition. Some sought equality for women. Artists and writers also began to develop a distinct style.

Chapter 13 In the mid-1800s, many Americans wanted the nation to expand westward to the Pacific Ocean. American settlers overcame hardships in making this happen.

Think Like a Historian

Read the Unit 4 Essential Question: **What forces unite and divide a nation?**

▶ Use the organizers on this page and the next to collect information to answer this question.

What forces united the nation? Some of them are listed in this chart. Review your section and chapter notes. Then complete the chart.

Factors That United the North and the South, 1800–1860	
Area	**Uniting Factors**
Economy	• transformed by the Industrial Revolution
Technology	• new methods of transportation: steamboat, railroad • •
Labor	•
Arts	•
Issues	• •

Look at the second part of the Unit Essential Question. It asks about the forces that divide a nation. The chart below gives you a part of the answer. Review your section and chapter notes. Then fill in the rest of the chart.

Factors That Divided the North and the South, 1800–1860		
Area	In North	In South
Economy	• industrial • based on manufacturing and trade	• agricultural • dependent on cotton
Key technology	• •	•
Where people lived and worked	• •	•
Source of labor	•	•
Reform movements	• •	•
Slavery	• •	• •

Civil War and Reunion

Chapter 14 With the addition of new western lands, tension over the slavery issue erupted into violence. The election of Abraham Lincoln led to seven states leaving the Union and marked the coming of the Civil War.

Chapter 15 People in the North and the South hoped for an early victory, but the Civil War went on for years. Hundreds of thousands of Americans were killed before the war ended.

Chapter 16 At the end of the Civil War, Americans faced the problem of how to reunite the nation. Disagreements over Reconstruction led to conflicts in government and in the South. With the end of Reconstruction, African Americans in the South lost many of the rights they had gained.

Focus Your Learning As you study this unit and take notes, you will find the information to answer the questions below. Answering the Chapter Essential Questions will help build your answer to the Unit Essential Question.

Chapter 14 Essential Question
How did the nation try but fail to deal with growing sectional differences?
(page 215)

Unit 5 Essential Question
How was the Civil War a political, economic, and social turning point?
(page 257)

Chapter 15 Essential Question
How did people, places, and things affect the outcome of the Civil War?
(page 229)

Chapter 16 Essential Question
What were the short-term and long-term effects of the Civil War? (page 246)

Chapter 14

The Nation Divided (1846–1861)

What You Will Learn

With the addition of new western lands, tension over the slavery issue erupted into violence. The election of Abraham Lincoln led to seven states leaving the Union and marked the coming of the Civil War.

Chapter 14 Focus Question

As you read through this chapter, keep this question in mind: **How did the nation try but fail to deal with growing sectional differences?**

Section 1

Growing Tensions Over Slavery

Section 1 Focus Question

How did the question of admission of new states to the Union fuel the debate over slavery and states' rights? To begin answering this question,

- Learn about slavery and the Mexican-American War.
- Explore the bitter debate over slavery in the United States.

Section 1 Summary

The vast new lands the United States won in the Mexican-American War recharged the national debate on slavery.

Slavery and the Mexican-American War

Between 1820 and 1848, the balance between free and slave states was maintained. However, the Missouri Compromise did not apply to the huge territory gained from Mexico in 1848. Would this territory be organized as states that allowed slavery?

The issue was important to northerners who wanted to stop slavery from spreading. Fearing that the South would gain too much power, Representative David Wilmot of Pennsylvania proposed in 1846 that Congress ban slavery in all southwestern lands that might become states. This was called the Wilmot Proviso. The proviso passed in the House, but not the Senate. Slaveholding states saw it as a northern attack on slavery.

Neither the Democrats nor the Whigs wanted to take a strong stand on slavery. Each party needed support in both the North and the South to win the presidential election of 1848.

The Democratic presidential candidate in 1848 was Senator Lewis Cass of Michigan. He came up with a slavery plan he

Key Events

1852 — Harriet Beecher Stowe publishes *Uncle Tom's Cabin*.

1857 — Supreme Court ruling in Dred Scott case declares Missouri Compromise unconstitutional.

1861 — The Civil War begins with Confederate bombardment of Fort Sumter.

Sovereign comes from a Latin word meaning "above." If the states were sovereign, and made their own laws, what law would they be above?

_____

_____

✓ **Checkpoint**

List the three parties and their candidates in the 1848 election.

_____

_____

_____

✓ **Checkpoint**

List two issues that caused debate in the Congress.

_____

_____

_____

_____

thought would work in both the North and South. His idea was to let people in each new territory that applied for statehood decide for themselves whether to allow slavery. This **popular sovereignty** meant that people in each territory would vote directly on the issue, rather than having their elected representatives decide for them.

Many antislavery Whigs and Democrats wanted to take a stronger stand. They created their own party, called the Free-Soil Party. They wanted to ban slavery in all territory gained in the Mexican-American War—to make it "free soil." The party chose former Democratic President Martin Van Buren as its candidate. Although Van Buren did poorly in the election, he took enough votes from Cass to keep him from winning. General Zachary Taylor of the Whig Party became President. ✓

A Bitter Debate

Both sides realized that California's entrance into the Union would upset the balance of free and slave states. Southerners feared that if free states gained the majority in the Senate, the South could no longer block antislavery proposals. Southern leaders threatened to **secede,** or withdraw, from the Union if California were admitted as a free state.

There were other bitter divisions between North and South. Northerners wanted the slave trade abolished in Washington, D.C. Southerners wanted laws forcing northerners to return **fugitive,** or runaway, enslaved people.

For a time, it seemed that a satisfactory conclusion was not possible. Then in January 1850, Senator **Henry Clay** of Kentucky made a series of proposals to save the Union, which led to a great Senate debate. South Carolina Senator **John C. Calhoun** was against Clay's compromises. He wrote that if California joined the Union as a free state, only a constitutional amendment protecting states' rights or secession could save the South's way of life.

Arguing the other side, Senator **Daniel Webster** of Massachusetts stated that Clay's compromises were necessary to preserve the Union. Both sides seemed deadlocked. ✓

Check Your Progress

1. What was the Wilmot Proviso?

_____

_____

_____

2. Why did southerners fear California entering the Union as a free state?

_____

_____

_____

Question to Think About As you read Section 1 in your textbook and take notes, keep this question in mind: **How did the question of admission of new states to the Union fuel the debate over slavery and states' rights?**

▶ Use this chart to record key information from the section. Some information has been filled in to get you started.

The Debate Over Slavery and States' Rights		
If	**Then**	**Who Benefits?**
The Wilmot Proviso passes,	1. slavery will be banned in all territory from the Mexican-American War that becomes part of the United States; slave states will be outnumbered and weakened.	North
Lewis Cass (Democrat) becomes President,	2. _____ _____ _____	
Martin Van Buren (Free-Soil) becomes President,	3. _____ _____ _____	
Zachary Taylor (Whig) becomes President,	4. _____ _____ _____	
California enters the Union as a free state,	5. _____ _____ _____	
Fugitive slave laws are enforced,	6. slavery is enforced in the North and the South.	South
Henry Clay's proposals are accepted,	7. according to Calhoun, the South _____ _____ _____ _____ _____	
Slavery remains an unresolved issue,	8. _____ _____ _____	

Refer to this page to answer the Chapter 14 Focus Question on page 228.

Key Events

1852	Harriet Beecher Stowe publishes *Uncle Tom's Cabin.*
1857	Supreme Court ruling in Dred Scott case declares Missouri Compromise unconstitutional.
1861	The Civil War begins with Confederate bombardment of Fort Sumter.

✓ Checkpoint

Name two parts of the Fugitive Slave Act.

_____

_____

_____

_____

✓ Checkpoint

What was the reaction of many northerners to *Uncle Tom's Cabin*?

_____

_____

Section 2 Focus Question

What was the Compromise of 1850, and why did it fail? To begin answering this question,

*   Learn about the Compromise of 1850.
*   Find out about the impact of *Uncle Tom's Cabin.*
*   Learn about the Kansas-Nebraska Act.
*   Read about the violence in Bleeding Kansas.

Section 2 Summary

Efforts to calm the slavery debate, such as the Compromise of 1850, ultimately failed, and the debate only grew fiercer.

The Compromise of 1850

In 1850, Congress passed and President Millard Fillmore signed a series of five bills known as the Compromise of 1850 that were based on Henry Clay's proposals. To please the North, California was admitted as a free state, and the slave trade was banned in the nation's capital. To please the South, popular sovereignty would be used to decide the slavery issue in the rest of the Mexican Cession. Southerners also got a tough fugitive slave law.

The Fugitive Slave Act of 1850 allowed government officials to arrest any person accused of being a runaway slave. Suspects had no right to prove they had been falsely accused in a trial. All that was needed to deprive someone of his or her freedom was the word of one white person. In addition, northerners were required to help capture runaway slaves if authorities requested assistance.

The Fugitive Slave Act became the most controversial part of the Compromise of 1850. Northerners hated the new law. Many swore they would resist it. They were outraged to see African Americans suddenly arrested and shipped South. Thousands of northern African Americans fled to Canada for safety, including many who had never been enslaved. ✓

Uncle Tom's Cabin

Harriet Beecher Stowe was a northerner committed to fighting slavery. In 1852, she published *Uncle Tom's Cabin*, about a kind slave who is abused by a cruel master. Many white southerners attacked the book as **propaganda,** false or misleading information that is spread to further a cause. The book was a bestseller in the North. It shocked thousands of people who were previously unconcerned about slavery. Stowe's book showed that slavery was not just a political conflict, but a real human problem. ✓

The Kansas-Nebraska Act

In 1853, Illinois Senator **Stephen A. Douglas** suggested forming two new territories—the Kansas Territory and the Nebraska Territory. Southerners objected because both territories lay in an area closed to slavery by the Missouri Compromise. This meant that the states created from these territories would enter the Union as free states.

To win southern support, Douglas proposed that slavery in the new territories be decided by popular sovereignty. In effect, this undid the Missouri Compromise. Northerners were angered that the slavery issue was to be reopened in the territories. Southerners, however, supported Douglas's proposal, which enabled the Kansas-Nebraska Act to pass in both houses of Congress in 1854. ✓

Bleeding Kansas

Both proslavery and antislavery settlers flooded into Kansas within weeks after Douglas's bill became law. Each side was determined to hold the majority in the territory when it came time to vote.

In March 1855, Kansas held a vote on whether to enter the Union as a free or slave state. Thousands of proslavery people from Missouri voted illegally. Kansas had only 3,000 voters, but 8,000 votes were cast. A proslavery government was elected. Antislavery Kansans refused to accept these results and put a second government in place.

Violence soon broke out. Pro- and antislavery groups terrorized the countryside, attacking and killing settlers. It was so bad that the territory earned the name Bleeding Kansas.

Violence even spilled onto the floor of the U.S. Senate. After Massachusetts Senator Charles Sumner attacked a South Carolina senator in a fiery speech, the senator's nephew attacked Sumner in the Senate chamber. Many southerners felt that Sumner got what he deserved. To northerners, however, it was further evidence that slavery was brutal and inhumane. ✓

Check Your Progress

1. What did each side get in the Compromise of 1850?

_____

_____

_____

2. What was the effect of the Kansas-Nebraska Act?

_____

_____

_____

Circle the definition of *propose* that most closely matches the meaning used in the underlined sentence.

A. to put forward for consideration
B. to nominate for an office
C. to make an offer of marriage

✓ Checkpoint

Name the method used to determine the status of slavery in the Kansas and Nebraska territories.

_____

✓ Checkpoint

Kansas election of 1855:

Number of voters:

_____

Number of votes cast:

_____

Section 2 Notetaking Study Guide

Question to Think About As you read Section 2 in your textbook and take notes, keep this section focus question in mind: **What was the Compromise of 1850, and why did it fail?**

▶ Use this chart to record key information from the section. Some information has been filled in to get you started.

Compromises Fail		
Compromise of 1850 Proposed by _____	**Terms:** • California admitted as a _____ • Slave trade banned in _____ • _____ would decide slavery in the rest of the Mexican Cession. • Southerners got a tough new _____	**Goal of Compromise:** To end slavery crisis by giving supporters and opponents of slavery some of what they wanted.
Fugitive Slave Act of 1850	**Terms:** • Government officials may arrest any person accused of being a _____ _____ by any white person. • Suspects had no right to a _____. • _____ were required to help authorities capture accused runaway slaves if asked.	**Results:** • Most_____ part of the Compromise of 1850 • Thousands of northern African Americans fled to _____.
Kansas-Nebraska Act of 1854 Proposed by _____	**Terms:** • Slavery in the new Kansas and Nebraska territories was to be decided by _____.	**Results:** • Undid the _____ _____ • Reopened the issue of _____ in territories • _____ outraged
Kansas Election of 1855	**Events:** • Both proslavery and antislavery settlers flooded Kansas and wanted to hold the _____ in the territory. • Thousands of Missourians entered Kansas illegally to select a _____. • Antislavery settlers held a second _____.	**Results:** • Kansas now had two _____. • Violence broke out and earned Kansas the name _____.

Refer to this page to answer the Chapter 14 Focus Question on page 228.

Section 3

The Crisis Deepens

Section 3 Focus Question

Why did the Lincoln-Douglas debates and John Brown's raid increase tensions between the North and South? To begin answering this question,

- Learn how a new antislavery party came to be.
- Explore the impact of the Dred Scott decision.
- Find out about the Lincoln-Douglas debates.
- Learn about John Brown's raid.

Section 3 Summary

The Lincoln-Douglas debates and John Brown's raid caused more controversy and anger over slavery.

A New Antislavery Party

The Whig Party split apart in 1854 when Whigs who were willing to take a strong antislavery stand joined the new Republican Party. Its main platform was to keep slavery from spreading to the western territories.

Joined by northern Democrats and by Free-Soilers, the Republican Party quickly became powerful. It won 105 of 245 seats in the House in the election of 1854. In 1856, John C. Frémont was the first Republican candidate for President. Although Frémont won 11 of the 16 free states, the Democrat candidate, James Buchanan, was elected President. ✓

The Dred Scott Decision

In 1857, the Supreme Court delivered a blow to antislavery forces. It decided the case of *Dred Scott* v. *Sandford*. **Dred Scott** was an enslaved person who sued for his freedom because he had lived with his master in states where slavery was illegal.

Supreme Court Chief Justice **Roger B. Taney** ruled that Scott had no right to sue in federal court because African Americans were not citizens. Taney also declared that living in a free state did not make enslaved people free. They were property, and the property rights of their owners were protected in all states.

This meant that Congress did not have the power to prohibit slavery in any territory, and that the Missouri Compromise was unconstitutional. Slavery was legal again in all territories. Supporters of slavery rejoiced at this ruling. Northerners, however, were stunned. ✓

The Lincoln-Douglas Debates

Abraham Lincoln, an Illinois attorney, was elected to the House as a Whig, where he voted for the Wilmot Proviso. After one term, he returned to his Springfield law practice.

Key Events

1852	Harriet Beecher Stowe publishes *Uncle Tom's Cabin*.
1857	Supreme Court ruling in Dred Scott case declares Missouri Compromise unconstitutional.
1861	The Civil War begins with Confederate bombardment of Fort Sumter.

✓ Chcokpoint

List three groups that joined the Republican Party.

_____

_____

_____

✓ Checkpoint

Name the kind of right that protected slavery in all states, according to the Dred Scott decision.

_____

Vocabulary Builder

Entitle, in the underlined sentence, means "to give a right to something." What does this tell you about the way Lincoln felt about the rights of African Americans?

_____

_____

✓ Checkpoint

List two points Lincoln made in the debates about slavery and African Americans.

_____

_____

_____

_____

✓ Checkpoint

Name the part of the country in which John Brown was considered a hero.

_____

Lincoln's opposition to the Kansas-Nebraska Act brought him back into politics. In 1858, Lincoln ran for the Illinois Senate seat against Stephen Douglas, the author of the Kansas-Nebraska Act. When Lincoln accepted the Republican nomination, he made a stirring speech in favor of the Union. He said the country could not survive "half slave and half free."

Many southerners believed that Lincoln was an abolitionist. Lincoln then challenged Douglas to a series of public debates, and thousands gathered to hear them speak.

Douglas strongly defended popular sovereignty. He said people in each state could decide the slavery issue for themselves and shouldn't worry about what other states did. He also painted Lincoln as a dangerous abolitionist who wanted equality for African Americans.

Lincoln declared, "If slavery is not wrong, nothing is wrong." He predicted that slavery would die on its own. In the meantime, slavery had to be kept out of the West. While Lincoln did not promote equal rights for African Americans, he stated that they should be "entitled to all the rights" in the Declaration of Independence.

Douglas won the Senate election, but the debates made Lincoln nationally known. Two years later, the men would be rivals again for the presidency. ✓

John Brown's Raid

John Brown was an abolitionist who had been driven out of Kansas after the Pottawatomie Massacre. He returned to New England and hatched a plot to raise an army to free people in the South who were enslaved. In 1859, Brown and a small band of supporters attacked Harpers Ferry, Virginia. His goal was to seize guns the U.S. Army stored there. He would give the arms to enslaved African Americans and lead them in a revolt.

Brown and his men were captured. Brown was executed, but his cause was celebrated in the North, where many considered him to be a hero. More than ever, southerners were convinced that the North was out to destroy their way of life. ✓

Check Your Progress

1. What was the Republican Party's main platform?

_____

_____

_____

2. Why did John Brown attack Harpers Ferry?

_____

_____

_____

Question to Think About As you read Section 3 in your textbook and take notes, keep this section focus question in mind: **Why did the Lincoln-Douglas debates and John Brown's raid increase tensions between the North and South?**

▶ Use these charts to record key information from the section. Some information has been filled in to get you started.

The Dred Scott Decision
• Dred Scott was an enslaved person who sued for his freedom.   • Supreme Court Chief Justice _____ ruled that Scott had no right to sue in federal court because African Americans were not _____.   • Slaves were property, and the _____ of their owners were protected in all states.   • This meant Congress did not have the power to prohibit slavery in any territory, and the _____ was unconstitutional.   • Supporters of slavery _____ at this ruling but northerners were _____.

Abraham Lincoln-Stephen Douglas Debates
• Occurred during Illinois Senate race in the year_____.   • Lincoln's opposition to the _____ led him to run as a Republican against Senator Stephen Douglas, the author of the _____.   • The goal of the new Republican Party was to _____ _____.

Douglas's stand on popular sovereignty:	Lincoln's stand on African Americans:	Lincoln's stand on slavery:	Lincoln's position on the Union:
_____ _____ _____ _____ _____ _____ _____	a. _____ _____ _____ b. _____ _____ _____	a. _____ _____ b. _____ _____ c. _____ _____	_____ _____ _____ _____ _____ _____

John Brown's Raid		
Who was John Brown? _____ _____ _____ _____	**His plan in 1859:** _____ _____ _____	**Southerners were worried because:** _____ _____ _____

Refer to this page to answer the Chapter 14 Focus Question on page 228.

Key Events

1852 — Harriet Beecher Stowe publishes *Uncle Tom's Cabin*.

1857 — Supreme Court ruling in Dred Scott case declares Missouri Compromise unconstitutional.

1861 — The Civil War begins with Confederate bombardment of Fort Sumter.

Vocabulary Builder

Confederate comes from a Latin word meaning "to unite." The Confederate States of America, then, means what?

_____

_____

✓ Checkpoint

List the four presidential candidates in 1860.

_____

_____

_____

_____

Section 4

The Coming of the Civil War

Section 4 Focus Question

Why did the election of Abraham Lincoln spark the secession of southern states? To begin answering this question,
- Learn how the nation divided.
- Find out how the Civil War began.

Section 4 Summary

By the time Lincoln became President, the division over slavery was too deep to heal. The Civil War began.

The Nation Divides

As the election of 1860 drew near, Americans everywhere felt a sense of crisis. The long and bitter debate over slavery had left the nation seriously divided. Southern Democrats wanted the party to support slavery in the territories. But northerners refused to do so, and the party split in two.

Northern Democrats nominated Stephen Douglas. But southern Democrats picked Vice President John Breckinridge from Kentucky. Some southerners still hoped to heal the split between North and South. They formed the Constitutional Union Party and nominated John Bell of Tennessee, who promised to protect slavery *and* keep the nation together. The Republicans chose Abraham Lincoln as their candidate. His criticisms of slavery during his debates with Stephen Douglas made him popular in the North.

The election showed just how fragmented the nation had become. Lincoln won every free state. Breckinridge won every slaveholding state except four. Bell won Kentucky, Tennessee, and Virginia. Douglas won only Missouri. Although he carried only 40 percent of the popular vote, Lincoln received enough electoral votes to win the presidency.

To many southerners, Lincoln's election meant that the South no longer had a voice in the national government. They believed that the President and Congress were set against their interests. South Carolina was the first southern state to secede from the Union. Six more states followed.

Not all southerners favored secession. But they were overwhelmed by those who did. By February 1861, leaders from the seven seceding states had met in Montgomery, Alabama, and formed a new nation they called the Confederate States of America. By the time Lincoln took office in March, the Confederate leaders had written a constitution and named former Mississippi Senator Jefferson Davis as their president. ✓

The Civil War Begins

In Lincoln's inaugural address, he assured the seceding states that he meant them no harm. He stated that he had no plan to abolish slavery where it already existed. Lincoln's assurance of friendship was rejected. The seceding states took over post offices, forts, and other federal property within their borders.

One of those forts was Fort Sumter, on an island in the harbor of Charleston, South Carolina. The fort's commander would not surrender. South Carolina authorities decided to starve the fort's troops into surrender. They had been cut off from supplies since late December and could not hold out much longer.

Lincoln did not want to give up the fort, but he feared that sending troops might cause other states to secede. He decided to send food to the fort, but on supply ships carrying no troops or guns. Confederate leaders decided to capture the fort while it was still cut off from supplies. On April 12, they opened fire. After 34 hours, with the fort on fire, the troops inside finally surrendered.

This attack marked the beginning of the American Civil War. A **civil war** is a war between opposing groups of citizens of the same country.

The Civil War probably attracts more public interest today than any other event in American history. Americans continue to debate whether it could have been avoided.

In 1850, southerners might have been satisfied if they had been left alone. But by 1861, the North and South were so bitterly opposed that most Americans saw war as inevitable. At stake was the nation's future. ✔

✓ **Checkpoint**

Name the event that marked the beginning of the American Civil War.

_____

Check Your Progress

1. How did Lincoln win the presidential election without receiving a majority of the popular vote?

_____

_____

_____

2. What is a civil war?

_____

_____

_____

Section 4 Notetaking Study Guide

Question to Think About As you read Section 4 in your textbook and take notes, keep this question in mind: **Why did the election of Abraham Lincoln spark the secession of southern states?**

► Use this chart to record key information from the section. Some information has been filled in to get you started.

Chain of Events Leading to Civil War	

The Election of 1860	• There were four candidates in the election because _____.
	
	   • Northern Democratic candidate:_____
	   • Southern Democratic candidate: _____
	   • Constitutional Union candidate: _____
	   • Republican candidate: _____
	• Although he did not receive a majority of the popular vote, Lincoln received enough _____ to win the election.
	• The election showed how _____ the nation was.

Secession	• After South Carolina learned that Lincoln had won the election, it responded by _____
	• Southern leaders who opposed secession:
	   1. _____
	   2. _____
	• First state to secede from the Union: _____
	• Name of the new southern nation: _____
	• President of the southern nation:_____
	• Lincoln's message to seceding states: _____
	   _____
	   _____
	• Response of seceding states to Lincoln's message:
	   1. _____
	   2. _____

Fort Sumter	• Lincoln's plan to deal with the siege of Fort Sumter:_____
	   _____
	   _____
	   _____
	• South Carolina's response to Lincoln's plan:_____
	   _____
	   _____

Refer to this page to answer the Chapter 14 Focus Question on page 228.

Chapter 14 Assessment

Directions: Circle the letter of the correct answer.

1. The main question raised by the Southwest territory was
   A   should slavery be abolished?
   B   should the Missouri Compromise be used?
   C   would slavery be allowed in the West?
   D   should California come in as a free state?

2. What was an effect of the Kansas-Nebraska Act?
   A   *Uncle Tom's Cabin* gained popularity.   C   The Free-Soil Party was formed.
   B   It undid the Missouri Compromise.   D   Abraham Lincoln became President.

3. The Republicans' first presidential candidate was
   A   Abraham Lincoln.   C   Martin Van Buren.
   B   Stephen Douglas.   D   John C. Frémont.

4. Most southerners believed Lincoln
   A   would abolish slavery.   C   would accept secession.
   B   would defend Fort Sumter.   D   would not become President.

Directions: Follow the steps to answer this question:

How did the issue of slavery bitterly divide the nation?

Step 1: Recall information: Describe each of the following pieces of legislation.

Legislation	What It Said
Wilmot Proviso	
Fugitive Slave Act of 1850	

Step 2: How did these acts affect the nation?

_____

_____

_____

Step 3: Complete the topic sentence that follows. Then write two or three more sentences that support your topic sentence.

Legislation like the Wilmot Proviso and the Fugitive Slave Act of 1850 _____

_____

_____

_____

_____

Chapter 14 Notetaking Study Guide

Now you are ready to answer the Chapter 14 Focus Question: **How did the nation try but fail to deal with growing sectional differences?**

▶ Complete the following chart to help you answer this question. Use the notes that you took for each section.

The Nation Divided	
Growing Tensions Over Slavery	
The Wilmot Proviso • Description: _____ _____ Its fate: Blocked in _____, slaveholding states saw it as an _____ on slavery.	*California* • Both sides realized its admission to the Union would upset the balance of free and slave states. • The South threatens: _____
Compromises Fail	
To please the North, the Compromise of 1850 • admitted California as a free state. •	To please the South, the Compromise of 1850 • •
The Kansas-Nebraska Act essentially undid _____.	
Harriet Beecher Stowe published _____ in 1852. A bestseller in the North, it was written off as _____ in the South.	
The Crisis Deepens	
In the Dred Scott case, the Supreme Court declared _____ unconstitutional and opened all territories _____.	
• Abraham Lincoln ran against _____ for the Illinois Senate in 1858. • In their debates, Lincoln took a stand against slavery, saying African Americans should be entitled to the rights stated in _____. • After he was executed for raiding Harpers Ferry and trying to lead a slave revolt, _____ was considered a hero by many northerners.	
The Coming of the Civil War	
To many southerners, the election of Lincoln meant that the South no longer had a voice in _____.	Lincoln's assurance of friendship in his inaugural address was _____ by the seceding states.
The Confederate attack on _____ marked the beginning of the Civil War.	

Refer to this page to answer the Unit 5 Focus Question on page 257.

What You Will Learn

People in the North and the South hoped for an early victory, but the Civil War went on for years. Hundreds of thousands of Americans were killed before the war ended.

Chapter 15 Focus Question

As you read this chapter, keep this question in mind: **How did people, places, and things affect the outcome of the Civil War?**

Section 1
The Call to Arms

Section 1 Focus Question

Why did each side in the Civil War think the war would be won easily? To begin answering this question,
- Discover how sides were taken in the war.
- Explore the strengths of the North and the South.
- Learn the two sides' strategies.
- Find out about the First Battle of Bull Run.
- Explore the details of a soldier's life.

Section 1 Summary

As the Civil War began, North and South prepared for a short war. They soon realized they were in for a long struggle.

Taking Sides in the War

After Fort Sumter was captured, President Lincoln declared that a rebellion existed in the South. He requested troops to subdue the Confederacy. Some states supplied more than enough volunteers, some refused to comply, and some did not respond. More southern states seceded.

There were four **border states**—slave states that did not secede. These were Delaware, Kentucky, Missouri, and Maryland. Delaware supported the Union. Kentucky started out **neutral,** not favoring either side, but it supported the Union after it was invaded by southern forces in September 1861.

Most people in Maryland and Missouri favored the South. Lincoln sent troops to occupy Missouri. If Maryland seceded, the U.S. capital would be in Confederate territory, so eastern Maryland was put under **martial law.** This is a type of rule in which the military is in charge and citizens' rights are suspended. ✓

Key Events

1861	Eleven states secede from the Union, creating the Confederacy.
1863	Lincoln delivers the Emancipation Proclamation.
1864	Grant invades South and lays siege to Petersburg.
1865	Lee's surrender at Appomattox brings Union victory.

✓ Checkpoint

List the four border states.

_____

_____

_____

_____

North Against South

When the war began, people on both sides were confident of victory. To win the war, the North had to invade the South. Southerners would be fighting on their own territory, and they would be led by some of the nation's best officers. The North also had some advantages. It had a larger population, more farmland, and more factories.

Two thirds of northern men aged 18 to 45 served in the military. In the South, three fourths of free men the same age served. But the North had 3.5 million men in this age group, whereas the South had only 1 million. The North thus had a much larger army than the South. ✓

The Two Sides Plan Strategies

To isolate the South, the North set up a naval **blockade**, a military action to prevent traffic to and from an area. If the South could not sell cotton to Britain, it would run out of money to fight. The North planned to control the Mississippi River and seize Richmond, Virginia, the Confederate capital.

Southerners had a simple strategy: defend their land until northerners gave up. They would finance the war with continued trade with Britain. They also hoped Britain would support the South. ✓

First Battle of Bull Run

Northerners wanted to end the war quickly with a decisive battle. Popular demand led Union General Irvin McDowell to march into Virginia before his troops were fully trained. The First Battle of Bull Run was fought along Bull Run, a river near Manassas, Virginia, on July 21, 1861. The South held firm, and the poorly trained Union troops panicked and retreated. ✓

A Soldier's Life

Soldiers spent most of their time in camp, not fighting. They spent much of the time training. Camp conditions were often miserable, especially in wet weather. Soldiers often did not have clean water, which led to outbreaks of disease.

Conditions in prison camps were even worse. In overcrowded camps, prisoners died each day from starvation and exposure. ✓

Check Your Progress

1. What were the Union and Confederate war strategies?

_____

_____

_____

2. What was the result of the First Battle of Bull Run?

_____

_____

Question to Think About As you read Section 1 in your textbook and take notes, keep this section focus question in mind: **Why did each side in the Civil War think the war would be won easily?**

▶ Use this chart to record key information from the section. Some information has been filled in to get you started.

The Call to Arms

The North	The South
1. How did two border states bolster northern confidence? <u>Kentucky and Delaware supported the Union.</u>	1. How did two border states bolster southern confidence? <u>Maryland and Missouri supported the South, and northern troops had to be used to subdue them.</u>
2. What Virginia event helped the North? _____ _____ _____	2. Which generals left the U.S. Army to join the Confederate Army? _____ _____
3. What four things did the North have much more of than the South had? _____ _____ _____	3. What were two advantages the South had? _____ _____
4. What were three parts of the Northern strategy? _____ _____ _____ _____	4. What was the South's strategy? _____ _____ _____
5. Who was the Union general in the First Battle of Bull Run? _____	5. Why was the South hopeful that Britain would support it? <u>because Britain was a major trading partner that needed southern cotton</u>

Hardships of Both Sides

1. What effect did the war have on American families?
_____

2. What were the camp conditions for soldiers?
<u>often miserable and diseased, lack of clean water</u>

3. What were the conditions for prisoners of war in the North and the South?
_____

Refer to this page to answer the Chapter 15 Focus Question on page 245.

Early Years of the War

Section 2 Focus Question

How did each side in the war try to gain an advantage over the other? To begin answering this question,

- Learn about new technology of the war.
- Read about the war in the East.
- Find out about the war in the West.

Section 2 Summary

Unable to win a quick victory, Union forces met Confederate troops in a series of battles made more bloody by new technology.

New Technology in the War

New weapons made the Civil War more deadly than any previous war. Traditionally, generals had relied on an all-out charge of troops to overwhelm the enemy. But new rifles and cannons were far more accurate and had a greater range than the old muskets and artillery. They could also be loaded much faster. As a result, the attacking army could be bombarded long before it arrived at the defenders' position.

Unfortunately, Civil War generals were slow to recognize the problem and change tactics. Thus, thousands of soldiers died charging across open fields during the Civil War.

Ironclads, or warships covered with protective iron plates, were another new invention. Cannonfire bounced harmlessly off these ships. The Confederacy used ironclads against the Union's naval blockade, and the Union used them in their efforts to control the Mississippi River. ✔

The War in the East

After its demoralizing defeat at Bull Run, the Union army got a new commander, General **George McClellan.** He was an excellent organizer, but he was also a very cautious leader. He spent seven months training his army instead of attacking the Confederate enemy. In March 1862, he finally moved 100,000 soldiers by boat to a point southeast of Richmond. He knew that his troops could easily have defeated the 15,000 Confederate soldiers facing them, but the cautious McClellan stopped to ask Lincoln to send him more men. Almost a month passed before he resumed the march.

This delay gave the Confederates plenty of time to reinforce their small army. They stopped McClellan's advancing forces outside Richmond on May 31, 1862, then forced the Union army to retreat in late June.

General Lee decided to invade the North, reasoning that a victory on Union soil would win the Confederacy European support. He moved his army into western Maryland.

Key Events

1861 Eleven states secede from the Union, creating the Confederacy.

1863 Lincoln delivers the Emancipation Proclamation.

1864 Grant invades South and lays siege to Petersburg.

1865 Lee's surrender at Appomattox brings Union victory.

✓ Checkpoint

List three ways rifles were better than older guns.

_____

_____

_____

Vocabulary Builder

Fill in the first blank below with a synonym for _reinforce_. Fill in the second blank with an antonym for _reinforce_.

Union delays allowed Confederates to _____ their army near Richmond. McClellan thought that not having enough troops would _____ his army.

When McClellan learned that Lee had divided his army, he attacked the larger half at Antietam Creek near Sharpsburg, Maryland, on September 17, 1862. It was the bloodiest day of the Civil War. In attack after attack, McClellan's troops charged into the gunfire that came from the Confederate lines. The Union suffered 12,000 **casualties**, which is a military term for persons killed, wounded, or missing in action. The South lost nearly 14,000 soldiers, and Lee began a forced retreat back to Virginia. McClellan could have pursued Lee's battered army, but he did not. ✓

The War in the West

In the West, Union generals were not so cautious. General **Ulysses S. Grant,** the most successful of these generals, was a man who took chances. In February 1862, Grant captured Fort Henry, just south of the Kentucky-Tennessee border. Then he took Fort Donelson. These victories opened the South up to invasion from two different water routes. Grant's forces continued south along the Tennessee River to Corinth, Mississippi, an important railroad center.

Before Grant could advance on Corinth, Confederate General Albert Sidney Johnston attacked. On April 6, 1862, he surprised Grant's forces at the town of Shiloh. The Battle of Shiloh was costly for both sides. The South suffered nearly 11,000 casualties. The toll for the North was more than 13,000. However, the Union army was successful in forcing the Confederate army to withdraw from the railroad center, and in the process, it won control of Corinth. The Union now controlled western Tennessee and part of the Mississippi River.

Two weeks after the Battle of Shiloh, Union commander David Farragut entered the Mississippi River from the Gulf of Mexico and captured New Orleans. By the summer of 1862, the Union controlled almost all of the Mississippi River. ✓

Check Your Progress

1. What effect did rifles have at the beginning of the Civil War?

_____

_____

_____

_____

2. What two events show the differences between Grant's and McClellan's approaches after victory?

_____

_____

_____

_____

✓ Checkpoint

Name the error McClellan made before facing Lee's troops near Richmond.

_____

_____

✓ Checkpoint

List three key places Grant and his troops captured.

_____

_____

_____

Section 2 Notetaking Study Guide

Question to Think About As you read Section 2 in your textbook and take notes, keep this section focus question in mind: **How did each side in the war try to gain an advantage over the other?**

▶ Use this chart to record key information from the section. Some information has been filled in to get you started.

Early Years of the War		
New Technology		
New _____ and _____ were more accurate and had greater range than previous weapons. _____ were a great improvement over older wooden warships.		
Event	**Military Leader**	**Outcome**
Forts Henry and Donelson, February 1862	Union: <u>Grant</u>	• <u>The Union takes control of two water routes into the western Confederacy</u>.
Use of ironclads		• _____ • _____
Battle of Shiloh, April 1862	Union: <u>Grant</u> Confederacy: <u>A. S. Johnston</u>	• _____
New Orleans, April 1862	Union:	• The North controls almost all of the Mississippi River.
Outside Richmond, Virginia, May and June 1862	Union:	• _____
Battle of Antietam, September 1862	Union: Confederacy:	• _____

Refer to this page to answer the Chapter 15 Focus Question on page 245.

Section 3

The Emancipation Proclamation

Section 3 Focus Question

What were the causes and effects of the Emancipation Proclamation? To begin answering this question,

- Find out about emancipating the enslaved.
- Learn how African Americans helped the Union.

Section 3 Summary

After the Emancipation Proclamation was issued, the Civil War became a struggle to end slavery as well as a battle to save the Union.

Emancipating the Enslaved

Northern abolitionists assumed that Lincoln's main war goal was to end slavery because that was what they wanted most. But Lincoln's main goal was to preserve the Union. If that could be done without outlawing slavery, Lincoln would not outlaw slavery. He did not want to free the slaves at the outset of the war because it might provoke the border states into secession. Furthermore, he knew that most northerners did not care enough about slavery to fight a war to end it. Lincoln had no plan to **emancipate,** or free, enslaved people in 1861.

But by mid-1862, Lincoln realized that slavery was important to the southern war effort. Slaves kept farms and factories producing when their owners were away fighting the war. Lincoln decided slavery had to end.

On January 1, 1863, Lincoln issued the Emancipation Proclamation. He had been ready to do this in the summer of 1862, but nervous Cabinet members, fearing that the people would not like it, had urged him to wait until the Union army had more victories under its belt. Then northerners would still be willing to fight, even if they did not care about ending slavery.

The proclamation was not the sweeping rejection of slavery abolitionists wanted and expected. It freed slaves only in areas that were fighting the Union. Slaves in border states and the West were not affected, and southern states already under Union control were not affected. States that had seceded did not have to obey the law because they did not recognize the U.S. government. In short, very few slaves were actually freed in 1863.

Some abolitionists protested that the proclamation did not go far enough; others accepted it as a start. Northern African Americans rejoiced, while white southerners claimed Lincoln was trying to start a slave rebellion. For the most part, Union soldiers supported the law because they knew it dealt a blow to the South's ability to fight. Whether people embraced the proclamation or not,

Key Events

1861 Eleven states secede from the Union, creating the Confederacy.

1863 Lincoln delivers the Emancipation Proclamation.

1864 Grant invades South and lays siege to Petersburg.

1865 Lee's surrender at Appomattox brings Union victory.

Vocabulary Builder

Proclamation comes from a Latin word that means "to cry out." Use context clues from this section to write your own short definition of *proclamation*.

_____

_____

_____

List four ways that African Americans served in the Union army and navy.

_____

_____

_____

_____

it changed the nature of the Civil War. It was no longer just a fight to save the nation. It was now also a war to end slavery.

Also, the proclamation ended all hope the South had of being supported by Britain. Britain would not support a government identified as fighting for slavery. ✓

African Americans Help the Union

African Americans in the North were not allowed to fight in the Union army at first. Even after Congress allowed it in 1862, few state governments mobilized African American volunteers. After the Emancipation Proclamation, it was easier for African Americans to enlist. By the end of the war, 189,000 had served in the army or navy. Over half of these soldiers were former slaves who had escaped or been freed by Union soldiers when they took over southern territory.

All African Americans fighting in the Civil War faced grave danger—slavery or death—if taken prisoner by southerners. They served in all-black regiments in the army and served alongside whites in the navy. They were paid less than white soldiers. Still, they fought bravely, often deep in southern territory. Free northern and emancipated southern African Americans also served in the Union army as cooks, wagon drivers, and hospital aides.

People enslaved in the South during the war did what they could to hurt the Confederate war effort. Some provided information to the Union army. Enslaved people had always quietly resisted slavery by deliberately working slowly or damaging equipment. But with many slaveholders off fighting the war, large numbers of slaves refused to work. ✓

Check Your Progress

1. How did the Emancipation Proclamation change the Civil War?

_____

_____

2. What were some of the extra risks African Americans took by serving in the Union army?

_____

_____

Question to Think About As you read Section 3 in your textbook and take notes, keep this section focus question in mind: **What were the causes and effects of the Emancipation Proclamation?**

▶ Use this chart to record key information from the section. Some information has been filled in to get you started.

The Emancipation Proclamation
Emancipating the Enslaved
Lincoln's main war goal was to _____. He did not free slaves at the beginning of the war in order to avoid _____ _____.
Lincoln issued the _____ on January 1, 1863. However, it only freed slaves in _____, so very few enslaved people were immediately freed. Most Union soldiers supported the proclamation because it _____.
The _____Emancipation Proclamation_____ caused the Civil War to become a _____. It also kept Britain from _____.
African Americans Help the Union
More than half of African American volunteers serving in the Union army were _____.
Confederates did not treat captured African American soldiers as _____; they faced _____.
Noncombat positions held by free African Americans in the Union army: • • wagon drivers •
Ways enslaved African Americans hurt the Confederate war effort: • •

Refer to this page to answer the Chapter 15 Focus Question on page 245.

The Civil War and American Life

Section 4 Focus Question

How did the war affect people and politics in the North and the South? To begin answering this question,

- Explore divisions over the war.
- Find out about the draft laws.
- Learn about the economic strains caused by the war.
- Explore the role of women in the Civil War.

Section 4 Summary

Neither the North nor the South presented a united front in the war. Divisions existed between states and social classes.

Divisions Over the War

The North may have faced the South in the war, but each side experienced divisions over the war and slavery. Not all northerners supported a war to end slavery. Many opposed the Emancipation Proclamation. Nor did all northerners support restoring the Union. Some felt the South should be allowed to secede. Some northerners blamed Lincoln and the Republicans for forcing the South into a war. Northern Democrats who opposed the war were called Copperheads, after the poisonous snake. Copperheads criticized the war and called for peace with the Confederacy.

Not all southerners supported slavery or secession. Poor backcountry regions with few enslaved people were less supportive of the war than regions with large slaveholding populations. Strong support for states' rights created other divisions. For example, the governors of Georgia and North Carolina did not want the Confederate government to force men from their states to do military service.

People on both sides tried to disrupt the war effort by helping prisoners of war escape, encouraging soldiers to desert, and holding peace protests. Both Abraham Lincoln and Jefferson Davis tried to keep order by suspending the right of **habeas corpus,** the constitutional protection against unlawful imprisonment, during the war. ✔

The Draft Laws

Desertion was a problem for both sides. Between 300,000 and 550,000 Union and Confederate soldiers left their units and went home. Some returned after their crops were planted or harvested. To meet the need for troops, both North and South established a **draft,** a system of required military service. The southern draft began in 1862, and the northern draft began in 1863; all eligible men were required to enlist in the army or navy.

Key Events

1861 Eleven states secede from the Union, creating the Confederacy.

1863 Lincoln delivers the Emancipation Proclamation.

1864 Grant invades South and lays siege to Petersburg.

1865 Lee's surrender at Appomattox brings Union victory.

Vocabulary Builder

The term *habeas corpus* comes from a Latin phrase meaning "to have the body." Why would the term *habeas corpus* be used to describe imprisonment?

_____

_____

_____

✓ Checkpoint

Name three ways people disrupted the war effort.

_____

_____

_____

But there were ways around the draft. The wealthy could hire substitutes to serve for them. In the South, a man who held at least 20 enslaved people did not have to serve. In the North, anyone who paid $300 to the government was allowed to stay home. Only the well-off could afford this amount.

People on both sides objected that poor people were fighting the war. Draft riots broke out in many northern cities in 1863 as poor people who could not pay their way out of the draft destroyed draft offices and other property. ✔

The War and Economic Strains

While northern industries thrived on war production, the amount of money coming in to the government did not cover the costs of the war, so Congress introduced the first **income tax** in August 1861. This is a tax on the money people receive. Congress also printed $400 million in paper money. This was the first federal paper money, and it led to **inflation,** or a general rise in prices. In the North, prices went up 80 percent on average.

The Union blockade prevented the South from raising money by selling cotton overseas. Shortages of goods became severe as income from cotton dropped ever lower. On top of this, food production fell as Union armies invaded farmland. Food shortages led to riots in southern cities. ✔

Women in the Civil War

Women in the North and South contributed to the war effort in many ways. Some disguised themselves as men and enlisted in the army, and some were spies. But most women took up the roles their male family members had played in society. Women ran businesses and farms, worked in factories, taught school, and served on the battlefield, in army camps, and in hospitals. Elizabeth Blackwell, the first American woman to earn a medical degree, trained nurses for the Union army. Clara Barton cared for Union soldiers on the battlefield and later founded the American Red Cross. ✔

Check Your Progress

1. Why would suspending habeas corpus help keep the peace?

_____

_____

2. How did most women support the war effort?

_____

_____

✓ **Checkpoint**

List three ways someone could avoid the draft.

_____

_____

_____

✓ **Checkpoint**

Name the effect the printing of paper money had in the North.

_____

✓ **Checkpoint**

Name two women who helped heal soldiers during the war.

_____

_____

Section 4 Notetaking Study Guide

Question to Think About As you read Section 4 in your textbook, keep this section focus question in mind: **How did the war affect people and politics in the North and the South?**

▶ Use this chart to record key information from the section.

The Civil War's Effect on American Life

Divisions

In the North, some people:	Areas of South less supportive of war:
•	•
• believed the South had the right to secede	Opposition to the war was strongest in _____ and _____.
•	Divisions were also created by strong support for _____.
Northern Democrats opposed to the war were called _____.	

Disruptions

Ways people disrupted the war effort:
- encouraged soldiers to desert
-
-
-

Both sides dealt with disruptions in some areas by _____.

Draft Laws

- _____ was a problem for both sides. Many soldiers left their units to _____.
- Each side established a _____, a system of required _____. Anger at exceptions to this requirement caused _____ in many places.

Economic Strains

Congress levied the first ___income tax___ to pay for the war.
The Union printed large amounts of _____, causing the cost of goods to _____.
Union blockades of the South caused _____ that made goods _____.

Women in the Civil War

Women's contributions to the war effort on both sides:
- disguised themselves as men to join the army
-
-
-

Barriers for women fell, especially in the field of _____.

Refer to this page to answer the Chapter 15 Focus Question on page 245.

Section 5

Decisive Battles

Section 5 Focus Question

How did Lincoln and his generals turn the tide of the war? To begin answering this question,

- Learn about the turning points of the war.
- Find out how the Union closed in on the Confederacy.
- Discover how peace came at last.

Section 5 Summary

Under Grant's leadership, the Union finally defeated the Confederacy. Both sides suffered terrible losses in the final two years of the war.

The Tide Turns

The Union army had a new commander in 1862, General Ambrose Burnside, who was determined to act more boldly than General McClellan had. Burnside marched toward Richmond in December 1862 to attack Confederate General Lee's army. Burnside ordered traditional charges, sending thousands of men running into Confederate gunfire. The Union lost 13,000 men in the Battle of Fredericksburg. The South lost 5,000.

Burnside was replaced by General Joseph Hooker, who also marched toward Richmond. In May 1863, his army was defeated at the Battle of Chancellorsville by a southern force half its size. The South, however, lost General Stonewall Jackson in the battle.

After these victories, Lee determined once more to launch an attack in the North. His forces were outside the town of Gettysburg, Pennsylvania, on July 1, 1863, when they encountered Union troops, now led by General George Meade. Fighting broke out that lasted for three days. When the Battle of Gettysburg was over, the Union had won. The South had lost 28,000 men, and the North had lost 23,000.

The day after the Battle of Gettysburg ended, the city of Vicksburg, Mississippi—one of the last cities on the river still in southern hands—fell to Union General Grant. Grant had laid **siege** to the city for two months. A siege is an attempt to capture a place by surrounding it with troops and cutting it off until its people surrender. Grant's victory at Vicksburg and Lee's defeat at Gettysburg were the turning points of the war, giving the Union the advantage. ✓

Closing In on the Confederacy

President Lincoln decided to put General Grant in charge of the Union army. Grant marched toward Richmond, fighting a series of battles in Virginia in the spring of 1864 in which he lost about 55,000 men. The Confederacy lost 35,000. Grant knew his men

Key Events

1861	Eleven states secede from the Union, creating the Confederacy.
1863	Lincoln delivers the Emancipation Proclamation.
1864	Grant invades South and lays siege to Petersburg.
1865	Lee's surrender at Appomattox brings Union victory.

✓ Checkpoint

Name three Union commanders.

_____

_____

_____

could be replaced, but he also knew that the South was running out of soldiers and supplies. He settled into a siege at Petersburg, south of Richmond, to wait the Confederates out.

During this siege, another Union general, **William Tecumseh Sherman,** was driving his army across the South. In his march, he practiced **total war,** or all-out attacks aimed at destroying not only an enemy's army, but also its resources and its people's will to fight. His troops set fire to buildings, seized crops and livestock, and pulled up railroad tracks. Sherman captured Atlanta on September 2, 1864. He then marched east toward the Atlantic Ocean. Sherman's "March to the Sea" brought devastation to a path 60 miles wide.

Steps to a Union Victory

1. Meade defeats Lee at Gettysburg.
2. Vicksburg falls to Grant.
3. Grant is made commander of the Union army.
4. Grant fights a series of battles that cost Lee soldiers who cannot be replaced.
5. Sherman's "March to the Sea" devastates land, resources, and people.
6. Grant reinforces his army and captures Richmond.

Peace at Last

By March 1865, Grant had extended his armies, encircling Lee. Lee knew that the war was lost. Lincoln knew it too and asked the American people to welcome the South back to the Union. He said, "with malice toward none, [and] charity for all; . . . let us strive together . . . to bind up the nation's wounds."

On April 2, Grant broke the Confederate line and captured Richmond. After briefly retreating west, Lee offered to surrender. On April 9, Grant and Lee met in a home in the town of Appomattox Court House, Virginia, to sign the surrender agreement. The Union generously allowed the Confederates to return home without punishment.

The war was over, but its effects lasted long afterward. Around 260,000 southerners had died, along with over 360,000 northerners, including 37,000 African Americans. ✓

Check Your Progress

1. Why did Burnside suffer such high casualties?

_____

_____

2. What happened to Confederate soldiers under the terms of the surrender agreement?

_____

_____

✓ **Checkpoint**

Name the general who practiced total war and led the Union "March to the Sea."

_____

Vocabulary Builder

Using everyday language, write your own version of Lincoln's statement "with malice toward none, and charity for all; … let us strive together … to bind up the nation's wounds."

_____

_____

_____

✓ **Checkpoint**

How many soldiers died in the Civil War?

Northerners: _____

Southerners: _____

Question to Think About As you read Section 5 in your textbook and take notes, keep this section focus question in mind: **How did Lincoln and his generals turn the tide of the war?**

▶ Use these charts to record key information from the section.

Turning the Tide of War		
General	**Battle(s)**	**Result**
1. Ambrose Burnside	_____	_____ _____
2. Joseph Hooker	_____	_____ _____ _____
3. George Meade	Gettysburg	Union victory that forced Lee out of the North and cost Lee nearly a third of his soldiers, who could not be replaced.
4. Ulysses Grant	Vicksburg	_____ _____ _____
5. Ulysses Grant	_____	_____ _____
6. _____	Atlanta	_____ _____ _____
7. William Sherman	"March to the Sea"	_____ _____ _____
8. _____	Richmond	Confederate national capital is taken and Lee is forced to surrender his army.

The End of the War

Lincoln looked ahead to victory in a speech in 1863 called _____.
The capture of Atlanta gave Lincoln a _____.
Number of Union soldiers killed in the Civil War: _____
Number of Confederate soldiers killed in the Civil War: _____
Key results of the Civil War:
   •
   • It put an end to slavery.

Refer to this page to answer the Chapter 15 Focus Question on page 245.

Chapter 15 Assessment

Directions: Circle the letter of the correct answer.

1. Which does *not* describe public reaction to the start of the Civil War?
    A   Most believed the war would be short.
    B   The border states all sided with the Confederacy.
    C   Not everyone supported the war.
    D   Most people in Maryland and Missouri favored the South.

2. Where were slaves actually freed by the Emancipation Proclamation?
    A   areas outside of Union control
    B   parts of the South already under Union control
    C   the border states
    D   the western territories

3. In what year did the Union take the upper hand in the Civil War?
    A   1862   B   1863   C   1864   D   1865

Directions: Follow the steps to answer this question:

How did the North finally gain the upper hand in the Civil War?

Step 1: Recall information: In the chart, fill in the result of each Union victory.

Event	Result
Gettysburg	1.
Vicksburg	2.
Battles in northern Virginia	3.
Sherman's "March to the Sea"	4.

Step 2: How did these events affect the North and the South?

Events' Effects on North and South	
North	
South	

Step 3: Complete the topic sentence that follows. Then write two or three more sentences that support your topic sentence.

By 1864, the tide had turned in the North's favor because _____

_____

_____

_____

Now you are ready to answer the Chapter 15 Focus Question: **How did people, places, and things affect the outcome of the Civil War?**

▶ Complete the following chart to help you answer this question. Use the notes that you took for each section.

People, Places, and Things That Affected the Outcome of the Civil War		
People	**Places**	**Things**
Lincoln: • His main goal was to restore the Union. • Effects of the Emancipation Proclamation: 1. 2.	Border states: The Union's control over these states helped the Union war effort.	Railroads: The North had many more miles of railroad tracks than the South.
	First Battle of Bull Run: _____ _____	Manufacturing: _____ _____
	Shiloh: _____ _____ _____	New rifles and cannons were deadlier than earlier weapons: • more accurate • had a longer range
Ulysses S. Grant: • Attacks in the West led to Union control of the Mississippi. • He became the Union army's top commander.	Antietam: _____ _____ _____	• Ironclads: • protected from cannon fire
African Americans served in the army and navy as: • • • •	Gettysburg: important Union victory stopped the Confederate advance into northern territory	• used against Union naval blockade •
	Vicksburg: led to _____ _____	Economic challenges: In the North: • Congress levied the first income tax to pay war costs. • Increased currency supply led to inflation and higher prices. In the South: • •
How women participated: • • • •	Battles in northern Virginia/ Petersburg: • •	

Refer to this page to answer the Unit 5 Focus Question on page 257.

Chapter 16

Reconstruction and the New South

(1863–1896)

What You Will Learn

At the end of the Civil War, Americans faced the problem of how to reunite the nation. Disagreements over Reconstruction led to conflicts in government and in the South. With the end of Reconstruction, African Americans in the South lost many of the rights they had gained.

Chapter 16 Focus Question

As you read through this chapter, keep this question in mind: **What were the short-term and long-term effects of the Civil War?**

Key Events

1863	President Lincoln proposes a mild Reconstruction plan.
1867	Radical Reconstruction begins.
1870	The 15th Amendment is ratified by the states.
1896	Supreme Court rules to permit separate facilities for blacks and whites.

Section 1

Rebuilding the Nation

Section 1 Focus Question

How did the government try to solve key problems facing the nation after the Civil War? To begin answering this question,
- Explore the challenges of preparing the nation for reunion.
- Learn about the services of the Freedmen's Bureau.
- Find out about Lincoln's assassination and its aftermath.

Summary

As the Civil War came to a close, the United States faced the enormous challenge of reuniting the nation. **Abraham Lincoln and Congress were divided on how to do this.** With the assassination of President Lincoln in 1865, hopes of a lenient Reconstruction policy faded.

Vocabulary Builder

If *strict* is the opposite of *lenient*, what do you think *lenient* as used in the underlined sentence means?

_____

_____

_____

Preparing for Reunion

As the Civil War ended, enormous problems faced the nation. Much of the South lay in ruins, the homeless needed food and shelter, and many in the North and the South held hard feelings toward their former foes. The process of bringing the North and the South back together again, known as Reconstruction, would occupy the nation for years to come.

Lincoln and some fellow Republicans thought a lenient Reconstruction policy would strengthen the Republican Party in the South. The Radical Republicans disagreed and claimed only a "hard," or strict, Reconstruction policy would keep the South from rising again.

Reconstruction	
Lenient	**Strict**
Lincoln: Ten Percent Plan - loyalty oath from 10% of state's voters needed to create new state government - abolition of slavery by state government - former Confederates who swear loyalty pardoned	**Radical Republicans: Wade-Davis Bill** - loyalty oath from 50% of state's voters needed before reentering Union - abolition of slavery by state government - Confederate volunteers barred from voting and holding office

✓

The Freedmen's Bureau

It was urgent to deal with the needs of the **freedmen,** enslaved people who had been freed by war, as well as other war refugees. Congress created the Freedmen's Bureau in March of 1865. The bureau's first duty was to provide emergency relief to people displaced by war.

The Freedmen's Bureau set up schools to teach freedmen to read and write, and it helped to start schools at which African Americans could extend their education. The Freedmen's Bureau also helped freedmen find jobs and settled disputes between blacks and whites. ✓

Lincoln Is Murdered

As the war drew to a close, President Lincoln hoped for a peaceful Reconstruction. But Lincoln had no chance to put his plans into practice. He was shot on April 14, 1865, by **John Wilkes Booth,** a Confederate sympathizer. Lincoln died a few hours later.

News of Lincoln's death shocked the nation. His successor as President was Andrew Johnson from Tennessee. A southern Democrat who had remained loyal to the Union, Johnson had expressed bitterness toward the Confederates. Many expected him to take a hard line on Reconstruction. ✓

Check Your Progress

1. What were two major differences between the Ten Percent Plan and the Wade-Davis Bill?

_____

_____

2. How did the Freedmen's Bureau help former slaves?

_____

_____

✓ Checkpoint

List two problems that faced the nation during Reconstruction.

_____

_____

✓ Checkpoint

What was the main purpose of the Freedmen's Bureau?

_____

_____

_____

✓ Checkpoint

Name the person who succeeded Abraham Lincoln as President.

_____

Question to Think About As you read Section 1 in your textbook and take notes, keep this section focus question in mind: **How did the government try to solve key problems facing the nation after the Civil War?**

▶ Use this chart to record key information from the section. Some of the information has been filled in to get you started.

Rebuilding a Nation	
Challenges That the Nation Faced	**Proposed Solutions**
1. How would Confederate states and sympathizers be treated?	a. Lincoln's Ten Percent Plan • loyalty oath: <u>10% of each state's voters must take oath</u> • slavery: <u>each state's government must abolish slavery</u> • former Confederates: <u>pardoned if signed loyalty oath</u>
	b. The Wade-Davis Bill • loyalty oath: • former Confederates:

2. What provisions would be made for those freed from slavery?	The Freedmen's Bureau
	a. main purpose:
	
	b. examples:
	   •
	
	   •
	
	   •

Murder of Abraham Lincoln		Vice President Becomes President	
When	April 14, 1865	Who	Andrew Johnson
How		From where	
By whom		Political party	
National reaction		Expected impact on Reconstruction	

Refer to this page to answer the Chapter 16 Focus Question on page 256.

The Battle Over Reconstruction

Section 2 Focus Question

How did disagreements over Reconstruction lead to conflict in government and in the South? To begin to answer this question,

- Learn how conflict grew between the President and Congress during Reconstruction.
- Discover the significance of the Fourteenth Amendment.
- Understand the policies of Radical Reconstruction.

Summary

As the struggle for Reconstruction continued into Johnson's presidency, there were many clashes between Congress and the President. The Radical Republicans took hold of Congress, and African Americans made strides into politics for the first time.

A Growing Conflict

Like President Lincoln, **Andrew Johnson** wanted to restore the Union quickly and easily, so he proposed a lenient plan for Reconstruction. Johnson's plan required southern states to ratify the Thirteenth Amendment, which banned slavery and forced labor. His plan also offered amnesty to most Confederates and allowed southern states to form new governments and to elect representatives to Congress.

Congress rejected Johnson's plan and appointed a committee to form a new plan for the South. The committee learned that some southern states passed **black codes**, or laws to control African Americans. In response, Congress adopted a harder line against the South. The Radical Republicans took the hardest stance. They wanted to prevent former Confederates from regaining control of southern politics and to make sure that freedmen had the right to vote. ☑

The Fourteenth Amendment

The struggle for Reconstruction was focused on the President and Congress during 1866. Congress passed the Civil Rights Act of 1866, but President Johnson vetoed it and another bill extending the Freedmen's Bureau. Congress overturned both vetoes.

Congress also drew up the Fourteenth Amendment, which declared all people born or naturalized in the United States to be citizens. It barred the states from passing laws to take away a citizen's rights. The Fourteenth Amendment also stopped states from taking away property or liberty "without due process of law." In addition, any state that stopped its adult males from voting would have its representation in Congress reduced. Despite opposition from President Johnson, the amendment was ratified in 1868. ☑

Key Events

1863	President Lincoln proposes a mild Reconstruction plan.
1867	Radical Reconstruction begins.
1870	The 15th Amendment is ratified by the states.
1896	Supreme Court rules to permit separate facilities for blacks and whites.

✓ Checkpoint

List two goals of the Radical Republicans.

_____

_____

_____

_____

✓ Checkpoint

Name two elements of the Fourteenth Amendment.

_____

_____

_____

_____

Radical Reconstruction

As the elections of 1866 approached, violence directed at African Americans erupted in southern cities. Outrage at this violence led Congress to push a stricter form of Reconstruction, called Radical Reconstruction. The Reconstruction Act of 1867 threw out the governments of all states that refused to adopt the Fourteenth Amendment. It also imposed military rule on these states. By June of 1868, all of these states had ratified the Fourteenth Amendment and written new constitutions. They also allowed African Americans to vote.

For the first time, African Americans in the South played an important role in politics, serving as sheriffs, mayors, judges, and legislators. Sixteen African Americans served in the House of Representatives and two served in the Senate. Some other accomplishments of Radical Reconstruction included public schools opening in southern states, evenly spread taxation, and property rights to women. Bridges, roads, and buildings destroyed by the war were rebuilt.

Meanwhile, the Radical Republicans **impeached** and tried to convict President Johnson in order to remove him from office. To impeach means to bring formal charges against an elected official. Johnson barely escaped removal by one vote.

Ulysses S. Grant won the presidential election for the Republicans in 1868. With the South under military rule, some 500,000 African Americans voted. Grant was a war hero and a moderate with support from many northern business owners. Radicals then began to lose their grip on the Republican Party.

Despite Democratic opposition, Congress approved the Fifteenth Amendment in 1869. It barred all states from denying the right to vote "on account of race, color, or previous condition of <u>servitude</u>."

Angry at being shut out of power, some whites resorted to violence. They formed secret societies, such as the Ku Klux Klan, to terrorize African Americans and their white allies. Congress passed laws barring the use of force against voters, but the damage had been done. In the face of threats and violence from the Klan and other groups, voting by African Americans declined. The stage was set for the end of Reconstruction. ✔

Check Your Progress

1. What were the main features of Andrew Johnson's plan for Reconstruction?

_____

_____

2. List three accomplishments of Reconstruction.

_____

_____

_____

Vocabulary Builder

Servitude comes from the Latin word *servus*, which means "slave." What do you think *servitude* means?

_____

_____

✓ Checkpoint

List two effects of the Reconstruction Act of 1867.

_____

_____

_____

_____

Question to Think About As you read Section 2 in your textbook and take notes, keep this section focus question in mind: **How did disagreements over Reconstruction lead to conflict in government and in the South?**

▶ Use these organizers to record key facts from the section. Some information has been filled in to get you started.

Reconstruction

Johnson's Plan

- issued broad amnesty to Confederates _____
- allowed southern states to organize new governments and _____

Congress

- refused to seat southern representatives
- appointed committee to _____ _____
- passed _____ of 1866, which granted citizenship to African Americans and guaranteed their civil rights

Johnson

- _____ the Civil Rights Act of 1866
- vetoed a bill that extended the life of _____

Congress

- _____ Johnson's vetoes
- passed _____
  - All people born or naturalized in the United States are citizens.
  - All citizens are guaranteed rights.
  - Citizens are promised due process of law.
  - Denying the vote to any male citizen will reduce a state's representation in Congress.

Radical Reconstruction

Actions of the Radicals

- imposed _____military rule_____ on states that rejected _____ _____
- to join the Union, states had to:
  1. _____
  2. _____
- allowed _____ to register to vote
- opened _____ in the South
- built a strong following with three key groups:
  1. _____
  2. _____
  3. _____
- spread out _____ more evenly
- gave _____ to women
- impeached _____
- passed _____
  - states could not deny the right to vote based on _____, _____, or previous condition of servitude

Responses to Radicals

- General _____ elected President in 1868
- _____ terrorized African Americans and their white allies

Refer to this page to answer the Chapter 16 Focus Question on page 256.

1863 President Lincoln proposes a mild Reconstruction plan.

1867 Radical Reconstruction begins.

1870 The 15th Amendment is ratified by the states.

1896 Supreme Court rules to permit separate facilities for blacks and whites.

✓ Checkpoint

List two reasons that Reconstruction came to an end.

_____

_____

_____

_____

Section 3 Focus Question

What were the effects of Reconstruction? To begin to answer this question,

- Understand why support for Reconstruction declined.
- Learn how African Americans lost many rights with the end of Reconstruction.
- Discover how many freedmen and whites became locked in a cycle of poverty.
- Find out how the end of Reconstruction marked a start of industrial growth in the South.

Summary

Support for Radical Republicans and their policies declined. Reconstruction came to a halt with the election of 1876. Southern African Americans gradually lost their rights and fell into a cycle of poverty. Meanwhile, the South's economy flourished.

Reconstruction's Conclusion

Support for Radical Republicans declined as Americans shifted focus from the Civil War to their own lives. Many northerners lost faith in the Republicans and their policies as the Grant presidency suffered from controversy and corruption. Meanwhile, many northerners and southerners alike were calling for the withdrawal of federal troops from the South and amnesty for former Confederates. Beginning in 1869, Democrats regained power in the South state by state. Slowly they chipped away at the rights of African Americans.

The end of Reconstruction was finalized with the election of Rutherford B. Hayes in 1876. Although he was a Republican, he vowed to end Reconstruction to avoid a challenge to his election by Democrats. Hayes removed all federal troops from the South. ✓

African Americans Lose Rights

With the end of Reconstruction, African Americans began losing their remaining political and civil rights in the South. Southern whites passed a number of laws to prevent blacks from voting. As these laws could apply to blacks and whites, they did not violate the Fifteenth Amendment. A **poll tax,** or a tax to be paid before voting, kept many blacks and poor whites from voting. Another law required voters to pass a **literacy test,** or a test to see if a person could read or write, before voting. Most southern blacks had not been educated and could not pass the test. In addition, whites whose fathers or grandfathers could vote in the South on January 1, 1867, did not have to take the test.

Southern states created laws, known as Jim Crow laws, requiring **segregation,** or enforced separation of races. In *Plessy* v. *Ferguson*, the Supreme Court ruled that law could require "separate" facilities as long as they were "equal." The "separate but equal" rule was in effect until the 1950s, but the facilities for African Americans were rarely equal. ✓

A Cycle of Poverty

At emancipation, most freedmen were very poor. Most freedmen in rural areas became sharecroppers. A **sharecropper** is a farmer who rents land and pays a share of each year's crop as rent. Sharecroppers hoped to save money and eventually buy land of their own. But weather conditions and the ups and downs of crop prices often caused sharecroppers to lose money and become locked in a cycle of debt. They would then become poorer and poorer each year.

Opportunities also dwindled for African Americans in southern cities and towns. African Americans skilled in crafts and trades found such jobs closed to them in the segregated South. Those who were educated could possibly become schoolteachers, lawyers, or preachers in the black community. However, most urban African Americans had to take whatever menial jobs they could find. ✓

Industrial Growth

During Reconstruction, the South's economy slowly began to recover. By the 1880s, new industries appeared. Agriculture was the first industry to recover, with cotton production setting new records by 1875. Farmers also started to put more land into tobacco production, and output grew.

Industries that turn raw materials into finished products, such as the textile industry, came to play an important role in the South's economy. New mills and factories also grew to use the South's natural resources, such as iron, timber, and oil. By 1900, the South was no longer dependent on "King Cotton." A "New South" based on manufacturing was emerging. ✓

Check Your Progress

1. How did the rights of African Americans change after the end of Radical Reconstruction?

_____

_____

_____

2. What led to southern industrial growth in the 1880s?

_____

_____

✓ Checkpoint

Name two ways that southern African Americans were prevented from voting.

_____

_____

Vocabulary Builder

Use the context clues in the paragraph in brackets to write a definition of the word *menial*.

_____

_____

✓ Checkpoint

List two reasons that sharecropping was not profitable.

_____

_____

✓ Checkpoint

Name three industries that contributed to the South's economic recovery.

_____

_____

_____

Question to Think About As you read Section 3 in your textbook and take notes, keep this section focus question in mind: **What were the effects of Reconstruction?**

▶ Use this organizer to record key information from the section. Some information has been filled in to get you started.

The End of Reconstruction

African Americans' Rights

- Southern states passed laws to prevent African Americans from voting. These included
  - _____
  - _____
  - grandfather clauses

- Southern states passed _____ laws, which enforced _____.

Freedmen in Poverty

- Most rural freedmen became
  _____.
  - rented land and paid with
    _____
  - dependent on _____ and crop prices

- Opportunities declined for urban African Americans.
  - skilled labor jobs closed to African Americans

Reconstruction's Conclusion

- Support for Radical Republicans declined.
- Many people called for:
  - withdrawal of troops from the South
  - _____
- Disputed Election of 1876
  - _____ vowed to end Reconstruction
  - all troops removed

Industrial Growth in the South

- Investors started or expanded industries to turn _____ into _____.
- The _____ industry came to play an important role in the southern economy.
- New mills and factories grew up to use the South's _____, _____, and _____.

Refer to this page to answer the Chapter 16 Focus Question on page 256.

Chapter 16 Assessment

Directions: Circle the letter of the correct answer.

1. The case of *Plessy* v. *Ferguson* provided the legal basis for
   A   poll taxes.   C   impeachment.
   B   sharecropping.   D   segregation.

2. Which of the following was a result of the Ku Klux Klan's campaign of violence?
   A   Andrew Johnson was impeached.
   B   Rutherford B. Hayes was elected President.
   C   The South became more industrialized.
   D   Fewer African Americans voted.

3. Slavery and forced labor were banned by the
   A   Emancipation Proclamation.
   B   Freedmen's Bureau Bill.
   C   Thirteenth Amendment.
   D   Reconstruction Act of 1867.

4. The process of bringing the North and the South together after the Civil War became known as
   A   Reconstruction.   C   Radicalization.
   B   Emancipation.   D   Bureaucratization.

Directions: Follow the steps to answer this question:

What do the differences between Johnson's plan and Radical Reconstruction say about their supporters' attitudes about the South?

Step 1: Recall information: List two policies of Johnson's plan. Then list two policies of Radical Reconstruction.

Johnson's Plan	Radical Reconstruction
• •	• •

Step 2: Compare these policies in the chart.

How Plans Differ	What Differences Suggest

Step 3: Complete the topic sentence that follows. Then write two or three more sentences that support your topic sentence.

The details of Johnson's plan and Radical Reconstruction reveal that _____

_____

_____

_____

Chapter 16 Notetaking Study Guide

Now you are ready to answer the Chapter 16 Focus Question: **What were the short-term and long-term effects of the Civil War?**

► Complete the following chart to help you answer this question. Use the notes that you took for each section.

Rebuilding a Nation	
As the Civil War ended, the nation faced enormous challenges: • much of the South lay in ruins • •	
Lincoln's Plan	**Radical Republican Plan**
Ten Percent Plan • • • 10% state voter loyalty oath	Wade-Davis Bill • • •
The first duty of the Freedmen's Bureau was to _____ _____.	
Battle Over Reconstruction	
Johnson's Plan • Southern states ratify Thirteenth Amendment • •	Radical Republican Goals • • •
Radical Reconstruction	
• _____ imposed military rule on all southern governments that did not ratify the Fourteenth Amendment. • During Radical Reconstruction, _____ played an important role in politics, and women were given _____. • Southern states opened _____ for the first time. • Legislators spread _____ more evenly and made fairer _____.	
End of Reconstruction	
As Radical Republican support died, many called for local self-government and _____. The end of Reconstruction was finalized with _____.	
Southern whites prevented African Americans from voting with techniques such as _____ and _____.	The South's economy began to _____ due to industries based on _____.

Refer to this page to answer the Unit 5 Focus Question on page 257.

Unit 5 Pulling It Together Activity

What You Have Learned

Chapter 14 With the addition of new western lands, tension over the slavery issue erupted into violence. The election of Abraham Lincoln led to seven states leaving the Union and marked the coming of the Civil War.

Chapter 15 People in the North and the South hoped for an early victory, but the Civil War went on for years. Hundreds of thousands of Americans were killed before the war ended.

Chapter 16 At the end of the Civil War, Americans faced the problem of how to reunite the nation. Disagreements over Reconstruction led to conflicts in government and in the South. With the end of Reconstruction, African Americans in the South lost many of the rights they had gained.

Think Like a Historian

Read the Unit 5 Essential Question: **How was the Civil War a political, economic, and social turning point?**

▶ Use the organizers on this page and the next to collect information to answer this question.

What political, economic, and social factors existed before the Civil War? Some of them are listed in this organizer. Review your section and chapter notes. Then complete the organizer.

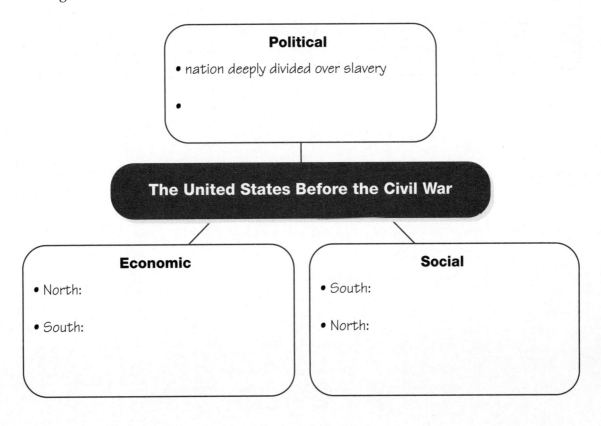

Political
- nation deeply divided over slavery
-

The United States Before the Civil War

Economic
- North:
- South:

Social
- South:
- North:

What political, economic, and social factors changed because of the Civil War? The organizer below gives you a part of the answer. Review your section and chapter notes. Then fill in the rest of the organizer.

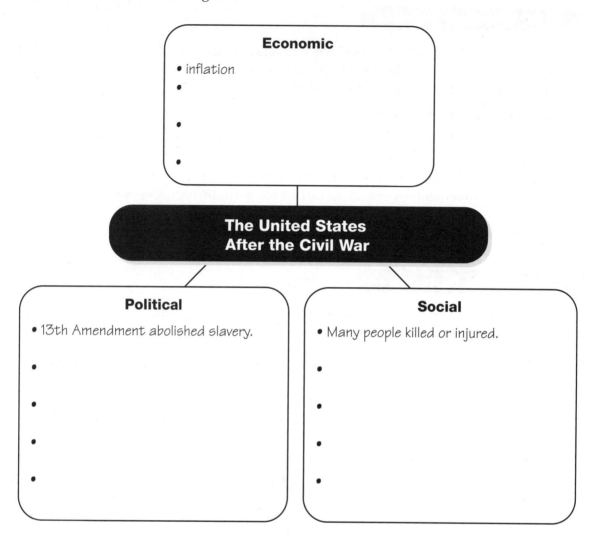

Economic
- inflation
-
-
-

The United States After the Civil War

Political
- 13th Amendment abolished slavery.
-
-
-
-

Social
- Many people killed or injured.
-
-
-

Unit 6

An Age of Industry

Chapter 17 Miners and railroad builders led to settlement of the West. Native Americans struggled to maintain their way of life. Western farmers faced many challenges.

Chapter 18 In the late 1800s, industrialization caused urban growth, altered the way business was run, and prompted reforms in education. A new wave of immigration to America occurred during this period.

Chapter 19 During the late 1800s and early 1900s, Americans organized to press for reforms in many areas of government and society.

Focus Your Learning As you study this unit and take notes, you will find the information to answer the questions below. Answering the Chapter Essential Questions will help build your answer to the Unit Essential Question.

Chapter 17 Essential Question
How did the growth of big business affect the development of the West?
(page 260)

Chapter 18 Essential Question
How did industrialization increase the speed of change?
(page 274)

Unit 6 Essential Question
How did the industrialization of the United States change the economy, society, and politics of the nation?
(page 305)

Chapter 19 Essential Question
How did society and politics change during the Progressive Era?
(page 291)

What You Will Learn

Miners and railroad builders led to settlement of the West. Native Americans struggled to maintain their way of life. Western farmers faced many challenges.

Chapter 17 Focus Question

As you read this chapter, keep this question in mind: **How did the growth of big business affect the development of the West?**

Section 1
Mining and Railroads

Section 1 Focus Question

How did mining and railroads draw people to the West? To begin answering this question,
- Find out about the boom and bust of the gold and silver rushes.
- Learn about the railroad boom.

Section 1 Summary

Americans rushed west after gold was discovered. Railroad companies helped open up the West to settlement.

Boom and Bust

After the Civil War, the western frontier stretched from the Mississippi River to the Pacific Ocean. It took in mountains, prairies, and forests. It was home to Spanish settlers and Native Americans. Settlers heading west passed over the Great Plains, which they thought were barren.

The trickle of settlers headed west became a flood when gold was discovered in California in 1849. Would-be miners spread from California to South Dakota.

In 1859, silver was found in the Sierra Nevada on land claimed by Henry Comstock. The Comstock Lode became one of the richest silver mines in the world, worth $300 million. But the money did not go to Henry Comstock. Only big mining companies had the expensive machinery required to mine the ore deep underground. Comstock sold his mining rights for just $11,000. By the 1880s, western mining had become big business.

Miners lived in boomtowns that sprang up overnight and often disappeared just as quickly. Boomtowns provided food,

---

Key Events

1867 First cattle drive on Chisholm Trail.

1887 Dawes Act breaks up Native American tribal lands.

1889 Oklahoma opens to homesteaders.

Vocabulary Builder

Based on context clues in your reading, write your own definition of a boom.

board, and equipment, all at greatly inflated prices. Women who joined the mining boom could make a good living running restaurants, laundries, and boarding houses.

Almost half of all miners were foreign-born. Foreign miners often faced hostility. For example, laws restricted Chinese miners to claims abandoned by others.

Mining towns sprouted so fast that law and order were hard to find. People formed groups of **vigilantes,** or self-appointed law keepers, to hunt down people they considered criminals and to punish people as they saw fit. Eventually, residents of western towns brought in judges and sheriffs as part of their push to become U.S. territories.

In some mining towns, all the ore was soon extracted. Mines shut down and miners moved away. Businesses failed and merchants left. Boomtowns became ghost towns. ☑

The Railroad Boom

Before 1860, the railroads stopped at the Mississippi River. The federal government offered the railroad companies **subsidies,** or grants of land and money, to extend their lines. For every mile of track they laid, railroads got ten square miles of land next to the track. Very quickly, the railroads owned over 180 million acres, an area the size of Texas. They also received federal loans.

In 1862, Leland Stanford and his partners won the right to build a railroad line eastward from Sacramento. Their company, called the Central Pacific Railroad, was to build the western portion of the **transcontinental railroad,** a railroad line that spanned the continent. At the same time, the Union Pacific Railroad was building west from Omaha. The two railroads hired thousands of workers, including native-born whites, Mexican Americans, African Americans, and immigrants from Mexico, Ireland, or China, to build each line. The work was hazardous, and the pay was low. Finally, on May 10, 1869, the lines met in Promontory, Utah.

With the transcontinental railroad in place, the West became a fixed part of the U.S. economy. Goods flowed between the East and the West, and railway stops turned into towns that grew rapidly. Eight western territories became states in the period from 1864 to 1890. ☑

Check Your Progress

1. What was the Comstock Lode?

_____

_____

2. How did railroads come to own millions of acres of land?

_____

_____

✓ **Checkpoint**

List three kinds of businesses women ran in boomtowns.

_____

_____

_____

✓ **Checkpoint**

Name the two companies that built the transcontinental railroad.

_____

_____

Question to Think About As you read Section 1 in your textbook and take notes, keep this section focus question in mind: **How did mining and railroads draw people to the West?**

▶ Use these charts to record key information from the section. Some information has been filled in to get you started.

The Discovery of Gold and Silver in the West
The Comstock Lode   • Discovered in Nevada in 1859   • Importance: one of the richest _____   • Effect: made <u>Nevada</u> a center for _____
The Boom Spreads   • Few prospectors became rich because _____   _____.   • By the 1880s, western mining had become _____.

Life in Mining Towns
 • Tent cities arose around mining camps and quickly became boomtowns.
 • Nearly half of all miners were _____.
 • Because mining towns grew so quickly, it was hard to find _____ and _____.
  So, miners formed groups of _____, who _____
  and _____.
 • As towns grew, local residents looked for more lasting forms of _____.
 • In some towns, all the ore was soon extracted, and mines _____, miners _____, businesses _____, and merchants _____.

The Railroad Boom
Aid to Railroads   • To encourage the growth of railroads, the _____ offered railroads _____, which are _____.   • Railroads also received _____.
The Transcontinental Railroad   • A transcontinental railroad is a railroad line that _____.   • In <u>1862</u>, the _____ Railroad won the right to build a line eastward from _____. The _____ Railroad would build west from _____.   • The railroads hired thousands of workers, including 10,000 _____.   • On May 10, _____, the two lines met in _____, _____.
Effects of the Railroads   • On population: _____   • Political changes: _____   _____

Refer to this page to answer the Chapter 17 Focus Question on page 273.

Native Americans Struggle to Survive

Section 2 Focus Question

What were the consequences of the conflict between the Native Americans and white settlers? To begin answering this question,

- Discover who the people of the Plains were.
- Find out about broken treaties.
- Learn about the last stand for Custer and the Sioux.
- Read about Native American efforts at resistance.
- Understand the failure of reform.

Section 2 Summary

The gold rush and the railroads meant disaster for Native Americans of the West.

People of the Plains

People of the Plains lived by gathering wild foods, by hunting, and by fishing. Some raised crops. When Europeans arrived, they introduced horses and guns to Native Americans. This allowed Native Americans to kill more game, as well as travel faster and farther. Many Plains nations followed the buffalo herds. As a result, buffalo hunting played a key role in people's survival.

In many Plains nations, women managed village life. They cared for children, prepared food, carved tools, and made clothing and **tepees**. Tepees are cone-shaped tents made of buffalo skins. Men were hunters and warriors. Often, they also led religious life. ✓

Broken Treaties

U.S. treaties promised to safeguard Native American lands. As miners and settlers pushed west, they broke the treaties. In 1851, Plains nations signed the Fort Laramie Treaty. This treaty said their lands would be protected by the United States forever if they stopped following the buffalo. No sooner had Native Americans signed the treaty than settlers moved onto their land.

In the early 1860s, new treaties forced Native Americans to give up land around Pikes Peak. Native Americans protested by attacking supply trains and settlers' homes. In response, Colonel John Chivington and 700 volunteers attacked a band of Cheyenne under army protection at Sand Creek in eastern Colorado in 1864. The Cheyenne waved a white flag, but Chivington attacked anyway. The Sand Creek Massacre helped to ignite an era of war. ✓

Key Events

1867	First cattle drive on Chisholm Trail.
1887	Dawes Act breaks up Native American tribal lands.
1889	Oklahoma opens to homesteaders.

✓ Checkpoint

Describe the roles of women and men in the Plains nations.

Women: _____

_____

Men: _____

_____

✓ Checkpoint

Name the event that helped start an era of war.

_____

✓ Checkpoint

Name two Native American leaders who resisted the reservation system.

_____

_____

Last Stand for Custer and the Sioux

Native Americans were moved to **reservations**, or land set aside for Native Americans to live on. But life on these reservations was a disaster. The poor soil of Oklahoma made farming extremely difficult. If gold was discovered on reservation land, a flood of miners would invade their land.

In June 1876, Colonel George Custer attacked a band of Sioux and Cheyenne in an attempt to force them onto a reservation. Chiefs **Sitting Bull** and Crazy Horse won this Battle of Little Bighorn, but the Sioux and Cheyennes were rounded up a winter or two later by a larger force. ✓

Other Efforts at Resistance

Under pressure, many Nez Percés agreed to go to a reservation. But Chief Joseph tried to flee to Canada rather than face this humiliation. He and his people were hunted down and finally caught near the Canadian border.

The Navajos of the Southwest resisted removal to reservations until 1864, when they were sent to the Pecos River in Arizona. The Apaches, led by Geronimo, fought until 1886, when they were sent to a reservation in Oklahoma.

In the 1880s, soldiers worried about the Ghost Dance, which Native Americans said gave them visions of returning to their old ways. In 1890, Sitting Bull was killed by Native American police sent to stop the dance. Then soldiers surrounded a group of Sioux fleeing to avoid more violence. While the Sioux were giving up their guns, a shot was fired. The army opened fire, killing nearly 200 Sioux men, women, and children. This Battle of Wounded Knee ended the Indian Wars. ✓

The Failure of Reform

Reformers criticized the government for its harsh treatment of Native American nations. Susette La Flesche told of the destruction of native culture in lectures and articles. Helen Hunt Jackson and Alice Fletcher promoted Native American rights.

Hoping to improve Native American life, Congress passed the Dawes Act in 1887. It tried to end Native Americans' wandering and turn them into farmers. The act set up schools and gave Native American men 160 acres to farm. But few Native Americans took to farming, and with the buffalo hunt gone, they remained poor. Many grew dependent on the government for food and supplies. ✓

Check Your Progress

1. What changed the western Native American way of life?

_____

_____

2. Why did the Dawes Act fail?

_____

_____

Question to Think About As you read Section 2 in your textbook and take notes, keep this section focus question in mind: **What were the consequences of the conflict between the Native Americans and white settlers?**

► Use this chart to record key information from the section. Some information has been filled in to get you started.

Native Americans in the West

People of the Plains
- For centuries, the Plains people lived by gathering wild foods, hunting, and fishing.
- The Europeans introduced _____ and _____.
- Many Plains nations began _____.

Broken Treaties
- As Americans moved west, U.S. officials tried to convince the Plains nations to stop _____ and _settle down permanently_.
- In 1851, Native American leaders signed the _____ Treaty. The U.S. government promised to _____. However, after the treaty was signed, _____.
- In 1864, _____ attacked a band of _____ at _____. The _____ helped ignite an era of war.

Native American Resistance
- Southern Plains nations were moved to reservations in Oklahoma. Life there was a disaster because _____.
- Many Sioux and Cheyennes gathered on land set aside for them in the _____ of _____. When a _____ in 1874 brought _____ to the area, _____ and _____ led attacks to keep whites out.
- In 1876, _____ tried to force Native Americans onto a reservation. He and all his men died in the Battle of _____.
- Chief Joseph led the _____ to _____. The U.S. Army _____, and Chief Joseph _____.
- After years of war, the _____ were defeated in 1864 in Arizona, and they were forced to move to a spot near the _____.
- In the late 1880s, Native Americans began performing the _____, which they believed would make their _____ and the _____ return and would cause _____ to leave the Plains. Soldiers saw this as the beginning of an _____. In a struggle, _____ was killed. Later, troops killed nearly _____ Sioux men, women, and children at the Battle of _____.

Efforts at Reform
- Congress passed the _____ Act in 1887, which gave Native American men _____ and set up _____. The measure failed because few Native Americans _____.

Refer to this page to answer the Chapter 17 Focus Question on page 273.

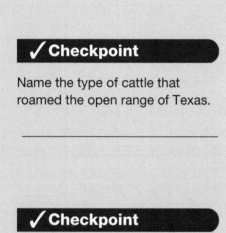

Key Events

1867 First cattle drive on Chisholm Trail.

1887 Dawes Act breaks up Native American tribal lands.

1889 Oklahoma opens to homesteaders.

✓ Checkpoint

Name the type of cattle that roamed the open range of Texas.

_____

_____

✓ Checkpoint

Name three types of clothes American cowhands borrowed from the vaqueros.

_____

_____

_____

Section 3
The Cattle Kingdom

Section 3 Focus Question
What factors led to boom and bust in the cattle industry? To begin answering this question,

- Find out about the rise of the cattle industry.
- Explore life on the trail.
- Learn about the Wild West.
- Learn why the cattle boom went bust.

Section 3 Summary

Cattle towns and the life of the cowhand on the trail helped create the legend of the Wild West. But the boom was short-lived.

The Rise of the Cattle Industry
Wild longhorn cattle had roamed the **open range,** or unfenced land, of Texas for years. When the railroads crossed the Plains in the 1860s, Texas ranchers at last saw a way to get these cattle to market. They could drive the cattle to the railroad towns, where they would be shipped by rail to slaughterhouses and then sold in the East.

These **cattle drives** meant herding and moving cattle over very long distances. Texan cattle were driven as far as 1,000 miles to rail lines. ✓

Life on the Trail
Cowhands who drove the cattle had to have nerves of steel. They had to control thousands of cows and keep the herds together through rivers, fires, and droughts. Cowhands earned less than a dollar a day.

The first cowhands were the Spanish and Mexican **vaqueros** (vah KAYR os). This Spanish word for cowhand or cowboy comes from *vaca*, the Spanish word for "cow." Americans learned how to ride, rope, and brand from vaqueros, and they adopted their spurs, chaps, and cowboy hats. About one third of all cowhands on the trails were Mexican, while many others were African American or white Civil War veterans. ✓

The Wild West
Railroad towns were the final destination of the cattle drives. Abilene, Kansas, was the first big **cow town,** or settlement at the end of a cattle trail. It was founded in 1867 by Joseph McCoy. He figured that after months on the trail, cowhands would spend their hard-earned money on a bath, a meal, a soft bed, and some fun. McCoy founded Abilene where the Chisholm Trail met the Kansas Pacific Railroad.

Cow towns were filled with unruly men. They were places of violence, adventure, and opportunity. There were saloons, dance halls, drinking, gambling, and gun fighting. These helped spread the myth of the Wild West.

William "Buffalo Bill" Cody did his best to promote the fantasy of the Wild West. He started his traveling Wild West show in 1883. It featured gun-slinging cowboys, Native Americans on horseback, and reenactments of battles from the Indian Wars. But even as Cody's show packed in eastern audiences, the West was being steadily <u>transformed</u>. It was changing into a place where Native Americans were forced onto reservations and big companies ran mining and ranching. Even cow towns were quieting down, a result of settlers and ministers who wanted peaceful communities. ☑

Boom and Bust in the Cattle Kingdom

The cattle boom lasted from the 1860s to the 1880s. At its height, ranchers could buy a calf for $5 and sell a grown steer for $60. Investors created huge cattle companies. One covered almost 800 square miles in three states. The ranching region, dominated by the cattle industry and its ranches, trails, and cow towns, became known as the **cattle kingdom**.

By the mid-1880s, more than 7 million cattle were on the open range. It was more than the land could support. Two years of hard weather in 1886 and 1887 killed millions of cattle. A depression in eastern cities lowered demand for beef, and farmers fenced in the open range. As railroads expanded and their lines moved closer to ranches, long cattle drives ended. All these factors led to the end of the cattle boom. ☑

Check Your Progress

1. Why did ranchers have to drive their cattle so far?

_____

_____

2. How was Buffalo Bill's Wild West show out of date?

_____

_____

_____

_____

Reread the bracketed paragraph. Based on context clues in the paragraph, write a definition of the word *transform*.

_____

_____

✓ Checkpoint

List three ways the West was changing in the 1880s.

_____

_____

_____

_____

_____

_____

✓ Checkpoint

List three factors that hurt the cattle industry.

_____

_____

_____

Question to Think About As you read Section 3 in your textbook and take notes, keep this section focus question in mind: **What factors led to boom and bust in the cattle industry?**

▶ Use this chart to record key information from the section. Some information has been filled in to get you started.

The Cattle Kingdom: Causes and Effects	
Causes	**Effects**
1. Railroads swept across the Plains.	1. Texas ranchers began driving cattle to the rail lines to get cattle to distant _____. Cowhands followed trails such as the _____ Trail and the _____ Trail.
2. Cowhands who drove cattle needed to unwind at the end of the trail, where they faced dangers such as panicked animals, stampedes, fires, and thieves.	2. _____ sprang up along rail lines. Here, _____, _____, _____, and _____ served the cowhands.
3. Cowhands borrowed much from early _____ and _____ _____.	3. Cowhands learned how to ride, rope, and brand. They wore spurs and chaps and broad-brimmed hats.
4. _____ created a traveling _____ show.	4. The myth of the Wild West as a place of violence, adventure, and endless opportunity was spread.
5. _Profits_ rose. New breeds of cattle had fewer _____ and more _____ than longhorns.	5. The cattle industry booms. Backers from the East and Europe invested _____ in _____.
6. In the 1880s, there was bad weather, economic depression, lower demand for beef, and competition with sheep. Farmers fenced in the open range.	6. The cattle industry _____.
7. Railroads expanded and their lines moved closer to the ranches.	7. Large _roundups_ and long _____ vanished. The cattle boom _____.

Refer to this page to answer the Chapter 17 Focus Question on page 273.

Section 4

Farming in the West

Section 4 Focus Question

How did farmers on the Plains struggle to make a living? To begin answering this question,

- Find out about the impact of homesteading.
- Discover the hardships of life on the Plains.
- Learn about the last rush for land.
- Read about how farmers organized politically.

Section 4 Summary

Homesteading boomed in the West after the Civil War, but times were not easy for farmers.

Homesteading

During the Civil War, Congress passed the Homestead Act of 1862. It offered 160 acres on the Great Plains to those who agreed to live on the land and farm it for five years. This gave thousands of poor people the chance to be **homesteaders,** settlers who acquired free land offered by the government.

But only one third of homesteaders on the Great Plains lasted the required five years. On the dry Plains, 160 acres was not enough land to support a family.

The railroads also promoted farming on the Plains. The railroads owned millions of acres thanks to land grants. They recruited people to farm them because more farms meant more shipping for the railroads. ✓

A Hard Life on the Plains

Life on the Great Plains was not easy. Water was scarce, and crops were hard to grow. The soil of the Plains was fertile, but the tough **sod,** a thick layer of roots of grasses tangled with soil, had to be removed to expose clear soil for planting. Plains farmers were called **sodbusters** for this reason.

New farming methods helped Plains farmers. They used steel plows, which were stronger and lighter than other plows. New drills allowed them to bury seeds deep in the ground, where there was moisture. They used both windmills to pump water that lay hundreds of feet below ground and barbed wire to keep cattle from trampling their crops. Whole families, including young children, worked long days on the farm to keep it going.

Thousands of African Americans, many former slaves, also settled on the Plains. By the 1880s, 70,000 African Americans had settled in Kansas. They were known as Exodusters because they believed they were like the Jews who fled slavery in Egypt, a biblical story told in the book of Exodus.

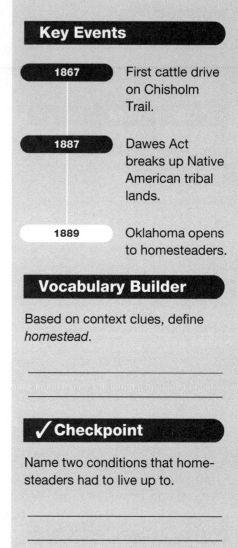

Key Events

1867 First cattle drive on Chisholm Trail.

1887 Dawes Act breaks up Native American tribal lands.

1889 Oklahoma opens to homesteaders.

Vocabulary Builder

Based on context clues, define *homestead*.

_____

_____

✓ Checkpoint

Name two conditions that homesteaders had to live up to.

_____

_____

✓ Checkpoint

List two things that made farming the Plains so difficult.

_____

_____

✓ Checkpoint

How much land was up for grabs in the Oklahoma Land Rush?

_____

✓ Checkpoint

Name two things that Populists wanted.

_____

_____

_____

_____

In the Spanish Southwest, the Spanish-speaking farmers and shepherds who had lived in the region for centuries were overrun by American settlers and immigrants from Mexico brought in to build railroad lines. ✓

A Last Rush for Land

By the late 1880s, free western land was finally running out. In 1889, nearly 100,000 people gathered at a line near present-day Oklahoma City to claim some of the two million acres of free land being offered in what was once Indian Territory. A few people, known as **sooners,** had already sneaked onto the land, and they came out of hiding to claim it. By 1890, the United States no longer had free land to give. ✓

Farmers Organize

As in mining and ranching, farming had a few big organizations that did well, while small farmers scraped by. Overproduction drove down prices. Small farmers borrowed money to expand or to buy new equipment. When prices for their crops fell, the farmers could not pay off the loans, and they lost their land.

Many farmers living in poverty and isolation formed **granges,** groups of farmers who met for lectures, sewing bees, and other events. In 1867, local granges joined to form the National Grange. In the 1870s and 1880s, National Grange members were demanding the same low rates from railroads and grain warehouses that big farmers received. They elected state officials who backed their views. The Farmers' Alliance was organized in the 1870s to set up **farm cooperatives**. These were groups of farmers who pooled their money to make large purchases of tools, seed, and other supplies at a discount.

In 1892, unhappy farmers joined labor unions to form the Populist Party. They pushed for social reforms like public ownership of railroads and warehouses to control rates, an income tax to replace property taxes, and an eight-hour workday. Populists also wanted the government to back the dollar with silver as well as gold. They hoped this would bring on **inflation,** or a general rise in prices, raising crop prices.

In the presidential election of 1896, Populists backed **William Jennings Bryan,** a Democrat who supported the silver plan. But Republican gold-alone backer William McKinley won, and Populism faded away. ✓

Check Your Progress

1. Why did railroads support farming on the Plains?

_____

_____

2. What did the National Grange demand?

_____

_____

Question to Think About As you read Section 4 in your textbook and take notes, keep this question in mind: **How did farmers on the Plains struggle to make a living?**

► Use this chart to record key information from the section.

Farming in the West	
Homestead Act of 1862	• Offered _160_ acres to anyone who resided on the land for five years • Thousands became homesteaders, which were _____ _____.
Railroads	• To the railroads, more farms meant more _____. • So railroads gave away _____ _____.
New Farming Methods	• _Steel plows_ that could break through sod • _____ to bury seed • _____ to harvest crops • _____ to beat off the hard coverings of grain
Farm Families	• Role of men: _____ • Role of children: _____ • Role of women: _____ _____
Exodusters	• Thousands of _____ came to the Plains. • They were known as Exodusters because _____ _____.
Spanish-speaking Farmers	• Many had been there since before _____. • Mexican immigrants arrived with the coming of the _____. • Large landowners were known as _____.
Sooners	• The federal government opened up what was once _____ in _____ to homesteaders in April 1889. • A few people known as sooners _____.
Farmers Organize	• Granges were groups of farmers who met for lectures, sewing bees, and other events. In 1867, local granges _____ _____. • Grangers demanded _____ _____ . • Farm cooperatives were groups of farmers who pooled their money to _____. • _Unhappy farmers_ joined with _____ to form the Populist Party, which pushed for _____.

Refer to this page to answer the Chapter 17 Focus Question on page 273.

Chapter 17 Assessment

Directions: Circle the letter of the correct answer.

1. Which of the following was true of miners in the late 1800s?
    - **A** Most worked for big mining companies.
    - **B** Most received government subsidies.
    - **C** Almost half were foreign-born.
    - **D** Almost half became wealthy.

2. What was the goal of the Dawes Act?
    - **A** to protect Native Americans' way of life
    - **B** to turn Native Americans into farmers
    - **C** to prohibit settlers from trespassing on Native American lands
    - **D** to offer employment opportunities to Native Americans

3. Which did *not* cause the end of the cattle kingdom?
    - **A** two years of bad weather
    - **B** extension of railroad lines into Texas
    - **C** oversupply of cattle
    - **D** an economic depression

4. Why did Populist farmers want inflation?
    - **A** to increase demand for crops
    - **B** to lower equipment prices
    - **C** to hurt big farmers
    - **D** to raise crop prices

Directions: Follow the steps to answer this question:

What was the main issue that led to the outbreak of the Indian Wars?

Step 1: Recall information: In the chart, recall the issues behind the events leading up to the Indian Wars.

Fort Laramie Treaty	Sand Creek Massacre
• Provision for Native Americans: _____ _____ • In return, the U.S. wanted: _____ _____ • What happened: _____ _____	• Events leading up to massacre: _____ _____ • What happened: _____ • Result: _____ _____

Step 2: Decide: What was the basic conflict between the U.S. government and Native Americans? _____

Step 3: Complete the topic sentence that follows. Then write two or three more sentences that support your topic sentence.

The Indian Wars were caused by a conflict over _____

_____

_____

_____

_____

Now you are ready to answer the Chapter 17 Focus Question: **How did the growth of big business affect the development of the West?**

▶ Complete the following organizers to help you answer this question. Use the notes that you took for each section.

Mining and Railroads	Effects on Native Americans
Gold and silver rushes • People raced to the West to mine. • By the 1880s, big businesses had taken over mining.	**Gold discoveries** • Led miners onto traditional Native American lands • Conflict erupted
Railroads laid tracks to mines and boomtowns. Effects: • • Western population grew rapidly.	**Railroad expansion and the buffalo** Railroads had buffalo killed to • • Effect:
	Westward settlement • Native Americans were forced onto _____, or areas set aside for them to live.

The Influence of Big Business on the West

Cattle Kingdoms	Farming in the West
Effect of railroads: •	**Railroads promoted farming by** •
Reasons the cattle industry boomed: • •	**Big farmers versus small farmers:** • Big farms tended to do well, while many small farms struggled.
Reasons the cattle boom ended: • • •	**Farm groups pushed for silver standard** • Why farmers wanted this: • Why banks and businesses opposed:
Reason cattle drives ended: •	• Result:

Refer to this page to answer the Unit 6 Focus Question on page 305.

Chapter 18

Industry and Urban Growth (1865–1915)

What You Will Learn

In the late 1800s, industrialization caused urban growth, altered the way business was run, and prompted reforms in education. A new wave of immigration into America occurred during this period.

Chapter 18 Focus Question

As you read this chapter, keep this question in mind: **How did industrialization increase the speed of change?**

Section 1

A New Industrial Revolution

Section 1 Focus Question

What conditions spurred the growth of industry? To begin answering this question,
- Find out why industry boomed.
- Learn about inventors and inventions.
- Explore a transportation revolution of the late 1800s.

Section 1 Summary

After the Civil War, the United States experienced rapid industrial growth. Westward expansion, government policy, and new technology helped the nation become an industrial power.

Why Industry Boomed

As the nation expanded westward, industry grew. Enormous deposits of coal, iron, lead, and copper were now within reach. Government policy also helped to spur growth by giving generous land grants to railroads and businesses and by placing high tariffs on imports. Tariffs helped American industry by raising the price of foreign goods.

New technology also spurred industrial growth. Inventors developed the Bessemer process, a method to make stronger steel at a low cost. Steel replaced iron as the basic building material of cities and industry.

The oil industry developed refining methods to turn crude oil into lubricants for machines. "Black gold," as oil was called, later became gasoline to power engines and cars.

Railroads fueled the new Industrial Revolution. Trains transported goods and people to the West and raw materials to the

Key Events

1869 Knights of Labor, a major labor union, is formed.

1889 Jane Addams founds Hull House to help city poor.

1892 Ellis Island opens as major entry station for European immigrants.

1913 Henry Ford sets up assembly line to mass produce automobiles.

East. Big rail lines sought ways to limit competition and keep prices high. Many small farmers became angry over high rail rates to transport their goods, and many joined the Granger and Populist movements. ✓

Inventors and Inventions

In the late 1800s, Americans created a flood of new inventions. In 1897, more government **patents,** or documents giving someone the sole right to make and sell an invention, were issued than in the ten years before the Civil War.

At **Thomas Edison**'s "invention factory," scientists produced such inventions as the light bulb and motion picture camera. In 1882, Edison opened the nation's first electrical power plant. Soon plants all over the country provided power to homes, streetcars, and factories.

Inventions that improved communication prompted growth in business. Telegraphs transmitted messages from Europe more quickly. **Alexander Graham Bell**'s invention of the telephone in 1876 helped speed up the pace of business. The patent for the telephone was the most valuable patent ever issued. The typewriter improved office efficiency. African Americans such as Jan Matzeliger also contributed to the flood of inventions. ✓

A Transportation Revolution

Technology revolutionized transportation. The invention of the automobile ushered in an era of faster and faster transportation. Only 8,000 Americans owned automobiles in 1900. Then, an American manufacturer, **Henry Ford**, made the automobile affordable to millions by perfecting a system to mass produce cars. Ford introduced the **assembly line,** a manufacturing method in which a product is put together as it moves along a belt.

Another transportation revolution was taking place at this time. In 1903, **Wilbur and Orville Wright**'s gas-powered airplane took flight. <u>By 1920, airplanes began to alter the world by making travel quicker and easier.</u> ✓

Check Your Progress

1. How did government policy influence industrial growth?

_____

_____

_____

2. How did Henry Ford make the automobile affordable to millions of people?

_____

_____

✓ Checkpoint

List three factors that influenced industrial growth.

_____

_____

_____

✓ Checkpoint

Name three inventions that helped businesses to grow.

_____

_____

_____

Vocabulary Builder

Reread the underlined sentence. Think about how airplanes affected travel. Based on this information, what do you think the word *alter* means?

_____

✓ Checkpoint

List two inventions that made transportation faster.

_____

_____

Question to Think About As you read Section 1 in your textbook and take notes, keep this question in mind: **What conditions spurred the growth of industry?**

► Use these charts to record key information from the section.

Factors Leading to the Industrial Boom	
Factor	**Effect**
Westward expansion	• provided access to vast deposits of _coal_, _____, _____, and _____ • Pacific Northwest furnished _____ for _____
Government policies	• Congress gave _____ and other _____ to _____ and other _____. • kept _____ high, which made _____ expensive
Railroads	• Trains carried _____ and _____ west.

Inventions That Spurred Industry, Business, and Transportation	
Invention	**Impact**
Bessemer process	• allowed people to make stronger _steel_ at a lower cost • Steel replaced iron as the basic building material of industry.
Oil refining methods	Crude oil refined into and _____
Electrical power plant	• _____ opened first one in _____ in _____ • allowed people to use inventions such as the _____ , the _____ , and the _____
Telegraph	• improved communication for _____
Underwater telegraph	• sped up communications with _____
Telephone	• invented by _____ in _____ • device that carried _____
Typewriter	• made office work _____ and _____
Automobile	• ushered in an era of _____ and _____ transportation
Assembly line	• introduced by _____ in _____ to mass produce _____
Gas-powered airplane	• first tested by _____ in _____ • later used by the _____ during _____

Refer to this page to answer the Chapter 18 Focus Question on page 290.

Big Business and Organized Labor

Section 2 Focus Question

How did big business change the workplace and give rise to labor unions? To begin answering this question,

- Learn about new ways of doing business.
- Find out about growth in "big business."
- Explore changes in the workplace.
- Learn how workers organized.

Section 2 Summary

Without government regulation, big business grew out of control. A few owners accumulated incredible wealth while factory workers tried to form unions to improve poor working conditions.

New Ways of Doing Business

Entrepreneurs (ahn treh preh NYOORZ) led business expansion. An **entrepreneur** is someone who sets up a business to make a profit. These entrepreneurs needed capital, or money, to expand. To raise this capital, Americans adopted new ways of organizing business. Many businesses became **corporations,** or businesses owned by many investors. Corporations raise large amounts of capital by selling stock, or shares in a business. Stockholders receive a share of profits and pick directors to run the company.

Banks lent money to corporations and industries to spur faster growth. One banker, J. P. Morgan, became the most powerful force in the American economy by gaining control of key industries such as railroads and steel mills. ✓

Growth of Big Business

Congress seldom made laws to regulate business practices. This encouraged the growth of what came to be known as "big business." Entrepreneurs formed giant corporations and monopolies. A **monopoly** is a company that controls all or nearly all business in a particular industry.

Andrew Carnegie's companies controlled every step of making steel. The Carnegie Steel Company produced more steel than all the mills of England combined. **John D. Rockefeller** ended competition in the oil industry by creating the Standard Oil Trust. A **trust** is a group of corporations run by a single board of directors. He bought out his competitors and slashed prices to drive his rivals out of business. By 1900, trusts dominated many of the nation's industries.

Some Americans criticized big business practices as threats to **free enterprise,** the system in which privately owned businesses compete freely. Others praised big business for expanding the economy, creating jobs, and lowering prices.

Key Events

1869	Knights of Labor, a major labor union, is formed.
1889	Jane Addams founds Hull House to help city poor.
1892	Ellis Island opens as major entry station for European immigrants.
1913	Henry Ford sets up assembly line to mass produce automobiles.

✓ Checkpoint

Name two industries that J. P. Morgan controlled.

_____

_____

Vocabulary Builder

Mono comes from the Greek word meaning "one." *Poly* comes from the Greek word meaning "many." What do you think the word *monopoly* means?

_____

_____

_____

Name the people who held monopolies in the steel and oil industries.

_____

_____

List three reasons used to justify the poor conditions of factories.

_____

_____

_____

Name three issues that workers organized to change.

_____

_____

_____

A new philosophy called Social Darwinism supported the trend toward trusts. Scientist Charles Darwin had said that, in nature, forms of life survived if they could adapt to change better than others. Social Darwinists applied this idea of "survival of the fittest" to human affairs. When applied to business, the "fittest" meant the entrepreneurs who beat out competition. ✓

Changes in the Workplace

Industry attracted millions of workers who toiled in dangerous conditions for low wages. Even young children worked in hazardous jobs. Employers did not have to pay employees if they were injured at work. Factory owners justified the harsh conditions by referring to Social Darwinism. The bad conditions of factories, they held, were necessary to cut costs, to increase production, and to ensure survival of the business.

An accident at a New York garment factory called attention to the dangers workers faced. In 1911, nearly 150 people, most of them young women, died in a fire at the Triangle Shirtwaist Factory. As a result, New York and other states began to pass laws protecting factory workers. ✓

Workers Organize

Although striking was illegal, workers attempted to organize against unsafe working conditions, low wages, and long hours. In 1869, workers in Philadelphia formed a union called the Knights of Labor. The union admitted both skilled and unskilled workers.

However, violent labor disputes undercut the union's successes. The American Federation of Labor replaced the Knights of Labor as the country's leading union. It admitted only skilled workers, who were difficult to replace. The AFL relied on collective bargaining to achieve its goals. In collective bargaining, unions negotiate with management for workers as a group.

In 1893, the nation plunged into an economic depression. Many business owners fired workers and cut wages. A wave of violent strikes swept the country. Federal troops were used to end some strikes, which often resulted in more violence. Most Americans sided with owners because they saw unions as radical and violent. ✓

Check Your Progress

1. What were the two differing views of big business?

_____

_____

_____

_____

2. Why did most Americans not favor unions?

_____

_____

Question to Think About As you read Section 2 in your textbook and take notes, keep this question in mind: **How did big business change the workplace and give rise to labor unions?**

▶ Use these organizers to record key information from the section.

Big Business	
Corporation	• businesses owned by _investors_ • raised capital by _____ • run by a _____ • limited risk for _____ • shareholders received _____
Trust	• consisted of a group of corporations run by a _____ • by 1900, dominated _____ • used _____ to justify efforts to limit competition
Monopoly	a company that controls _____
Banks	• huge loans helped industry _____ • J. Pierpont Morgan: most powerful force in _____
Andrew Carnegie	• controlled _steel industry_ • according to Carnegie's Gospel of Wealth philosophy, _____ _____
John D. Rockefeller	• used profits from investing in an _____ to buy other oil companies • formed _____ , which _____ _____
Debate over big business	Arguments for: Arguments against: • _lowered the price of goods_ • _____ • _____ • _____ • _____

Workplace Conditions and Labor Unions	
Workplace	**Labor Unions**
Hours: _long_ Pay: _____ Conditions: _____ Employers not required to _____ _____ for workplace injuries	Goals: safer working conditions, _____ , _____ Early unions: • _____ • _____

Refer to this page to answer the Chapter 18 Focus Question on page 290.

Cities Grow and Change

Key Events

1869 Knights of Labor, a major labor union, is formed.

1889 Jane Addams founds Hull House to help city poor.

1892 Ellis Island opens as major entry station for European immigrants.

1913 Henry Ford sets up assembly line to mass produce automobiles.

Section 3 Focus Question
What were the causes and effects of the rapid growth of cities? To begin answering this question,
- Learn about the rapid growth of cities.
- Find out about problems of urban life.
- Explore the excitement of city life.

Section 3 Summary

The Industrial Revolution reshaped American cities. Millions of people moved to cities in search of jobs. Cities and reformers battled the problems caused by such rapid growth while American urban dwellers discovered the excitement of city life.

Rapid Growth of Cities
The rate of urbanization during the late 1800s was astonishing. **Urbanization** is the rapid growth of city populations. Cities attracted industry, and industry attracted people. Farmers, immigrants, and African Americans from the South all migrated to cities in search of jobs and excitement.

Cities near waterways drew industry because they provided easy transport for goods. New York City and San Francisco had excellent ocean harbors. Chicago rose on the shores of Lake Michigan. Technology also helped cities grow. Electric streetcars and subways made it easier for people to get around. Growing urban populations and public transportation gave rise to suburbs, or living areas on the outskirts of a city. Cities began to expand upward as well as outward. By 1900, skyscrapers towered over city streets.

Living patterns in cities also changed. The poor crowded into the old downtown sections of cities while the middle class lived in outlying row houses or apartments. The wealthy built fine homes on the cities' outskirts. ✓

Problems of Urban Life
Rapid urbanization created many problems. Fire was a constant threat to tightly packed neighborhoods. In downtown slums, the poor lived in crowded tenements. **Tenements** are buildings divided into many tiny apartments. Many apartments had no windows, heat, or indoor plumbing. As many as 10 people might live in a single room. Sanitation was perhaps the worst problem. Streets in slums were strewn with garbage, and outbreaks of cholera and other diseases were common. Babies ran the greatest risk. In one Chicago slum, half of all babies died before the age of one.

✓ Checkpoint

List three effects of urbanization.

_____

_____

_____

To improve urban life, cities set up police, fire, and sanitation departments. They paved streets and installed street lights while public health officials waged war on disease. Religious groups served the poor. Some set up hospitals and clinics, or places where people could receive medical treatment for little or no money, for people who could not afford a doctor. Others provided food and shelter to the homeless. Reformers like **Jane Addams** worked hard for poor city dwellers. She opened Hull House, one of America's first settlement houses. **Settlement houses** were centers offering help to the urban poor. Volunteers taught immigrants English and provided entertainment for young people and nurseries for children of working mothers. Addams and other settlement house leaders also pressured state legislative leaders to outlaw child labor. ☑

The Excitement of City Life

Despite hardships, cities offered attractions and excitement not available in the country. Newcomers were awed by electric lights, elevated railroads, and tall buildings that seemed to pierce the clouds.

Downtown shopping areas attracted hordes of people. Merchants developed a new type of store, the department store. These stores offered many types of goods in separate sections of the same store.

Long hours on the job made people value their free time. This strict division between work and play led to a new interest in leisure. To meet this need, cities provided a wealth of entertainment. Attractions included museums, orchestras, theatres, and circuses. City parks, zoos, and gardens allowed city dwellers to take a break from crowded city streets.

After the Civil War, professional sports teams began to spring up in cities. The most popular professional sport was baseball. Football gained popularity in American colleges. In 1891, James Naismith invented basketball. It quickly became a favorite winter sport. ☑

Check Your Progress

1. How did living patterns change in cities during the Industrial Revolution?

_____

_____

2. What services did settlement houses provide?

_____

_____

✓ **Checkpoint**

Name three problems created by urbanization.

_____

_____

_____

Vocabulary Builder

The text states that people found leisure in a city's entertainment. Based on the context clues, write a definition of the word *leisure*.

_____

✓ **Checkpoint**

List three attractions found in cities.

_____

_____

_____

Question to Think About As you read Section 3 in your textbook and take notes, keep this section focus question in mind: **What were the causes and effects of the rapid growth of cities?**

▶ Use these charts to record key information from the section.

Growth of Cities		
Urbanization	**Expanding Cities**	**Living Patterns**
Urbanization: the rapid growth of _____ _____	Public transportation: _subways_ , _____ ,	Lived in oldest sections at cities' centers: _____
Why people were attracted to cities: _____ _____	Public transportation gave rise to new living areas called _____. _____ helped speed up the growth of suburbs.	Lived away from city centers in row houses and apartments: _middle class_
To meet the needs of shoppers, merchants developed _____, which _____ _____.	New types of buildings: _____ _____	Lived in fine homes on outskirts of cities: _____
Kinds of leisure activities cities offered: _____ _____ _____ _____		

Urban Problems and Solutions	
Problems of Urban Life	**Solutions to Problems**
Fires endangered _____ _____. Tenement life was _____. Slum streets were _____ with _____. Disease was caused by _____ _____.	Provided by cities: • _____ • _____ • _____ Provided by religious groups: • _____ • _____ Provided by reformers: • _____ _____

Refer to this page to answer the Chapter 18 Focus Question on page 290.

Section 4

The New Immigrants

Section 4 Focus Question

How was the experience of immigrants both positive and negative? To begin answering this question,

- Learn why immigrants sought a fresh start in America.
- Explore how immigrants started a new life.
- Find out how immigrants became American.
- Learn about a new wave of nativism.

Section 4 Summary

Starting in the late 1800s, millions of immigrants came to America seeking freedom and opportunities. Immigrant labor was essential to the economy. Many immigrants wanted to assimilate to American culture.

A Fresh Start

The industrial age changed the population. Some 25 million immigrants entered the country between 1865 and 1915. Some people emigrated from their homelands in search of employment or to escape political and religious persecution. Jews fled Russia after becoming the targets of government-sponsored pogroms, or violent attacks against Jews. A revolution in Mexico in 1910 pushed many political refugees into the United States.

The wave of "new immigrants" in the late 1800s came from southern and eastern Europe, as well as from Asia and the Pacific. Few of the new immigrants understood English or had experience living in a democracy. ✔

Starting a New Life

The passage to America was miserable. Most immigrants came to the United States crammed into the steerage of ships. **Steerage** consisted of large compartments that usually held cattle. After 1892, most people from Europe went through the receiving center on Ellis Island in New York. Asian immigrants entered through Angel Island in San Francisco Bay. About two thirds of immigrants settled in cities. Many immigrants settled near other people from the same country in ethnic neighborhoods. Here, they could speak their native languages and observe familiar holidays. ✔

Becoming American

Many newcomers to America clung to their traditional ways while trying to assimilate. **Assimilation** is the process of becoming part of another culture. Surrounded by English-speakers at school, children of immigrants learned the language more quickly and were more easily assimilated.

Key Events

1869 Knights of Labor, a major labor union, is formed.

1889 Jane Addams founds Hull House to help city poor.

1892 Ellis Island opens as major entry station for European immigrants.

1913 Henry Ford sets up assembly line to mass produce automobiles.

✓ Checkpoint

List three regions from where the "new immigrants" came.

_____

_____

_____

✓ Checkpoint

About what fraction of immigrants settled in cities?

_____

Vocabulary Strategy

Assimilate means "to make similar." If you assimilate, you become similar to something. How does the immigrant experience reflect this meaning?

_____

_____

_____

Immigrant labor was essential to the new economy. Immigrants worked in steel mills, meat-packing plants, and garment factories. They helped build skyscrapers, railroads, subways, and bridges. With hard work and saving, immigrants slowly advanced economically.

Some Notable Immigrants

Immigrant	Place of Origin	Important Contribution
Alexander Graham Bell	Scotland	invented the telephone
Andrew Carnegie	Scotland	steel magnate; donated money to charities
Samuel Goldwyn & Louis Mayer	Eastern Europe	helped establish the motion picture industry in California
Arturo Toscanini	Italy	orchestra conductor
Leo Baekeland	Belgium	invented plastic

✓

✓ **Checkpoint**

Which immigrant invented the telephone?

_____

_____

✓ **Checkpoint**

List two restrictions placed on immigration.

_____

_____

_____

_____

A New Wave of Nativism

As immigration increased, a new wave of nativists sought to preserve the country for native-born Americans. Nativists charged that foreigners would never assimilate and also that they took jobs from Americans. Many Americans associated immigrants with anarchy, crime, and violence. An **anarchist** is a person who opposes all forms of government.

In the West, nativist feelings against Chinese drove many Chinese immigrants from mining camps and cities. The Chinese Exclusion Act of 1882 excluded, or kept out, Chinese laborers from the United States until it was repealed in 1943. In 1917, Congress passed a law that barred those who could not read their own language from immigrating to the United States. ✓

Check Your Progress

1. Why was it easier for children of immigrants to assimilate?

_____

_____

2. Why did nativists oppose immigration?

_____

_____

Question to Think About As you read Section 4 in your textbook and take notes, keep this section focus question in mind: **How was the experience of immigrants both positive and negative?**

▶ Fill in these charts to record key information from the section.

Reasons for Migration
• __Employment opportunities__
• _____ persecution: Russian Jews were the victims of _____.
• Political unrest: Many Mexicans were driven out of their homes because of _____.
• Most "new immigrants" came from southern Europe and _____. Smaller numbers came from _____ and the Pacific.

Starting New Lives
• Most immigrants were received at _____ and _____.
• About two thirds of immigrants settled in _____.
• Living in ethnic neighborhoods, immigrants could speak _____ and celebrate _____.

Becoming American
• Assimilation is the process of _____.
• Children of immigrants assimilated more quickly because _____ _____ _____.
• Immigrants worked in _____ , _____ , _____ , and _____. They helped build _____ , _____ , _____ , and _____.
• Many immigrants advanced economically by _____
• Immigrants who made major contributions: _____ , _____ , _____ , _____ , _____.

A New Wave of Nativism
• Nativists sought to _____.
• Nativists charged that immigrants took away jobs from _____.
• Many Americans associated immigrants with _____ , _____ , and _____.
• The Chinese Exclusion Act of 1882 _____
• In 1917, Congress passed a law that denied entry to immigrants who could not _____

Refer to this page to answer the Chapter 18 Focus Question on page 290.

Key Events

1869	Knights of Labor, a major labor union, is formed.
1889	Jane Addams founds Hull House to help city poor.
1892	Ellis Island opens as major entry station for European immigrants.
1913	Henry Ford sets up assembly line to mass produce automobiles.

Vocabulary Strategy

Reread the underlined sentence. What meaning would be lost if the word *compulsory* were replaced with the word *voluntary*?

_____

_____

_____

✓ Checkpoint

Which states were reluctant to pass compulsory education laws?

_____

Section 5 Focus Question

What were the causes and effects of an expanded educational system? To begin answering this question,

- Learn about American education.
- Find out about new American writers.
- Explore the newspaper boom.

Section 5 Summary

Public education expanded during the economic boom. Compulsory education eventually became commonplace in all states. With better education, Americans took more interest in reading. Newspapers vied for readers' attention with sensational headlines and colorful features.

Educating Americans

Before 1870, fewer than half of all American children went to school. Addressing the need for an educated workforce for the nation's growing industry, states improved public schools. In 1852, Massachusetts passed the first compulsory education law. **Compulsory education** is the requirement that children attend school up to a certain age. Southern states were more reluctant to pass compulsory education laws than states in the North or West. But by 1918, compulsory education became the norm in all states.

By 1900, there were 6,000 high schools in the country. Higher education also expanded. Private colleges for men and women opened, and states built universities that offered free or low-cost education.

Education for adults also improved. Wealthy people such as Andrew Carnegie gave money to build public libraries. These made speakers as well as books and magazines available to adults. The Chautauqua (shuh TAWK wuh) Society in New York, which began as a summer school for Bible teachers, was opened to the public. Middle class men and women of all ages turned out to hear lectures on a variety of subjects. ✔

New American Writers

As education became available to more people, reading habits changed. Americans began to read more books and magazines. In the 1880s, a new crop of American writers appeared. Many were **realists**, writers who try to show life as it is. Stephen Crane wrote about the hardships of city slums. Californian Jack London wrote about miners and sailors on the West Coast who put their lives at risk. Kate Chopin shocked readers by writing about an unhappily married woman. Paul Laurence Dunbar was the first African American to make a living as a writer.

Mark Twain, the pen name of Samuel Clemens, was the most popular writer of the time. Twain made his stories, such as *Huckleberry Finn*, realistic by capturing the speech patterns of southerners living and working along the Mississippi River. Today, many critics consider *Huckleberry Finn* to be one of the greatest American novels. ✔

A Newspaper Boom

The number of American newspapers increased dramatically in the late 1800s. By 1900, half of the newspapers in the world were printed in the United States.

The spread of education was one cause of growth in the newspaper industry. As more Americans could read, they bought more newspapers and magazines. Urbanization was another reason for the newspaper boom. In small towns, news spread by word of mouth, but people in cities depended on newspapers to stay informed.

Immigrant **Joseph Pulitzer** created the first modern, mass-circulation newspaper. In 1883, he purchased the *New York World* and cut the price of the newspaper to make it more affordable.

Pulitzer added crowd-pleasing features to his newspaper, including color comics. The Yellow Kid, a tough but sweet slum boy, became the first popular American comic strip character. The *New York World* also became known for its sensational headlines. As a result, readership of the *New York World* skyrocketed, and other newspapers tried to follow suit.

Because of the Yellow Kid, critics of the *New York World* coined the term **yellow journalism** to describe the sensational reporting style of the *New York World* and other papers. ✔

Check Your Progress

1. Why did education become such an important issue in the late 1880s?

_____

_____

2. What caused the newspaper boom?

_____

_____

_____

✔ **Checkpoint**

List three well-known writers of the time.

_____

_____

_____

✔ **Checkpoint**

Name three ways in which Joseph Pulitzer changed the newspaper industry.

_____

_____

_____

Question to Think About As you read Section 5 in your textbook and take notes, keep this section focus question in mind: **What were the causes and effects of an expanded educational system?**

▶ Use these organizers to record key information from the section.

Education and Culture
Better-Educated Americans

- States improved public schools because _____.
- States in the _____ were more reluctant to pass compulsory education laws than states in the _____ and _____. Still, by _____ every state required children to attend school.
- Elementary school students learned reading, _____, and _____.
- _____ offered free or low-cost higher education.
- Wealthy individuals funded the building of _____ in cities and towns.
- The Chautauqua Society offered _____ and later began _____.

Americans Read More Books and Magazines		A Newspaper Boom

Americans Read More Books and Magazines

What or Who People Read	Description or Accomplishment
Many bestsellers	low-priced paperbacks that told tales of the "Wild West" or "rags-to-riches" stories
Realists	
Stephen Crane	
Jack London	wrote about the lives of miners and sailors
Kate Chopin	
Paul Dunbar	
Mark Twain	

A Newspaper Boom

By 1900, half the newspapers in the world were printed in the United States.

Causes:
- spread of education
- _____

New York World
- first modern _____ newspaper
- created by _____, who cut _____ so people could _____ the paper
- known for _____ and _____
- term used to describe its reporting style: _____

Refer to this page to answer the Chapter 18 Focus Question on page 290.

Chapter 18 Assessment

Directions: Circle the letter of the correct answer.

1. Which of the following created a trust in the oil industry?
   A J. P. Morgan
   B John D. Rockefeller
   C Andrew Carnegie
   D Joseph Pulitzer

2. Westward expansion was important to industrial growth because
   A it provided new land on which to build factories.
   B it created the need for more automobiles.
   C it made raw materials readily available.
   D it eased overcrowding in urban areas.

3. The sensational reporting style of the *New York World* and other newspapers became known as
   A yellow journalism.
   B trustbusting.
   C Chautauqua journalism.
   D realism.

4. Which of the following was *not* a result of urbanization?
   A rise of the newspaper industry
   B building of skyscrapers
   C overcrowding in cities
   D rise in the price of oil

Directions: Follow the steps to complete this task:

Decide whether the changes to cities were positive or negative.

Step 1: Recall information: In the chart, list ways rapid urbanization changed cities and the way people lived in them.

Changes to Cities	Effect on City Dwellers

Step 2: Analyze effects: which were positive? Which were negative?

_____

_____

Step 3: Explore consequences: Complete the topic sentence that follows. Then write two or three more sentences that support your topic sentence.

The rapid growth of cities led to _____

_____

_____

_____

Chapter 18 Notetaking Study Guide

Now you are ready to answer the Chapter 18 Focus Question: **How did industrialization increase the speed of change?**

▶ Fill in the following organizer to help you answer this question.

Industrial Growth

Caused by:
- Westward expansion: Industries gained access to natural resources, including
  _____, _____, _____, _____, and _____.
- Government policies: Congress gave _____ and other subsidies
  to _____ and other businesses. The government also kept high
  _____ on imports, making foreign goods _____.
- Technology: The _____ process made stronger _____ at a lower cost.
  _____ was increasingly used to fuel machines and became a valuable resource.
- Improvements in transportation: _____ carried people and goods
  to the West and raw materials to eastern _____.

Furthered by Inventions:
- light bulb
- _____
- _____

- electric power plant
- _____
- _____

Supported by Labor from Immigration:
- The "new immigrants" came from _____
  _____.
- Many immigrants came to America in search of _____. Others wanted to escape
  religious persecution or _____ in their home countries.
- Many immigrants tried to maintain familiar traditions while trying to _____
  to American culture.
- Immigrants worked in _____, _____, _____, and
  _____. They built _____,
  _____, _____, and _____.

The Growth of Cities	The Rise of Big Business	Improved Educational System
Problems of cities • poor sanitation • _____ • _____ Attractions and leisure activities: • department stores • _____ • _____ • _____	• Role of corporations and trusts: _____ _____ _____ • Conditions of factory work:_____ _____ _____ • Labor unions were formed to: _____ _____	• Why education was needed: _____ _____ _____ • Better educated Americans took more interest in reading. This spurred a boom in _____.

Refer to this page to answer the Unit 6 Focus Question on page 305.

Chapter 19

Political Reform and the Progressive Era (1870–1920)

What You Will Learn

During the late 1800s and early 1900s, Americans organized in support of several different kinds of reform.

Chapter 19 Focus Question

As you read through this chapter, keep this question in mind: **How did society and politics change during the Progressive Era?**

Section 1

The Gilded Age and Progressive Reform

Section 1 Focus Question

How did reformers try to end government corruption and limit the influence of big business? To begin answering this question,
- Learn about reform during the Gilded Age.
- Find out about the Progressives' political reforms.
- Learn about the muckrakers.

Section 1 Summary

The Progressives supported various reforms aimed at ending government corruption and limiting the influence of big business.

Reform in the Gilded Age

The period after the Civil War was called the <u>Gilded</u> Age. It was a time of rapid economic growth. It was also a time of serious problems in society. One problem was the spoils system, which is the rewarding of political supporters with government jobs, a practice that started during Andrew Jackson's presidency. Many believed the spoils system encouraged corruption.

Support for reforming the spoils system grew when President James Garfield was assassinated by a disappointed office seeker. The Pendleton Act (1883) created the Civil Service Commission. The **civil service** is a system that includes most government jobs, except elected positions, judges, and soldiers. Jobseekers were to be hired on merit instead of their political connections.

During the late 1800s, big businesses often bribed members of Congress to get favorable laws passed. The Constitution gave the federal government the power to regulate interstate commerce, or trade that crossed state lines. The Interstate Commerce Act (1887) prohibited rebates. It also set up the Interstate Commerce Com-

Vocabulary Builder

Gilded means "coated with a thin layer of gold paint." How was this appropriate for describing America after the Civil War?

_____

_____

mission to regulate railroads. The Sherman Antitrust Act (1890) was supposed to prohibit businesses from using trusts to destroy competition, but it was hard to enforce. Instead the law was mainly used to limit the power of labor unions.

Corruption was a serious problem in city governments. Politicians called bosses demanded bribes from businesses that wanted work from the city. Immigrants often supported political bosses in exchange for favors. ✓

Progressives and Political Reform

The Progressive movement aimed to stop corruption and promote the public interest, or the good of all. The Wisconsin Idea was a set of reforms of state government. They included getting rid of political bosses and using commissions to solve problems. One important reform was the **primary**, or election in which voters, rather than party leaders, choose their party's candidate for an election.

There were other important political reforms to give more power to voters. One was the **recall**, a process by which people may vote to remove an elected official from office. Another reform was the **initiative**, a process that allows voters to put a bill before a state legislature. A third political reform was the **referendum**, a way for people to vote directly on a proposed law. Many reformers supported the Sixteenth and Seventeenth amendments. The Sixteenth Amendment (1913) gave Congress the power to pass a federal income tax. The Seventeenth Amendment (1913) required the direct election of U.S. senators by the people instead of state legislatures. ✓

The Muckrakers

The press played an important role in exposing corruption. **Muckraker** became a term for a crusading journalist.

Muckrakers	Exposed
Ida Tarbell	unfair business practices
Jacob Riis	city slums
Upton Sinclair	meatpacking industry

Check Your Progress

1. What was the practice of rewarding political supporters with government jobs?

_____

2. What were the two constitutional amendments supported by Progressive reformers, and what did each amendment do?

_____

_____

Question to Think About As you read Section 1 in your textbook and take notes, keep this section focus question in mind: **How did reformers try to end government corruption and limit the influence of big business?**

▶ Use this chart to record key information from the section. Some information has been filled in to get you started.

The Gilded Age and Progressive Reform
Reform in the Gilded Age

Two Political Concerns of the Gilded Age
- The wealthy were making themselves rich at the _public's expense_.
- There was widespread _____ in government.

Reforming the Spoils System
- The spoils system _____ political supporters with _____.
- In 1883, the _____ created the _____, which filled jobs on the basis of merit.

Controlling Big Business
- In 1887, the Interstate Commerce Act forbade _____ and set up the _____ to oversee railroads.
- Although difficult to enforce, the Sherman Antitrust Act of 1890 was designed to _____.

Corruption: A Serious Problem in City Government
- Politicians called _____ controlled work locally and demanded _____ from businesses.

Progressives and Political Reform

The Progressive Movement
- The _____ Idea was a set of Progressive reforms proposed by Governor _Robert La Follette_. These reforms included the creation of _____, made up of experts, to solve problems.
- Some states instituted reforms to put more power in the hands of _____. These included the recall, the _____, and the _____.

Constitutional Amendments
- The Sixteenth Amendment gave Congress the power to _____.
- The _____ (1913) required the direct election of U.S. senators.

Muckrakers

- Muckraker became a term for a _____.
- Muckrakers played an important role in exposing _____ and other problems.
- Three well known muckrakers were _____, _____, and _____.

Refer to this page to answer the Chapter 19 Focus Question on page 304.

Section 2 Focus Question

How did the Progressive Presidents extend reforms? To begin answering this question,

- Learn about Theodore Roosevelt, the first Progressive President.
- Find out about Roosevelt's Square Deal.
- Explore Taft and Wilson's accomplishments.

Section 2 Summary

The Progressive Presidents were Theodore Roosevelt, William Howard Taft, and Woodrow Wilson. New areas of reform included conservation of natural resources, consumer protection laws, and banking reform.

The First Progressive President

Theodore Roosevelt was the first Progressive President. A former war hero and governor, Vice President Roosevelt took office after the assassination of President McKinley.

Roosevelt was a **trustbuster,** a person who worked to destroy monopolies and trusts. He distinguished between "good trusts" that were fair and efficient, or acted in a way that minimized waste, and "bad trusts" that cheated the public and took advantage of workers. Roosevelt argued that the government must control bad trusts or break them up. In a case involving the Northern Securities trust, the Supreme Court used the Sherman Antitrust Act to break up a trust because it limited free trade. It was the first time the act had been used to break up trusts, not unions. Roosevelt used the decision to push for the breakup of other trusts. Roosevelt also forced mine owners to negotiate with striking coal miners. ✔

The Square Deal

The Square Deal, Roosevelt's <u>platform</u> during the presidential election of 1904, promised that everyone, not just big businesses, would have the same opportunity to succeed. It helped him win an overwhelming victory.

Roosevelt was a strong advocate of **conservation,** or the protection of natural resources. He created the U.S. Forest Service to manage the nation's woodlands. He also created **national parks,** or natural areas protected and managed by the federal government.

Roosevelt also supported reforms to protect consumers from unsafe food and drugs. He was influenced by Upton Sinclair's book *The Jungle,* which exposed the meatpacking industry's

---

Key Events

1890 Sherman Antitrust Act bars businesses from limiting competition.

1909 Reformers found the NAACP to promote rights of African Americans.

1920 Nineteenth Amendment guarantees women the right to vote.

✓ Checkpoint

Why was the Northern Securities court case important?

_____

_____

_____

Vocabulary Builder

Platform in this context means a set of policies that a politician or political party proposes.

unhealthy practices. Roosevelt made public a report exposing unhealthy conditions in meatpacking plants. As a result, Congress was forced to pass a law allowing closer inspections of meatpacking houses. Muckrakers also exposed companies for making false claims about medicines and adding harmful chemicals to food. In response, Congress passed the Pure Food and Drug Act, which required food and drug makers to list all ingredients on packages. ✓

Taft and Wilson

Roosevelt supported **William Howard Taft** for President in the election of 1908. Taft won easily. His approach differed from Roosevelt's. He was quiet and more cautious. Nevertheless, Taft supported many Progressive causes. He broke up more trusts than Roosevelt. He also favored a graduated income tax, approved new mine safety rules, and started to regulate child labor. However, Taft lost Progressive support by raising tariffs, which raised the price of consumer goods, and modifying some of Roosevelt's conservation policies.

In the election of 1912, Roosevelt ran against Taft for the Republican presidential nomination. Republican leaders sided with Taft and made him the nominee. Roosevelt then formed the Progressive, or Bull Moose, Party so he could run. Meanwhile, the Democrats nominated **Woodrow Wilson** as their candidate. A cautious reformer, Wilson was often criticized for being too rigid, or strict, and uncompromising. Wilson won the election of 1912 because Taft and Roosevelt split the Republican vote.

President Wilson created a program called the New Freedom. It sought to restore free competition among American corporations. The Federal Trade Commission (1914) helped restore competition by investigating and then stopping companies that used unfair trade practices. The Clayton Antitrust Act (1914) banned other business practices that harmed free competition. It also stopped antitrust laws from being used against labor unions. The Federal Reserve Act (1913) set up a system of federal banks and gave the government the power to change interest rates and control the money supply. ✓

Check Your Progress

1. How did President Roosevelt promote conservation?

_____

_____

2. Why did Woodrow Wilson win the election of 1912?

_____

_____

✓ Checkpoint

List two causes that Roosevelt supported.

_____

_____

✓ Checkpoint

List three parts of Wilson's New Freedom program.

_____

_____

_____

Question to Think About As you read Section 2 and take notes, keep this section focus question in mind: **How did the Progressive Presidents extend reforms?**

▶ Use this chart to record key information from the section. Some information has been filled in to get you started.

The Progressive Presidents
Theodore Roosevelt

- war hero, former governor, Vice President
- became President in 1901 after _____
- believed the government had to <u>control</u> or _____ bad trusts
- launched lawsuits against _____
- Northern Securities: first time that _____
  _____
- 1902 Pennsylvania coal miners strike: first time that _____
  _____
- During the 1904 presidential campaign, Roosevelt promised Americans a Square Deal. By this, he meant _____.
- Conservation is _____.
- In 1905, Roosevelt created _____ to conserve the nation's wood- lands. He had _____ of land set aside for _____.
- Roosevelt supported consumer protection reforms. The _____ required food and drug makers to list all ingredients on packages.

William Howard Taft

- Roosevelt's secretary of war, won presidency in 1908 with Roosevelt's support
- Unlike Roosevelt, Taft was _____.
- supported Progressive reforms: graduated _____, new rules for mines, government workers, child labor
- lost Progressive support because he _____ and modified _____ policies
- Roosevelt broke with Taft and started the _____.
- In the presidential election of 1912, Roosevelt and Taft _____, so Woodrow Wilson won.

Woodrow Wilson

- had served as a university president and a _____
- was known as a brilliant scholar and a <u>cautious reformer</u>
- His program to restore free competition was called _____. It included the creation of the Federal Trade Commission (1914), the _____ , and the _____.

Refer to this page to answer the Chapter 19 Focus Question on page 304.

The Rights of Women

Section 3 Focus Question

How did women gain new rights? To begin answering this question,

- Learn about the women's suffrage movement.
- Find out about new opportunities for women.
- Learn about the temperance movement.

Section 3 Summary

After decades of effort, the movement for women's rights won the right to vote. New educational and career opportunities also opened for women.

Women Win the Vote

The Seneca Falls Convention of 1848 marked the start of an organized women's rights movement in the United States. After the Civil War, Elizabeth Cady Stanton and Susan B. Anthony organized the National Woman Suffrage Association. It pushed for a constitutional amendment to give women the right to vote.

In most states, leading politicians opposed women's suffrage. Still, the suffrage movement had its first successes in the late 1800s in four western states: Wyoming, Utah, Colorado, and Idaho. By giving women the right to vote, at least in local or state elections, these states recognized the contributions of pioneer women to the settlement of the West.

In the early 1900s, support for women's suffrage grew. One reason was that more women were beginning to work outside the home. Although women were paid less than men, wages gave them some power. Women wage earners believed that they deserved to be able to vote on laws that affected them.

A new generation of leaders took over after the deaths of Stanton and Anthony. **Carrie Chapman Catt** created a strategy for winning suffrage state by state. The plan <u>coordinated</u> the work of **suffragists,** or people who worked for women's right to vote, across the nation.

One by one, states in the West and Midwest began giving women the right to vote. Still, in some of these states, women could not vote in federal elections. More women joined the call for a federal amendment to allow them to vote in all elections. **Alice Paul** and other suffragists met with President Wilson on the matter. Wilson pledged his support for a constitutional amendment. The ratification of the Nineteenth Amendment gave women the right to vote in federal elections. ✓

Key Events

1890	Sherman Antitrust Act bars businesses from limiting competition.
1909	Reformers found the NAACP to promote rights of African Americans.
1920	Nineteenth Amendment guarantees women the right to vote.

Vocabulary Builder

A synonym is a word that is similar in meaning to another word. Which of the following words is a synonym for *coordinated*: organized, ruined, or finished?

_____

✓ Checkpoint

Name the change that increased support for women's suffrage in the early 1900s.

_____

_____

_____

New Opportunities for Women

Women also struggled for access to better jobs and educational opportunities. Starting with the first granting of a Ph.D. to a woman in the late 1870s, increasing numbers of women earned advanced degrees at graduate schools. By 1900, there were thousands of women doctors and lawyers.

During the late 1800s, many middle-class women joined clubs. The earliest clubs were formed to help women improve their minds by, for instance, meeting to discuss books. Women's clubs gradually became more concerned with improving society. They raised money for libraries, schools, and parks, and pushed for laws to protect women and children, to ensure pure food and drugs, and to win the right to vote.

African American women also formed clubs. The National Association of Colored Women sought to end segregation and violence against African Americans. Its members also supported the women's suffrage movement.

Many women became reformers during the Progressive Era. Florence Kelley fought for safe working conditions and organized a boycott of manufacturers who used child labor. In time, she was made the chief factory inspector for Illinois. Some women entered the field of social work, helping poor city-dwellers. ✓

The Crusade Against Alcohol

Women took a leading role in the temperance movement. The campaign against alcohol gained strength in the late 1800s.

The Woman's Christian Temperance Union was founded in 1874. Its president **Frances Willard** encouraged women to also support women's suffrage. Carry Nation was a more radical crusader for temperance. She gained publicity for the movement by attacking saloons, or places that sold liquor, with a hatchet.

After years of effort, temperance leaders persuaded Congress to pass the Eighteenth Amendment in 1917. The amendment enforced **prohibition,** a ban on the sale and consumption of alcohol. The amendment was ratified in 1919. ✓

Check Your Progress

1. Where did women first gain the right to vote? Why?

_____

_____

_____

2. How did the concerns of women's clubs change over time?

_____

_____

_____

✓ **Checkpoint**

List three fields women entered.

_____

_____

_____

✓ **Checkpoint**

Name two leaders of the temperance movement.

_____

_____

Section 3 Notetaking Study Guide

Question to Think About As you read Section 3 in your textbook and take notes, keep this section focus question in mind: **How did women gain new rights?**

▶ Use these charts to record key information from the section. Some information has been filled in to get you started.

Women's Suffrage	
Seneca Falls Convention (1848)	Importance: Marked the start of _an organized women's rights movement_ in the United States
National Woman Suffrage Association	Goal: Passage of _____ _____ Founders: _____, _____
Western states	By the late 1800s, women won voting rights in _____, _____, _____, and _____.
Reasons for increased support for women's suffrage	• More women _____ and demanded _____. • New leaders: _____, _____ • A detailed strategy to _____
Nineteenth Amendment	Ratified: _1920_ What it did: _____

New Opportunities

Higher Education
• Women began to earn _advanced degrees_.
Clubs and Reform
• At first women's clubs focused on advancing _____.
• The focus of many switched to social reforms:
  1. raised money for _____, _____, and _____.
  2. pressed for laws to _____, to _____, and to _____.
• Racial barriers forced _____ to form their own clubs.

Temperance	
Temperance	Campaign against _____
Woman's Christian Temperance Union	Goal: _____ Led by: _____, _____
Eighteenth Amendment	Ratified: _____ What it did: _____

Refer to this page to answer the Chapter 19 Focus Question on page 304.

Struggles for Justice

Key Events

1890 Sherman Antitrust Act bars businesses from limiting competition.

1909 Reformers found the NAACP to promote rights of African Americans.

1920 Nineteenth Amendment guarantees women the right to vote.

Vocabulary Builder

Reread the underlined sentence. One meaning of *discriminate* is "to treat differently." In the context of this sentence, does *discrimination* mean African Americans were treated better or worse than white Americans?

_____

_____

✓ Checkpoint

Name Ida B. Wells' main goal.

_____

_____

Section 4 Focus Question

What challenges faced minority groups? To begin answering this question,

- Learn how African Americans responded to discrimination.
- Explore how Mexican Americans lived.
- Find out about challenges faced by Asian Americans.
- Learn about prejudice facing religious minorities.

Section 4 Summary

African Americans and other groups faced discrimination with little support from Progressives.

African Americans

After the Civil War, African Americans faced discrimination in the North and South. They were denied housing in white areas and confined to the lowest paying jobs. Most white Progressives ignored the problems of African Americans. And President Wilson segregated workers in the federal civil service.

Booker T. Washington, a former slave, educator, and early leader in the struggle for African American rights, urged African Americans to learn trades and seek to move up gradually in society. Eventually, they would have the money and power to demand equality.

Washington founded the Tuskegee Institute in Alabama. The school trained African Americans in the industrial and agricultural skills they needed to get better jobs. Many white businessmen supported Washington's moderate approach.

The scholar **W.E.B. Du Bois** was the first African American to get a Ph.D. from Harvard. He had a different approach than Booker T. Washington. He urged blacks to fight discrimination rather than yield to it. Du Bois helped found the National Association for the Advancement of Colored People, or NAACP, to fight for equal rights.

The African American woman Ida B. Wells tried to stop **lynching,** or the murder by a mob, of African Americans. She encouraged African Americans to protest lynching and to boycott white-owned stores and segregated streetcars.

Despite many obstacles, some African Americans succeeded. The scientist George Washington Carver discovered new uses for peanuts and other crops. Sarah Walker started a successful line of hair care products for African American women that made her the first American woman to make $1 million. Many black-owned businesses also served the African American community, and churches helped train new leaders. ✓

Mexican Americans

By 1900, about half a million Mexican Americans lived in the United States. They also faced legal segregation. Around 1910, famine and the Mexican Revolution forced many more Mexicans to settle in the United States. They first moved to the Southwest, then to the Midwest and Rocky Mountain region. Mexican Americans were confined to unskilled jobs and were paid less than Anglo workers.

Many Mexican Americans lived in barrios, or ethnic Mexican American neighborhoods, which helped preserve their language and culture. The largest barrio was in Los Angeles. In the barrio, mutualistas, or mutual aid groups, were formed. They helped provide insurance and legal advice and collected money to care for the sick and needy. ✔

Asian Americans

When the Chinese Exclusion Act of 1882 stopped Chinese immigration to the United States, employers on the West Coast hired workers from other parts of Asia, mainly the Philippines and Japan.

Many Japanese settled in California where they became successful farmers. When San Francisco forced all Asians into segregated schools, Japan protested the insult. Unions and other groups pressured President Roosevelt to limit Japanese immigration. A "Gentlemen's Agreement" was made. Japan agreed to stop workers from moving to the United States. In exchange, the American government allowed Japanese women whose husbands had already migrated to the United States to join them. ✔

Religious Minorities

Religious minorities also faced prejudice. Nativist groups worked to restrict immigration of Roman Catholics and Jews. Both native-born and immigrant Catholics and Jews faced discrimination in housing and jobs.

To avoid prejudice in schools, Catholics set up church-sponsored schools. Jewish Americans founded the Anti-Defamation League to promote understanding and fight prejudice. (Defamation is the spreading of false or hateful information.) ✔

Check Your Progress

1. How did Washington's and Du Bois's views on ending discrimination differ?

_____

_____

_____

2. What was one way that Mexican Americans preserved their language and culture?

_____

_____

✓ Checkpoint

Name three ways mutualistas helped residents of barrios.

_____

_____

_____

✓ Checkpoint

List the terms of the "Gentlemen's Agreement" between Japan and the United States.

_____

_____

_____

✓ Checkpoint

List two religious minorities that faced discrimination.

_____

_____

Section 4 Notetaking Study Guide

Question to Think About As you read Section 4 in your textbook and take notes, keep this section focus question in mind: **What challenges faced minority groups?**

▶ Use this chart to record key information from the section. Some information has been filled in to get you started.

Struggles for Justice

African Americans

- Booker T. Washington founded the _____. He advised African Americans to _learn trades_ and move up gradually in society.

- W.E.B. Du Bois helped found the _____. He urged African Americans to _____.

- _____ fought against lynching, or _____.

Mexican Americans

- Before 1900, about _half a million_ Mexican Americans lived in the United States. Like _____, they faced legal _____.
- In 1910, _____ and _____ swept Mexico. As a result, thousands of Mexicans fled into the United States.
- Mexican Americans created barrios, or _____.
- Mexican immigrants and Mexican Americans formed _____, or mutual aid groups. Members pooled money to pay for _____ and _____. They also collected money for the sick and needy.

Asian Americans

- More than _____ Japanese entered the United States in the early 1900s.
- Most first went to _____ to work on _____.
- In 1906, the city of _____ forced Asian students to attend separate _____.
- This led to a compromise called the _____ between the United States and Japan. Japan would stop any more _____ from going to the United States. The United States, in exchange, allowed _____.

Religious Minorities

- _____ groups worked to restrict immigration. Even _____ and _____ who were not immigrants faced discrimination in _____ and _____.
- American Catholics set up _____ schools.
- American Jews set up the _____, which worked to fight _____, or prejudice against Jews.

Refer to this page to answer the Chapter 19 Focus Question on page 304.

Directions: Circle the letter of the correct answer.

1. Which did President Theodore Roosevelt strongly support?
   A women's rights   C banking reform
   B conservation   D African American rights

2. Women first won voting rights in several states in the
   A Northeast.   C South.
   B Midwest.   D West.

3. Which reformer urged African Americans to fight discrimination?
   A Upton Sinclair   C W.E.B. Du Bois
   B Carry Nation   D Booker T. Washington

Directions: Follow the steps to answer this question.

How did the reforms of the Wisconsin Idea help to achieve its goals?

Step 1: Recall information: What was the Wisconsin Idea and its goals?

The Wisconsin Idea	
Description	
Goals	• •

Step 2: Describe these reforms associated with the Wisconsin Idea.

The Wisconsin Idea Reforms	
Reform	**Description**
Primary	
Initiative	
Recall	
Referendum	

Step 3: Complete the topic sentence that follows. Then write two or three more sentences that support your topic sentence.

The Wisconsin Idea reforms _____

_____

_____

_____

_____

_____

_____

Chapter 19 Notetaking Study Guide

Now you are ready to answer the Chapter 19 Focus Question: **How did society and politics change during the Progressive Era?**

► Complete the following chart to help you answer this question. Use the notes that you took for each section.

Change in the Progressive Era

The Gilded Age and Progressive Reform

- _____, or dishonesty in _government_, was widespread.
- Critics said a key part of the problem was the _____.

Efforts to Control Big Business	Political Reforms
• _____	• Wisconsin Idea _____
• Interstate Commerce Commission	• _____
• _____	• _____

Progressive Presidents

Theodore Roosevelt
- In 1904, he campaigned on the promise of a _____ for all Americans.
- He also pressed for _____, or the protection of natural _resources_. He had thousands of acres set aside to become _____.

William H. Taft	Woodrow Wilson
• reputation: _____	• reputation: _____
• Despite strong Progressive policy record, he lost Progressive support.	• Goal of New Freedom program: _____ _____

Rights of Women

Two significant suffragist leaders: _____ and _____.	The _____ guaranteed women the right to vote.

Struggles for Justice

Booker T. Washington	W.E.B. Du Bois
• founded: _____	• helped found: _____
• believed: _____ _____	• believed: _____ _____

Mexican Americans	Asian Americans
• Barrio: _____ _____	• Gentlemen's Agreement: _____ _____

Two religious minorities who faced discrimination: _____ and _____

Refer to this page to answer the Unit 6 Focus Question on page 305.

Unit 6 Pulling It Together Activity

What You Have Learned

Chapter 17 Miners and railroad builders led to settlement of the West. Native Americans struggled to maintain their way of life. Western farmers faced many challenges.

Chapter 18 In the late 1800s, industrialization caused urban growth, altered the way business was run, and prompted reforms in education. A new wave of immigration to America occurred during this period.

Chapter 19 During the late 1800s and early 1900s, Americans organized to press for reforms in many areas of government and society.

Think Like a Historian

Read the Unit 6 Essential Question: **How did the industrialization of the United States change the economy, society, and politics of the nation?**

▶ Use the organizers on this page and the next to collect information to answer this question.

What were some developments made during the industrialization of the United States? Some of them are listed in this chart. Review your section and chapter notes. Then complete the chart.

Growth of U.S. Industry		
Inventions	**Transportation**	**Other Industries**
• phonograph • camera • • • •	• • •	• cattle • • •

What aspects of the industrialization of the United States caused changes in territorial expansion, growth of cities, and the Progressive movement and labor unions? The organizer below gives you a part of the answer. Review your section and chapter notes. Then fill in the rest of the organizer.

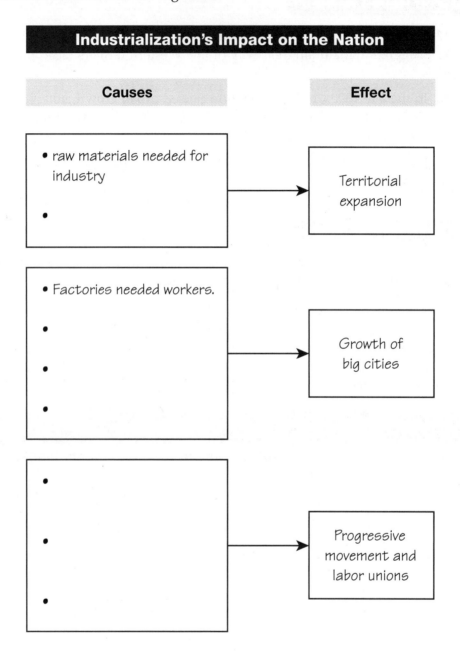

Industrialization's Impact on the Nation

Causes

Effect

- raw materials needed for industry
-

→ Territorial expansion

- Factories needed workers.
-
-
-

→ Growth of big cities

-
-
-

→ Progressive movement and labor unions

A New Role in the World

What You Will Learn

Chapter 20 By the late 1800s, the United States was taking a larger role in world affairs. The nation acquired new territories in the Pacific and strengthened its trade ties with Asia. The Spanish-American War led to increased involvement in Latin America.

Chapter 21 In 1914, a war broke out in Europe. Although the United States at first remained neutral, it eventually joined the war. The conflict, which we now call World War I, had important effects both in the United States and in the rest of the world.

Chapter 22 The decade following World War I marked dramatic changes for the United States. Republicans in charge of the government returned the country to pre-war isolationism and supported big business. Cultural changes affecting the lives and values of Americans sparked conflicts and tensions.

Focus Your Learning As you study this unit and take notes, you will find the information to answer the questions below. Answering the Chapter Essential Questions will help build your answer to the Unit Essential Question.

Chapter 20 Essential Question
How did the United States demonstrate its growing interest in the Pacific and in Latin America? (page 308)

Unit 7 Essential Question
How did a more powerful United States expand its role in the world? (page 347)

Chapter 21 Essential Question
What were the causes and effects of World War I?
(page 319)

Chapter 22 Essential Question
How did the nation react to change in the 1920s?
(page 333)

The United States Looks Overseas

(1853–1915)

What You Will Learn

By the late 1800s, the United States acquired new territories in the Pacific and strengthened its trade ties with Asia. The Spanish-American War led to increased involvement in Latin America.

Chapter 20 Focus Question

As you read this chapter, keep this question in mind: **How did the United States demonstrate its growing interest in the Pacific and in Latin America?**

Section 1

Eyes on the Pacific

Section 1 Focus Question

How did the United States acquire new territory and expand trade in the Asia-Pacific region? To begin answering this question,

- Learn about trade with Japan and the purchase of Alaska.
- Understand the country's expansionist mood.
- Learn how the U.S. gained footholds in the Pacific region.
- Find out about interventions in China.

Section 1 Summary

With its financial and military might, and the support of many U.S. leaders, the United States expands its trade, its territory, and its influence in Asia, the Pacific, and Latin America.

The United States Looks Overseas

In the mid-1800s, the United States began to take on new challenges, establishing new trading partners and acquiring new land. Since about 1600, Japan's doors had been closed to foreign trade. In 1853, Commodore **Matthew C. Perry** sailed U.S. warships into Tokyo Bay. He called on the Japanese to reopen foreign trade. The Japanese were awed by U.S. power and realized they had a lot to gain from trade. The next year, they signed a trade treaty with the United States.

In 1867, Russia was looking to sell its colony of Alaska. U.S. Secretary of State William Seward believed buying Alaska was a way to open trade in Asia and the Pacific. He paid $7.2 million for the territory, or about 2 cents an acre. Many Americans called the purchase "Seward's Folly," because they saw Alaska as a frozen wasteland. They changed their tune when gold was discovered there. ✓

Key Events

1893	American planters stage a revolt in Hawaii.
1898	United States wins the Spanish-American War.
1904	United States begins to build the Panama Canal.

✓ Checkpoint

Name two people who helped develop U.S. influence in the Pacific.

_____

_____

The Expansionist Mood

Until the late 1800s, the United States maintained a course of **isolationism.** It avoided involvement in the affairs of other countries. Several European nations, however, began a policy of **imperialism,** or building empires by establishing political and economic control over peoples around the world. In 1893, historian **Frederick Jackson Turner** announced that there was no more western frontier. Many U.S. leaders believed that imperialism could provide a new sort of Manifest Destiny. The United States could find new natural resources and markets for its products, as well as spread "American values." ✓

Gaining Footholds in the Pacific

American expansionists became interested in two groups of islands in the Pacific—Samoa and Hawaii. Britain and Germany were also interested in Samoa as a place where their ships could refuel. All three countries sent warships to claim the islands. In 1889, a typhoon hit the islands and destroyed the warships. Ten years later, Germany and the United States agreed to divide Samoa.

By 1887, American planters in Hawaii had already gained great influence over the government. Queen **Liliuokalani,** who took the throne of Hawaii in 1891, tried to prevent Hawaii from losing its independence. The planters tried to overthrow the queen with help from U.S. Marines, but the revolt was not supported by President Grover Cleveland. President William McKinley was in favor of annexation, however, and in 1898, Congress voted to make Hawaii a U.S. territory. ✓

Carving Up China

In the late 1800s, Japan and European powers divided China into **spheres of influence,** or areas where another nation has economic and political control. U.S. leaders feared exclusion from the China trade, so Secretary of State John Hay issued the Open Door Policy. It called for all nations to be able to trade in China on an equal basis. The Chinese hated foreign influence and began a rebellion in the spring of 1900. A secret society known as the Boxers attacked westerners and Chinese Christians. The United States and other countries sent troops and crushed the Boxer Rebellion. Secretary Hay then issued a second Open Door message that stated China should remain one country. ✓

Check Your Progress

1. What three new lands did the United States acquire?

_____

_____

2. What nations became new trading partners with the United States?

_____

_____

✓ Checkpoint

Give two reasons why imperialism appealed to some U.S. leaders.

_____

_____

✓ Checkpoint

Name the two Pacific island groups that became U.S. possessions.

_____

_____

✓ Checkpoint

Explain what caused the Boxer Rebellion.

_____

_____

Question to Think About As you read Section 1 in your textbook and take notes, keep this section focus question in mind: **How did the United States acquire new territory and expand trade in the Asia-Pacific region?**

▶ Use this chart to record key information from the section. Some information has been filled in to get you started.

The United States Looks Overseas	
Japan • The United States could not trade with Japan because Japan _____ _____ and _____. • _Commodore Perry_ sailed warships into _____. The Japanese were awed by his _____ and _____. • As a result, the Japanese _____ _____.	**Alaska** • Secretary of State _____ bought Alaska from _Russia_ for _____ in 1867. • Many people called Alaska _____ _____ because they thought it was a _____. • They changed their tune when _____ _____ led to the _____ of 1897–1898.
The Expansionist Mood • In the late 1800s, the idea of _expansionism_ replaced _____. • Historian _____ concluded that the American _____ was gone. • American leaders thought if the United States did not act soon, it might be shut out of _____ and denied _____. • Alfred T. Mahan said that future U.S. prosperity depended on building up _____, and the key was a _____. • Many Americans believed they had a divine duty to spread _____ and _____ around the world.	
Gaining Footholds in the Pacific Expansionists wanted more U.S. influence and trade in the _____.	
Samoa • Besides the United States, _____ and _____ wanted possession of Samoa. • After a _____ prevented a war, _____ and _____ divided Samoa.	**Hawaii** • In 1887, _____ forced the Hawaiian king to accept a new constitution. • Queen _____ refused to recognize the constitution. • On July 7, 1898, the U.S. Congress voted to_____.
The Boxer Rebellion A secret Chinese society, called the Boxers, tried to _____. Outside powers _____. To prevent other powers from seizing more Chinese territory, _____.	

Refer to this page to answer the Chapter 20 Focus Question on page 318.

Section 2

The Spanish-American War

Section 2 Focus Question

What were the causes and effects of the Spanish-American War?
To begin answering this question,
- Understand American interest in the Cuban rebellion.
- Learn what caused the United States to declare war on Spain.
- Find out how the United States governed its newly won territories.

Section 2 Summary

When war broke out between Cuba and Spain, many Americans wanted to protect U.S. business interests in Cuba. The United States sent the battleship *Maine* to Havana to protect American lives and property. When the *Maine* exploded, America blamed Spain and declared war. The United States defeated Spain, gaining territories in the Caribbean and the Pacific.

War Clouds Loom

Cubans had been under Spanish rule since the landing of Columbus in 1492. In 1868, they staged a revolt that was put down ten years later. In 1895, a new revolt broke out. Spain responded with a policy of **reconcentration,** or the forced movement of large numbers of people into detention camps for military or political reasons. After about 200,000 Cubans died in the camps, Cuban exile **José Martí** appealed to the United States for help. Many Americans were sympathetic toward the Cuban cause. Others, who had money invested in Cuba, wanted the United States to intervene to protect their interests.

Neither President Cleveland nor President McKinley would intervene, but newspaper publishers **William Randolph Hearst** and Joseph Pulitzer tried to incite American citizens to call for war. Through yellow journalism, they ran headlines and stories that played up the horror in Cuba. Finally, when fighting broke out in Havana, Cuba's capital city, President McKinley sent the battleship *Maine* to protect American lives and property. On February 15, 1898, the great ship exploded and sank, taking the lives of 260 men. Americans blamed Spain, and "Remember the *Maine*" became the battle cry of revenge. ✓

The United States Goes to War

Although President McKinley wanted to make peace with Spain, he finally gave in and asked Congress to declare war on April 11, 1898. Surprisingly, the first battle was fought not in Cuba, but in the Philippines, another Spanish colony. Assistant Secretary of the

Key Events

1893	American planters stage a revolt in Hawaii.
1898	United States wins the Spanish-American War.
1904	United States begins to build the Panama Canal.

Vocabulary Builder

Intervene comes from the Latin words *inter* ("between") and *venere* ("to come"). Using these meanings and the context clues in the text, explain what some Americans wanted the United States to do in Cuba.

_____

_____

✓ Checkpoint

Name the two publishers who fanned the flames of war in their newspapers.

_____

_____

telegraphed Commodore George Dewey, head of the Pacific fleet.
Roosevelt ordered Dewey to move American ships to the Philippines. On May 1, Dewey's small fleet entered Manila Bay and
sank all of the Spanish ships there without losing one U.S. ship or
life. Dewey then received help from a Philippine rebel leader,
Emilio Aguinaldo, who was already fighting to rid his land of
Spanish rule. The Americans were soon in control of the islands.

When the war shifted to Cuba, the main fighting took place
near the city of Santiago and at sea. Theodore Roosevelt, who had
given up his navy post, led the Rough Riders unit in a successful
charge up San Juan Hill, which became a highlight of the war. The
U.S. Navy then destroyed the Spanish fleet trapped in Santiago
Harbor. Within two weeks, the Spanish surrendered Cuba. Soon,
the United States invaded the Spanish island of Puerto Rico and
brought it under U.S. control. ✔

An American Empire

In December 1898, the United States and Spain signed a peace
treaty. Cuba gained its independence. The United States paid
Spain $20 million and took control of Puerto Rico, the Philippines,
and the Pacific islands of Guam and Wake. Many Americans were
unhappy about acquiring colonies, but not the expansionists.
They were eager to open new businesses and to spread the idea of
democratic government.

The United States replaced Spain as a colonial power in the
Caribbean. Cuba was independent in name only. Congress forced
the Cuban government to adopt the Platt Amendment in its
constitution. This amendment limited Cuba's power and made it
a U.S. **protectorate,** an independent country whose policies are
controlled by an outside power. The Foraker Act of 1900 gave
Puerto Rico limited self-rule, and its people became U.S. citizens.
Many of the islanders wanted their freedom, however. And in the
Philippines, Emilio Aguinaldo, still seeking independence from
foreign rule, led a revolt that resulted in many deaths. In 1901, he
was captured and the fighting ended. ✔

Check Your Progress

1. Why were expansionists eager to acquire colonies?

   _____

   _____

2. What new territories did the United States acquire?

   _____

   _____

✓ Checkpoint

List the three Spanish possessions
where fighting occurred in the
Spanish-American War.

_____

_____

_____

✓ Checkpoint

Name the rebel leader who led
Filipinos against American rule.

_____

Question to Think About As you read Section 2 in your textbook and take notes, keep this section focus question in mind: **What were the causes and effects of the Spanish-American War?**

▶ Use this chart to record key information from the section. Some information has been filled in to get you started.

The Spanish-American War	
Cause	**Effect**
Cubans rose up against Spanish rule in 1895.	Spain began a policy of <u>reconcentration</u>.
Many Americans were sympathetic toward Cuba. Others wanted to safeguard American investments in Cuba.	_____ _____ _____
• Yellow journalists _____ _____. • Americans blamed Spain for _____ _____.	Americans called for the United States to declare war on Spain.
• Dewey's warships sank the Spanish squadron at _____. • With help from _____, Dewey seized Manila.	The United States gained control of the Philippine Islands.
In a battle along the Cuban coast, U.S. ships destroyed the Spanish fleet.	_____ _____
Spain and the United States signed a peace treaty.	• Spain accepted _____. • Spain granted _____ _____ to the United States. • The United States paid _____.
The United States forced Cuba to add the Platt Amendment to its constitution.	• Limited Cuba's _____ _____ • Gave the United States _____ _____ • Allowed the United States to _____ _____
The Foraker Act of 1900 was passed, setting up a government in Puerto Rico.	• Gave Puerto Ricans _____ _____
Filipino rebels renewed their fight for independence.	• After 3 years of fighting, _____ _____ was captured and fighting _____.

Refer to this page to answer the Chapter 20 Focus Question on page 318.

The United States and Latin America

Key Events

1893 American planters stage a revolt in Hawaii.

1898 United States wins the Spanish-American War.

1904 United States begins to build the Panama Canal.

✓ Checkpoint

Explain why the United States backed the Panamanian rebels.

_____

_____

_____

Section 3 Focus Question

How did the United States use the Monroe Doctrine to justify intervention in Latin America? To begin answering this question,
- Learn why the United States built the Panama Canal.
- Understand how President Theodore Roosevelt dealt with European interference in Latin America.
- Learn about President Taft's "dollar diplomacy."
- Read about President Wilson's troubles with Mexico.

Section 3 Summary

The United States intervened in Latin American conflicts. Building the Panama Canal was central to its goals in world trade and managing distant possessions.

Linking the Oceans

Before the 1900s, the shortest sea route from San Francisco to Cuba was around the tip of South America. The 14,000-mile journey took over two months. The United States needed an inland canal connecting the Atlantic and the Pacific oceans. A canal would improve international shipping and would help the United States police its new empire.

In 1902, the **Isthmus** of Panama, a narrow strip of land between the Caribbean Sea and the Pacific Ocean, was a province of Colombia. The United States offered Colombia $10 million in cash and a yearly rent of $250,000 for the use of the isthmus, but Colombia wanted more money. To avoid lengthy bargaining, President Theodore Roosevelt urged Panamanians to claim independence from Colombian rule. The Panamanian revolt, supported by the U.S. military, took place on November 3, 1903. Three days later, the United States took control of the 10-mile-wide zone across the Isthmus of Panama in exchange for $10 million plus $250,000 yearly rent. ✓

The Panama Canal

Work on the Panama Canal began in 1904. The first big problem in digging the "big ditch" was disease. Malaria and yellow fever sickened many workers and halted work. Both diseases were mosquito-transmitted. **William C. Gorgas,** an American expert on tropical diseases, came to Panama. He had workers drain swamps and clear brush to wipe out mosquitoes' breeding grounds. By 1906, Gorgas had greatly reduced malaria and yellow fever in Panama.

Canal construction proceeded with difficulty. Six thousand workers died as they cut through the earth, constructed dams, and built giant locks to raise and lower the water level. Many more thousands of men, most of them West Indians of African heritage, transformed miles of mud into the great canal. The canal opened on August 15, 1914. ☑

Wielding a "Big Stick" in Latin America

President Theodore Roosevelt was fond of saying an old West African proverb, "Speak softly and carry a big stick; you will go far." In other words, if diplomacy failed, the United States would not hesitate to use military force. In 1904, Roosevelt applied his "big stick" policy in Latin America. He announced that the United States had the right to use police power against foreign nations that get involved in disputes with Latin America. The policy came to be known as the Roosevelt Corollary to the Monroe Doctrine. A **corollary** is a logical extension of a doctrine or proposition.

President Taft, Roosevelt's successor, had a different approach. He believed in **dollar diplomacy,** a policy based on the idea that economic ties were the best way to expand American influence. He urged businesses to invest heavily in Asia and Latin America. Taft's dollar diplomacy led to as many military interventions in Latin American as Roosevelt's "big stick" policy. American troops occupied Nicaragua, Haiti, and Honduras. ☑

Relations With Mexico

Woodrow Wilson became President in 1913 with his own foreign policy goal. He aimed to support and nurture democracy throughout the world. Wilson's ideas were first tested in Mexico, which was involved in a violent revolution after a dictator was overthrown. Wilson did not want to intervene. He adopted a "watchful waiting" policy, hoping that Mexico would become a democratic nation. But when two U.S. sailors were briefly arrested in Mexico, Wilson sent in the navy and almost caused a war. Two years later, the rebel general **Francisco "Pancho" Villa** attacked and burned a town in New Mexico, killing 18 Americans. General John J. Pershing led U.S. troops into Mexico looking for Villa, but failed to capture him. ☑

Check Your Progress

1. Why did Roosevelt want to build the Panama Canal?

_____

_____

_____

2. What was meant by Roosevelt's "big stick" policy?

_____

_____

_____

✓ Checkpoint

Name the first obstacle that interfered with building the Panama Canal.

_____

Vocabulary Builder

A *succession* is the following of one thing after another. What, then, is the meaning of a *successor*?

_____

_____

_____

✓ Checkpoint

Name the earlier policy that the Roosevelt Corollary extended.

_____

✓ Checkpoint

Explain Wilson's foreign policy goal.

_____

_____

Question to Think About As you read Section 3 in your textbook and take notes, keep this section focus question in mind: **How did the United States use the Monroe Doctrine to justify intervention in Latin America?**

▶ Use this chart to record key information from the section. Some information has been filled in to get you started.

The United States and Latin America
The United States and Panama
<ul><li>In 1902, the United States wanted to build a canal across Panama linking the _____ and _____ oceans.</li><li>After helping Panama win its independence from <u>Colombia</u>, the United States and Panama signed a treaty that gave the United States _____ _____.</li><li>In return, the United States paid Panama _____.</li><li>Construction of the _____ began in 1904 and was completed in _____.</li></ul>
Roosevelt's Foreign Policy
<ul><li>Roosevelt wanted the world to know that the United States _____ _____.</li><li>In 1904, European nations considered _____ in the Dominican Republic. Roosevelt wanted to prevent this. He announced a new policy that became known as the _____ to the _____.</li><li>This policy stated that the United States had the right to _____ _____.</li></ul>
Taft's Dollar Diplomacy
<ul><li>Dollar diplomacy was based on the idea that _____ were the best way to expand American influence.</li><li>As a result, American bankers and business leaders _____ _____.</li><li>Dollar diplomacy led to U.S. military intervention in _____, _____, and _____.</li></ul>
Woodrow Wilson's Foreign Policy
<ul><li>Wilson believed that U.S. foreign policy should _____ _____.</li><li>After Porfírio Díaz was overthrown, Wilson's policy toward Mexico was one of _____.</li><li>In 1914, Wilson intervened in Mexico after _____.</li><li>In 1916, the United States was drawn into Mexican affairs again when _____.</li><li>The United States responded by _____.</li></ul>

Refer to this page to answer the Chapter 20 Focus Question on page 318.

Chapter 20 Assessment

Directions: Circle the letter of the correct answer.

1. Which best describes the change that the United States went through in the late 1800s and early 1900s?

   A from isolationism to the Monroe Doctrine

   B from expansionism to isolationism

   C from trade to "gunboat diplomacy"

   D from isolationism to expansionism

2. With which countries did the United States engage in battle?

   A Japan and China

   B China and Mexico

   C Japan and Spain

   D China and Spain

3. Woodrow Wilson supported

   A isolationism.

   B spreading democracy.

   C gunboat diplomacy.

   D dollar diplomacy.

Directions: Follow the steps to answer this question:

How were U.S. policies between 1853 and 1915 toward countries in the Pacific and in Latin America similar and different?

Step 1: Recall information: In the chart, list U.S. actions in each area.

Japan	
Alaska	
Hawaii	
China	
Cuba	
Panama	
Mexico	

Step 2: Write each country under the type of U.S. action that occurred there.

Peaceful Intervention	Military Intervention

Step 3: Complete the topic sentence that follows. Then write two or three sentences summarizing how U.S. actions were similar and different.

Between 1853 and 1915, U.S. actions were _____

_____

_____

_____

Chapter 20 Notetaking Study Guide

Now you are ready to answer the Chapter 20 Focus Question: **How did the United States demonstrate its growing interest in the Pacific and in Latin America?**

▶ Complete the following chart to help you answer this question. Use the notes that you took for each section.

The United States Looks Overseas	
Commodore Perry's mission to Japan	• Opened up _____ with Japan • Effect on Japan: <u>set out to transform its feudal society into an industrial nation</u>
The purchase of Alaska and the annexation of Hawaii	• Secretary of State _____ saw Alaska as a stepping stone for trade with _____ and the _____. • Why expansionists were interested in Hawaii: _____ _____ • How Hawaii became a U.S. territory: _____ _____
Open Door Policy in China	• The first Open Door Policy: _____ _____ • The second Open Door Policy: _____ _____
Spanish-American War	• The United States intervened in the conflict in Cuba to protect _____. • Terms of the treaty ending the war: _____ _____
Panama Canal	• The United States gained access to the Isthmus of Panama after helping Panama gain its independence from _____. • The canal linked the _____ and _____.
Foreign relations under Theodore Roosevelt	• Roosevelt's Big Stick Policy: _____ _____ • The Roosevelt Corollary: _____ _____
Foreign relations under Taft	• Taft's policy was called _____. • What it was: _____ _____
Foreign relations under Wilson	• Wilson's foreign policy: _____ _____ • Led to two incidents in _____

Refer to this page to answer the Unit 7 Focus Question on page 347.

Chapter 21

World War I (1914–1919)

What You Will Learn

In 1914, a war broke out in Europe. Although the United States at first remained neutral, it eventually joined the war. World War I had important effects in America and in the rest of the world.

Chapter 21 Focus Question
As you read this chapter, keep this question in mind: **What were the causes and effects of World War I?**

Section 1

The Road to War

Section 1 Focus Question
What were the causes of World War I? To begin answering this question,
- Understand the factors that led to the outbreak of war.
- Learn why World War I was so deadly.
- Find out how American neutrality was tested.
- Understand the events that brought the United States into the war.

Section 1 Summary

As competition for colonies increased, so did national pride and military power. European nations began to take sides in case war broke out. When war finally erupted, the United States tried to remain neutral. Events pulled the United States in with the Allies.

Origins of World War I
European **militarism,** or the glorification of the military, grew in the early 1900s as competition for overseas colonies increased. **Nationalism,** or pride in one's national or ethnic group, also rose dramatically. The Balkan countries became especially tense as Russia urged Balkan nationalists to seek independence from Austria-Hungry. As tensions mounted, two alliance systems formed among European nations. Members of each alliance promised to support one another in case of attack.

On June 28, 1914, a Serbian nationalist killed the heir to the Austro-Hungarian throne, Archduke Franz Ferdinand. In July, Austria-Hungary invaded Serbia. The alliance system soon drew more than twenty nations into the war. Britain, France, and Russia led the Allies. They fought against the Central powers of Germany, Austria-Hungary, and the Ottoman Empire. ✔

Key Events

1914	World War I begins in Europe.
1917	United States declares war on Germany.
1918	Armistice ends World War I.
1919	U.S. Senate rejects the Treaty of Versailles.

✓ Checkpoint

Name the two sides in World War I.

_____

_____

✓ Checkpoint

List three factors that made World War I much deadlier than previous wars.

_____

_____

_____

✓ Checkpoint

Name two ethnic American groups that supported the Central powers.

_____

_____

✓ Checkpoint

State the event that prevented the United States from allying with a tyrant.

_____

The Deadliest War

Everyone hoped for a quick victory, but both sides implemented new kinds of warfare that made the battles more lethal and prolonged the war. Airplanes, tanks, rapid-fire guns, and heavy artillery took a heavy toll. **Trench warfare,** in which soldiers fired on one another from opposite lines of dugouts, was brutal. It became especially deadly when men charged into the "no man's land" between the trenches. The most feared new weapon, however, was poison gas. ✓

American Neutrality

Officially, the United States remained neutral, yet German Americans often supported the Central powers. Many Irish Americans, who hated Britain's long occupation of their homeland, also supported the Central powers. Americans of British, Italian, and Slavic heritage generally supported the Allies. To strengthen American support, Britain used **propaganda,** or spreading stories about enemy brutality that were often exaggerated or made up.

American banks made loans to the Allies. U.S. businesses, although free to sell supplies to both sides, traded mostly with the Allies. And in any case, Britain's naval blockade of Germany prevented U.S. merchant ships from entering German ports.

Germany announced it would use U-boats, or submarines, to blockade Britain and France. On May 7, 1915, a U-boat sank the British passenger ship *Lusitania,* with 128 Americans aboard. Fearing the United States would enter the war, Germany promised not to target neutral merchant ships or passenger liners. ✓

Entering the War

Wilson was reelected in 1916 on the slogan "He kept us out of war." But in February 1917, the British intercepted the Zimmermann Telegram, in which Germany asked Mexico to join the Central powers in exchange for help in regaining New Mexico, Texas, and Arizona. Americans were outraged. Then U-boats sank three American ships. In March, the Russian Revolution overthrew the tsar, Nicholas II, which meant Wilson no longer had to justify fighting on the same side as a tyrant. On April 2, 1917, Wilson asked Congress to declare war on the Central powers to "make the world safe for democracy." ✓

Check Your Progress

1. What event sparked World War I on June 28, 1914?

_____

2. What three events led the United States into the war?

_____

_____

Section 1 Notetaking Study Guide

Question to Think About As you read Section 1 in your textbook and take notes, keep this section focus question in mind: **What were the causes of World War I?**

▶ Use this chart to record key information from the section. Some information has been filled in to get you started.

Events Leading to U.S. Entry into World War I	
Prior to June 1914	European imperialism led to a rise in __militarism__ and __nationalism__. European nations formed alliances: • _____: Germany allied with _____ and _____ • _____: France allied with _____ and _____
June 28, 1914	A Serbian nationalist assassinated _____, heir to the _____.
July 29, 1914	Austria-Hungary invaded _____.
July 31, 1914	Russia _____.
August 1, 1914	Germany declared war on _____.
August 3, 1914	Germany declared war on _____.
August 4, 1914	Germany invaded _____. _____ declared war on Germany.
May 1915	A German U-boat sank the passenger ship _____, then told the United States that _____ _____.
November 1916	_____ is reelected on the slogan " _____."
February 1917	Britain intercepted the _____ in which _____. Other events followed: • The Germans _____. • In Russia, _____.
April 1917	Wilson asks _____ to make the world " _____."

Refer to this page to answer the Chapter 21 Focus Question on page 332.

Supporting the War Effort

Section 2 Focus Question

What steps did the U.S. government take to prepare the nation for war? To begin answering this question,

- Find out how the United States quickly mobilized.
- Learn about the agencies that helped to manage the war.
- Read how antiwar opinions were suppressed.

Section 2 Summary

With the declaration of war on the Central powers, the United States faced an enormous task. It had to raise, train, and equip an army; coordinate the efforts of industrial production; and continue to boost public support.

Building the Military

Although the United States had a large navy, its army was small. The nation had to quickly **mobilize,** or prepare for war. Many young men volunteered to fight, but there were too few to build an army. Consequently, Congress passed the Selective Service Act, which required men between the ages of 21 and 30 to register for the draft. By the end of the war, almost four million Americans had entered the armed services.

Women were not drafted, but more than 30,000 of them volunteered, most of them as nurses for the army and navy. Others did clerical work as members of the navy and marines. Some leading women were against the war. **Jeannette Rankin,** the first woman elected to Congress, refused to send men to fight because she, as a woman, was unable to do so. Suffragists, however, urged women to support the war effort, hoping that their contributions would accelerate their drive to gain the right to vote.

Many Native Americans, not yet citizens of the United States, volunteered. Some 380,000 African Americans also served, but only 10 percent saw combat. They were placed in segregated units. Several members of a unit known as the Harlem Hell Fighters received France's highest medal for bravery.

For many soldiers from poor rural areas, the military was a great educator. In addition to teaching fighting skills, the military taught these soldiers how to read. The soldiers also learned about nutrition, personal hygiene, and patriotism. ✓

Managing the War Effort

President Wilson chose **Herbert Hoover** to head a new Food Administration in order to make sure that there was enough food

---

1914 — World War I begins in Europe.

1917 — United States declares war on Germany.

1918 — Armistice ends World War I.

1919 — U.S. Senate rejects the Treaty of Versailles.

✓ Checkpoint

Name three groups of people who were not subject to the draft yet chose to volunteer for military service.

_____

_____

_____

for both the troops and civilians. Many people planted "victory gardens" to provide food for their own table. Wilson also created the War Industries Board headed by Bernard Baruch. The Board told industries what and how much to produce, and how much to charge.

Because of a steep drop in immigration and the rise in the number of men in the military, industries experienced a severe labor shortage. Women and African Americans, who migrated to factories in the Midwest and Northeast, filled many of the vacated jobs. ✓

Shaping Public Opinion

Another government agency, the Committee on Public Information, maintained public support for the war. It recruited "Four-Minute Men" to give patriotic speeches at movie theaters and ballparks. It hired artists to produce pro-war cartoons and posters, and movie stars to sell war bonds.

Criticism of the war was sternly suppressed. The Espionage Act of 1917 and the Sedition Act of 1918 closed newspapers and jailed people for expressing antiwar opinions. **Eugene V. Debs**, a labor leader and Socialist Party candidate for president, was among those jailed. Debs, who urged people not to support the war, made this ironic comment: "It is extremely dangerous to exercise the constitutional right of free speech in a country fighting to make democracy safe in the world."

Private organizations encouraged people to spy on their neighbors and report anyone who did not <u>comply</u> with pro-war behavior. The American Protective League enlisted 200,000 people to open mail, tap phones, and pry into medical records. German Americans, who were shunned, harassed, and even attacked, probably suffered worst of all. ✓

Check Your Progress

1. What was the purpose of the Selective Service Act?

_____

_____

2. What steps did the Committee on Public Information take to promote pro-war support?

_____

_____

✓ Checkpoint

List two government agencies that helped manage resources during the war.

_____

_____

Vocabulary Builder

When you *comply* with something, you go along with it. With what did the American people need to comply?

_____

_____

✓ Checkpoint

Name two acts that punished the expression of antiwar views.

_____

_____

Question to Think About As you read Section 2 in your textbook and take notes, keep this section focus question in mind: **What steps did the U.S. government take to prepare the nation for war?**

▶ Use this chart to record key information from the section. Some information has been filled in to get you started.

Building the Military

- Many men volunteered to fight but there were too few to form an army, so _Congress passed the Selective Service Act_. Men between _the ages of 21 and 30_ had to _____.

- Women were not drafted, but more than 30,000 _____. Suffragists hoped women's wartime service would help them _____ after the war.
- Other volunteers included _____ and _____.
- For poor, rural recruits, the war was a great _____ because _____ _____.

Managing the War Effort

- Herbert Hoover was appointed to head the _____ in order to _____.

- People grew _____ in order to _____.
- Wilson also created the _____ to oversee the shift to _____.

- A drop in immigration and _____ led to a _____. Women and _____ filled many of the vacancies.

Shaping Public Opinion

- The Committee on Public Information recruited "_____" to deliver _____. It also hired _artists_ to produce _____ and movie stars to _____.
- Two Acts were passed to suppress criticism of the war: the _____ and the _____, which _____ _____.

- At times, war fever collided with personal freedoms. Private organizations, such as the _____, enlisted people to _____.

Refer to this page to answer the Chapter 21 Focus Question on page 332.

Section 3

Americans at War

Section 3 Focus Question

How did the arrival of American troops in Europe affect the course of the war? To begin answering this question,

- Learn how the first American troops to arrive in Europe were received.
- Find out how the American troops aided the Allies.
- Read about President Wilson's contribution to the armistice.

Section 3 Summary

The first American troops to arrive in France greatly boosted European morale. But the Allies suffered a great setback when Russia made a treaty with Germany and withdrew from the war, giving Germany a stronger military advantage. When America joined the Allies, the combined troops turned the tide, and the Central powers fell. The Allies dictated a harsh peace agreement with Germany.

Joining the Fight

From February through April 1917, German submarines sank 844 Allied ships. To get much needed supplies from the United States, the Allies developed a **convoy** system in which Allied destroyers accompanied large groups of merchant ships sailing together. The convoy system greatly decreased Allied losses.

Meanwhile, American forces prepared to enter the war. The American Expeditionary Force, as it was called in Europe, was under the leadership of **John J. Pershing.** On President Wilson's orders, Pershing insisted that American troops not integrate with Allied units. Wilson wanted the United States to make its own victorious showing, thereby allowing the United States to influence the peace settlement. The first troops to arrive in Europe in June were not ready for combat. They did, however, lift French morale as they entered Paris, confirming America's commitment to the war. ✔

Setbacks and Advances

While the Allies waited for more American troops to arrive, their situation grew desperate. Fighting bogged down on the Western Front. The Central powers scored a major victory in Italy.

Then Russia's new government, under Bolshevik leader **Vladimir Lenin,** pulled out of the war and signed a peace treaty with Germany. Lenin wanted to concentrate on taking his country toward **communism,** an economic and political system based on

Key Events

1914	World War I begins in Europe.
1917	United States declares war on Germany.
1918	Armistice ends World War I.
1919	U.S. Senate rejects the Treaty of Versailles.

✓ Checkpoint

Describe two ways the United States assisted the Allies.

_____

_____

_____

the idea that social classes and private property should be eliminated. Russia and Germany signed the Treaty of Brest-Litovsk in March 1918. The treaty gave Germany about 30 percent of Russia's territory. Peace with Russia allowed Germany to transfer a huge number of troops to the Western Front. With this increase of military force, Germany hoped to defeat the Allies before the American troops arrived.

On March 21, 1918, the Germans launched a series of daring attacks. They moved through Belgium and into France. The situation became so grave that General Pershing turned over all U.S. resources to the French, even allowing the French to command American troops. It was a good decision. Twice during that summer, American and Allied troops pushed the Germans back from the Marne River, which was located less than 50 miles from Paris. By September, the Allies—including one million American soldiers—advanced against fortified German positions in northeastern France. By November, the German defenses had crumbled. ☑

The Armistice

Germany's leaders decided to seek an **armistice,** a halt in fighting, to discuss the conditions of a peace treaty. Without Germany's help, the remaining Central powers could no longer carry on the war. They, too, agreed to an armistice. Germany had hoped the settlement would be based on Wilson's peace plan, founded on principles of international cooperation. In the end, however, Wilson's plan had little impact on the deliberations. Britain and France dictated the terms. Germany had to pull its troops from the Western Front, cancel the Treaty of Brest-Litovsk, and surrender all of its U-boats. At Wilson's insistence, Kaiser Wilhelm II had to <u>abdicate</u> his throne so Germany could develop a republic.

The armistice went into effect on November 11, 1918, at 11 A.M. The bloodiest and most brutal war the world had yet seen was over. About 10 million soldiers had died. Millions of other soldiers were maimed for life. In addition, some historians think the number of civilian deaths was equal to the number of military deaths. ☑

Check Your Progress

1. Why did Russia pull out of the war?

_____

_____

_____

2. What were the terms of the armistice?

_____

_____

_____

✓ Checkpoint

Name the treaty that allowed Germany to concentrate solely on the Western Front.

_____

_____

Vocabulary Builder

To *abdicate* means "to give up a high position in government." What position did Wilhelm II abdicate?

_____

_____

✓ Checkpoint

Name the two nations that dictated the terms of the armistice.

_____

_____

Question to Think About As you read Section 3 in your textbook and take notes, keep this section focus question in mind: **How did the arrival of American troops in Europe affect the course of the war?**

▶ Use this chart to record key information from the section. Some information has been filled in to get you started.

Americans at War	
Cause	**Effect**
1. German U-boats destroy many Allied ships.	• <u>U.S. supplies cannot get to the Allies</u> • _____ _____
2. President Wilson wants the United States to make its own victorious showing.	• _____ _____
3. First Division of the American Expeditionary Force arrives in Paris.	• _____ _____
4. Russia signs a peace agreement with Germany.	• _____ _____
5. Daring German attacks create a grave situation for the Allies.	• _____ _____
6. Allied forces push forward along a line that stretches from the North Sea to Verdun.	• <u>German defenses crumble</u> • _____

Terms of the armistice:
• _____
• _____
• _____
• <u>Kaiser Wilhelm II forced to abdicate throne</u>

War dead:
Total military personnel _____
France _____
Britain _____
Germany _____
Russia _____
American _____
Civilian _____

Refer to this page to answer the Chapter 21 Focus Question on page 332.

Key Events

1914	World War I begins in Europe.
1917	United States declares war on Germany.
1918	Armistice ends World War I.
1919	U.S. Senate rejects the Treaty of Versailles.

✓ Checkpoint

List the three main ideas that the Fourteen Points addressed.

_____

_____

_____

Section 4 Focus Question

How did the Treaty of Versailles and the League of Nations disappoint President Wilson? To answer this question,
- Learn about President Wilson's Fourteen Points.
- Find out how the Treaty of Versailles punished Germany.
- Understand why Congress rejected the League of Nations.

Section 4 Summary

President Wilson's peace plan, known as the Fourteen Points, was a blueprint to try to avoid future wars. The most important point, in Wilson's mind, was the creation of an international peacekeeping body. Wilson agreed to the harsh demands of the armistice to insure the creation of this organization, but Congress rejected U.S. membership in the League of Nations.

The Fourteen Points

President Wilson presented his peace plan, the Fourteen Points, to Congress before the war even ended. The first five points dealt with some of the causes of the war. He called for an end to secret agreements, freedom of the seas, free trade among nations, a reduction in the military, and a settlement of colonial claims. The next eight points dealt with territorial issues created by the war, especially **self-determination** for minority groups in Austria-Hungary and the Ottoman Empire. Under Wilson's plan, they would be able to decide for themselves what kind of government they would have. The fourteenth point was a call for an international peacekeeping body. ✓

Peace Conference in Paris

President Wilson arrived in Paris in January 1919 to cheering crowds. The war-weary population approved of Wilson's Fourteen Points. Not in agreement were the other three members of the "Big Four"—prime ministers Georges Clemenceau of France, David Lloyd George of Britain, and Vittorio Orlando of Italy. They had already signed secret treaties dividing up the territories and colonies of the Central powers.

The final peace agreement, known as the Treaty of Versailles (ver SI), forced Germany to accept full responsibility for the war and to pay huge **reparations,** or payments to cover war damages. Wilson disagreed with the Allies, but he complied in order to win his international peacekeeping organization. The Versailles Treaty included an organization similar to the one in Wilson's plan. It was called the League of Nations. On June 28, 1919, Germany signed the treaty.

Separate treaties with the other Central powers redrew the map of Europe. Austria, Hungary, and Czechoslovakia became separate states. The Balkan peoples formed Yugoslavia. Poland became independent. Britain and France divided Germany's African colonies and the Middle Eastern lands of the Ottoman Empire. The Ottoman Empire became the new republic of Turkey. ✓

Battle Over the League

The U.S. Senate was strongly opposed to the Treaty of Versailles. Senator **Henry Cabot Lodge** of Massachusetts led the opposition. Lodge felt the Treaty's most controversial element, the League of Nations, would limit the ability of the United States to act independently in its own interests. He requested changes that would reduce United States ties to the League. Wilson would not compromise. Instead, he tried to rally public support for the League. He gave speeches around the country, traveling 8,000 miles in three weeks. Despite Wilson's efforts to save the League, he failed. The Senate voted against the Treaty of Versailles, a decision that crippled the League of Nations' peacekeeping power. ✓

Postwar Troubles

The postwar years were troubled times. A worldwide epidemic of influenza (flu) killed more people than the war had. Soldiers returning home from the war could not find jobs. Great numbers of union workers demanding higher wages went on strike. Many Americans thought the Communists, or "Reds," were behind the labor troubles. On the orders of Attorney General Palmer, thousands of immigrants suspected of Communist or other <u>radical</u> sympathies were sent back to their home countries. Eventually the public turned against Palmer's tactics and the panic ended. ✓

Check Your Progress

1. Why did Wilson's Fourteen Points have little influence during the armistice?

   _____

   _____

2. Why did Wilson agree to the harsh terms of the Treaty of Versailles?

   _____

   _____

✓ Checkpoint

Name the "Big Four" and the nations they represented.

_____

_____

_____

_____

✓ Checkpoint

Name the U.S. senator who led the opposition to the Treaty of Versailles.

_____

_____

Vocabulary Builder

A person with *radical* views usually promotes extreme political, economic, or social changes. What radical view did the Americans fear during the postwar years?

_____

✓ Checkpoint

List three major problems the United States faced after World War I.

_____

_____

_____

Section 4 Notetaking Study Guide

Question to Think About As you read Section 4 in your textbook and take notes, keep this section focus question in mind: **How did the Treaty of Versailles and the League of Nations disappoint President Wilson?**

▶ Use this chart to record key information from the section. Some information has been filled in to get you started.

Shaping the Peace
The "Big Four" met in Paris in 1919.   U.S. President: _____   Prime Minister of France: _____   Prime Minister of Britain: _____   Prime Minister of Italy: _____

Wilson's Goals	What Eventually Resulted
End to secret international agreements →	Britain, France, and Italy signed secret agreements dividing up territories and colonies of the Central powers.
Deal fairly with Germany →	_____ _____ _____
Self-determination for minority peoples →	• Austria, _____, and _____ became seperate states. • Balkan people _____ • Poland _____ • _____ replaced the Ottoman Empire • Britain and France divided _____ _____
International peacekeeping body →	_____
Ratification of the Treaty of Versailles →	_____

U.S. Opposition to The Treaty of Versailles
The United States opposed the Treaty of Versailles. Senator _____ objected to the Treaty's peacekeeping body, the _____, because _____.   Wilson campaigned to _____, but his efforts _____.

Refer to this page to answer the Chapter 21 Focus Question on page 332.

Chapter 21 Assessment

Directions: Circle the letter of the correct answer.

1. Who made up the Central powers?
   - **A** Germany, Austria-Hungary, Italy
   - **B** Germany, Austria-Hungary, Ottoman Empire
   - **C** Germany, Italy, Japan
   - **D** Germany, Austria-Hungary, Russia

2. Which of the following was *not* a result of World War I?
   - **A** Communist ideology
   - **B** the League of Nations
   - **C** Germany's loss of its colonies
   - **D** the breakup of the Ottoman Empire

3. Woodrow Wilson supported
   - **A** dividing up Germany's colonies.
   - **B** having Germany pay huge reparations.
   - **C** secret treaties.
   - **D** the League of Nations.

Directions: Follow the steps to answer this question:

Which minority peoples of Central Europe gained the right to determine their own government as a result of the Treaty of Versailles?

Step 1: Recall information: In the chart, list the colonial status before and after the war.

Nation	Pre-War Colonies	Post-War Changes
Germany	Controlled colonies in _____	Lost _____
Austria-Hungary	Controlled _____	Lost _____ Became_____
Ottoman Empire	Controlled _____	Lost _____ Became_____
Britain	had colonial empire throughout world	Gained half of _____ _____
France	had colonies in West Africa and West Indies	Gained half of_____ _____

Step 2: List the minority peoples who gained self-determination after the war.

Gained Self-determination	Did Not Gain Self-determination

Step 3: Complete the topic sentence that follows. Then write two or three sentences summarizing the degree to which Wilson's point calling for self-determined governments was fulfilled.

The Treaty of Versailles allowed _____

_____

_____

Now you are ready to answer the Chapter 21 Focus Question: **What were the causes and effects of World War I?**

► Complete the charts to help you answer this question. Use the notes that you took for each section.

Causes of World War I

Imperialism
- Germany had colonies in _____ _____.
- Austria-Hungary ruled _____ _____.
- Ottoman Empire ruled _____ _____.

Nationalism
Ethnic groups in the <u>Balkan region</u> wanted to free themselves of _____ _____.

Alliance Systems
- _____, _____, and _____ formed the Central powers.
- The nations of _____, _____, and _____ formed the Allies.

World War I Begins

On June 28, 1914, a Serbian nationalist assassinated _____ of Austria-Hungary. As a result, Austria-Hungary declared war on _____. Britain, France, and _____ came to its aid. Germany, and later the Ottoman Empire, _____.

Events that Brought America into the War

At first, America _____, allowing it to trade with both sides, although most American trade and banking helped the _____. President Wilson cut off diplomatic relations with Germany when Germany _____

America finally entered the war after Germany _____ _____ and _____.

Results of the Allied Victory

The Treaty of Versailles punished _____ and changed the map of Europe. Germany had to pay _____ and lost _____. Austria-Hungary and the Ottoman Empire were _____. The Treaty established a peacekeeping organization called the _____. The U.S. rejected _____ because _____.

Refer to this page to answer the Unit 7 Focus Question on page 347.

Chapter 22

The Roaring Twenties

(1919–1929)

What You Will Learn

After World War I, U.S. presidents shifted the country's focus to domestic issues. Accompanied by a burst of creativity that transformed mass culture, plus rapid changes in the lives of women and African Americans, the decade was prosperous—but serious economic problems lay just beneath the surface.

Chapter 22 Focus Question
As you read this chapter, keep this question in mind: **How did the nation react to change in the 1920s?**

Section 1

Adjusting to Peacetime

Section 1 Focus Question
What problems at home and abroad challenged the nation after World War I? To begin answering this question,
- Learn about the administrations of Hoover and Coolidge.
- Understand what postwar isolationism meant.
- Read about the Red Scare.

Section 1 Summary

Due to the failure of the Treaty of Versailles, a poor economy, and threats of violence, people voted largely Republican in the election of 1920. This began a decade that favored big business, isolationism, and immigration restrictions.

Return to Normalcy
President Wilson had expected to return home from the Paris Peace Conference a hero, but the failure of the United States to sign the Treaty of Versailles, plus an economic decline, cost his Democratic Party the election of 1920. The change from wartime to peacetime industry as well as violent labor strikes led to an economic recession. Threats of communism and racial violence also disturbed the American public. The voters hoped new leadership would lead the <u>decade</u> into peace and prosperity.

President **Warren Harding** of Ohio promised a return to "normalcy." For the two years he was in office, until his death in 1923, he supported business interests and appointed wealthy businessmen to revive the economy. He also appointed friends who used their jobs to make personal fortunes. As a result, the

Key Events

1919 18th Amendment prohibits the consumption and sale of alcoholic beverages.

1924 Teapot Dome and other government scandals become public.

1927 Lindbergh flies alone across the Atlantic.

Vocabulary Builder

Decade comes from *decem*, the Latin word for "ten." How many years are in a decade?

_____

✓ Checkpoint

List two ways the United States participated in international affairs during the Coolidge administration.

_____

_____

Harding administration was rocked by scandal. Upon Harding's death, Vice President **Calvin Coolidge** became President. The public saw him as an honest man, and he won the 1924 election by a large margin. During Coolidge's presidency, the economy revived and the 1920s began to "roar." ✓

Foreign Policy

Although World War I had made the United States an international power, government leaders and most Americans favored isolationism. Nevertheless, the United States did not cut itself off from world affairs. It participated in international conferences to promote **disarmament**, or the reduction of weapons. With France, the United States sponsored the Kellogg-Briand Pact, which condemned military aggression and outlawed war. In addition, Coolidge felt the United States could intervene in foreign disputes when America's business interests were threatened, and he did so several times in Latin America. ✓

The Red Scare

Under President Wilson's administration, the United States had refused to diplomatically recognize the Soviet Union's new Communist government. **Communism** is an anti-democratic political system in which the single-party government controls all means of production. The fear of Communists, or Red Scare, reached a peak in 1919. In addition, **anarchists,** or people who oppose organized government, set off a series of bombings. Many anarchists were foreign born. American fear of radical foreigners spread to include Communists. Thousands of anarchists and "Reds" were deported from the country.

The 1920 trial of Sacco and Vanzetti symbolized the public hysteria of the time. Two men, Nicola Sacco and Bartolomeo Vanzetti, were charged with murder. There was little evidence of their guilt, but they were convicted on the fact that they were foreigners and anarchists. Both men were executed.

Fear of radical immigrants, along with fear of losing jobs to newcomers, led Congress to pass an emergency immigration law in 1921. The law limited immigration from Europe and prohibited all immigration from Asia. Immigrations from Mexico and Canada, however, were allowed to continue. ✓

Check Your Progress

1. What did Harding promise that won him the presidency?

_____

_____

2. What two actions did the U.S. government take to curb the perceived threat of anarchists and Communists?

_____

_____

Question to Think About As you read Section 1 in your textbook and take notes, keep this section focus question in mind: **What problems at home and abroad challenged the nation after World War I?**

▶ Use this chart to record key information from the section. Some information has been filled in to get you started.

Adjusting to Peacetime
Return to Normalcy
President Wilson expected to return home a hero, but several factors put Democrats out of power:
• Mishandling of _____, an economic _____, labor disputes that led to _____, and fear that _____ would overthrow the government
Harding Administration
• Harding promised a _____.
• Appointed businessmen, including _____ as secretary of the treasury
• Slashed the _____
• Scandals marred Harding's presidency, including the __Teapot Dome scandal__, after which _____ became the first Cabinet member sent to prison.
• After Harding died, Vice President _____ took office.
Foreign Policy
Most Americans favored _____ after World War I.
The United States, however, continued to participate in world affairs:
• Encouraged _____, or limiting weapons
• Joined the _____, limiting powerful navies
• Sponsored the _____, which outlawed war
• Coolidge sent troops to _____ to __protect American business interests__.
The Red Scare
Alarm about _____ affected American foreign policy and events at home.
• Postwar strikes led Americans to believe that a _____.
• A series of bombings by _____ led to many Communists being hunted down, arrested, and _____.
• Two Italian immigrants, _____ and _____, were arrested and executed based on the fact that both were _____ and _____.
• Immigration was limited because of fears about _____, and American workers feared for their jobs.
• Immigration law limited people from _____ and prohibited immigration from _____.

Refer to this page to answer the Chapter 22 Focus Question on page 346.

Key Events

1919	18th Amendment prohibits the consumption and sale of alcoholic beverages.
1924	Teapot Dome and other government scandals become public.
1927	Lindbergh flies alone across the Atlantic.

✓ Checkpoint

Name the amendments that established and repealed Prohibition.

_____

_____

Vocabulary Builder

Retrict means "to confine or restrain." Give three examples from the bracketed sentences that show restrictions on women's lives.

_____

_____

_____

Section 2 Focus Question

How did social change and social conflict mark the 1920s? To begin answering this question,

- Find out how Prohibition affected the nation.
- Learn about the changing social position of women.
- Read about inventions that created a new mass culture.
- Understand the conflicts created by rapid change.

Section 2 Summary

Along with the political changes of the 1920s came a number of social changes in American society. Prohibition laws led to illegal activities and organized crime. Women got the right to vote along with increasing social independence, but they still suffered old restrictions. Social divisions split the nation.

Prohibition

During World War I, the temperance movement to ban alcohol gained public support. In 1919, the states ratified the Eighteenth Amendment, which prohibited the making, selling, and transporting of alcohol. The new law ushered in the age of Prohibition. Saloons closed, but illegal ones called **speakeasies** took their place. A smuggling industry known as bootlegging arose. **Bootleggers** transported alcohol from Canada and the Caribbean into the country. Organized crime made huge amounts of money from bootlegging. As a result, gang warfare and general lawlessness increased.

Eventually it was clear that Prohibition could not be enforced. In February 1933, the Twenty-first Amendment repealed Prohibition. ✓

Changing Lives of Women

The Nineteenth Amendment, which gave women the right to vote, was ratified prior to the 1920 election. Women exercised that right for the first time in the presidential election of 1920. Before long they were joining political parties. Some were elected to office. Both Wyoming and Texas elected women governors. In spite of these new freedoms, women's lives remained restricted in other ways. Many universities and professional schools, such as medical schools, still did not admit them. In some states, they could not serve on juries or, if they were married, could not keep the money they earned. More women were holding jobs, however.

Meanwhile, a younger generation of women was exhibiting another kind of independence. They donned short dresses and "bobbed" their hair. These young women, called "flappers," shocked their elders with their actions and became the symbol for women of the 1920s. ✓

A New Mass Culture

Another symbol of the 1920s' individual freedom and independence was the automobile. Henry Ford introduced the assembly line, which reduced the amount of time it took to produce the Model T Ford and made the automobile more affordable for people to buy. An increase in new roads lined with gas stations, restaurants, and cabins encouraged travel and tourism.

The first commercial radio station began broadcasting in 1920. By 1926, more than 700 stations and a national radio network were bringing the same radio shows into millions of homes. Motion pictures became a popular entertainment, and millions of people paid to see a movie every week. ✓

Social Conflict

Rapid change created conflict between old and new social values. This conflict was evident in the 1925 Scopes trial. John Scopes, a high school biology teacher in Dayton, Tennessee, defied both state religious leaders and state law by teaching Charles Darwin's theory of evolution to his students. The trial became the focus of national attention as Clarence Darrow, a famous Chicago lawyer, defended Scopes. Darrow lost the case, and Scopes lost his job. The trial, however, ridiculed the old way of thinking.

Racial conflict became another problem. Hoping for a higher standard of living, many African Americans moved from the South to northern cities in what was called the Great Migration. Mounting racial tensions resulted in violent riots. In response to the violence, Marcus Garvey, an immigrant from Jamaica, created the Universal Negro Improvement Association (UNIA) to promote black pride and black unity. At the same time, the Ku Klux Klan—an organization opposed to blacks, immigrants, Catholics, and Jews—gained power. It spread from the South to the Midwest and the West before its decline. ✓

Check Your Progress

1. What were three main social conflicts during the 1920s?

_____

_____

2. What effect did the Model T Ford have on American culture?

_____

_____

✓ **Checkpoint**

Identify the purpose of the Nineteenth Amendment.

_____

_____

✓ **Checkpoint**

List two forms of media that contributed to a mass culture in the 1920s.

_____

_____

✓ **Checkpoint**

Name the organization founded by Marcus Garvey.

_____

_____

Question to Think About As you read Section 2 in your textbook and take notes, keep this section focus question in mind: **How did social change and social conflict mark the 1920s?**

▶ Use this chart to record key information from the section. Some information has been filled in to get you started.

Changes in American Society
Prohibition
During World War I, prohibition was supported as a way to conserve _____. • In 1919, the states ratified the _____, which prohibited _____. • Saloons closed, but the law proved impossible to _____. • _____ made huge profits importing illegal alcohol. • Every large town had a _____. • Prohibition led to the growth of _____. • In February 1933, Prohibition was repealed by the _____.
Changing Lives of Women
• _____ gave women the right to vote in the 1920 presidential election. • Two women governors: _____ and _____. • In some states, women could not serve on _____ or keep their _____. • Younger women known as _____ became the symbol of women in the 1920s.
A New Mass Culture
• Henry Ford introduced the _____, which made the price for a Model T_____. • The automobile became the symbol of _____. • New businesses created by the automobile: _____ • Cars made it easier for families to move to _____, and people in rural areas were less _____. Cars also encouraged _____. • The first commercial radio station:_____ • Families listened to _____ and <u>political conventions</u>. • The first major "talking" movie: _____
Social Conflict
• The Scopes trial pitted <u>religion</u> against <u>scientific theory</u>. • Many African Americans moved north in the _____. • Race riots broke out, with the worst occurring in _____ in 1919. • Jamaican immigrant _____ created the _____ _____. It promoted_____ and encouraged African Americans to _____. • Social tensions led to the growth of _____.

Refer to this page to answer the Chapter 22 Focus Question on page 346.

Section 3 Focus Question

What arts and culture symbolized the Jazz Age? To begin answering this question,

- Read about the new pastimes of the 1920s.
- Learn about a uniquely American musical sound.
- Find out about writers who chronicled the social values of the 1920s.
- Understand the Harlem Renaissance.

Section 3 Summary

During the 1920s, American culture was bursting with a new energy and artistic expression. From fads and heroes to dance, music, and literature, America's popular culture expressed both the hopes and the conflicts of a new generation.

Fads and Heroes

The 1920s was a decade of prosperity that fostered many new enthusiasms. Lively dances, such as the Charleston, the Lindy Hop, the Black Bottom, and the Breakaway, were all the rage. Fads such as flagpole sitting and dance marathons, in which couples danced for hours, swept the country. The Chinese game of mah-jongg also became a popular pastime.

A new kind of celebrity captured American hearts during the 1920s: the sports hero. Athletes such as baseball's Babe Ruth, swimmer Johnny Weissmuller, and champion golfer Bobby Jones became famous. The most popular celebrity of all was **Charles Lindbergh**, who made the first solo nonstop flight across the Atlantic. His nickname was Lucky Lindy, and he came to symbolize the optimism of the decade. ✔

An American Sound

Jazz is a style of music that combined rhythms from West Africa and the Caribbean, work chants and spirituals from the rural South, and harmonies from Europe. African American musicians developed jazz in the nightclubs and dance halls of New Orleans. From there, jazz moved north with the Great Migration. African American musicians spread jazz to St. Louis, New York, Chicago, Kansas City, and Detroit. Among the most famous jazz stars were Louis Armstrong, Bessie Smith, and Duke Ellington, all of whom had southern roots.

Radio helped spread jazz, too. White composers and band-leaders, such as George Gershwin and Paul Whiteman, embraced the style and gave it their own stamp. Jazz became one of the most important American contributions to world culture. So popular did jazz become that the 1920s are known as the Jazz Age.

Key Events

1919	18th Amendment prohibits the consumption and sale of alcoholic beverages.
1924	Teapot Dome and other government scandals become public.
1927	Lindbergh flies alone across the Atlantic.

✓ Checkpoint

List three fads that were popular in the 1920s.

_____

_____

_____

_____

_____

Vocabulary Builder

The word *renaissance* means "rebirth." Why do you think the Harlem Renaissance was given this name?

_____

_____

_____

✓ Checkpoint

List three major novelists of the 1920s.

_____

_____

_____

Like many other cultural movements, however, it widened the divide between older and younger generations. ✓

Literature of the 1920s

American literature in the 1920s reflected both the decade's energy and its excesses. The novels of F. Scott Fitzgerald, Ernest Hemingway, and **Sinclair Lewis** were as much social criticisms as they were fictional stories. Fitzgerald's *The Great Gatsby* expressed disillusionment with the emptiness of rich people's lives. Hemingway's *The Sun Also Rises* and *A Farewell to Arms* captured growing antiwar sentiment. Lewis's *Babbitt* criticized the loose values and hypocrisy of middle-class culture. Fitzgerald and Hemingway, among others, actually left the United States to live abroad for extended periods.

During the 1920s, a vibrant African American culture known as the Harlem <u>Renaissance</u> emerged. Harlem was a large African American neighborhood of New York City, and it attracted thousands of African Americans from the South. A different kind of social criticism arose among the black writers, musicians, and poets who settled in Harlem. Their moving works were a reaction to racial prejudice as well as an expression of hope. **Langston Hughes** expressed black pride in poetry that he hoped would capture the beat of jazz. James Weldon Johnson combined poetry and politics. He wrote editorials for the *New York Age*, an important black-owned newspaper. He also worked for the NAACP, an organization dedicated to the advancement of African Americans. Novelist and anthropologist Zora Neale Hurston recorded and analyzed many African American folk songs and folk tales. ✓

Check Your Progress

1. Who was the favorite celebrity of the 1920s and why?

_____

_____

_____

2. Who were some of the major figures of the Harlem Renaissance?

_____

_____

_____

_____

Question to Think About As you read Section 3 in your textbook and take notes, keep this section focus question in mind: **What arts and culture symbolized the Jazz Age?**

▶ Use this chart to record key information from the section. Some information has been filled in to get you started.

Arts and Popular Culture of the Jazz Age
Fads Dance fads that expressed the energy and optimism of the 1920s included the ___Charleston___ , _____ , _____ , and _____ . Other fads included _____ , _____ , and _____ .
Heroes of the 1920s • Baseball player ___Babe Ruth___ • Swimmer _____ • Football player _____ • Golf champion _____ • Tennis stars _____ • Boxer _____ The most loved hero of the decade was _____ , whose Atlantic flight symbolized _____ .
Jazz Greats Jazz was born in the nightclubs and dance halls of _____ . It combined _____ , _____ , and _____ . Famous jazz artists included _____ , _____ , and _____ . Jazz emphasizes _____ and _____ .
Notable Writers Some novels reflected _____ of the era as well as criticized its _____ , such as F. Scott Fitzgerald's _____ and Sinclair Lewis's _____ . Ernest Hemingway's novel _____ captured _____ . In a New York City neighborhood, a vibrant African American culture known as the _____ occurred. African American writers reacted to _____ . The works of writers such as _____ , _____ , and _____ expressed _____ .

Refer to this page to answer the Chapter 22 Focus Question on page 346.

The Economy of the 1920s

Key Events

1919	18th Amendment prohibits the consumption and sale of alcoholic beverages.
1924	Teapot Dome and other government scandals become public.
1927	Lindbergh flies alone across the Atlantic.

Section 4 Focus Question

What economic problems threatened the economic boom of the 1920s? To begin answering this question,
- Learn about the decade's industrial growth.
- Find out about margin buying on the stock market.
- Understand Americans' failure to see the signs of economic trouble.
- Read about the election of Herbert Hoover.

Section 4 Summary

Many people regarded the economic changes of the 1920s as a long period of prosperity, but others were concerned that problems lay hidden beneath the surface. Heavy consumer purchasing and a booming stock market existed alongside rural poverty and unemployment.

Industrial Growth

A huge increase in industrial production pulled the nation out of the postwar economic recession. As more goods came to market, prices dropped. Advertisements, chain stores, and mail-order catalogs presented labor-saving devices for the home, such as washing machines, vacuum cleaners, and toasters. These enticed consumers to spend their money. **Installment buying**, or buying on credit, meant that people could enjoy expensive purchases such as cars, refrigerators, and radios long before they had paid for them in full.

Government policies kept the economy going. High taxes on imported goods favored American companies. Tax cuts for the wealthy encouraged spending. These measures stimulated the economy, but at the same time they encouraged reckless spending. ✓

A Booming Stock Market

In a strong economy, more people are able to afford to buy stocks, or shares of companies. During the 1920s, the stock market became a **bull market**, meaning that stock values rose. Investors began **buying on margin**, which meant they paid a percentage of the stock's cost when they bought it, and paid the rest when they sold it. As long as the market value continued to rise, this was not a risk. If the market fell, however, investors could be left owing money for devalued stock. Some economists began to worry about margin buying. Most people, however, listened to positive economists such as Irwin Fisher who said, "The nation is marching along

✓ Checkpoint

List three reasons for increased consumer spending in the 1920s.

_____

_____

_____

a permanently high plateau of prosperity." Unfortunately, this statement did not match the reality of the country. Wealthy Americans made up only 5 percent of the population. Many of the rest worked hard yet barely survived. ✓

Signs of Trouble
Among the people who did not share in the decade's prosperity were farmers. Before World War I, they had sold their surplus crops to foreign markets. During the pre-war years, farmers took out loans to buy land and equipment. However, many postwar nations were too poor to purchase surplus crops. With the drop in income, farmers were unable to pay their debts.

Some factory workers fared well, but others did not. Some companies offered their employees benefits such as vacations and pensions. With the rise of the assembly line, however, unskilled workers were taking the jobs of skilled workers for less pay. Unemployment was high even during the more prosperous years. ✓

The Election of 1928
The Republicans, who held the presidency throughout the 1920s, took credit for the decade of prosperity. Republican Secretary of Commerce Herbert Hoover ran for President in 1928. His Democratic opponent, Alfred E. Smith, was the first Catholic to run for President. Religion and the economy became the major issues in the election. Hoover won with the slogan "a chicken in every pot and a car in every garage." Although Hoover lost the largest cities, he carried 41 states. This was a <u>significant</u> victory for Republicans. It showed that many poor, rural voters still placed their hopes in the Republican Party. Herbert Hoover came to the White House believing he could satisfy those hopes. ✓

Check Your Progress
1. What were two factors in the economy that indicated a period of prosperity?

_____

_____

_____

2. What two groups in American society did not share in the prosperity of the 1920s?

_____

_____

✓ Checkpoint

Explain why buying stocks on margin could be a risky practice.

_____

_____

✓ Checkpoint

Explain why farmers were unable to repay their loans.

_____

_____

Vocabulary Builder

Something that is *significant* has a major or important effect. Why was Hoover's victory significant?

_____

_____

✓ Checkpoint

Name the two major issues in the election of 1928.

_____

_____

Question to Think About As you read Section 4 in your textbook and take notes, keep this section focus question in mind: **What economic problems threatened the economic boom of the 1920s?**

▶ Use this chart to record key information from the section. Some information has been filled in to get you started.

The Economy of the 1920s	
Industrial Growth • From 1922 to 1928, _____ _____ climbed 70 percent. • As more goods came to market, _____. • _Rising incomes_ gave consumers more to spend. • To encourage spending, businesses offered _____. • Chain stores and _____ made it easier for people to buy goods. • A new _____ culture arose. • High tariffs on _____ stopped competition with domestic products. • Taxes on the wealthy were_____ to encourage spending. • Americans developed a _____ about spending.	**A Booming Stock Market** • Many people could now afford to _____ _____, or shares of companies. • A _bull market_ occurred, and stocks were so profitable that people began _____. • Some economists began to worry, and a few experts warned that _____ _____. • Most investors _____ the warnings. • Most people at the time were not _____. • The wealthiest Americans made up _____ of the population.

Signs of Trouble	
Farmers Many farmers lived in poverty. Reasons for an agricultural depression: • Farmers grew more than the _____ _____ could consume. • After World War I, other nations were too poor to buy farmers' _____ crops. • Many farmers were unable to pay off their _____.	**Workers** • Workers' _____ were rising. • Some companies offered _____, such as _pensions_ and _____. • Unemployment was _____. • Unskilled workers who worked on an _____ were squeezing out skilled labor for less wages.

Election of 1928
• The _____ Party held the presidency throughout the 1920s.   • The Republican candidate for the 1928 presidential election: _____   • The Democratic candidate for the 1928 presidential election: _____   • Two issues highlighted in the election: _____   • Winner: _____; Slogan: _____

Refer to this page to answer the Chapter 22 Focus Question on page 346.

Directions: Circle the letter of the correct answer.

1. Who were the Republican Presidents of the 1920s?
   - **A** Wilson, Coolidge, Hoover
   - **B** Harding, Coolidge, Hoover
   - **C** Wilson, Harding, Coolidge
   - **D** Wilson, Harding, Hoover

2. Which amendment to the Constitution gave women the right to vote?
   - **A** Eighteenth
   - **B** Nineteenth
   - **C** Twentieth
   - **D** Twenty-first

3. What was the Great Migration?
   - **A** Midwestern farmers leaving rural areas for urban ones
   - **B** Eastern Europeans leaving for America
   - **C** Mexicans crossing the border into California
   - **D** Southern African Americans leaving for northern cities

4. Who of the following was *not* a writer of the 1920s?
   - **A** Langston Hughes
   - **B** Sinclair Lewis
   - **C** Louis Armstrong
   - **D** James Weldon Johnson

Directions: Follow the steps to answer this question:

How might American culture be different if three major events had not occurred in the 1920s?

Step 1: Recall information: List one effect each event below had on American culture.

Three Major Events of the 1920s	Effect
• Increase of installment buying • Nineteenth Amendment passed into law • Birth of Jazz	• • •

Step 2: Hypothesize: Now imagine three ways the American culture would be different today if these events had never occurred.

Differences in American Culture Without Those Events
• • •

Step 3: Complete the topic sentence that follows. Then write two or three sentences that support the topic sentence.

American culture today would be much different if _____

_____

_____

_____

Now you are ready to answer the Chapter 22 Focus Question: **How did the nation react to change in the 1920s?**

▶ Fill in the following chart to help you answer this question. Use the notes that you took for each section.

Change in the 1920s	
Areas of Change	**Results of Change**
The Red Scare and Immigration	• Thousands of radical anarchists, Communists, and other foreigners are deported from the country. • • •
Ratification of Amendments • Eighteenth Amendment • Nineteenth Amendment	• •
Mass Culture • Automobile • Entertainment	• •
The Great Migration	• • •
Arts and Culture • Literature • Music	• • •
The Economy • Consumer market • Stock market • Job market	• • •

Refer to this page to answer the Unit 7 Focus Question on page 347.

Unit 7 Pulling It Together Activity

What You Have Learned

Chapter 20 By the late 1800s, the United States had acquired new territories in the Pacific and strengthened its trade ties with Asia. The Spanish-American War led to increased involvement in Latin America.

Chapter 21 In 1914, a war broke out in Europe. The United States remained neutral at first, but it eventually joined the war. The conflict, which we now call World War I, had important effects both in the United States and in the rest of the world.

Chapter 22 The decade following World War I marked dramatic changes for the United States. Republicans returned the country to pre-war isolationism and supported big business. Cultural changes affecting the lives of Americans sparked conflicts.

Think Like a Historian

Read the Unit 7 Essential Question: **How did a more powerful United States expand its role in the world?**

▶ Use the organizers on this page and the next to collect information to answer this question.

How did the United States expand its territorial, economic, and political roles? Some of the answers are listed in the charts. Review your section and chapter notes. Then complete the charts.

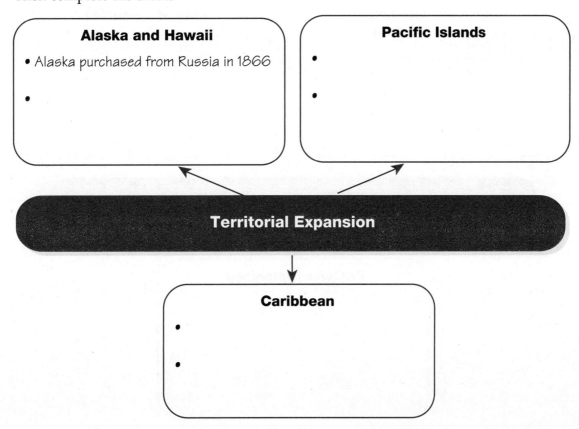

Alaska and Hawaii
- Alaska purchased from Russia in 1866
-

Pacific Islands
-
-

Territorial Expansion

Caribbean
-
-

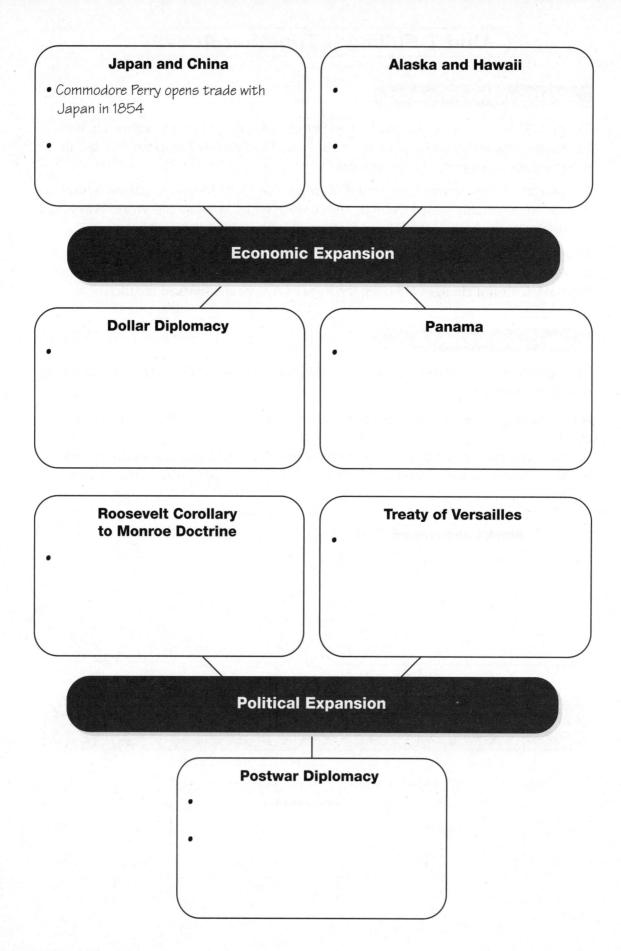

Japan and China

- Commodore Perry opens trade with Japan in 1854

-

Alaska and Hawaii

-

-

Economic Expansion

Dollar Diplomacy

-

Panama

-

Roosevelt Corollary to Monroe Doctrine

-

Treaty of Versailles

-

Political Expansion

Postwar Diplomacy

-

-

Depression and War

Chapter 23 Millions of people lost their jobs, homes, and savings during the Great Depression. President Franklin Roosevelt responded with a wide range of measures called the New Deal that had long-lasting effects.

Chapter 24 The United States finally came out of the Great Depression as its factories produced the "arsenal of democracy" for fighting World War II, the bloodiest conflict in history. Both U.S. soldiers and civilians at home made major contributions to winning the war.

Chapter 25 After World War II, the United States faced new challenges in the world and economic and social changes at home. Conflict with the Soviet Union developed into a Cold War. U.S. policy aimed to contain the spread of communism, using military force when necessary.

Focus Your Learning As you study this unit and take notes, you will find the information to answer the questions below. Answering the Chapter Essential Questions will help build your answer to the Unit Essential Question.

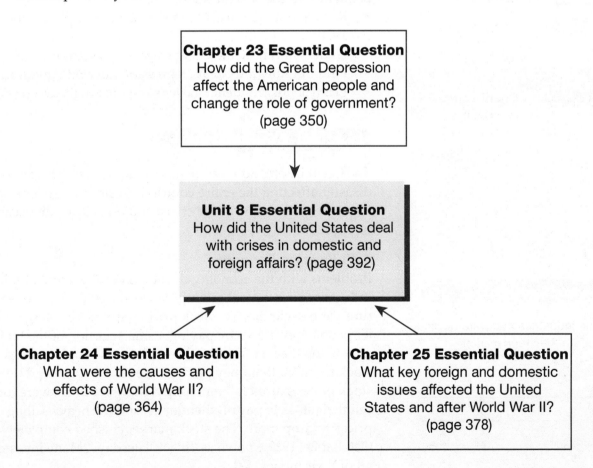

Chapter 23 Essential Question
How did the Great Depression affect the American people and change the role of government?
(page 350)

Unit 8 Essential Question
How did the United States deal with crises in domestic and foreign affairs? (page 392)

Chapter 24 Essential Question
What were the causes and effects of World War II?
(page 364)

Chapter 25 Essential Question
What key foreign and domestic issues affected the United States and after World War II?
(page 378)

The Great Depression and the New Deal

(1929–1941)

What You Will Learn

The Great Depression was the worst economic crisis in American history. Millions of people lost their jobs, homes, and savings. President Franklin Roosevelt responded with the New Deal.

Chapter 23 Focus Question

As you read this chapter, keep this question in mind: **How did the Great Depression affect the American people and change the role of government?**

Section 1

Hoover and the Crash

Section 1 Focus Question

Why did the economy collapse after the stock market crash? To begin answering this question,

- Read about America's economic problems during the late 1920s.
- Understand how the Great Depression started.
- Find out how the Great Depression affected Americans.
- Learn about President Hoover's response to the Depression.

Section 1 Summary

The Great Depression was an economic crisis that became a social disaster affecting the entire country. President Hoover's responses failed to stop the crisis, and he became increasingly unpopular.

A Collapsing Economy

Problems with the economy developed in the late 1920s. Major industries such as coal mining, railroads, clothing, and agriculture were declining. Yet stock prices kept rising. Margin buying let people buy stocks by paying a small portion of the total cost and owing the rest. That worked as long as people could sell their stock for more than they paid. However, on October 23, 1929, stock prices started falling rapidly. Margin buyers were forced to sell their stock to pay off their loans, and the heavy selling caused prices to drop more. The stock market crashed completely on October 29, 1929, known as "Black Tuesday." Many investors lost all of their money. ✓

Key Events

1929	Stock market crash marks the beginning of the Great Depression.
1933	President Roosevelt launches the New Deal.
1935	Congress passes the Social Security Act.
1941	Great Depression ends as the United States prepares for war.

✓ Checkpoint

List the industries that were declining before the stock market crashed.

_____

_____

_____

_____

The Great Depression Begins

The stock market crash contributed to economic problems that caused the Great Depression, which lasted 12 years and had far-reaching effects. One cause of the Depression was **overproduction,** which occurs when there are too many goods produced and not enough buyers. A banking crisis was another cause. Rural banks lost money because many farms were failing, and many urban banks lost huge sums in the stock market crash. Thousands of banks closed, and depositors lost their money.

A downward spiral developed. People had less money to buy goods, so factories cut jobs or closed. In turn, jobless people had even less to spend, making the situation worse. Many companies declared **bankruptcy,** or financial failure caused by a company's inability to pay its debts. Eventually, because of international loans and trade, the Depression spread worldwide. Some European countries **defaulted,** or failed to repay their loans. ✓

The Human Cost

Between 1929 and 1933, unemployment rose from 3 percent to 25 percent, with some 13 million people out of work. The urban unemployed were hit hardest, because they had no money for food and no land on which to grow their own. Salaries were cut, so that even people with jobs made significantly less money. Widespread poverty and misery gripped the country. Many people lost their homes and lived in makeshift dwellings. The magnitude of the crisis was so great that many schools closed from lack of funds. ✓

Hoover Responds

Hoover's advisers thought the economy would bounce back naturally. When it did not, Hoover still hesitated to have the federal government take action. Instead, he encouraged businesses and local governments and charities to help those in need. It was not enough. In 1932, Hoover created a federal agency, the Reconstruction Finance Corporation, to provide money to local governments and key industries. The Depression continued to worsen, however, and Hoover was blamed. His popularity plummeted after the Bonus Army incident in June 1932. World War I veterans marched on Washington to demand early receipt of a $1,000 **bonus,** or extra payment, promised for their military service. Some veterans refused to leave, and government forces fired on them, which outraged the country. ✓

Check Your Progress

1. What were two causes of the Great Depression that started before the stock market crash?

   _____

   _____

2. How did the loss of jobs make the Depression worse?

   _____

✓ Checkpoint

Explain why the Depression spread worldwide.

_____

_____

Vocabulary Builder

Magnitude means "great size, significance, or importance." List two examples of how human suffering showed the magnitude of the Depression.

_____

_____

✓ Checkpoint

Identify the unemployment figures of the Great Depression.

_____

_____

✓ Checkpoint

Name two measures President Hoover took in response to the Depression.

_____

_____

Question to Think About As you read Section 1 in your textbook and take notes, keep this section focus question in mind: **Why did the economy collapse after the stock market crash?**

▶ Use this chart to record key information from the section. Some information has been filled in to get you started.

Hoover and the Crash
The Collapsing Economy
• Problems with the U.S. economy started __in the late 1920s__.   • Major industries were declining, but stock prices were still _____. This encouraged risky investments by _____.   • When stock prices started falling, margin buyers _____ _____.   • The stock market crashed on _____, known as Black Tuesday.
The Great Depression Begins
• The Great Depression was a major _economic_ and _____ disaster that affected the entire country.   • The Great Depression lasted _____ years and was triggered by the _____.   • One problem that caused the Great Depression was _____. Factories produced more goods than people could afford to buy.   • The _____ crisis also contributed to the Depression. Banks closed because _____.   • People had less money because _____.
The Human Cost
• From 1929 to 1933, the unemployment rate went from _____ to _____ percent.   • The number of people without jobs was about _____.   • With little or no money, many people lacked adequate _food, shelter, and clothing_.   • The Great Depression was a time of widespread _____.
Hoover Responds
• At first, President Hoover's advisers recommended doing _____. They believed the Depression was __temporary__.   • Hoover's first measures encouraged businesses and local governments—but not the _____ government—to take the lead to help people. He also urged private _____ to set up _____.   • As the Depression worsened, he created the _____ in 1932 to provide _____ to key industries and local governments.   • The treatment of the _____ further damaged Hoover's popularity.

Refer to this page to answer the Chapter 23 Focus Question on page 363.

Section 2

Roosevelt and the New Deal

Section 2 Focus Question

How did President Roosevelt respond to the Great Depression?
To begin answering this question,

- Learn how Franklin Roosevelt won the 1932 presidential election.
- Find out how the New Deal tried to promote economic recovery.
- Understand what new laws regulated America's economic system.
- Identify obstacles and criticisms faced by the New Deal.

Section 2 Summary

Franklin D. Roosevelt, known as FDR, took office in 1933 and provided hope and action. His program, the New Deal, included many measures and reforms. The New Deal had critics and mixed results, yet FDR became a popular President.

Franklin D. Roosevelt

Roosevelt, a Democrat and governor of New York, was elected President in 1932. FDR was a wealthy cousin of Theodore Roosevelt. He was disabled from polio, yet he was never shown in his wheelchair and most Americans never knew their president could not walk unaided. In his 1933 inaugural speech, he offered hope in a famous phrase: "the only thing we have to fear is fear itself. . . ."His first action targeted the banking crisis with a bank holiday, a four-day closing of all banks. He then introduced government regulation with the Emergency Banking Relief Act, which restored confidence in the nation's banks. FDR also began his **fireside chats,** which were national radio broadcasts to explain his measures and reassure the public. ✔

Relief for the Jobless

FDR's New Deal measures had three key goals: relief for the jobless, economic recovery, and reforms to prevent future depressions. Fifteen new bills were passed and signed in the first hundred days of his presidency. The Federal Emergency Relief Administration (FERA) provided financial help for the unemployed. Jobs programs offered employment. The Civilian Conservation Corps (CCC) hired jobless men in cities to work on environmental projects in national parks, forests, and wilderness areas. The Works Progress Administration (WPA) hired people to build or repair schools, post offices, roads, bridges, and airports. Even artists and writers were employed for government arts and writing projects. ✔

Key Events

1929 — Stock market crash marks the beginning of the Great Depression.

1933 — President Roosevelt launches the New Deal.

1935 — Congress passes the Social Security Act.

1941 — Great Depression ends as the United States prepares for war.

✓ Checkpoint

Name the method FDR used to reassure the public.

_____

_____

✓ Checkpoint

Name two federal programs that gave work to the jobless.

_____

_____

Promoting Economic Recovery

FDR established federal agencies to help two main sectors of the economy: industry and agriculture. The National Recovery Administration (NRA) aimed to keep prices stable while increasing employment. The goal was for companies to make enough money to be able to hire more workers and pay decent wages. The Public Works Administration (PWA) hired people for major public works projects, such as building the Lincoln Tunnel in New York City. The Tennessee Valley Authority (TVA) built dams along the Tennessee River to provide jobs and electricity in a poverty-stricken region. These government programs generally accomplished their goals. They failed to significantly improve the economy, however. ✓

Reforming the Economic System

FDR's reform measures aimed to prevent another depression. Companies were now required to report honestly about their stock. People received protection for their bank deposits through the Federal Deposit Insurance Corporation (FDIC). Federal agencies were established or strengthened to set fairness and safety standards for various industries. ✓

Obstacles to the New Deal

Many Americans supported FDR's New Deal, and he easily won reelection in 1936. Yet, he faced roadblocks. One challenge came from the judicial branch. The Supreme Court declared some of his programs unconstitutional. In response, FDR tried to "pack" the court by proposing to add six additional judges who would support him. Congress defeated the plan, but FDR was able to appoint a liberal justice when a conservative resigned in 1937.

FDR's critics included conservatives who complained about regulations on business, as well as liberals who wanted more done for the poor. Among his most vocal critics was Louisiana Senator **Huey Long,** a fellow Democrat who called for taxing the rich and distributing their wealth to the poor. Still, FDR remained popular and kept most of the country's trust. ✓

Check Your Progress

1. What was President Roosevelt's first action after taking office?

2. What were the three goals of FDR's New Deal program?

✓ Checkpoint

Identify FDR's two priorities for economic recovery.

✓ Checkpoint

Explain why the FDIC was established.

Vocabulary Builder

Judicial is an adjective that means "relating to judges or a court of law." What court does it refer to here?

✓ Checkpoint

List three critics of FDR's New Deal.

Question to Think About As you read Section 2 in your textbook and take notes, keep this section focus question in mind: **How did President Roosevelt respond to the Great Depression?**

▶ Use the chart to record key information from the section. Some information has been filled in to get you started.

Roosevelt and the New Deal

Franklin D. Roosevelt took office in _____. Three goals of FDR's New Deal measures:
- _____
- _____
- _____

New Deal Measures		
Act	Abbreviation	Purpose
Emergency Banking Relief Act	(none)	Provided more careful government regulation of banks
Federal Emergency Relief Administration		
	CCC	
	WPA	
National Recovery Administration		
	PWA	
	TVA	
Truth-in-Securities Act	(none)	
Federal Deposit Insurance Corporation		
Federal Power Commission		

Obstacles to the New Deal

Roosevelt was reelected in __1936__, showing that many Americans _____ the New Deal. However, the Supreme Court declared the _____ and other measures _____. When FDR tried to add justices who would support his programs, his plan to _____ the court was defeated. Three famous critics of the New Deal were _____, _____, and _____.

Refer to this page to answer the Chapter 23 Focus Question on page 363.

Key Events

| 1929 | Stock market crash marks the beginning of the Great Depression. |

| 1933 | President Roosevelt launches the New Deal. |

| 1935 | Congress passes the Social Security Act. |

| 1941 | Great Depression ends as the United States prepares for war. |

✓ Checkpoint

Explain what First Lady Eleanor Roosevelt did to help during the Depression.

_____

_____

_____

Section 3 Focus Question

How did the Great Depression affect daily life? To begin answering this question,

- Discover how the Great Depression and the New Deal affected women, African Americans, Mexican Americans, and Native Americans.
- Learn about the causes and effects of the Dust Bowl.
- Understand how art, radio, and movies informed and entertained people during the Depression.

Section 3 Summary

The Great Depression made life more difficult for nearly everyone. However, some people experienced special hardships because of their gender, racial or ethnic background, or where they lived.

Women in the Depression

Women had special hardships and took on additional responsibilities during the Great Depression. Many had to take jobs to support their families. They benefited from positions such as secretaries and salesclerks, which were more secure than men's factory jobs. However, when the Depression started, women in factory jobs were usually cut before men, and those who were maids and housekeepers lost positions when families could no longer afford paid help. At home, women took on extra chores, such as making their family's clothing, to save money. One very busy woman during the Depression was First Lady **Eleanor Roosevelt.** She traveled the country to report conditions to the President and to help evaluate needs. She was an activist First Lady who supported women's rights and racial equality. ✓

African Americans in the Depression

African Americans experienced more hardships than most whites during the Depression. Whites competed for jobs that African Americans traditionally held. African American workers were often the first to be cut in layoffs. As a result, African American unemployment was 50 percent or higher in the South and in northern cities like New York. Through the influence of the First Lady, FDR appointed some 100 African American leaders to government posts. Some served as his informal "Black Cabinet." Still, FDR did not push for more **civil rights,** or rights guaranteed in the Constitution, for African Americans. He needed southern senators' support for the New Deal. A concert at the Lincoln

Memorial by African American singer **Marian Anderson** became a civil rights symbol. ✓

Other Americans in the Depression

Mexican Americans and Native Americans also faced special challenges. Mexicans who were **migrant workers,** or those who moved about picking crops, were threatened by whites who wanted their jobs. Many Mexicans, including some who were U.S. citizens, were deported. Native Americans were already among the poorest citizens before the Depression. A program called the Indian New Deal provided jobs for them. It also aimed to give them greater control of their reservations, encouraged Indian schools, and stopped the sale of tribal lands. Still, Native Americans remained desperately poor. ✓

The Dust Bowl

Farmers in the southwestern Plains faced a new problem when a severe drought hit in 1930. Crops failed, and with no plants to hold the topsoil in place, it blew away in giant dust storms called "black blizzards." This environmental disaster lasted five years and turned the region into what was called the Dust Bowl. Farming methods that had cleared huge acres of land contributed to the calamity. Oklahoma was especially hard hit. Thousands of "Okies" abandoned their ruined farms and moved to California to find work. There they suffered more hardships as they competed for low-paying jobs. ✓

Arts and Media of the Depression

Some artists and writers used the Depression as a theme in their work. Photographers and painters captured visually the suffering of people. **John Steinbeck's** *The Grapes of Wrath* chronicled the experiences of Dust Bowl Okies in California. Some movies also depicted people's struggles, but most helped ordinary Americans escape their miseries. Mickey Mouse and child star Shirley Temple were particularly popular. People listened to radio for entertainment but also for news and FDR's fireside chats. Continuing dramas sponsored by soap companies created the birth of soap operas. ✓

Check Your Progress

1. List the people who were hardest hit by the Depression.

_____

_____

2. Name three groups of people who captured the experience of the Great Depression.

_____

_____

✓ **Checkpoint**

Give two reasons for high unemployment among African Americans.

_____

_____

✓ **Checkpoint**

Explain why many Mexican Americans were deported.

_____

_____

✓ **Checkpoint**

Name the region that became the Dust Bowl.

_____

✓ **Checkpoint**

List three reasons why people listened to the radio.

_____

_____

_____

Question to Think About As you read Section 3 in your textbook and take notes, keep this section focus question in mind: **How did the Great Depression affect daily life?**

▶ Use this chart to record key information from the section. Some information has been filled in to get you started.

Life in the Great Depression

Women in the Depression
Women who were __secretaries__ and _____ often kept their jobs, but those who were _____ or _____ workers lost theirs.

African Americans in the Depression
African Americans suffered more __unemployment__, _____, _____, and _____ than did whites.

Other Americans in the Depression
Mexicans and Mexican Americans were forced out of _____ and sometimes _____. Native Americans were among the _____ when the Depression began.

The Dust Bowl was located in the _____. The dust storms began in __1930__ and lasted _____, turning _____ into wasteland. Many farm families were forced to go to _____ to find work.

Arts and Media of the Depression
The movies helped people _____, while radio was a vital part of _____.

Important People of the Depression		
Key Person	Position or Role	Why Important
1.	First Lady	Championed women's and minorities' rights
2. Mary McLeod Bethune	Educator and member of FDR's "Black Cabinet"	
3.		Promoted the "Indian New Deal"
4. John Steinbeck		
5.	Photographer for Farm Security Administration	
6.		WPA murals captured lives of ordinary people
7.	Popular child actress	

Refer to this page to answer the Chapter 23 Focus Question on page 365.

Section 4

Legacy of the New Deal

Section 4 Focus Question

What were the long-term effects of the New Deal? To begin answering this question,
- Find out how Social Security began.
- Learn how the New Deal reformed labor relations.
- Identify the main arguments for and against the New Deal.

Section 4 Summary

Social and labor reforms contributed to changes in the size and influence of the federal government, which gave the New Deal its lasting legacy.

Social Security

One of the most important legacies of the New Deal is Social Security. The Social Security Act was passed in 1935 to give the federal government a major role in helping the neediest in society: old people, children, the disabled, and the unemployed. Old-Age Insurance was a key part of the Social Security Act. It guaranteed a pension to retired people. The pension was funded by a **payroll tax,** or a tax that removes money directly from workers' paychecks. Businesses were required to match the amount withheld from their employees, and they objected to keeping this much money out of the economy.

The Social Security Act also included Aid to Dependent Children (ADC), which provided money for children without fathers at home or whose fathers were unemployed. In addition, it enabled mothers to stay home to raise their children. Social Security also gave financial help to disabled people and offered the states federal money to give short-term payments to workers who were unemployed. ✔

Lasting Labor Reforms

FDR had the first woman Cabinet member, **Frances Perkins.** As secretary of labor, she supported reforms that gave workers more rights. The 1935 National Labor Relations Act, called the Wagner Act, guaranteed the right to organize employee unions and banned unfair firing of union members. It also allowed **collective bargaining,** or the right of unions to speak for all workers in labor negotiations. The 1938 Fair Labor Standards Act guaranteed a minimum wage and maximum hours for the work week. It established overtime pay and ended some kinds of child labor.

Union membership increased as unions became more powerful. More women and African Americans became union members through the new Congress of Industrial Organizations (CIO).

Key Events

1929 Stock market crash marks the beginning of the Great Depression.

1933 President Roosevelt launches the New Deal.

1935 Congress passes the Social Security Act.

1941 Great Depression ends as the United States prepares for war.

✔ Checkpoint

List four types of payments that Social Security provided.

_____

_____

_____

_____

_____

_____

_____

Vocabulary Builder

Synonyms for the word *impact* include "influence" and "effect." List two influences or effects of the New Deal on government.

_____

_____

✓ Checkpoint

State when the Great Depression finally ended, and why.

_____

_____

_____

Formed by **John L. Lewis,** the CIO included all workers, skilled and unskilled, in each industry for union membership. A new labor tactic was the **sit-down strike,** in which employees would stay on the job but stop working. The sit-down strike was successful for auto workers, although it was later ruled illegal by the Supreme Court. ☑

Scorecard on the New Deal

The New Deal had a strong and lasting impact on the federal government. The size of government was increased along with its role in solving social problems. There was much debate over whether this was a good or a bad development. Arguments against the New Deal included concerns that a powerful federal government threatened individual freedom and free enterprise. The cost of the New Deal programs led to **deficit spending,** where the government spends more money than it receives in taxes. Some critics also questioned the effectiveness of New Deal programs. They argued that preparing for war in 1941—not New Deal programs—pulled the country out of the Depression.

Supporters of the New Deal pointed to the millions of new jobs it created, how it ended the banking crisis and reformed the stock market, and how it improved working conditions. Buildings, roads, and bridges were improved or created. About 12 million acres of national parks were improved through New Deal programs. Rural America had electricity for the first time, and lasting works of art emerged. Many Americans also felt greater confidence in their government and great personal loyalty to President Roosevelt. Supporters of the New Deal believed that the programs helped save democracy in the United States, when other countries in Europe and Asia turned to dictatorships. ☑

Check Your Progress

1. Explain why the New Deal had a lasting legacy.

_____

_____

2. Identify at least two arguments for and two arguments against the New Deal.

_____

_____

_____

_____

Question to Think About As you read Section 4 in your textbook and take notes, keep this section focus question in mind: **What were the long-term effects of the New Deal?**

▶ Use these charts to record key information from the section. Some information has been filled in to get you started.

Social Security		Labor Reforms
Lasting effects: • Retirement pensions paid for by _____ on workers and matching payments by _____ • Aid to Dependent _____ • _____ aid to the disabled • _____ payments for unemployed people	**Legacy of the New Deal**	Lasting effects: • Workers' right to organize into _____ • Right to _____ bargaining • Federally set minimum _____ • Time-and-a-half pay for _____ • Working to end _____ labor • Growth of union _____ among skilled and unskilled workers

Scorecard on the New Deal	
Arguments against the New Deal	**Arguments in favor of the New Deal**
Powerful federal government threatened ___individual freedom___	Employed millions and improved _____ conditions on the job
Powerful federal government threatened free _____	Ended the _____ crisis and reformed the _____ market
Increase in national debt through _____ spending	• Built dams and bridges • Preserved _____ million acres of parkland • Provided _____ to rural areas
New Deal programs did not fulfill their goal of full _____	Restored Americans' _____ in government

Refer to this page to answer the Chapter 23 Focus Question on page 363.

Chapter 23 Assessment

Directions: Circle the letter of the correct answer.

1. Which of the following did *not* cause the Great Depression?
   - A The stock market crashed on October 29, 1929.
   - B Banks failed across the country, and depositors lost savings.
   - C Bonus Army veterans demanded their payments.
   - D Overproduction forced jobs to be cut and factories to close.

2. All of the following were goals of FDR's New Deal program *except*
   - A cleaning up the Dust Bowl.
   - B helping jobless Americans.
   - C preventing another Great Depression.
   - D helping industry and agriculture recover.

3. Which was *not* a problem that Americans faced during the Depression?
   - A schools closing from lack of money
   - B 50% unemployment for African Americans
   - C widespread homelessness and hunger
   - D soap companies sponsoring soap operas

Directions: Follow the steps to answer this question:

How might the outcome of the Great Depression have been different if Franklin Roosevelt had not been elected President in 1932?

Step 1: Recall information: In the chart below, list three major problems in the country that developed from 1929 to 1932. Include statistics that you remember.

Downward Spiral from 1929 to 1932
•
•
•

Step 2: Describe: In the chart below, list examples of how FDR provided hope and took action to solve these problems when he assumed the office of President in 1933.

FDR Takes Office in 1933
• Hope:
• Action:

Step 3: Complete the topic sentence that follows. Then write two or three more sentences that support your topic sentence.

The outcome of the Great Depression might have been different without FDR as President because _____

_____

_____

_____

Now you are ready to answer the Chapter 23 Focus Question: **How did the Great Depression affect the American people and change the role of government?**

▶ Complete the charts to help you answer this question. Use the notes that you took for each section.

Great Depression: Effects on American People		
Aspect of Life	**Problems Caused by the Great Depression**	**Improvements as a Result of New Deal**
Jobs	• Widespread job loss • High unemployment with no relief for the unemployed • Poverty and _____	• Job programs provided employment • Labor reforms provided a _____ wage and workers' right to join _____ • Federal money to states provided _____ funds to the unemployed
Communities	• People lived in makeshift areas called _____ • Dust Bowl farms _____ _____ • Schools _____ _____	• WPA projects built _____ _____ • PWA financed large _public-works projects_ • TVA provided _____ _____
Savings and investments	• Margin buying in stocks wiped out investors' money • Banks _____ _____	• FDIC_____ _____ • Truth-in-Securities Act _____ _____

Changing Role of Government		
Aspect of Federal Government	**Before the Great Depression**	**After the Great Depression**
Size	Smaller	
Role in solving economic and social problems	Local governments, charities, and businesses solved problems	
Control of business practices and industry standards	• Risky stock speculating allowed • Overproduction in manufacturing unchecked	
Relationship of people to federal government	Less connection and involvement in people's lives	

Refer to this page to answer the Unit 8 Focus Question on page 392.

The World War II Era (1935–1945)

What You Will Learn

The United States was pulled out of the Great Depression as its factories produced "the great arsenal of democracy" for fighting World War II. Both U.S. soldiers and civilians at home made major contributions to winning the war.

Chapter 24 Focus Question

As you read this chapter, keep this question in mind: **What were the causes and effects of World War II?**

Section 1

Aggression Leads to War

Section 1 Focus Question

What events led to the outbreak of World War II? To begin answering this question,

- Learn why dictators gained power after World War I.
- Find out how Germany, Italy, and Japan embarked on a path of military conquest.
- Learn how the U.S. tried to remain neutral in a new conflict.
- Understand how World War II began in Europe.

Section 1 Summary

The Great Depression in the 1930s led to dictatorships in Germany, Italy, and Japan. Those dictators led their nations into military actions against other countries, eventually igniting World War II. American policy aimed to remain neutral.

The Rise of Dictators

After World War I, many nations thought democracy was too weak to solve their hardships. In the Soviet Union, Italy, Germany, and Japan, the citizens turned to dictators to rule their countries. These brutal dictators imprisoned or killed any citizen who opposed them. In the Soviet Union, **Josef Stalin** held total control of the country. In Italy, **Benito Mussolini** used **fascism**—a form of rule based on militarism, radical nationalism, and blind loyalty—to assume absolute power. In Germany, **Adolf Hitler** and his Nazi Party rose to power. Nazism was a form of fascism. Hitler argued that Germans were a "master race," and he preached a racist theory of anti-Semitism, or hatred of Jews. Once in power, he began a policy of violent persecution of Jews. In Japan, military leaders gained control and used racism to justify the invasion of nearby countries. ✔

Key Events

1939	Germany invades Poland; World War II begins.
1941	United States enters war after Japan attacks Pearl Harbor.
1945	U.S. plane drops atomic bomb on Hiroshima. World War II ends.

✓ Checkpoint

Name the dictator in each country.

Soviet Union: _____

Germany: _____

Italy: _____

Military Aggression

The League of Nations was founded after World War I to stop **aggression,** or warlike actions against another country without cause. But the League failed to act when Japan, Italy, and Germany invaded other countries. In 1931, Japan took over Manchuria in China. In late 1937, Japanese troops pillaged China, killing about 250,000 people in the city of Nanjing alone. Italy was also on the march and, in 1935, invaded Ethiopia in Africa. Hitler rebuilt Germany's military might, enabling the invasion of the Rhineland in 1936 and Austria in 1938. When he threatened Czechoslovakia, Britain and France finally stepped in. To avoid war, they tried to appease Hitler and signed the Munich Pact, which gave him a German-speaking area of Czechoslovakia. Defying the pact, Germany soon took all of Czechoslovakia. ✓

American Neutrality

The United States declared itself neutral in order to avoid being drawn into the growing worldwide conflicts. The Neutrality Act of 1935 forbade providing loans, arms, or other assistance to any nation at war. The country also took steps to improve relations with Latin America. Under President Hoover, the United States had renounced the right to get involved in Latin American affairs. President Franklin Roosevelt initiated the Good Neighbor Policy, which withdrew U.S. troops from Nicaragua and Haiti. ✓

War Begins in Europe

As Hitler eyed Poland, France and Britain recognized that their policy of **appeasement,** or agreeing to <u>tolerate</u> aggression to avoid war, had failed. Germany and the Soviet Union, former enemies, signed a pact pledging not to attack each other. Secretly, they agreed that the Soviet Union would take eastern Poland when Germany invaded. On September 1, 1939, German troops attacked Poland. Britain and France then declared war on Germany. Hitler's army proved unstoppable, quickly crushing Poland and much of western Europe. France fell in June 1940. Only Britain remained unconquered. Led by Prime Minister **Winston Churchill,** the British withstood German bombing with such unshakable resistance that Hitler gave up his invasion plans. In June 1941, he attacked the Soviet Union, which soon allied with Britain. ✓

Check Your Progress

1. How did the rise of dictators lead to World War II?

_____

_____

2. Why was appeasement a failure in preventing war?

_____

_____

✓ **Checkpoint**

Name the country that invaded each nation.

Austria: _____

Manchuria: _____

Czechoslovakia: _____

China: _____

Ethiopia: _____

✓ **Checkpoint**

Explain what the Neutrality Act of 1935 did not allow.

_____

_____

Vocabulary Builder

Tolerate means "to allow something to exist." What did France and Britain tolerate, and why?

_____

_____

✓ **Checkpoint**

Name the British leader who withstood Germany.

_____

Question to Think About As you read Section 1 in your textbook and take notes, keep this section focus question in mind: **What events led to the outbreak of World War II?**

► Use this chart to record key information from the section. Some information has been filled in to get you started.

Aggression Leads to War	
Event	**How It Contributed to World War II**
1. Economic problems and social unrest after World War I	Encouraged the rise of ___dictators who took control of their countries_____.
2. Fascism takes hold in Italy and Germany.	_____ was appointed Italy's prime minister. He turned Italy into a Fascist state, which is a political system based on _militarism_, extreme nationalism, and _____.
3. Adolf Hitler becomes the leader of Germany.	He created a _____ state and passed _____ against the Jews.
4. Japan invades China.	Japan became an aggressive force in the _____ region.
5. Italy invades Ethiopia.	The emperor, _____, appealed to the League of Nations for aid, but Ethiopia fell to Italy.
6. Hitler violates the Treaty of Versailles without punishment and rebuilds Germany's armed forces.	It gave Germany _____ might and it showed Hitler that the _____ were weak.
7. Britain and France sign the Munich Pact with Germany.	They were following a policy of_____ that failed to stop Hitler's aggression. Hitler occupied the _____ in Czechoslovakia.
8. U.S. Congress passes the Neutrality Act.	Forbade the United States from _____ _____ involved in war.
9. Germany and the Soviet Union sign the Nazi-Soviet Pact.	They pledged not to _____ and secretly agreed to _____.
10. Britain and France pledge support to Poland.	When Germany attacked Poland on _____, they _____.

War Begins in Europe
- By June 1940, Britain _____.
- In June 1941, Hitler invaded _____.

Refer to this page to answer the Chapter 24 Focus Question on page 377.

Section 2

The United States at War

Section 2 Focus Question

How did the United States move from neutrality to full involvement in the war? To begin answering this question,

- Understand how the United States prepared for war and strengthened its ties with the Allies.
- Discover why the United States finally entered World War II.
- Learn how, after many early setbacks, the Allies began to turn the tide of battle in North Africa and the Pacific.

Key Events

1939	Germany invades Poland; World War II begins.
1941	United States enters war after Japan attacks Pearl Harbor.
1945	U.S. plane drops atomic bomb on Hiroshima. World War II ends.

Section 2 Summary

The United States stayed out of World War II until it was directly attacked by Japan in late 1941. Soon the United States was fighting with the Allies against Germany in Europe and against Japan in the Pacific. After sustained losses, key victories in 1942 and 1943 began to change the war in favor of the Allies.

Moving Toward War

In 1940, Franklin Roosevelt became the first American President to run for and win a third term in office. He promised that the United States would remain neutral. However, when Britain stood alone against Germany, the United States allowed the British to buy war goods, and then, through the Lend-Lease Act of 1941, to "borrow" them. Under the Lend-Lease plan, the United States became "the great arsenal of democracy."

America also quietly stepped up its war readiness by instituting the first peacetime draft in 1940. At the same time, the Tuskegee Airmen were organized as the first African American combat unit under the command of black officers.

In August 1941, Roosevelt and Britain's Prime Minister Winston Churchill issued the Atlantic Charter, which set postwar goals. Both countries agreed that they would not seek territory after the war, and they called for an effective international organization to replace the League of Nations. ✔

The United States Enters the War

It was Japanese aggression that forced the United States to enter World War II. The Japanese invaded Indochina in July 1941, prompting President Roosevelt to ban exports of scrap metals and to restrict oil to Japan. <u>Facing shortages for their navy propelled Japan to set a course for war with the United States</u>. On December 7, 1941, Japanese planes attacked the American naval fleet at Pearl Harbor, Hawaii. Roosevelt rallied the country, calling December 7 "a date which will live in infamy."

✓ Checkpoint

List two "firsts" that occurred in 1940 that showed the United States was moving toward war.

_____

_____

Vocabulary Builder

Which of the following words is the best synonym for the word *propelled* as used in the underlined sentence?

a. forced
b. steered
c. targeted

_____

✓ **Checkpoint**

Name two battles that helped turn the tide of war against Germany.

_____

_____

✓ **Checkpoint**

Name the general who vowed to return to the Philippines.

_____

Soon the United States was in a global fight. Germany, Italy, Japan, and six other nations made up the Axis powers. America joined some 50 countries that made up the Allies. Together, all were involved in **total war,** as not only armies, but as civilians, too, were caught up in the conflict. ☑

Europe and North Africa

In Europe, Germany's early victories and large gains of territory made the war a hard and bloody struggle. However, the Allies made some gains. In late 1941, Soviet fighters and the fierce Russian winter halted the Germans outside of Moscow. After a second major defeat at Stalingrad in 1942, Hitler's army lost ground. It began to be pushed back by the Soviets.

In October 1942, the British defeated the German forces at the Battle of El Alamein in Egypt. The German tank commander Erwin Rommel was pushed westward. General **Dwight D. Eisenhower** arrived with fresh American troops in November and occupied Morocco and Algeria. Hemmed in by both the Americans and the British, Rommel's army surrendered in May 1943. ☑

Japan Sweeps Through the Pacific

Following Pearl Harbor, Japan swiftly attacked other Allies in the Pacific and threatened to invade Australia. The Japanese bombed and then invaded the U.S.-governed Philippine Islands. A Filipino-American force under General **Douglas MacArthur** resisted bravely. MacArthur was ordered to leave the Philippines but vowed to return. Some 70,000 soldiers and civilians eventually surrendered. Their forced 65-mile march to a Japanese prison camp became the "Bataan Death March."

In May 1942, naval battles helped turn the tide. The Battle of the Coral Sea became the first battle fought by planes launched from aircraft carriers instead of ships firing at each other. At the Battle of Midway Island in June, American forces sank four Japanese carriers and shot down 322 planes. Japan's navy had been delivered a severe blow. ☑

Check Your Progress

1. How did the Lend-Lease Act of 1941 show U.S. support of one side of the war in Europe?

_____

_____

2. Why did the United States end its neutrality and enter World War II?

_____

_____

Question to Think About As you read Section 2 in your textbook and take notes, keep this section focus question in mind: **How did the United States move from neutrality to full involvement in the war?**

▶ Use this chart to record key information from the section. Some information has been filled in to get you started.

The United States at War
Moving Toward War
• President Roosevelt was reelected for a third term in __1940__. He sympathized with the _____ in Europe.   • The _____ supported the British by allowing them to obtain American war goods without paying for them directly.   • Meanwhile, the United States passed the first _____ to build up its armed forces.   • Roosevelt and British Prime Minister _____ showed their alliance by meeting and issuing the _____.   • On _____, the _____ waged a surprise attack on U.S. naval forces at _____. As a result, __the United States declared war__.   • In turn, _____ and _____ declared war on the United States.   • The main Axis powers were Germany, Italy, and _____.   • The main Allied powers were Britain, France, _____, _____, and _____.
Europe and North Africa
• In the Soviet Union, key victories that stopped the German push took place near __Moscow__ in 1941 and at _____ in 1942.   • In North Africa, the British began pushing back the German tank corps after the victory at _____ in Egypt.   • The United States entered its first ground combat troops and occupied _____ and _____ under the command of _____.
Japan Sweeps Through the Pacific
• Japanese troops invaded country after country in the Pacific region, including _____, which were governed by the United States and had __U.S. bases__.   • General _____ became commander of the U.S. troops in the region.   • The Bataan Death March followed the defeat in _____ and took the lives of U.S. and _____ prisoners.   • Two historic naval battles that turned the tide of the war in the Pacific were the Battles of _____ and _____. Both were important because the United States _____.

Refer to this page to answer the Chapter 24 Focus Question on page 377.

Key Events

1939	Germany invades Poland; World War II begins.
1941	United States enters war after Japan attacks Pearl Harbor.
1945	U.S. plane drops atomic bomb on Hiroshima. World War II ends.

✓ Checkpoint

Name three ways that Americans on the home front contributed to the fight.

_____

_____

_____

✓ Checkpoint

Identify two benefits women gained as a result of their wartime work.

_____

_____

Section 3 Focus Question

How did the home front respond to American participation in the war? To begin answering this question,

- Find out how the United States built its military and converted its economy to meet wartime needs.
- Learn how American women contributed to the war effort.
- Discover how World War II affected Japanese Americans and other groups of people at home.

Section 3 Summary

Daily life in the United States changed dramatically after war was declared in 1941. Millions of men joined the service, while women stepped in to fill male jobs in wartime factories. For some Americans, the war brought serious restrictions and new tensions at home.

Organizing for War

Americans quickly realized that all of the country's resources had to be committed to supporting the armed forces. Volunteers and draftees of all ethnic and religious backgrounds swelled the ranks of the military. Some 15 million men would fight, and hundreds of thousands of women served in noncombat roles. They served as nurses and also as pilots who ferried bombers, towed targets, and taught men to fly.

The War Production Board directed the change as factories shifted to producing war goods. Millions of new jobs ended the unemployment problems of the Great Depression. Americans accepted **rationing,** or setting limits on the purchase of specific items, such as certain foods, rubber, and gasoline that were needed for the war effort. Planting victory gardens and buying war bonds were other ways people contributed to the fight. ✓

Women in Industry

Along with minority workers, women went to work in industry. They took over traditionally male jobs in factories and shipyards, such as welders and riveters. "Rosie the Riveter" became a symbol of all women who worked for the war effort. Women also became the bus drivers, police officers, and other key workers in their communities. Millions of women were needed in these roles, and millions answered the call. As a result, women gained better working conditions and generally received the same pay as men for the same work. ✓

Ordeal for Japanese Americans

For Japanese Americans, World War II created a painful situation. Erroneous fears that they would spy for Japan fueled prejudice, and anti-Japanese sentiment was widespread. In February 1942, President Roosevelt issued an order to **intern,** or temporarily imprison, Japanese Americans in the United States. About 110,000 were forced to sell most of their possessions and live in internment camps until the end of the war. Barbed wire and guards made the camps seem very much like prison camps. No evidence of Japanese American disloyalty was ever found. On the contrary, the 17,000 Japanese Americans who fought in Europe were among the most honored for bravery. Both at the time and later, there was criticism of the internment. In 1990, the government formally apologized to Japanese Americans and provided each surviving internee with a $20,000 payment. ✓

Tensions at Home

German Americans and Italian Americans also faced some restrictions. Several thousand who were not U.S. citizens were held in camps as "enemy aliens." Despite job gains, African Americans still experienced discrimination in employment. The irony of the United States fighting for democracy overseas while allowing injustice at home drove some African American leaders to demand change. President Roosevelt set up the Fair Employment Practices Committee to enforce racial equality in hiring.

Young Mexican Americans also served in the armed forces. In the United States, Mexican Americans, as well as **braceros,** or Mexican laborers, supported the war effort. Yet their language, culture, and flashy "zoot suits" set them apart. When some Mexican Americans were attacked by sailors on leave in Los Angeles, riots followed. Eleanor Roosevelt boldly blamed long-standing discrimination against Mexican Americans for causing the "Zoot Suit Riots." ✓

Check Your Progress

1. What are some examples of American unity on the home front during World War II?

_____

_____

2. What are some examples of prejudice on the American home front during the war?

_____

_____

_____

Erroneous describes something that is based on an incorrect idea. Circle two sentences in the bracketed paragraph that explain why fears of Japanese Americans acting as spies were erroneous.

✓ Checkpoint

Explain why Japanese Americans were interned.

_____

_____

✓ Checkpoint

Name the committee that President Roosevelt set up to combat racial discrimination in hiring.

_____

_____

Question to Think About As you read Section 3 in your textbook and take notes, keep this section focus question in mind: **How did the home front respond to American participation in the war?**

▶ Use this chart to record key information from the section. Some information has been filled in to get you started.

The War at Home		
Building the Military	**The Wartime Economy**	**Supporting the War Effort**
• More than _____ men served in the U.S. military. • Hundreds of thousands of women served as _nurses_ and in _____ roles. For example, they _____ _____ _____ .	• U.S. factories shifted from producing _____ goods to creating _____ goods. • The _____ _____ was a government agency that supervised that change and set_____ . • U.S. military output nearly _____ .	• Americans followed _____ of scarce goods like _sugar, shoes, and gasoline_ . They used _____ to buy these goods. • They also bought_____ to show support. • Maintaining strong _____ at home was also key to fighting the war.

Americans on the Home Front		
Group	**Experience**	**Positive or Negative Outcomes**
Women	Millions went to work in industry to fill needed _____ in factories and _____ .	They gained: • • •
Japanese Americans	Some 110,000 were _____ _____ _____ .	They lost their freedom and _____ , even though there was never evidence of_____ against the United States.
African Americans	They still faced _____ _____ _____ .	The Fair Employment Practices Committee was set up to _____ _____ .
Mexican Americans	They experienced_____ in America. In Los Angeles, they were attacked by _____ _____ .	After the_____ , Eleanor Roosevelt called attention to the problem of _____ against them.

Refer to this page to answer the Chapter 24 Focus Question on page 377.

Section 4

Toward Victory

Section 4 Focus Question

How did the Allies win World War II and what were the results?
To begin answering this question,

- Learn how the Allies were finally able to defeat Germany.
- Discover how a powerful new weapon brought the war in the Pacific to a close.
- Explore the horrors of the Holocaust.
- Understand the immediate aftereffects of World War II.

Section 4 Summary

The battles that stopped the Axis powers in 1942 turned the tide of the war. With perseverance and sacrifice, the Allies achieved victory in 1945. The war's brutality, exemplified by Hitler's Holocaust on the Jews, prompted the Allies to take historic action against those defeated in war.

Victory in Europe

In 1942, German advances into the Soviet Union and North Africa had been checked. Russia was still facing heavy aggression from Germany, however. Stalin urged the Americans and the British to invade France to bring German troops west. Instead, the United States and Britain invaded Italy in July 1943, knocking Mussolini from power. German troops in Italy continued to fight there, however.

On June 6, 1944—D-Day—the long-awaited campaign to retake France began. Under Allied commander Dwight Eisenhower, American, British, and Canadian troops landed at Normandy, in western France. Some 2,500 American soldiers were killed that day on Omaha Beach. By August, however, the Allies were able to liberate Paris.

The German army regrouped for a last offensive at the Battle of the Bulge in December, but by then it was short of supplies and soldiers. In January 1945, Allied troops invaded Germany from the west as the Soviets closed in from the east. By April 1945, both Berlin and victory were in sight. Tragically, President Roosevelt died of a stroke on April 12. On April 30, Hitler committed suicide, freeing his generals to make an unconditional surrender. V-E Day, May 8, 1945, celebrated the end of war in Europe. ✔

Victory in the Pacific

The Japanese offensive was halted at the Battle of Midway in 1942. Japan had conquered much of the Pacific region, including

Key Events

1939 Germany invades Poland; World War II begins.

1941 United States enters war after Japan attacks Pearl Harbor.

1945 U.S. plane drops an atomic bomb on Hiroshima. World War II ends.

✔ Checkpoint

List three major events that led to Allied victory in Europe.

_____

_____

_____

The word *kamikaze* means "divine wind" in Japanese.

✓ **Checkpoint**

Explain the term "island hopping."

_____

_____

✓ **Checkpoint**

Identify the goal of Hitler's "final solution."

_____

_____

its many islands. The Allies used a strategy of **island hopping**, or capturing some Japanese-held islands and going around others, to create a path for an invasion of Japan. MacArthur made good on his promise to return to the Philippines in January 1945. Famous battles in the Pacific included Iow Jima and Okinawa, islands closest to Japan. Still, the Japanese were fierce fighters and the Pacific battles were especially bloody. Japanese **kamikaze** pilots willingly committed suicide by crashing into U.S. ships. The fear of continued high American casualties convinced the new President, **Harry Truman**, to drop a secret weapon, the atomic bomb, on the Japanese cities of Hiroshima and Nagasaki. An estimated 165,000 people died instantly in the two blasts. Five days after the second bomb was dropped, the Japanese surrendered on August 14, 1945, known as V-J Day. World War II finally ended with Japan's official surrender to General MacArthur on September 2, 1945. ✓

The Holocaust

World War II took the lives of up to 60 million people, including 400,000 Americans. After the Germans were defeated, the Allied armies made gruesome discoveries as they stumbled upon "death camps" in Poland. Hitler's early policy of racism and anti-Semitism had changed into a plan to exterminate all of Europe's Jews. His "final solution" was **genocide**, or the deliberate attempt to wipe out an entire nation or group of people. Railway cars carried men, women, and children to the death camps, where most were killed in gas chambers. Others were tortured and kept barely alive. Some six million Jews were murdered in the nightmare known as the Holocaust.

World War II was total war, and the level of brutality was extreme. The Allies charged the German and Japanese leaders with **war crimes**, or wartime acts of cruelty and brutality that are judged to be beyond the accepted rules of war and human behavior. Nuremberg, Germany, saw the first trials in history for war crimes, with trials also held in Tokyo and Manila. Several Axis leaders were sentenced to death. ✓

Check Your Progress

1. How did the Allies win the war in Europe?

_____

_____

2. How did the Allies win the war in the Pacific?

_____

_____

Question to Think About As you read Section 4 in your textbook and take notes, keep this section focus question in mind: **How did the Allies win World War II and what were the results?**

► Use this chart to record key information from the section. Some information has been filled in to get you started.

Toward Victory	
Victory in Europe	**Victory in the Pacific**
Italy Surrenders • Invasion of Sicily in __July 1943__ • Surrendered on _____ **D-Day** • Date: _____ • Commanded by __General Eisenhower__ • Goal: _____ • Americans landed on _____ . • Number killed: _____ • Success: Allies entered Paris on _____ **Battle of the Bulge** • Date: _____ • Outcome: Germany's defeat showed that the Allies had more_____ and _____ to keep fighting. **Germany Invaded** • Date: January _____ • Allies invaded from the _____ . • _____ invaded from the east. • Allies used ground troops and _____ . **Victory** V-E Day: _____ **Aftermath** • Nazi death camps discovered • Nazis who committed war crimes were tried at _____ .	**Island Hopping** • Strategy: Capture_____ _____ _____ **Battles:** • Guadalcanal • Luzon and _____ in the Philippines • Iwo Jima • _____ **The Atomic Bombs** • President _____ ordered bombings. • Goal: To avoid _____ _____ if United States invades Japan • First bomb: Hiroshima on _____ killed_____ • Second bomb: _____ on _____ killed 30,000 instantly **Victory** • V-J Day:_____ • Who announced surrender: __Emperor of Japan__ • Official end of World War II: General _____ accepted surrender on the battleship _____ . **Aftermath** • War crimes trials in _____ and Manila forced responsibility on the leaders who created the _____ machine.
• Which Allied leader did not live to see the end of World War II, and when did he die? _____	

Refer to this page to answer the Chapter 24 Focus Question on page 377.

Chapter 24 Assessment

Directions: Circle the letter of the correct answer.

1. Which world event contributed most directly to the start of World War II?
   A   Roosevelt was elected to a third term.
   B   Germany invaded Poland.
   C   Italy invaded Ethiopia.
   D   Military leaders came to power in Japan.

2. Which is *not* an accurate description of World War II?
   A   It demonstrated the failure of appeasement.
   B   It was total war.
   C   War production pulled the United States out of the Depression.
   D   The main allies were the United States and Britain.

3. Which is *not* true of the U.S. home front during World War II?
   A   Some foods and other items were rationed.
   B   Millions of women filled jobs in industry.
   C   There was proof of spying by Japanese Americans.
   D   The government fought job discrimination.

Directions: Follow the steps to answer this question:

How might the outcome of the war in Europe have changed if Germany had kept the nonaggression pact and not invaded the Soviet Union?

Step 1: Recall information: In the chart, identify details that describe the countries and their relationship before the war.

Germany and Russia Before the War
• Their Leaders: _____
_____
• Terms of Nazi-Soviet Pact: _____
_____

Step 2: List three examples of how the Soviet Union helped defeat Germany.

Soviet Union in the War
•
•
•

Step 3: Complete the topic sentence that follows. Then write two or three more sentences that support your topic sentence.

The outcome of the war in Europe might have been different if Germany had not attacked the Soviet Union because _____

_____

_____

Chapter 24 Notetaking Study Guide

Now you are ready to answer the Chapter 24 Focus Question: **What were the causes and effects of World War II?**

► Complete the charts to help you answer this question. Use the notes that you took for each section.

Causes			
Economic Factors	**Totalitarian Governments**	**Racist Theories**	**Failed Organizations and Policies**
_____ _____ caused people in many countires to lose faith in _____ governments.	Dictators took control in Germany, Italy, and _____. Militarism and _____, which promotes extreme nationalism and _____ took hold.	The idea of _____ peoples who have the right to conquer _____ ones spread in Italy, Japan, and Germany. Hitler preached extreme _____ against Jews.	The _____ failed to act to stop invasions of China and Ethiopia. Britain and France tried _____ with Hitler by signing the _____ _____.

↘ ↓ ↙ ↙

World War II

↓

Effects	
In the United States	**In the World**
• War production solved the unemployment problems of the _____. • Women gained _____ _____ because they were needed in industry. • _____ of scarce goods required sacrifice of all Americans. • Prejudice created shameful experiences for _____, _____, and _____. • The United States gained power as "the great arsenal of _____."	• Global conflict spread throughout _____ and _____. • Total war affected millions of _____ and _____. • Hitler's "final solution" murdered _____ Jews in the _____. • The first _____ were used in warfare, on _____ and _____. • The first trials to prosecute _____ followed victory by the Allies.

Refer to this page to answer the Unit 8 Focus Question on page 392.

The United States in the Cold War
(1945–1963)

Key Events

1947	The Truman Doctrine and Marshall Plan change U.S. foreign policy.
1950	The Korean War begins.
1962	The United States faces the Soviet Union in the Cuban missile crisis.

✓ Checkpoint

State the term Churchill used to describe Soviet expansion.

What You Will Learn

After World War II, the United States faced new challenges in the world as well as economic and social changes at home. Conflict with the Soviet Union developed into a Cold War. U.S. policy aimed to contain communism, using military force when necessary.

Chapter 25 Focus Question

As you read this chapter, keep this question in mind: **What key foreign and domestic issues affected the United States after World War II?**

Section 1
Roots of the Cold War

Section 1 Focus Question

How did the United States respond to the early stages of the Cold War? To begin answering this question,
* Learn about the growing distrust of Russia after the war.
* Discover how the United States tried to limit the spread of communism.
* Find out about three new international organizations.
* Understand how the events of 1949 shook America's confidence

Section 1 Summary

A new conflict developed immediately after World War II as the Soviet Union pushed the spread of communism. A Cold War of tension developed as the United States and its allies faced off with the Soviet Union and other Communist nations.

Growing Distrust

Soviet troops occupied most of Eastern Europe at the end of World War II. Stalin had agreed to allow free elections in those countries, but he broke his promise. His true goal was to make the Soviet Union the dominant world power. He wanted Communist governments in Eastern Europe to protect the Soviet Union's western border and expand Soviet influence. Churchill described the outcome as an "**iron curtain,**" or barrier to understanding and information, across Europe. By 1948, Eastern Europe was filled with Communist **satellites,** or countries ruled by another nation. The world dispute between the Communist and non-Communist nations became known as the Cold War. ✓

Containing Soviet Expansion

The Soviets tried to expand communism into Turkey and Iran. Greek Communists threatened to take over Greece. In response, President Truman outlined the "Truman Doctrine," which opposed the spread of communism. He established the policy of **containment**, or limiting Soviet expansion, using both military and economic aid. In 1947, the United States introduced the Marshall Plan to help European nations rebuild from the war and to weaken Communist influence.

The next standoff developed in Germany, which was divided into four military zones after the war. The Soviets controlled the eastern zone, which included the German capital, Berlin. It was also zoned, with the Soviets controlling East Berlin. When the Western powers wanted to reunify Germany in 1948, Stalin chose to confront the Allies. He set up a blockade to bar entry into West Berlin. The Allies responded with a massive **airlift**, sending cargo planes to deliver tons of supplies to West Berliners. In 1949, the Allies combined their zones into West Germany, and the Soviet zone became East Germany, with Berlin still divided. In 1961, the Communists began building a wall to keep East Berliners from escaping to the West. The Berlin Wall became an emotional symbol of the Cold War. ✔

International Organizations

The United States reversed its pre-war isolationism by leading the creation of the United Nations (UN) as an international organization to maintain peace and to settle disputes. The United States also joined a military alliance that developed from the Cold War. The Western powers formed the North Atlantic Treaty Organization (NATO). The Soviets and Eastern Europeans created the Warsaw Pact. ✔

The Shocks of 1949

In 1949, American security was shaken by two events. The Soviet Union exploded its own atomic bomb, and Communists came to power in China under Mao Zedong, who established the People's Republic of China. The Chinese Nationalists had been America's allies in World War II. They retreated to Taiwan and for years were viewed by the United States as the legal Chinese government. ✔

Check Your Progress

1. What was the purpose of the Truman Doctrine?

_____

_____

2. What two organizations signaled a U.S. turn from isolationism?

_____

_____

Vocabulary Builder

To *confront* is "to challenge face to face." Identify what Stalin did in 1948 to confront the Allies.

_____

_____

✓ Checkpoint

List two purposes of the Marshall Plan.

_____

_____

✓ Checkpoint

List two goals of the UN when it was founded.

_____

_____

✓ Checkpoint

Identify the two events in 1949 that shocked Americans.

_____

_____

Question to Think About As you read Section 1 in your textbook and take notes, keep this section focus question in mind: **How did the United States respond to the early stages of the Cold War?**

▶ Use these charts to record key information from the section. Some information has been filled in to get you started.

Roots of the Cold War
• Conflict developed immediately following World War II when the Soviet Union refused to allow free elections in _____ and created Communist __satellites__ there.
• Winston Churchill called the Soviet threat an _____ across Europe.

U.S. Responses to the Cold War	
U.S. Policies 1947 to 1949	**U.S. Actions 1947 to 1949**
• The Truman Doctrine stated that the United States would _____ _____. • The U.S. policy of limiting Communist expansion was called _____. • The United States demonstrated a turn away from __isolationism__ by supporting two organizations. • The United States took a leading role in creating the _____. Like all members, it had a vote in the _____. The United States became one of five countries that are permanent members of the more powerful _____. • The United States also helped establish a __military__ alliance with other Western nations known as NATO, the_____ _____ _____. Its purpose was to _____ _____.	• In 1947, President Truman requested military aid to stop Communist threats to Greece and _____ . • In 1947, Secretary of State George Marshall proposed the_____ to provide _____ to postwar Europe. Growing Communist parties in _____ and Italy was one reason the United States stepped in to help with $_____ in aid. • In 1948, the Soviet Union _____ _____ around West Berlin. The United States played a major role in the Berlin airlift by _____ _____ . • In 1949, the United States joined with Britain and France to combine the areas of Germany that they controlled into _____. In turn, the Soviets created __East Germany__ . • In 1949, Communists under _____ came to power in China. The United States refused to recognize the People's Republic of China, insisting that the government of _____ was the _____ Chinese government.

Refer to this page to answer the Chapter 25 Focus Question on page 391.

A Time of Prosperity

Section 2 Focus Question

How did the American economy and society change after World War II? To begin answering this question,

- Identify the problems of the postwar economy.
- Explain the effects of a changing society on the lives of Americans during the 1950s.
- Contrast life in the suburbs with life in the cities.

Section 2 Summary

The immediate postwar years were turbulent as the country adjusted to peacetime. By the 1950s, the economy was booming and more Americans were doing well. Television had an impact on families, while growing suburbs sent cities into decline.

Adjusting to Peacetime

With peace came significant changes on the U.S. home front. Millions of soldiers were returning, and Congress passed the GI Bill of Rights, which gave them money for starting businesses, buying homes, and paying for college. U.S. industry had to convert from producing military goods to producing consumer goods. After the sacrifices of the war years, consumer demand for goods was high and soon exceeded the supply. Inflation resulted, which caused prices to rise. This in turn caused workers to demand higher pay, and labor unrest followed. President Truman at first backed employers, fearing that higher wages would increase inflation even more. That made the unions angry. In contrast, when Truman supported higher wages and prices rose, consumers became angry.

Truman's Democrats lost the 1946 mid-term election, and Republicans gained control of Congress. The Republicans' aim was to undo many New Deal labor reforms. Over Truman's veto, Congress passed the Taft-Hartley Act, which cracked down on strikes. The act also banned the **closed shop**, a workplace in which only union members can be hired.

By the presidential election of 1948, Truman seemed unlikely to win. The Republicans nominated New York's governor, Thomas Dewey. Even Truman's party, the Democrats, was divided. However, Truman campaigned tirelessly and focused Americans on the problem of the "do-nothing" Republican Congress. In a surprise victory, Truman was reelected, and the Democrats regained control of Congress. With a friendlier Congress, Truman passed some of his "Fair Deal" proposals, such as a higher minimum wage and low-income housing.

Key Events

1947 — The Truman Doctrine and Marshall Plan change U.S. foreign policy.

1950 — The Korean War begins.

1962 — The United States faces the Soviet Union in the Cuban missile crisis.

Name the act that helped returning soldiers.

_____

_____

Vocabulary Builder

One meaning of *prosper* is "to be successful in a financial way." Use clues in the bracketed paragraphs to identify four types of purchases that reveal how Americans were prospering in the 1950s.

_____

_____

✓ **Checkpoint**

Identify two urban problems that resulted from the growth of suburbs.

_____

_____

In 1952, Truman chose not to run again. The presidency went to World War II General Dwight Eisenhower. He was more conservative and scaled back the government's role in economic matters. Eisenhower won again in 1956 on a campaign promise of "peace, progress, and prosperity." His achievements included the Interstate Highway Act of 1956, which provided funds for a vast system of highways linking the country. ✓

A Changing Society

The 1950s were good times for much of America. Employment grew and inflation fell as more goods became available. New technologies helped increase **productivity**, which meant that workers were able to work more efficiently and produce more goods. Many Americans prospered and purchased homes, filling them with freezers, clothes dryers, and air conditioners. The **standard of living** rose, which is the measure of how comfortable life is for a person, group, or country. The population grew as the postwar birthrate soared, a phenomenon called the **baby boom**. People lived longer thanks to new antibiotic medicines and vaccines.

For many Americans, the setting of their life was also changing. More families had cars, and with the new highway system, more people had the freedom to live outside of cities. Suburbs grew rapidly, especially in western states like California, Arizona, and Texas.

At home, television replaced the radio as the focus of family entertainment. By the early 1960s, most households had at least one television. Young people also enjoyed a new kind of music called **rock-and-roll**, a blend of blues and country music. The most popular rock-and-roll singer was **Elvis Presley**.

In many cities, however, life became worse. The tax base eroded as people moved to the suburbs. Without the money to make repairs and ensure city services, urban areas deteriorated. Crime rose. Those left behind in the **inner cities**, or centers of older cities, tended to be poorer and less educated. ✓

Check Your Progress

1. What were three effects of soaring inflation after the war?

_____

_____

2. What were some of the changes that families experienced in the 1950s?

_____

_____

Question to Think About As you read Section 2 in your textbook and take notes, keep this section focus question in mind: **How did the American economy and society change after World War II?**

► Use these charts to record key information from the section. Some information has been filled in to get you started.

Adjusting to Peacetime

- Two economic challenges that the United States faced after World War II were absorbing millions of _____ into a peacetime economy and changing the economy from producing war goods to _____.
- The _____ helped to solve the first problem by providing money for __starting businesses, buying homes, and paying for college__.
- Americans were eager to buy consumer goods, and demand soon exceeded _____, causing _____. As prices rose, workers demanded higher wages, and a wave of _____ swept the nation.
- When a Republican Congress took control, it passed the Taft-Hartley Act, which gave the government power to _____. Truman managed to win the presidential election in _____, and the _____ gained control of Congress. It passed Truman's "Fair Deal" proposals that helped workers, such as a higher _____.

A Changing Society

Dwight Eisenhower was elected president in _____ and reelected in _____. He believed in smaller government with less control of the _____.

Economic Changes in the 1950s	**Social Changes in the 1950s**
• Once the peacetime economy got underway, the 1950s were _____ _____ for many Americans. • Soaring <u>employment</u> and increased _____ helped workers produce more goods for consumers to buy. • The U.S. standard of living_____. More people owned their own _____ and _____ . • However, cities experienced an economic <u>downturn</u> as _____ and _____ moved to the suburbs, leaving _____ people behind. Cities lost money to pay for_____ and <u>services</u>, and _____ increased.	• A postwar increase in population was caused by a _____ and by new antibiotic medicines and _____that helped people live longer. • More <u>cars</u> and a new system of _____ linking America fueled the growth of suburbs located _____ cities. • Entertainment changed as _____ became the most important family activity, and new styles of music such as _____became popular. • Social critics worried that Americans were feeling more pressure to _____. They also criticized consumers' collecting of _____ possessions.

Refer to this page to answer the Chapter 25 Focus Question on page 391.

Key Events

1947 The Truman Doctrine and Marshall Plan change U.S. foreign policy.

1950 The Korean War begins.

1962 The United States faces the Soviet Union in the Cuban missile crisis.

Vocabulary Builder

Which of the following words is a synonym for the underlined word *retreating*: advancing, withdrawing, or repeating?

Section 3 Focus Question

How did the United States respond to the invasion of Korea and its aftermath? To begin answering this question,

- Learn how the invasion in Korea became the Korean War, the first military conflict of the Cold War.
- Describe how the Korean War ended.
- Explain how the Cold War led to a Red Scare in the United States.

Section 3 Summary

In 1950, the United States responded to aggression from Communist North Korea and led United Nations troops in the Korean War. Spy cases and a U.S. senator also fueled fear of Communists inside America.

Conflict in Korea

After World War II, Korea was divided into two countries along the 38th line of latitude. Communists backed by the Soviet Union took control in North Korea. On June 25, 1950, North Korean troops invaded South Korea. They reached Seoul (sole), South Korea's capital, within three days. President Truman urged the UN to rush military aid to South Korea. The UN force included soldiers from 16 different countries but was primarily made up of American troops. U.S. General Douglas MacArthur, the former World War II commander, led the force.

At first the war went badly for the UN troops. However, with more soldiers and supplies, they pushed the North Koreans back over the 38th parallel. MacArthur sent his forces after the <u>retreating</u> North Koreans, and the UN troops almost reached the Yalu River, the border between North Korea and Communist China. The Chinese were threatened and attacked with an overwhelming force. They pushed the UN troops back to the South Korean border and into a military **stalemate,** a situation in which neither side wins.

MacArthur was frustrated at this outcome and said publicly that bombing bases in China that were supplying the North Koreans could win the war. Truman wanted to avoid war with China, and he warned MacArthur to stop making public statements. When MacArthur complained that politicians were preventing him from winning in Korea, Truman fired him.

The Korean conflict remained a stalemate for two years, during which the killing continued while peace talks were held. Finally, in July 1953, a cease-fire was reached. Each side agreed to a **demilitarized zone,** an area that neither side controls, and which still separates North and South Korea today. About two million Koreans died in the war, many of them civilians. More than 30,000 Americans died, and another 100,000 were wounded. ✓

Fears at Home

With Cold War tensions high, fear of communism increased in the United States. Americans worried that the country could not defeat communism, or worse, that Communists inside the United States might overthrow the government. Those fears were fueled by two famous spy cases. In 1948, a former Communist named Whittaker Chambers accused a former State Department employee named Alger Hiss of passing secrets to the Soviets in the 1930s. Chambers produced copies of papers that Hiss gave him, saved on microfilm and hidden in a pumpkin in Chambers' garden. It was too late to convict Hiss of spying, but he was convicted of lying to Congress and spent several years in prison.

The second case made headlines in 1950, when Julius and Ethel Rosenberg were found guilty of passing secret information to the Soviets. They were executed in 1953. At the time, many people in the United States and throughout the world were outraged by the executions. Years later, however, the U.S. government released decoded messages that proved the guilt of the Rosenbergs and Hiss.

In the anxious environment of the 1950s, a U.S. senator from Wisconsin, **Joseph McCarthy,** gained fame and a following for hunting down Communists in government and other fields. He made sensational charges that were often unfounded, yet many lives were ruined by his accusations of Communist activity. After four years he lost popularity when, in televised Senate hearings, he made false charges against U.S. Army leaders. Congress voted to **censure,** or condemn, him for his behavior. Since that time, *McCarthyism* has come to mean accusing someone of disloyalty without evidence. ✓

Check Your Progress

1. How did the Korean War end?

_____

_____

2. What did many Americans fear most about the idea of having Communists in the United States?

_____

_____

✓ **Checkpoint**

Name the country that MacArthur wanted to bomb in order to win the Korean War.

_____

✓ **Checkpoint**

Name the person who led the hunt for Communists in America in the 1950s.

_____

Question to Think About As you read Section 3 in your textbook and take notes, keep this section focus question in mind: **How did the United States respond to the invasion of Korea and its aftermath?**

► Use these charts to record key information from the section. Some information has been filled in to get you started.

The Korean War		
Causes/Expansion	**Decisive Actions**	**Outcomes**
• After World War II, Korea was divided into _____ _____ and _____ at the __38th parallel__. • The Soviet Union backed a Communist government in _____. The United States backed _____. • On _____, __North Korea__ invaded __South Korea__. • President Truman called on the __United Nations__ to send military aid. The United States led a force of soldiers from _____ countries, although ____ were American. The commander was General _____.	• Within three days after the invasion, the North Koreans reached _____, the capital of South Korea. • The UN forces did badly at first. Then more soldiers and _____ arrived, and the UN _____ line held. • MacArthur ordered an advance that sent the North Koreans back over the _____. • MacArthur pushed his troops to the _____ border. • A counterattack by _____ and North Korean forces sent the UN troops back to _____.	• War ended in a _____. A cease-fire in 1953 created a _____ _____, an area that neither side controlled. • More than _____ Koreans died in the war, mainly_____. U.S. casualties were _____ killed and _____ wounded. • A disagreement between MacArthur and President Truman developed. Truman _____ MacArthur after he called for the bombing of _____. • Korea remained _____ _____.

Fears at Home		
Three events that caused Americans to become worried about Communists at home: • • •	Two famous spy cases that seized public attention: • •	• _____ gained a following of Americans by hunting Communists in _____ and in the U.S. Army. • The term _____ came to mean accusing someone without evidence.

Refer to this page to answer the Chapter 25 Focus Question on page 391.

Section 4

Global Concerns in the Cold War

Section 4 Focus Question
How did the Cold War increase tensions around the world? To begin answering this question,
- Explain how the Cold War turned into an arms race.
- Describe how the Cold War divided the emerging countries in Asia and Africa.
- Explain how communism gained influence in Latin America.
- Explain why Cuba became a crisis during the Cold War.

Section 4 Summary

In the 1950s and 1960s, the United States and the Soviet Union competed to have the most nuclear arms and influence in the world. The Cold War nearly exploded into a nuclear war over Cuba.

The Arms Race
The death of Stalin in 1953 brought Nikita Khrushchev (KROO shawt) to power. However, new leadership did not improve relations between the Soviet Union and America. Both countries had exploded an even more powerful nuclear weapon, the hydrogen bomb. Both were on their way to becoming **superpowers**, or countries whose military, economic, and political strength are so great that they can influence events worldwide. A dangerous competition developed in the form of an **arms race**—a contest in which nations compete to build more and more powerful weapons. China, France, and Britain joined the arms race when they developed nuclear weapons. No country wanted to use the weapons, so they **stockpiled**, or collected, them. The United States and the Soviet Union had enough missiles stockpiled to destroy each other many times.

In the late 1950s, space exploration also became an area of competition between the two countries. In October 1957, the Soviets successfully launched *Sputnik*, a satellite, into Earth's orbit. Congress responded by creating NASA, the National Aeronautics and Space Administration, to begin a U.S. space program. It also passed the National Defense Education Act to train more scientists and teachers. ✓

Emerging Nations
Following World War II, a wave of former colonies gained independence. These new countries became the target of U.S. efforts to contain communism—and the Soviet's aim to expand it. Military aid was not the only means the United States used to influence the world, however. In 1961, newly elected President **John F. Kennedy** proposed the Peace Corps to build friendships

Key Events

1947 — The Truman Doctrine and Marshall Plan change U.S. foreign policy.

1950 — The Korean War begins.

1962 — The United States faces the Soviet Union in the Cuban missile crisis.

✓ Checkpoint

Name the first satellite launched into space.

_____

✓ Checkpoint

List three countries in which forces supported by the United States fought Communist-backed forces.

_____

_____

_____

Vocabulary Builder

Potential refers to the possibility or capability of something happening. In the bracketed paragraph, identify one action by the United States and one by the Soviet Union that caused the potential for nuclear war to increase.

_____

_____

✓ Checkpoint

Name the failed invasion of Cuba.

_____

with developing countries. The Peace Corps sent skilled American volunteers to help in villages throughout Asia, Latin America, and Africa.

In Africa, the Congo was one area of conflict. After independence from Belgium, a civil war developed within the Congo for control of the government. The United States backed one side, and the Soviet Union supported the other. The war became more violent with the armaments supplied by the two superpowers.

In Asia, the United States gave independence to the Philippine Islands in 1946, but Communist rebels soon began fighting there. The rebels were defeated, yet the new government under Ferdinand Marcos in 1965 was less democratic. In the French colony of Indochina, the United States supported France in its battle with Ho Chi Minh, a Soviet-backed Communist who sought independence for Vietnam. In 1954, Ho's forces gained control of what would become North Vietnam. ✓

Latin America and the Cold War

Poverty created unrest in many Latin American countries. To protect American interests in Latin American businesses, the United States often helped military dictators stay or get into power. This led to hostile feelings toward the United States. In 1959, Fidel Castro staged a successful revolution in Cuba and set up a Communist government. The Soviet Union promised aid. Two years later, exiled Cubans tried to retake control of the island through a U.S.-supported invasion. Known as the "Bay of Pigs," the invasion failed miserably and made tensions higher.

The Soviet Union backed Castro's government with aid and arms, which led to the Cuban missile crisis of 1962. The United States gained evidence of nuclear missiles in Cuba. President Kennedy demanded that the weapons be removed and ordered a naval blockade of Cuba to stop Soviet ships from delivering more. The world watched in fear when the <u>potential</u> for nuclear war grew as Soviet ships steamed toward Cuba. Ultimately, the ships turned back, and a compromise was reached. The Soviet Union agreed to withdraw the missiles from Cuba, and the United States pledged not to invade there. ✓

Check Your Progress

1. What are two reasons why the arms race increased tensions in the world?

_____

_____

2. What agreement was reached between the United States and the Soviet Union that ended the Cuban missile crisis?

_____

_____

Question to Think About As you read Section 4 in your textbook and take notes, keep this section focus question in mind: **How did the Cold War increase tensions around the world?**

▶ Use this chart to record key information from the section. Some information has been filled in to get you started.

Global Concerns in the Cold War

The Arms Race

- Josef Stalin died in 1953 and was replaced by _____.
- Both the United States and Soviet Union exploded_____ in the early 1950s, starting a race to create more powerful weapons, which they _____ in dangerous collections.
- The arms race got more crowded as _____, _____, and _____ developed nuclear weapons.
- The Soviet Union launched _____, expanding the arms race. Now the goal was also to control _____.
- Two responses by the United States were the establishment of __NASA__ and the _____.

Emerging Nations

- The _____ was established for the purpose of building _____ with developing countries and encouraging their __economic growth__.
- New countries emerged following _____. Most were former colonies in _____ and _____ that gained independence.
- The United States backed one side and the Soviets the other in the __Congo__. Each side supplied _____, _____, and __technical advisers__. As a result, the war became more _____.
- The U.S. colony of _____ also gained independence. Communist rebels were _____ there.
- The United States backed _____ forces against a Communist fight for independence in __Vietnam__. Communists under _____ won control of _____.

Latin America and the Cold War

- Revolts in Latin America brought _____ groups to power.
- When _____ took power in Cuba, he created a _____ state and began encouraging __revolution__ in other parts of Latin America.
- The _____ invasion failed and made _____ more popular.
- Soviet aid to Cuba included building _____ and providing nuclear missiles.
- During the Cuban missile crisis, the two key opposing leaders were _____ and _____. There were fears of nuclear war if _____ ran the American blockade. The crisis ended when the Soviets agreed to _____ _____, and the United States agreed not to _____.

Refer to this page to answer the Chapter 25 Focus Question on page 391.

Directions: Circle the letter of the correct answer.

1. Which of the following was *not* a foreign policy issue for the United States after World War II?
   - **A** supporting the United Nations
   - **B** helping Europe recover economically
   - **C** fighting inflation
   - **D** building up nuclear arms

2. Which event did *not* happen in the United States during the 1950s?
   - **A** Julius and Ethel Rosenberg were arrested as spies.
   - **B** Joseph McCarthy led the hunt for U.S. Communists.
   - **C** Watching television took over family life.
   - **D** A baby boom forced a drop in the standard of living.

3. What caused the greatest threat to the United States during the Cold War?
   - **A** Communists in China
   - **B** Communists in Eastern Europe
   - **C** Communists in Cuba
   - **D** Communists in Vietnam

Directions: Follow the steps to answer this question:

Why was President Truman a good leader for the United States at the start of the Cold War?

Step 1: Recall information: In the chart, identify places in the world where communism spread while President Truman was in office.

Communism Spreads	
•	•
•	•
•	

Step 2: In the chart, explain how Truman responded to Cold War threats.

President Truman's Statements and Actions
• Statements:
• Actions:

Step 3: Complete the topic sentence that follows. Then write two or three more sentences that support your topic sentence.

President Truman was a good leader for the United States at the start of the Cold War because _____

_____

_____

_____

Now you are ready to answer the Chapter 25 Focus Question: **What key foreign and domestic issues affected the United States after World War II?**

► Complete the charts to help you answer this question. Use the notes that you took for each section.

Foreign Issues Affecting U.S.	How the United States Responded
Spread of communism	• Sets policy of _____ • Funds $12 billion _____ to prevent growth of communism in _____ Europe • Fights war in _____, with _____ Americans killed and _____ wounded
Arms race	• Explodes a more powerful _____ bomb • Competes with _____ in stockpiling _____ • Establishes _____ to compete in space • Comes to brink of nuclear war during the_____
International organizations	• Abandons policy of _____ • Leads in establishing _____ • Joins _____ to prevent Soviet attacks
Developing nations	• Spreads influence with military support against _____ forces • Establishes the _____, sending skilled _____ to promote friendships and provide _____ help

Domestic Issues Affecting U.S.	Positive or Negative Outcomes
Inflation	• Negative because:
Peacetime economy	• Positive when:
Growth of suburbs	• Positive for: • Negative for:
Fear of communism	• Negative because:

Refer to this page to answer the Unit 8 Focus Question on page 392.

Unit 8 Pulling It Together Activity

What You Have Learned

Chapter 23 The Great Depression was the worst economic crisis in American history. Millions of people lost their jobs, homes, and savings. President Franklin Roosevelt responded with a wide range of measures called the New Deal that had long-lasting effects.

Chapter 24 The United States finally came out of the Great Depression as its factories produced the "great arsenal of democracy" for fighting World War II, the bloodiest conflict in history. Both U.S. soldiers and civilians at home made major contributions to winning the war.

Chapter 25 After World War II, the United States faced new challenges in the world and economic and social changes at home. Conflict with the Soviet Union developed into a Cold War. U.S. policy aimed to contain the spread of communism, using military force when necessary.

Think Like a Historian

Read the Unit 8 Essential Question: **How did the United States deal with crises in domestic and foreign affairs?**

▶ Use the organizers on this page and the next to collect information to answer this question.

How did the United States deal with domestic crises in the Great Depression and war? Read the problems and issues identified on the organizer below. Then review your section and chapter notes to help you list the solutions to, or effects of, each.

U.S. Domestic Crises: Problems and Issues		
The Great Depression	**World War II Home Front**	**Postwar/Cold War Era**
• 25% unemployment	• Meeting war production	• Millions of returning soldiers
• Bankrupt businesses and industries	• Supporting the war effort	• Fear of Communists in the United States
• Stock market crash and bank failures	• Anti-Japanese feelings and fears	• Competing in the space race

What types of crises in foreign affairs did the United States deal with, and how did it respond? Major ones are identified here. Review your section and chapter notes to help you complete the organizer.

U.S. Foreign Crises: American Responses	
World War II	**The Cold War**
• German Aggression in Europe • Japanese Aggression in the Pacific	• Spreading Soviet Threat • Korean War • Cuban Missile Crisis

Unit 9

Moving Toward the Future

What You Will Learn

Chapter 26 In the 1950s and 1960s, the civil rights movement made great strides. President Johnson's "Great Society" program sought to end poverty and eliminate discrimination. African Americans and other groups organized for civil rights.

Chapter 27 Vietnam became a major battlefield in America's fight against communism. America's involvement in the Vietnam War grew during the 1960s, and opinion was divided on the war and how it ended.

Chapter 28 Ronald Reagan ushered in a conservative era. The Cold War ended during this period, leaving the United States as the sole remaining superpower. Tensions within the Middle East posed challenges.

Chapter 29 The terrorist attacks on September 11, 2001, led to a war on terrorism. Today, the United States faces a number of foreign policy, economic, and environmental challenges. Scientific and technological issues are being debated.

Focus Your Learning As you study this unit and take notes, you will find the information to answer the questions below. Answering the Chapter Essential Questions will help you build your answer to the Unit Essential Question.

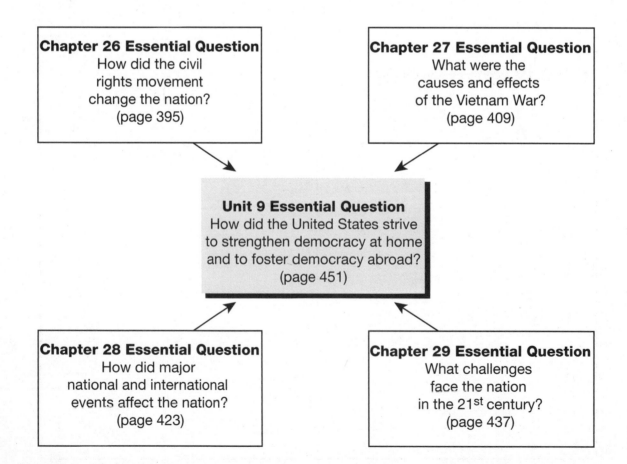

Chapter 26 Essential Question
How did the civil rights movement change the nation?
(page 395)

Chapter 27 Essential Question
What were the causes and effects of the Vietnam War?
(page 409)

Unit 9 Essential Question
How did the United States strive to strengthen democracy at home and to foster democracy abroad?
(page 451)

Chapter 28 Essential Question
How did major national and international events affect the nation?
(page 423)

Chapter 29 Essential Question
What challenges face the nation in the 21st century?
(page 437)

Chapter 26

The Civil Rights Era (1945–1975)

What You Will Learn

African Americans made important gains in their struggle for civil rights in the decades after World War II. Their civil rights movement inspired other groups, such as women, Latinos, and Native Americans, to protest for better treatment.

Chapter 26 Focus Question

As you read this chapter, keep this question in mind: **How did the civil rights movement change the nation?**

Section 1

Beginnings of the Civil Rights Movement

Section 1 Focus Question

What key events marked the beginning of the civil rights movement in the 1950s? To begin answering this question,

- Learn about barriers in the North and segregation in the South.
- Read about the integration of baseball and the military.
- Find out about *Brown* v. *Board of Education of Topeka*.
- Understand the significance of the Montgomery bus boycott.

Section 1 Summary

Racial obstacles for African Americans began to change after World War II, when professional baseball and the armed services desegregated. In the 1950s, the Supreme Court made decisions to desegregate schools and, after the Montgomery bus boycott, to end segregation on buses.

Separate but Unequal

African Americans faced racial barriers throughout the country. In the North, prejudice kept African Americans from getting good jobs or from buying homes in white neighborhoods. In the South, laws kept African Americans separate from whites in restaurants, hospitals, schools, and on public transportation.

The National Association for the Advancement of Colored People (NAACP) worked to end prejudice and segregation. This organization had an important victory in 1915, when the Supreme Court judged grandfather clauses to be unconstitutional. These clauses had been used to keep African Americans from voting. Beginning in 1938, the talented lawyer **Thurgood Marshall** took charge of the NAACP's legal efforts. He fought against segregation laws so that **integration,** or an end to racial segregation, could be achieved. ✔

Key Events

1954 — Supreme Court strikes down school segregation in *Brown* v. *Board of Education*.

1955 — African Americans stage a bus boycott in Montgomery, Alabama.

1965 — United Farm Workers union is founded.

1966 — National Organization for Women is founded.

✓ Checkpoint

Explain what the NAACP fought against.

_____

_____

African American soldiers fought bravely in World War II, as did other minorities. After the war, they wanted discrimination to end. The color barrier fell in Major League Baseball in 1947, when Brooklyn Dodgers manager Branch Rickey hired **Jackie Robinson** to play for his team. Robinson endured terrible treatment by other players and baseball fans. Eventually, however, his talent and courage earned him many admirers.

President Harry Truman was sympathetic to civil rights. He supported legislation against lynching and to end discrimination in voting and hiring. But Congress did not pass these laws. In 1948, Truman—as commander in chief—ordered an end to military segregation without needing congressional approval. ✓

Desegregating the Schools

In 1951, Oliver Brown sued the Topeka, Kansas, board of education because he thought his daughter should be allowed to attend a nearby public school. At the time, the school allowed only white students. Thurgood Marshall took the landmark civil rights case, *Brown* v. *Board of Education of Topeka,* before the Supreme Court. He argued that segregated schools were not equal to all-white schools, and they made African Americans feel inferior. The Court ruled that schools needed to be integrated.

In many places, there was harsh resistance to school integration. In 1957, when nine African Americans tried to attend an all-white high school in Little Rock, Arkansas, they faced hostile mobs. President Eisenhower eventually sent federal troops to protect the nine students. ✓

The Montgomery Bus Boycott

In 1955, **Rosa Parks** refused to give up her seat to white passengers on a bus in Montgomery, Alabama. She was arrested. To protest this injustice, the African American community **boycotted,** or refused to use, the city's buses. At the time, nearly 75 percent of Montgomery's bus riders were African Americans. Leaders like **Martin Luther King, Jr.,** urged the boycott to continue until bus segregation laws were repealed. Angry white citizens bombed King's house. Other leaders were arrested on false charges. Still, the boycott continued 381 days. In November 1956, the Supreme Court ruled against segregation on buses. ✓

Check Your Progress

1. How did the Supreme Court help to end segregation?

_____

_____

2. What led to the Montgomery bus boycott, and why was it effective?

_____

_____

✓ Checkpoint

Name two institutions that desegregated during the 1940s.

_____

_____

Vocabulary Builder

Reread the bracketed paragraph. Use context clues to write a definition of *hostile.*

_____

_____

✓ Checkpoint

State why Oliver Brown sued the Topeka board of education.

_____

_____

✓ Checkpoint

Name two people closely associated with the Montgomery bus boycott.

_____

_____

Question to Think About As you read Section 1 in your textbook and take notes, keep this section focus question in mind: **What key events marked the beginning of the civil rights movement in the 1950s?**

► Use this chart to record key information from the section. Some information has been filled in to get you started.

Beginnings of the Civil Rights Movement
• The 1896, the Supreme Court ruling _Plessy v. Ferguson_ strengthened _segregation_ .   • The _National Association for the Advancement of Colored People (NAACP)_ was organized to fight discrimination.

The 1940s
• After serving in the armed services in _____, minorities wanted justice between the races at home.   • When Branch Rickey hired _____, he helped to integrate _____ _____.   • President Harry Truman ordered desegregation of the _____.

The 1950s
Segregation in the Schools   • _Thurgood Marshall_ argued for school _____ in the Supreme Court case _____.   • In this case, the Court ruled to _____ school segregation.   • In 1957, nine African American students tried to enter Central High School in_____ _____.   • Governor _____ called in the state's National Guard to keep them out.   • President _____ called in federal troops to protect the students.   **Montgomery Bus Boycott**   • _____ was arrested when she refused _____ _____ on a bus to a white passenger.   • The Women's Political Council organized a _____ of buses on Parks' trial day.   • _____ urged African Americans to continue the boycott.   • Some white leaders were _____ by the boycott. Some even _____ King's home.   • After the boycott went on for more than a year, the Supreme Court ruled that _____.

Refer to this page to answer the Chapter 26 Focus Question on page 408.

An Expanding Role for Government

Section 2 Focus Question

What was the "Great Society"? To begin answering this question,
- Learn about the Supreme Court under Chief Justice Earl Warren.
- Find out about the domestic goals of President John F. Kennedy.
- Discover President Lyndon Johnson's interest in social reform.

Section 2 Summary

The role of the federal government expanded during the 1960s. This was partly due to the actions of the Supreme Court and partly due to legislation for social reform that was favored by President Kennedy and advanced by President Johnson.

The Warren Court

President Eisenhower appointed **Earl Warren** as Chief Justice of the Supreme Court in 1953. Warren broke with past decisions if he believed they were unfair. He did not depend on the precise words of the Constitution to make his decisions. This approach to law has become known as "judicial activism," and it remains controversial. It led to the landmark decision ending school segregation in *Brown* v. *Board of Education of Topeka*.

The Warren Court generally supported the rights of individuals. In the 1966 decision *Miranda* v. *Arizona*, the Supreme Court determined that police must inform arrested persons of their right to remain silent and to have a lawyer. This decision was criticized for making it harder to prosecute criminals. In the 1969 decision *Tinker* v. *Des Moines School District*, the Supreme Court expanded freedom of speech. The Court ruled that school administrators could not punish students for wearing black arm bands in protest of the Vietnam War. ✔

Kennedy's Brief Presidency

John F. Kennedy ran for President against Richard Nixon in 1960. Kennedy, a Roman Catholic, had to assure the public that he believed in the separation of church and state. Kennedy beat Nixon in a very close election, and he became the youngest President in U.S. history.

Kennedy believed that social reforms were necessary. He had a strong domestic agenda. Kennedy wanted people to have equal treatment under the law, and he wanted to <u>eradicate</u> poverty and improve health conditions. Congress did not pass most of his legislation, although they did approve some antipoverty programs. Kennedy's most successful accomplishment was the nation's

Key Events

1954	Supreme Court strikes down school segregation in *Brown* v. *Board of Education*.
1955	African Americans stage a bus boycott in Montgomery, Alabama.
1965	United Farm Workers union is founded.
1966	National Organization for Women is founded.

✓ Checkpoint

Name three cases decided by the Warren Court.

_____

_____

_____

Vocabulary Builder

Eradicate means "to get rid of." Find a synonym for *eradicate* in the bracketed paragraph on the next page.

_____

space program. His goal was to place a man on the moon by the end of the 1960s.

Kennedy's administration was brought to a tragic end when he was assassinated in Dallas, Texas, on November 22, 1963. Lee Harvey Oswald was arrested for the murder. He, too, was shot and killed two days later. Earl Warren headed a commission that reported Oswald as the sole shooter. ✓

Johnson's Great Society

After Kennedy was assassinated, Vice President **Lyndon Johnson** took over as President. In 1964, Johnson was elected President by a landslide. Johnson had grown up in a poor family in Texas, and he wanted to eliminate poverty in the United States.

Johnson began his presidency by advancing laws that Kennedy had promoted. Soon he came up with his own program, an ambitious plan for social and economic reform that he named the Great Society. As part of the Great Society, Johnson promoted an antipoverty agenda that he called the War on Poverty. The table below shows his major programs.

Great Society and the War on Poverty	
Program	**Purpose**
Economic Opportunity Act	To address causes of poverty
Head Start	To provide preschools for needy children
Food stamps	To provide food vouchers for the poor
Welfare	To give cash payments to the poor
Department of Housing and Urban Development	To build housing for the poor and middle-income
Medicare	To help the elderly pay medical bills
Medicaid	To help poor people (not covered by Medicare) pay medical bills

✓

Check Your Progress

1. Define "judicial activism." Name one of the cases decided by the Warren Court, and describe its impact.

_____

_____

_____

2. List some of the goals of Johnson's Great Society.

_____

_____

✓ Checkpoint

Name two issues that Kennedy was successful at promoting.

_____

_____

✓ Checkpoint

Name two programs that were part of Johnson's War on Poverty.

_____

_____

Question to Think About As you read Section 2 in your textbook and take notes, keep this section focus question in mind: **What was the "Great Society"?**

▶ Use this organizer to record key information from the section. Some information has been filled in to get you started.

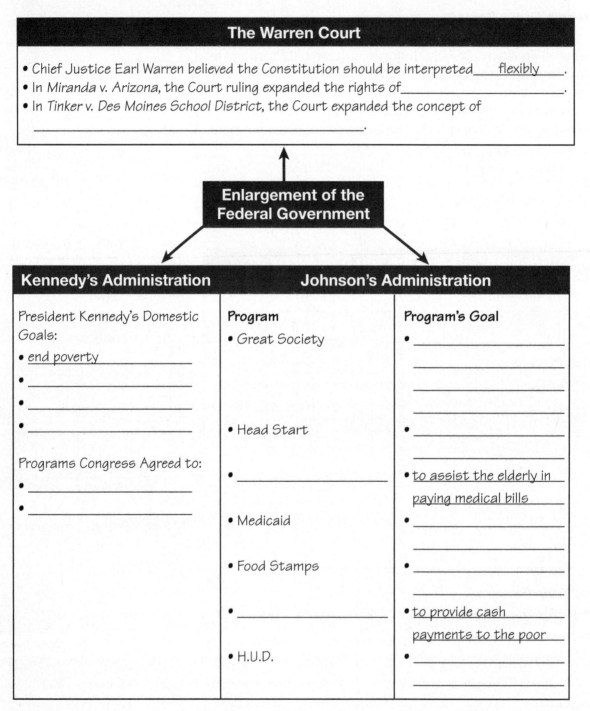

The Warren Court

- Chief Justice Earl Warren believed the Constitution should be interpreted ____flexibly____.
- In *Miranda v. Arizona*, the Court ruling expanded the rights of _____.
- In *Tinker v. Des Moines School District*, the Court expanded the concept of
  _____.

Enlargement of the Federal Government

Kennedy's Administration

President Kennedy's Domestic Goals:
- end poverty _____
- _____
- _____
- _____

Programs Congress Agreed to:
- _____
- _____

Johnson's Administration

Program
- Great Society

- Head Start

- _____

- Medicaid

- Food Stamps

- _____

- H.U.D.

Program's Goal
- _____
  _____
  _____
  _____
- _____
- to assist the elderly in
  paying medical bills
- _____
  _____
- _____
  _____
- to provide cash
  payments to the poor
- _____
  _____

Refer to this page to answer the Chapter 26 Focus Question on page 408.

The Civil Rights Movement Continues

Section 3 Focus Question

How did the civil rights movement gain momentum? To begin answering this question,

- Learn about Martin Luther King, Jr., and civil disobedience.
- Discover which legislation helped further civil rights.
- Read about how new leaders emerged in the movement, and find out about its lasting effects.

Section 3 Summary

Protests using King's ideas of civil disobedience led to important changes, but later, the civil rights movement splintered. President Johnson pushed important civil rights laws through Congress.

King's Strategy of Nonviolence

Martin Luther King, Jr., believed in **civil disobedience,** or peaceful refusal to obey unjust laws. King's philosophy came from Jesus and Christian teachings, and was influenced by Mohandas Gandhi's movement in India. King also took ideas from A. Philip Randolph, an African American labor leader. In 1957, King and other prominent African American church leaders came together to form the Southern Christian Leadership Conference (SCLC). This group led many 1960s protests for civil rights. ✓

Nonviolent Protest Spreads

African Americans protested segregation in several ways. One method was the **sit-in,** in which people sit and refuse to leave. This occurred at a "whites only" lunch counter in Greensboro, North Carolina, in 1960. After its effectiveness, sit-ins became common. Freedom Rides were another type of protest. African Americans rode buses with white colleagues to verify that the Supreme Court's order to desegregate interstate travel was followed. Freedom Riders often faced violence.

In 1963, the SCLC organized massive marches in Birmingham, Alabama, to protest the city's segregation policies. The city's police used violent means to try to stop the marches. Images of the brutality were broadcast throughout the United States, horrifying viewers. Birmingham finally agreed to desegregate because of lobbying from the business community.

During the same year, President Kennedy sought to get Congress to pass a sweeping civil rights act. To publicize the bill, the civil rights community organized the March on Washington. Almost 250,000 people came to the demonstration, where King moved the crowd with his famous speech, "I Have a Dream." ✓

Key Events

1954	Supreme Court strikes down school segregation in *Brown* v. *Board of Education*.
1955	African Americans stage a bus boycott in Montgomery, Alabama.
1965	United Farm Workers union is founded.
1966	National Organization for Women is founded.

✓ Checkpoint

Name three people who influenced Martin Luther King, Jr.

_____

_____

_____

✓ Checkpoint

Name two types of protests used during the early 1960s.

_____

_____

Civil Rights Legislation

President Johnson successfully pushed the Civil Rights Act of 1964 through Congress. This act integrated public facilities, outlawed job discrimination, sped up school desegregation, and helped to protect rights of voters. Even so, African Americans had trouble registering to vote in the South. In 1964, civil rights groups worked to register voters in Mississippi. Three volunteers were murdered. In 1965, King organized a march from Selma to Montgomery, Alabama, to publicize the voting rights problem. State troopers tear-gassed, whipped, and clubbed the peaceful marchers, all witnessed on the evening news. In response, Johnson pushed the Voting Rights Act of 1965 through Congress. This law banned discriminatory voting practices and allowed federal officials to register African Americans in the South. ✓

The Movement Splinters

Some African Americans began to disagree with King's slow, nonviolent approach. **Malcolm X** initially believed in total black separatism rather than integration. He later supported a white-black brotherhood, but he was murdered before his new ideas were fully formed. **Stokely Carmichael** believed in "black power," encouraging African Americans to support African American businesses and to feel pride in being black.

The movement focused on the South, but African Americans in the North had grievances, too. Many lived in **ghettos,** or poor, run-down neighborhoods. In Watts, a Los Angeles neighborhood, African Americans reacted to police brutality with massive rioting in 1965. More than 1,000 were killed or injured. Other cities also erupted in riots, and politicians struggled to find a solution. Things grew worse in 1968, when Martin Luther King, Jr., was shot to death. Riots took place all over the country. ✓

Summing Up the Civil Rights Era

The civil rights movement ended legal segregation, removed barriers to voting, and led to more African Americans holding political office. **Affirmative action,** a policy by which businesses and schools give preference to groups discriminated against in the past, increased the number of African Americans in colleges and in professions. Critics opposed affirmative action because they believed it unfairly benefited certain groups over others. ✓

Check Your Progress

1. What did the Civil Rights Act of 1964 do?

2. What were three achievements of the civil rights movement?

✓ **Checkpoint**

List two pieces of civil rights legislation passed under Johnson.

✓ **Checkpoint**

Name two leaders who disagreed with King's approach.

✓ **Checkpoint**

Define affirmative action.

Section 3 Notetaking Study Guide

Question to Think About As you read Section 3 in your textbook and take notes, keep this section focus question in mind: **How did the civil rights movement gain momentum?**

▶ Use this chart to record key information from the section. Some information has been filled in to get you started.

Date	Events
	**Timeline of the Civil Rights Movement**
1957	_Martin Luther King, Jr._ joins with other African American church leaders to form the _____.
1960	Four African American college students refuse to leave a lunch counter, starting a type of protest known as a _____.
1961	_____ take place to desegregate public transportation across state lines.
1962	_____ tries to attend the University of Mississippi, and riots break out.
1963	• Massive demonstrations take place in _Birmingham, Alabama_, and police respond with violence. • Nearly 250,000 people come together to support civil rights legislation in the famous _____.
1964	President _____ pushed the _____ through Congress. This act _____ _____.
1965	• In King's march for voting rights, people walk from _____ to _____. State troopers set upon marchers with _____. • Congress passes the _____, which _____. • _____, once a believer in black separatism, is killed. • Riots occur in the _____ neighborhood of Los Angeles in response to _____.
1967	_____ becomes the first African American Supreme Court justice.
1968	_____ is killed. _____ occur throughout the country.
1970s	_____, a program through which groups who were previously discriminated against get _____, is established. Critics argue that _____ .

Refer to this page to answer the Chapter 26 Focus Question on page 408.

Key Events

1954 Supreme Court strikes down school segregation in *Brown* v. *Board of Education*.

1955 African Americans stage a bus boycott in Montgomery, Alabama.

1965 United Farm Workers union is founded.

1966 National Organization for Women is founded.

Section 4 Focus Question

What other groups were swept up in the spirit of reform? To begin answering this question,

- Learn about the gains of the women's rights movement.
- Find out about Mexican Americans' struggles for change.
- Read how older Americans, the disabled, and Native Americans formed groups to seek fairer treatment.

Section 4 Summary

As African Americans struggled for civil rights, other groups also began to organize for better treatment. Women, Mexican Americans, Native Americans, the disabled, and older Americans tried to advance their own economic and social conditions.

Women's Rights Movement

In the 1960s, women began to question their place in society, inspired by **Betty Friedan's** book *The Feminine Mystique.* Friedan argued that women were unhappy because of their limited roles in society. Friedan and other leaders in the women's rights movement founded the National Organization for Women (NOW) in 1966. NOW fought for fairer treatment under the law, better professional opportunities, and day-care for working mothers. NOW also led the fight for the Equal Rights Amendment (ERA), which would outlaw sex discrimination. Congress passed the ERA in 1972, but 38 states had to ratify it for it to become law.

Critics of ERA worried that traditional values would be eroded. They feared that women might end up losing alimony and having to serve in combat. Critics also argued that the law was unnecessary, as other laws already existed to protect women from discrimination. Eventually, the ERA failed to be ratified by enough states, and it died.

The women's movement did have important successes. These included the 1963 Equal Pay Act, which ensured that men and women doing the same job received equal pay. The Civil Rights Act of 1965 banned discrimination based on sex. Additionally, more and more women went to college and got jobs outside of their homes. In the political realm, many women were elected to important offices. Shirley Chisholm was the first African American woman elected to Congress. Ella Grasso was the first woman elected governor without succeeding her husband. ✔

✓ Checkpoint

List three goals of the National Organization for Women.

_____

_____

_____

Civil Rights for Mexican Americans

Although no laws legally segregated Mexican Americans, segregation still existed in schools in the Southwest. Mexican American children had to attend <u>deficient</u> "Mexican schools." Mexican Americans also faced discrimination in housing and in the workplace. In 1948, Mexican American World War II veterans formed the American GI Forum to legally challenge discrimination. An important victory came in the Supreme Court case *Hernández* v. *Texas*. In *Hernández,* the Court determined that excluding Mexican Americans from juries was illegal.

In 1965, **César Chávez** helped to form the United Farm Workers (UFW), a labor union for migrant workers, many of whom were Mexican Americans. Growers refused to recognize the union, however. Chávez believed in nonviolent protest, and he organized a successful national boycott of California grapes. This boycott led to a union contract with growers to increase wages and improve working conditions for migrant workers.

The Voting Rights Act of 1975 ensured that Mexican Americans and other foreign-language speakers could vote by requiring bilingual elections. **Bilingual** means "in two languages." Legislation also passed to promote bilingual education. ✔

Organizing for Change

Other groups also formed to work for equal rights. Native Americans, some of the poorest people in America, formed the National Congress of American Indians to work to regain land, mineral, and water rights. The American Indian Movement (AIM) was a more militant group. AIM sought to make people realize how poorly the American government had historically treated Native Americans.

Older Americans formed the American Association of Retired Persons (AARP) in 1958 to promote health insurance for the elderly. AARP has continued to promote a great many causes for older Americans.

Americans with disabilities also fought for change, pushing for better access to public buildings. Congress passed laws that provided equal educational opportunities for disabled children. In 1990, Congress passed the Americans With Disabilities Act, which outlawed job discrimination against persons with physical or mental disabilities. ✔

Check Your Progress

1. What were some successes of the women's rights movement?

_____

_____

2. What groups fought for change during the 1960s and 1970s?

_____

_____

Vocabulary Builder

The word *deficient* comes from the Latin *deficiens*, which means "to be wanting." In what ways do you think the "Mexican schools" were found wanting?

_____

_____

✓ Checkpoint

Explain why the UFW organized a grape boycott.

_____

_____

✓ Checkpoint

Name one difference between the National Congress of American Indians and AIM.

_____

_____

Question to Think About As you read Section 4 in your textbook and take notes, keep this section focus question in mind: **What other groups were swept up in the spirit of reform?**

▶ Use this chart to record key information from the section. Some information has been filled in to get you started.

Reform Movements

The Women's Rights Movement
- Betty Friedan's _The Feminine Mystique_ criticized _women's limited role in society_ .
- NOW's goals were_____
   _____.
- Arguments for the ERA: _____
- Arguments against the ERA: _____
- The 1963 Equal Pay Act ensured _____.
- _____ of 1965 banned discrimination based on sex.
- In the 1960s and 1970s, the number of women working outside the home and attending college _____.

Mexican Americans
- In the Southwest, many Mexican American children went to _____, which were not as good as the all-white schools.
- Mexican American World War II veterans formed the _____ to challenge discrimination.
- In _Hernández v. Texas_, the Supreme Court ruled that _____.
- _____ was one of the founders of the United Farm Workers. He organized a nationwide boycott of California _____. The boycott led to _____.
- The Voting Rights Act of 1975 was important because_____.
- Legislation for _____ education was passed.

Native Americans
- _The National Congress of American Indians_ had some success in regaining land, _____, and _____ rights for Native Americans.
- The _____ was more militant. Armed members went to _____ _____. Its goal was _____.

Older Americans
- Mandatory retirement means _____.
- The _____ championed health insurance for retired Americans.
- Maggie Kuhn formed the _____ to fight age discrimination.

Americans With Disabilities
- Organizations for the disabled championed laws that_____.
- The Education for the Handicapped Act of 1975 guaranteed _____.
- The Americans With Disabilities Act made it illegal to_____.

Refer to this page to answer the Chapter 26 Focus Question on page 408.

Chapter 26 Assessment

Directions: Circle the letter of the correct answer.

1. Which of the following Supreme Court cases ended segregation in schools?
   A   *Hernández* v. *Texas*
   B   *Brown* v. *Board of Education of Topeka*
   C   *Plessy* v. *Ferguson*
   D   *Miranda* v. *Arizona*

2. Martin Luther King, Jr.'s, strategy for protest and change was known as
   A   civil disobedience.
   B   separatism.
   C   Black Power.
   D   militancy.

3. The organization founded by Betty Friedan and other leaders of the women's movement was named
   A   Women's Lib.
   B   UFW.
   C   the Great Society.
   D   National Organization for Women.

Directions: Follow the steps to answer this question:

In what ways did the American government help the civil rights movement to achieve its goals?

Step 1: Recall information: Briefly list some of the goals of the civil rights movement for African Americans.

Goals of Civil Rights Movement
•
•
•
•

Step 2: List court cases and legislation, and their effects, that were related to the civil rights movement.

Court Cases & Legislation	Effects

Step 3: Draw conclusions: Complete the topic sentence that follows. Then write two or three more sentences that support your topic sentence.

The American government helped the civil rights movement to achieve its goals in that

_____

_____

_____

Chapter 26 Notetaking Study Guide

Now you are ready to answer the Chapter 26 Focus Question: **How did the civil rights movement change the nation?**

▶ Fill in the following chart to help you answer this question. Use the notes that you took for each section.

Civil Rights Movements Change the Nation
Education
• In *Brown v. Board of Education of Topeka*, the Supreme Court ruled that _____ _____.
• Head Start, one of President Johnson's Great Society programs, provided _____ _____.
• When students get bilingual education, they are taught _____.
• The Education for the Handicapped Act of 1975 ensured _____ _____.
Transportation
• The Montgomery bus boycott started after _____ was arrested for refusing to _____.
• The Supreme Court decided that segregation on public buses was_____.
• Freedom Rides took place to_____.
Workplace
• The Civil Rights Act of 1964 banned_____.
• The 1964 Equal Pay Act stated that_____.
• César Chávez led the struggle for_____.
• The Americans With Disabilities Act made it illegal to_____ in hiring based on_____.
Public facilities
• At sit-ins, protesters _____.
• The Civil Rights Act of 1964 banned _____.
• Organizations for the disabled have successfully fought to have _____ to public facilities.
Voting
Purpose of the Voting Rights Act of 1965
• _____
• _____
Purpose of the Voting Rights Act of 1975
• _____
Public Health
• Medicare is a program that _____.
• Medicaid is a program that_____.
• The American Association of Retired Persons fought for _____.

Refer to this page to answer the Unit 9 Focus Question on page 451.

Chapter 27

The Vietnam Era (1954–1976)

What You Will Learn

The United States became involved in a civil war in Vietnam in order to stop the spread of communism. Americans were divided in their opinion of the war. After the United States withdrew, Vietnam was taken over by a Communist government. Richard Nixon's presidency, which occurred during the last years of the war, ended in scandal.

Chapter 27 Focus Question

As you read this chapter, keep this question in mind: **What were the causes and effects of the Vietnam War?**

Section 1

The War Begins

Section 1 Focus Question

How did Vietnam become a major battlefield in the war against communism? To begin answering this question,

- Learn how Vietnam became a focus of conflict after World War II.
- Find out why America was concerned about developments in Vietnam, and how U.S. involvement increased.

Section 1 Summary

The United States backed France in opposing Vietnamese independence. When the French were defeated, the United States feared the spread of communism and backed South Vietnam with military aid.

Origins of the Conflict

France had ruled Vietnam, a small country in Southeast Asia, since the 1800s as part of its Indochina colony. During World War II, Japan took over, but after the war, the French regained control. **Ho Chi Minh,** a Communist leader, fought for Vietnam's independence from France. He and his followers, known as the Vietminh, occupied Hanoi and proclaimed Vietnam's independence. France refused to recognize an independent Vietnam. Ho Chi Minh had asked the United States for help in his fight against France, but America distrusted Communists. Instead, the United States gave money and supplies to France. The fighting between the Vietminh and France lasted nearly eight years. During this war, Ho Chi Minh <u>acquired</u> more and more followers. In 1954, the Vietminh

Key Events

1961	Kennedy sends military advisers to South Vietnam.
1964	Congress passes the Gulf of Tonkin Resolution.
1968	Antiwar demonstrations disrupt the Democratic National Convention.
1974	Nixon resigns from office as a result of the Watergate scandal.

Vocabulary Builder

Use context clues to determine which of the following is a synonym for *acquired.*

a. collected
b. destroyed
c. supported

finally forced the French to surrender after a battle at Dien Bien Phu. After this major defeat, France agreed to negotiate an end to the war and its control of Vietnam. ✓

The War Spreads

After World War II, the United States worried about the Soviet Union's policy of spreading communism. When China was taken over by a Communist government in 1949, these worries intensified. In 1950, the Korean War began after Communist North Korea attacked South Korea. As leaders in the United States watched the Communists' power grow, they worried that if Ho Chi Minh gained control of Vietnam, much of Southeast Asia would fall under Communist rule. This argument, called the **domino theory**, reasoned that if one country fell to Communists, neighboring countries would follow.

When the French gave up power in Vietnam, an international conference took place in Geneva, Switzerland. Here it was decided under the Geneva Accords that Vietnam would be divided. Ho Chi Minh's Communist government would rule North Vietnam from its capital of Hanoi, while **Ngo Dinh Diem's** non-Communist government would hold power in South Vietnam from its capital of Saigon. Under the Geneva Accords, elections would be held to unite the country within a few years, but Diem's government prevented these elections from taking place. In 1959, dissatisfied South Vietnamese organized to oppose Diem. **Guerrillas,** or fighters who carry out hit-and-run attacks, began strikes against Diem's government. Called the Vietcong, these guerrillas were supplied with weapons by the North Vietnamese.

During both Eisenhower's and Kennedy's administrations, the United States supported South Vietnam with aid and military advisers. As time went on, however, it became clear to the United States that Diem's government was tyrannical and corrupt. Diem's actions were causing the Vietcong to gain followers. Finally, in 1963, Kennedy pulled his support from Diem. The South Vietnamese military then took over the government and shot Diem. Soon after, Kennedy was assassinated in the United States, and Vice President **Lyndon Johnson** became President. ✓

Check Your Progress

1. Why did Ho Chi Minh fight the French?

_____

_____

2. What happened to Vietnam as a result of the Geneva Accords?

_____

_____

Question to Think About As you read Section 1 in your textbook and take notes, keep this section focus question in mind: **How did Vietnam become a major battlefield in the war against communism?**

▶ Use this chart to record key information from the section. Some information has been filled in to get you started.

The War Begins
Vietnam's History

- Vietnam is located in ___Southeast Asia___.
- Since the 1800s, Vietnam had been ruled by the ___French___ as part of the colony of _____.
- In World War II, ___Japan___ gained control of Vietnam.
- After World War II, _____, a Communist leader, led the fight for Vietnamese independence. His followers were called _____.
- The United States supported _____ during the war in order to stop _____.
- The fighting lasted nearly _____ years.
- France's major defeat came at the battle of_____.

A Battleground Against Communism

- The domino theory argued that _____.
- Under the Geneva Accords, Vietnam _____.
- _____ was to rule North Vietnam from its capital of _____.
- _____ was to rule South Vietnam from its capital of _____.
- Guerrillas are_____.
- Guerrillas in South Vietnam were called _____.
- Ngo Dinh Diem's government in South Vietnam was _____.
- The United States responded to Diem's governing by _____.
- In November 1963, _____ of South Vietnam took over the government and shot Diem.
- Three weeks later, American President _____ was shot.
- Vice President _____ was sworn in as President.

Refer to this page to answer the Chapter 27 Focus Question on page 422.

American Involvement Grows

1961 — Kennedy sends military advisers to South Vietnam.

1964 — Congress passes the Gulf of Tonkin Resolution.

1968 — Antiwar demonstrations disrupt the Democratic National Convention.

1974 — Nixon resigns from office as a result of the Watergate scandal.

✓ Checkpoint

Name the act that gave President Johnson the authority to step up American involvement in Vietnam.

_____

_____

Section 2 Focus Question

How did the demands of greater involvement in Vietnam divide the nation? To begin answering this question,

- Learn how President Johnson increased American involvement in the war.
- Read about how the United States tried to win this unconventional war.
- Discover how hawks and doves in the United States reacted to the war.

Section 2 Summary

Determined not to lose Vietnam to communism, President Johnson sent hundreds of thousands of American troops to the war. In response to this escalation, some Americans protested for an end to American involvement, while others supported an even greater military response.

A Wider War

During President Johnson's early days in office, South Vietnam was in turmoil. One military government overthrew another, and no leader seemed strong enough to keep power for very long. The Vietcong, supported by the Soviet Union and China, were gaining strength. Johnson believed that saving South Vietnam from communism was vital, so he sent more money and military advisers there.

In August 1964, reports said that American destroyers were attacked twice by North Vietnamese torpedo boats in the Gulf of Tonkin. Although it was later revealed that the second attack may not have taken place, Johnson was determined to stage air strikes against North Vietnam. He asked Congress to pass a resolution that would permit the United States to respond to aggression. The act, called the Gulf of Tonkin Resolution, enabled Johnson to **escalate,** or step up, involvement in Vietnam. ✓

An Unconventional War

President Johnson successfully ran for reelection in 1964, indicating that he would not send American troops to Vietnam. When the Vietcong attacked an American base in South Vietnam and killed eight soldiers, Johnson responded with more air strikes against North Vietnam. After it became clear that air strikes alone would not be enough to stop North Vietnam, Johnson decided to send American soldiers to Vietnam. At first, American troops were sent there to defend the American base. Soon, however, they were directed to take part in attacks. By 1968, half a million American troops were in Vietnam.

In the meantime, South Vietnam grew more stable. Nguyen Cao Ky, a military leader, took over in 1965 and dealt harshly with his opponents. Because he seemed firmly in control, South Vietnam could focus more on the war. Americans used new weapons, such as bombs with **napalm,** a jellylike substance that burst into flames, sticking to people's bodies. Another weapon was Agent Orange, an herbicide that killed a vast amount of plant life to destroy enemy hiding places. Some claim that Agent Orange caused health troubles for Vietnamese and U.S. troops.

None of this stopped the Vietcong. They had the advantages of knowing the countryside and of being able to recognize their enemy. In contrast, it was hard for American troops to be sure who was a member of the Vietcong and who was not. Americans tried new strategies, including search and destroy missions. Instead of trying to gain territory, they tried to kill as many Vietcong as they could.

On January 31, 1968, the war took a surprising turn. That day was Tet, the Vietnamese New Year holiday. During the celebrations, the North Vietnamese and Vietcong launched massive attacks on every major city in South Vietnam. By the end of February, American and South Vietnamese forces had retaken the cities. However, the magnitude of the Tet offensive undermined American support for the war because people were no longer sure that the United States could win. ✓

A Nation Divided

As more troops were sent to Vietnam, the U.S. reaction was divided. **Hawks** supported the war, and some even wanted to increase U.S. military involvement. **Doves** believed the Vietnam War could not be won and was morally wrong. They wanted the United States to withdraw its troops. Doves engaged in huge protests against the war. Sometimes they came into conflict with police.

During this time, some young men resisted being drafted into the military by burning their draft cards. Others claimed to be **conscientious objectors,** or people who oppose war based on religious or philosophical beliefs. About 100,000 people went to live in Canada to avoid military service in Vietnam. Throughout the war, television brought horrible images of war into people's homes. ✓

Check Your Progress

1. Why did President Johnson escalate American involvement in Vietnam?

_____

_____

2. How did young Americans avoid going to war?

_____

_____

Vocabulary Builder

The word *magnitude* has different meanings depending on its context. Which definition below is closest to its usage in the underlined sentence?

a. volume of sound
b. greatness of size or extent

✓ Checkpoint

List two effects of the Tet offensive.

_____

_____

_____

✓ Checkpoint

Name the two "sides" at home that conflicted over the war.

_____

_____

Question to Think About As you read Section 2 in your textbook and take notes, keep this section focus question in mind: **How did the demands of greater involvement in Vietnam divide the nation?**

▶ Use this chart to record key information from the section. Some information has been filled in to get you started.

United States in Vietnam	
Event	**U.S. Response**
North Vietnam attacks American destroyers in the Gulf of Tonkin.	Johnson responds by calling for: • ___Gulf of Tonkin Resolution___ • ___air strikes against North Vietnam___
Johnson runs for reelection, vowing not to send Americans to Vietnam.	• Johnson _____ the 1964 election in a _____.
North Vietnam attacks American base at Pleiku.	• Johnson responds by launching more _____ _____.
The Vietcong continue their attacks.	• Americans develop new weapons, including _____ and _____. • Americans try to kill massive numbers of enemy troops in missions called _____.
The North Vietnamese launch the _____ on the New Year holiday.	• Americans and South Vietnamese troops _____ the battle. • Americans at home react with _____ _____.
The war continues for several years.	• Hawks _____ _____. • Doves _____ _____.
Opposition to the war increases.	• Some resisters _____ their draft cards. • Some claim to be _____, who disagree with war for religious or philosophical reasons. • Many flee to _____.
Antiwar movement evolves.	• First, protests are mainly _____. • Later, violence between protesters and _____ becomes more common.

Refer to this page to answer the Chapter 27 Focus Question on page 422.

Section 3
The War Ends

Section 3 Focus Question
What were the causes and effects of American withdrawal from Vietnam? To begin answering this question,
- Learn about the 1968 presidential election.
- Read about how American involvement changed under Nixon.
- Find out how South Vietnam came under Communist control.
- Discover some of the lasting effects of the war for both the United States and Vietnam.

Section 3 Summary

Richard Nixon won the presidential election of 1968, promising to bring peace. Antiwar protests in the United States continued, especially when war spread to Cambodia. U.S. troops withdrew, and two years later, Communists took over South Vietnam.

Election of 1968
With American support for the Vietnam War weakening, Lyndon Johnson decided not to run for reelection in 1968. Instead, Vice President Hubert Humphrey, who supported Johnson's policies, ran for the Democrats. At the Democratic nominating convention in Chicago, antiwar protesters staged a massive demonstration. When police attacked the protesters, the nation watched televised reports of the turmoil. The Republican candidate was **Richard Nixon,** who promised to bring "peace with honor" in Vietnam. In a close race, Nixon beat Humphrey. ✔

The War Winds Down
With a policy called Vietnamization, Nixon reduced America's role in Vietnam by having South Vietnamese troops take on more fighting. Yet Nixon expanded the war into Cambodia, bombing Communist bases there that supplied the Vietcong. Although this had little <u>impact</u> on the enemy, it did result in major protests at home. During antiwar protests at Kent State, the Ohio National Guard killed four students. Other protests also ended tragically.

Peace talks in Paris between the United States and North Vietnam dragged on for three years. **Henry Kissinger,** the national security adviser, met secretly with a North Vietnamese leader in 1970. By then, the United States had begun withdrawing thousands of troops. As the 1972 presidential election drew near, Kissinger maintained that the two sides were close to an agreement. South Vietnam did not agree to Kissinger's plan, but an agreement was finally signed on January 27, 1973. By March, the last American troops in Vietnam had come home. ✔

Key Events

1961	Kennedy sends military advisers to South Vietnam.
1964	Congress passes the Gulf of Tonkin Resolution.
1968	Antiwar demonstrations disrupt the Democratic National Convention.
1974	Nixon resigns from office as a result of the Watergate scandal.

✔ Checkpoint
State Nixon's campaign promise.

_____

_____

Vocabulary Builder

Impact means "having a strong effect." Why did Nixon think bombing Cambodian bases would impact the war?

_____

_____

✔ Checkpoint
Name Nixon's policy of giving South Vietnam responsibility of fighting the war.

_____

The Final Years of Conflict

After U.S. forces left Vietnam, conflict went on between the North and South Vietnamese governments. According to the Paris Peace Accords, the North Vietnamese could keep 150,000 troops in South Vietnam. Communists used these troops to take control of the country, attacking the South Vietnamese army and forcing them to retreat. This retreat, during which many South Vietnamese soldiers and civilians died, became known as the Convoy of Tears. When North Vietnamese troops got close to Saigon in April 1975, the United States sent helicopters to help 1,000 U.S. workers and 5,500 South Vietnamese supporters leave the country. U.S. ships rescued thousands of Vietnamese who fled on boats. The North Vietnamese gave Saigon a new name—Ho Chi Minh City. ✔

Vietnam Balance Sheet

For America, the Vietnam War had lasting effects. Americans were defeated in a foreign war for the first time. The defeat came at a terrible price—more than 58,000 Americans died in battle, and another 300,000 were injured. The huge amount of money that the United States spent on the war hurt the American economy for years. Veterans, who lacked support when they got home, also suffered. America's faith in its government grew weaker. Secret government documents, known as the Pentagon Papers, were published in 1971. They detailed U.S. involvement in Vietnam and revealed that U.S. leaders had misled Americans about the war.

To diminish presidential power, Congress passed the War Powers Act in 1973. This said that presidents needed the approval of Congress before sending U.S. troops into combat for longer than 60 days. The United States also passed the Twenty-sixth Amendment to the Constitution, lowering the legal voting age to 18.

In Vietnam, the war had awful costs. More than 350,000 South Vietnamese died in combat, while between 500,000 and a million North Vietnamese died. Bombing tore apart North Vietnam. In South Vietnam, 10 million people lost their homes. When Communists took power in 1975, over a million people tried to leave Vietnam. Those who attempted to escape in small boats were called **boat people,** and some 200,000 died. Many Vietnamese refugees came to the United States and other countries. ✔

Check Your Progress

1. What effects did bombing Cambodian bases have in the United States?

_____

_____

2. What happened after U.S. troops left Vietnam?

_____

_____

✓ Checkpoint

Explain what the Convoy of Tears was.

_____

_____

_____

✓ Checkpoint

List U.S. losses in the Vietnam War.

_____

_____

Question to Think About As you read Section 3 in your textbook and take notes, keep this section focus question in mind: **What were the causes and effects of American withdrawal from Vietnam?**

► Use this chart to record key information from the section. Some information has been filled in to get you started.

Events During the Vietnam War	
Cause	**Effect**
Johnson does not run for reelection.	• ___Hubert Humphrey___ runs for the Democrats.
Nixon promises to bring _"peace with honor."_	• _____ wins the 1968 presidential election.
Nixon pursues a policy of _____.	• American troops withdraw, giving the South Vietnamese more responsibility for the war.
Nixon calls for bombing Cambodian bases.	• For the outcome of the war, the effect is _small_____. • For Cambodia, the bombings cause _____ _____. • The attacks trigger_____ in the United States.
Henry Kissinger meets with a North Vietnamese leader to work out a peace agreement.	• Before the 1972 presidential election, Kissinger promises that _____. • In fact, the South Vietnamese_____ _____.
_____ are signed in January 1973.	• The last U.S. combat troops leave Vietnam by _____ _____.
North Vietnamese are allowed to keep 150,000 troops in South Vietnam.	• North Vietnamese troops proceed to _____ _____
South Vietnamese troops retreat.	• Thousands of soldiers die and civilians flee in what became known as the _____.
South Vietnamese government surrenders.	• Vietnam is united under a _____ government. • Saigon is renamed _____ .
Number of killed and wounded	• _____ Americans die in battle. • About _____ South Vietnamese die in battle. • North Vietnamese dead are between _____ . • _____ people in South Vietnam are left homeless.
Some South Vietnamese want to flee.	• Some try to escape by sea and are called _____ . • About _____ die at sea or in refugee camps.

Refer to this page to answer the Chapter 27 Focus Question on page 422.

Key Events

1961	Kennedy sends military advisers to South Vietnam.
1964	Congress passes the Gulf of Tonkin Resolution.
1968	Antiwar demonstrations disrupt the Democratic National Convention.
1974	Nixon resigns from office as a result of the Watergate scandal.

Vocabulary Builder

The word *priority* comes from the Latin word *prior*, meaning "first." Why do you think easing Cold War tensions might have been one of Nixon's first concerns?

_____

_____

✓ Checkpoint

State two of Nixon's successes.

_____

_____

Section 4 Focus Question

What successes and failures marked Nixon's presidency? To begin answering this question,

- Learn about Nixon's foreign and domestic policies.
- Find out about the Watergate scandal.
- Read about President Gerald Ford.

Section 4 Summary

Richard Nixon had successes in foreign policy, including easing tensions with China and the Soviet Union. He fought inflation unsuccessfully at home, however. After the Watergate scandal broke, Nixon was forced to resign, leaving Vice President Gerald Ford to serve as President.

Richard Nixon in Office

When Richard Nixon won the presidency in 1968, the country was in turmoil as a result of the Vietnam War. A bright spot occurred on July 20, 1969, when American astronaut Neil Armstrong became the first person to walk on the moon.

Most Americans, however, were concerned with the war and with **inflation,** or a steady rise in prices, which was hurting the economy. High unemployment and a recession also hurt the economy. To help ease inflation, Nixon took an unusual step, especially for a Republican. He froze prices, wages, and rents, but unfortunately, the freeze did not curb inflation. The freeze was short lived.

Nixon had greater success with some of his foreign policy actions. He opened relations between the United States and Communist China, which had long been strained. In 1972, Nixon visited mainland China, even meeting with Chairman Mao Zedong. Easing tensions with the Soviet Union also was a priority. Nixon signed the Strategic Arms Limitation Treaty (SALT), which limited how many and what kind of nuclear weapons the United States and the Soviet Union could build. ✓

Watergate Scandal

Nixon was reelected in the 1972 presidential election. Within months, however, a political scandal erupted that distracted the nation and ended Nixon's presidency.

During the presidential campaign, Nixon's team tried to gather information about their opposition, the Democrats. Police arrested five men who broke into the Democratic Party offices, which were in the Watergate apartment complex in Washington, D.C. Later, White House officials tried to pay the burglars so that they would not tell the story of the break-in. However, the story became public.

Senate hearings on the Watergate scandal took place in May 1973, and the nation watched these proceedings on television. A former White House counsel, John Dean, testified that Nixon was involved in the attempt to cover up the burglary. Another witness revealed that Nixon had tapes of all of his presidential conversations. The Supreme Court ordered Nixon to give up the tapes, and they showed that Nixon was indeed involved in the coverup operation. In July 1974, Nixon faced impeachment proceedings by the House of Representatives. He knew that there were enough votes to remove him from office, so within a month, Nixon resigned. ✔

The Ford Presidency

After Nixon resigned, Vice President **Gerald Ford** was sworn into office as President. He made the decision to pardon Richard Nixon, and that decision was unpopular.

When Ford took office, the economy was still in trouble with high inflation. Ford tried to lower inflation through Whip Inflation Now, a program of voluntary wage and price controls that met with little success. As the country slipped into a recession, Ford pushed Congress to cut taxes to help spur the economy. It took the economy a long time to recover from the recession.

Ford continued Nixon's policies in China and the Soviet Union, working to ease Cold War tensions. Although American troops were out of Vietnam, when Communist troops got near Saigon, Ford arranged an airlift that helped more than 50,000 South Vietnamese to leave the country. Ford had other crises as well. When Cambodian Communists seized an American merchant ship, Ford sent U.S. marines to Cambodia to save the crew. In the 1976 presidential election, Ford ran as the Republican candidate. Democratic candidate **Jimmy Carter** won the race, however. ✔

Check Your Progress

1. What led to Nixon's resignation?

_____

_____

_____

2. What prompted Ford to continue U.S. involvement in Southeast Asia?

_____

_____

✓ **Checkpoint**

Name the activity that Nixon tried to cover up.

_____

_____

✓ **Checkpoint**

Name Ford's program to beat inflation through voluntary price controls.

_____

_____

Question to Think About As you read Section 4 in your textbook and take notes, keep this section focus question in mind: **What successes and failures marked Nixon's presidency?**

▶ Use this chart to record key information from the section. Some information has been filled in to get you started.

President Richard Nixon

Important Events
- In 1969, Neil Armstrong became the first person to ___walk on the moon___.

Domestic Policy
- Throughout his presidency, Nixon had to deal with the following economic problems: _____, _____, and _____.
- Nixon _____ wages, rents, and prices to curb inflation. The policy _____ work.

Foreign Policy
- In 1972, Nixon visited _____, which surprised many people.
- While there, Nixon met with Chairman _____.
- Nixon and Soviet leaders signed the _____.
- The agreement that Nixon reached with Soviet leaders limited_____ _____.

Watergate
- In order to obtain information during the 1972 presidential elections, burglars broke into the _____ offices in the_____ apartment complex.
- _____ paid the burglars so that they would not tell the story of the burglary.
- _____ held hearings to investigate the scandal.
- _____, a former White House counsel, testified that Nixon had approved the coverup.
- The Supreme Court ordered Nixon to turn over _____.
- The House of Representatives took steps to _____ President Nixon.
- On August 9, 1974, Nixon _____.

President Gerald Ford

- The public felt less trust in Ford because he _____.
- Ford's voluntary program of wage and price controls was called _____.
- To spur the economy, Congress approved a _____.
- When Communist troops drew near to Saigon, Ford _____ _____.
- In 1976, Ford lost the presidential election to _____.

Refer to this page to answer the Chapter 27 Focus Question on page 422.

Directions: Circle the letter of the correct answer.

1. The idea that once one country falls to communism, neighboring countries will follow, is called
   A search and destroy.   C the domino theory.
   B Vietnamization.   D the Tet offensive.

2. In 1968, this candidate won the U.S. presidential election, saying he would bring "peace with honor."
   A Lyndon Johnson   C Hubert Humphrey
   B Richard Nixon   D Gerald Ford

3. When North Vietnamese and Vietcong troops coordinated attacks on major cities in South Vietnam, it was called
   A the Tet offensive.   C the Gulf of Tonkin attack.
   B the *Mayaguez* incident.   D Vietnamization.

Directions: Follow the steps to answer this question:

Why did the United States keep changing its goals throughout the Vietnam War?

Step 1: Recall information: Briefly list some of the goals of the United States during the Vietnam War.

U.S. Goals at Beginning of Vietnam War	U.S. Goals During the War Under Nixon
• Stop the spread of communism •	• •

Step 2: List factors that might have had an impact on these goals.

U.S. Difficulties in Vietnam	U.S. Reaction to War
• •	• •

Step 3: Complete the topic sentence that follows. Then write two or three more sentences that support your topic sentence.

The U.S. goals in Vietnam changed as time went on, from _____

_____

_____

_____

_____

Chapter 27 Notetaking Study Guide

Now you are ready to answer the Chapter 27 Focus Question: **What were the causes and effects of the Vietnam War?**

▶ Complete the charts to help you answer this question. Use the notes that you took for each section.

The Vietnam War
Causes
• Beginning in the 1800s, France ruled Vietnam as part of the colony of __Indochina__ .   • When France took control of Vietnam again after World War II, _____ led the Vietnamese fight for independence. His followers were called _____.   • The _____ were defeated at the battle of Dien Bien Phu.   • U.S. leaders believed that if one country fell to communism, its neighbors would follow, an idea known as _____.   • Vice President Lyndon Johnson became President after _____ _____.   • After North Vietnam attacked American destroyers, Congress passed the _____, allowing the President to use the military to respond to acts of aggression.   • New types of weapons were used by the U.S. military, including _____ and _____.
Effects
• U.S. opinion of the war was divided. _____ believed that the war was justified. _____ believed that the war was morally wrong.   • The antiwar movement grew, and _____ between protesters and police became more common.   • _____ realized how unpopular the war was, and he decided not to run for reelection.   • _____ won the presidential election of 1968 and pursued a policy of _____, whereby the South Vietnamese took on more responsibility for fighting.   • U.S. troops left Vietnam after the _____ Accords were signed in 1973.   • After U.S. troops left, North Vietnamese troops _____.   • In 1975, South Vietnam was united with North Vietnam under a _____ government.   • During the war, _____ American soldiers died in combat.   • The South Vietnamese lost _____ in battle.   • The North Vietnamese lost between _____ and _____ soldiers in battle.   • _____ tried to escape the new regime by sea.   • As a result of the war, some Americans lost faith in the government, and this feeling intensified as a result of Nixon's presidential scandal, known as _____.

Refer to this page to answer the Unit 9 Focus Question on page 451.

New Directions for a Nation (1977–2008)

What You Will Learn

With Ronald Reagan's 1980 defeat of President Jimmy Carter, a conservative movement gained momentum. During George H. W. Bush's presidency, the Soviet Union collapsed, ending the Cold War and changing America's foreign policy goals. The Middle East continues to pose grave challenges to the nation's leaders.

Chapter 28 Focus Question

As you read this chapter, keep this question in mind: **How did major national and international events affect the nation?**

Section 1

A Conservative Surge

Section 1 Focus Question

How did the growing conservative movement help reshape American politics? To begin answering this question,

- Learn about Jimmy Carter's difficult presidency.
- Read about the presidencies of Reagan and George H. W. Bush.
- Understand the prosperity and scandal of Clinton's presidency.
- Find out about the conservative agenda of George W. Bush.

Section 1 Summary

President Carter faced inflation at home and a hostage crisis abroad. Reagan began a conservative momentum in 1980. Clinton brought prosperity, but scandal weakened his presidency. George W. Bush made tax cuts and educational reforms.

Carter's Troubled Presidency

President Jimmy Carter was elected in 1976, and he had to confront inflation at home and difficult issues abroad. When Carter allowed the Shah of Iran to get medical care in the United States, revolutionaries seized the American embassy in Iran and held 53 American hostages. For over a year, Carter failed to gain the hostages' freedom, which weakened his presidency. ✓

The Conservative Movement

During the Carter years and after, liberals believed that the federal government could solve problems in the tradition of the New Deal. Political conservatives wanted to curb government power and lower taxes. Social conservatives felt that traditional

Key Events

1979	Militants take 53 Americans hostage in Iran.
1987	United States and Soviet Union agree on an arms control treaty.
1991	United States leads the coalition against Iraq in the Persian Gulf War.

Vocabulary Builder

Read the underlined sentence. Based on context clues, what do you think the word *confront* means?

_____

✓ Checkpoint

Name two challenges President Carter faced.

_____

_____

_____

_____

_____

_____

_____

_____

_____

family values, patriotism, and religion must be priorities. Jerry Falwell's Moral Majority organized around these principles. Conservatives gained control of the Republican Party by 1980, promising tax cuts, business deregulation, and a **balanced budget,** meaning that government spends only as much money as it collects. They nominated Ronald Reagan, who beat Carter. ✓

Reagan's Presidency

President **Ronald Reagan,** a former actor, became known as the Great Communicator. He promoted a conservative agenda, pushing large tax cuts through Congress. By slashing federal jobs and social programs, he cut $40 billion from the federal budget. He also **deregulated** industries, or scaled back federal rules for businesses. Reagan was a popular President elected for two terms, yet his tax cuts and spending on the military caused a huge federal **deficit,** in which government spent more money than it collected. Critics charged that he helped the wealthy but hurt the poor and the environment. Still, he limited the growth of federal government and cut inflation.

Reagan's Vice President, **George H. W. Bush,** was elected in 1988. After promising not to raise taxes, he realized later that he needed to do so in order to reduce the deficit. Conservatives were outraged. A **recession,** or temporary economic slump, took place. People blamed Bush's tax hike for rising unemployment. ✓

The Clinton Years and George W. Bush

In 1992, **Bill Clinton** defeated George H. W. Bush and became President. He ran as a "New Democrat," or more moderate than many liberals. By pushing through tax increases for the wealthy and reducing federal spending, Clinton reduced the size of the deficit. He also ended federal welfare payments, giving money to state and local antipoverty programs instead. Clinton's policies brought prosperity and, eventually, a government **surplus,** in which government collects more than it spends. A scandal during his second term weakened his presidency. Because he seemed to lie under oath, the House of Representatives voted to impeach him. The Senate did not convict Clinton, so he remained in office.

In 2000, Vice President Al Gore ran against **George W. Bush.** Although more people voted for Gore, Bush won the electoral vote in one of the most controversial elections in U.S. history. He pushed through tax cuts and education reforms. ✓

Check Your Progress

1. What were the strengths of Reagan's presidency?

_____

_____

2. What were the strengths of Clinton's presidency?

_____

_____

Question to Think About As you read Section 1 in your textbook and take notes, keep this section focus question in mind: **How did the growing conservative movement help reshape American politics?**

▶ Use this chart to record key information from the section. Some information has been filled in to get you started.

President Jimmy Carter
President Carter had to deal with the economic problem of __inflation_____ .
Carter's major foreign policy crisis was _____ .

The Conservative Movement and President Ronald Reagan
A political conservative believes ___in cutting federal government, deregulating business, and lowering taxes_____ .
A social conservative believes _____ .
Reagan's arguments for cutting government spending and taxes: _____ _____ _____
Reagan's successes include _____ _____ _____
Reagan's critics charged _____ .

President George H. W. Bush
Bush broke his promise not to raise taxes because _____ .
A recession is _____ .

President Bill Clinton
Bill Clinton was a "New Democrat." This meant that _____ _____ _____ .
Clinton's economic policies included _____ _____
Clinton's welfare reform included _____ .
A surplus is _____ .
Clinton's presidency was weakened during his second term when _____ _____ .

President George W. Bush
The presidential election of 2000 was controversial because _____ _____ _____ .
Bush's major domestic priorities included _____ .

Refer to this page to answer the Chapter 28 Focus Question on page 436.

Key Events

1979	Militants take 53 Americans hostage in Iran.
1987	United States and Soviet Union agree on an arms control treaty.
1991	United States leads the coalition against Iraq in the Persian Gulf War.

Vocabulary Builder

List three synonyms for the underlined word *marred*.

_____

_____

_____

✓ Checkpoint

List three actions Reagan took to fight communism.

_____

_____

_____

Section 2 Focus Question

How did the Cold War end? To begin answering this question,
- Learn how the policy of détente ended when the Soviet Union invaded Afghanistan.
- Read about how the Soviet Union weakened both economically and militarily, and how Gorbachev introduced reforms.
- Discover how the Cold War ended when the Soviet Union broke apart.

Section 2 Summary

President Carter pursued a policy of détente with the Soviet Union, until the Soviets invaded Afghanistan. President Reagan increased military spending, and when the Soviet Union tried to keep up, its economy fell into decline. The Soviet Union broke apart in 1991, which ended the Cold War.

The End of Détente

President Nixon, and then President Carter, believed in the policy of détente with the Soviet Union. But in 1979, the Soviet Union invaded Afghanistan. Carter showed his disapproval by pulling an arms agreement from the Senate, boycotting the 1980 Moscow Olympics, and imposing trade restrictions with the Soviet Union.

President Reagan supported the Afghanistan government and its Islamic fighters who fought the Soviet Union. He also greatly increased military spending and oversaw major weapons programs, including the stealth bomber. Reagan believed in funding the Strategic Defense Initiative, a defense system that would use lasers to shoot enemy missiles before they could hit the United States. Critics charged that the program was too expensive.

Reagan fought communism in Central America by secretly supporting the Contras, guerrillas who fought the Sandinistas in Nicaragua. The Sandinistas were tied to both Cuba and the Soviet Union. Because the Contras were believed to be brutal, Congress outlawed further support to them. When seven Americans were taken hostage in Lebanon, Reagan officials worked out a plan through which the hostages would be freed and support would be given to the Nicaraguan Contras. The officials sold arms to Iran and used the money to help the Contras. When this agreement, known as the "Iran-Contra deal," became public, many were scandalized. Seven government officials were convicted of covering up the deal and of lying to Congress. President Reagan claimed that he knew nothing of the agreement, but the controversy <u>marred</u> his second term. ✓

The Soviet Union in Decline

The Soviet Union met America's increased military spending with its own increase in funding the military. Because Soviets had already spent so much on the failed war in Afghanistan, this new buildup caused an economic decline. Meanwhile, resistance to Communist rule was growing in Eastern Europe. When **Mikhail Gorbachev** took over the Soviet government in 1985, he began economic reforms. He introduced a policy known as **glasnost,** or speaking openly about Soviet problems. Gorbachev met with President Reagan, and they agreed on a major arms control treaty calling for the destruction of short-range and intermediate-range nuclear missiles.

At the same time, the Soviet-controlled governments of Eastern Europe faced rising opposition. Communist governments gave up power first in Poland, then also in Hungary, Romania, and Czechoslovakia. Finally, in 1989, students and workers destroyed the Berlin Wall, which had been the symbol of Communist oppression. Soon, there was one united Germany. Other national borders changed as well. Czechoslovakia became the two countries of the Czech Republic and Slovakia. Yugoslavia divided into several loosely joined republics. ✔

The Cold War Ends

The fall of Communist governments in so many Eastern European countries sparked independence movements within several of the fifteen Soviet republics. As a result, the Soviet Union dissolved in 1991, and each republic became an independent state. Boris Yeltsin became president of Russia. He worked to strengthen the economy and achieve democratic reforms. Yet Russia still faced huge problems of crime and corruption. Some worried that democracy would not help Russia. Independence for the Yugoslav republics led to a four-year civil war in which hundreds of thousands of Croatians, Bosnians, and Albanians were killed.

The Cold War between the United States and the Soviet Union, which had lasted for 45 years, ended with the dissolution of the Soviet Union. Americans were relieved. The Cold War had cost the United States trillions of dollars in military spending. Worse, thousands had died in the conflicts of Korea and Vietnam. ✔

Check Your Progress

1. What happened to cause an end to détente?

_____

_____

2. How did Reagan's military policies affect the Soviet Union?

_____

_____

✓ **Checkpoint**

Name two important actions Gorbachev made as the leader of the Soviet Union.

_____

_____

✓ **Checkpoint**

Describe the American reaction to the end of the Cold War.

_____

_____

Question to Think About As you read Section 2 in your textbook and take notes, keep this section focus question in mind: **How did the Cold War end?**

▶ Use this chart to record key information from the section. Some information has been filled in to get you started.

The Cold War Ends	
Cause	**Effect**
Nixon and Carter pursue détente with Soviet Union.	Cold War tensions ___ease___.
Soviet Union invades Afghanistan.	President Carter responds by: • ___stopping arms control agreement___ • _____ • _____
Conservative Reagan is elected President of the United States.	Tries to fight communism by: • _____ • _____ • _____
Sandinistas overthrow Somoza in Nicaragua.	• Reagan responds by supporting _____ _____.
Seven Americans taken hostage in Lebanon by Iranian-backed militants.	• Reagan officials sell arms to_____ so that hostages will be freed. Officials use the money to buy arms for_____ _____.
Reagan builds up military.	• Soviet Union responds by _____ _____.
Soviet Union increases military spending.	• Soviet economy _____.
Gorbachev allows glasnost.	• Soviets want _____.
Gorbachev wants better relations with the West.	He meets with Reagan in 1987, and they agree on _____ treaty.
Soviet Union stops supporting unpopular Eastern European Communist leaders.	• Communism loses power in _____, _____, _____, _____, and _____. In East Germany, people tear down the_____.
Soviet republics want independence.	• Soviet Union_____.
The Cold War ends.	• Americans feel _____.

Refer to this page to answer the Chapter 28 Focus Question on page 436.

Section 3

A New Role in the World

Section 3 Focus Question

How did the United States use its influence after the Cold War ended? To begin answering this question,

- Learn about U.S. goals for peace and democracy.
- Read about how the United States attempted to promote change in South Africa, Northern Ireland, China, and Cuba.
- Discover how the United States dealt with the problem of nuclear arms.

Key Events

1979	Militants take 53 Americans hostage in Iran.
1987	United States and Soviet Union agree on an arms control treaty.
1991	United States leads the coalition against Iraq in the Persian Gulf War.

Section 3 Summary

President George H. W. Bush and President Clinton worked to achieve peace and the spread of democracy. The United States promoted change in South Africa, Northern Ireland, China, and Cuba. The United States also tried to halt the spread of nuclear weapons.

Promoting Democracy and Peace

After the Cold War ended, the United States became the world's only superpower. President George H. W. Bush and President Clinton believed that it was important to use that power wisely, in the causes of peace and democracy.

For years, American lawmakers wanted to do something about South Africa and its policy of **apartheid,** or racial separation and inequality. Despite a veto by President Reagan, Congress voted for **sanctions,** penalties applied against a country in order to pressure it to change its policies. The sanctions forbade U.S. businesses to invest in South Africa or to import its products. Other countries applied similar measures. In 1991, as a result of the sanctions and internal protests, South Africa ended apartheid. Free elections in 1994, which included nonwhites, put black leaders in office.

British-ruled Northern Ireland had also been a trouble spot for years, with violence between the Protestant majority and the Catholic minority. The United States helped negotiate a 1998 power-sharing agreement between these groups to help end violence.

In 1989, Chinese students and workers protested in Tiananmen Square for democratic reforms. The Communist government brutally assaulted the protesters. President George H. W. Bush responded by trying to persuade China to introduce reforms. Clinton continued to press China to change human rights policies.

Communist-led Cuba posed a different problem for the United States. After the Soviet Union broke apart, Cuba lost a major source of economic aid. When Cuba's economy crashed, the United States considered the possibility of resuming trade with its

Vocabulary Builder

When a computer "crashes," it fails completely. When an economy crashes, what do you think happens to the value of the currency, or money?

_____

_____

_____

✓ **Checkpoint**

Name the strategy the U.S. Congress used to pressure South Africa to change its policy of apartheid.

_____

_____

with its neighbor. However, George W. Bush has vowed to maintain economic sanctions against Cuba in order to weaken its Communist dictator Fidel Castro. ✓

Easing the Arms Race

The first arms control agreement between the Soviet Union and the United States was signed in 1972. Since then, both countries have worked on agreements to reduce their nuclear weapons.

Arms Control Agreements Between United States and Soviet Union		
Treaty	**Year Signed**	**Agreement**
Strategic Arms Limitation Treaty (SALT)	1972	Reduced number of nuclear warheads and long-range missiles to be built
SALT II	1977	None—Carter withdrew the treaty after the Soviet invasion of Afghanistan
Strategic Arms Reduction Treaty (START)	1991	Thirty percent reduction in existing nuclear weapons
START II	1993, revised 1997	Two-thirds reduction in existing long-range nuclear weapons

After the Cold War ended, new problems arose. The former Soviet Union had nuclear weapons in four now-independent republics. Each of these republics, including Russia, agreed to uphold the treaties that the Soviet Union had signed. The U.S. sent support so that the weapons could be safely stored or destroyed.

Britain, France, and China had held nuclear weapons for a long time. Israel had a nuclear weapon by the late 1960s. Nuclear arms continued to spread to other countries, increasing the danger of nuclear war. U.S. intelligence reports indicated that Iran and Iraq were trying to build nuclear weapons. Particularly worrisome was the fact that India and Pakistan, feuding neighbors, both built nuclear bombs. ✓

Check Your Progress

1. Name a country that the United States has tried to influence, and describe the progress it has made.

_____

_____

2. Why are nuclear weapons a continuing threat?

_____

_____

✓ **Checkpoint**

Name one difference between the START treaties and the SALT treaty.

_____

_____

Question to Think About As you read Section 3 in your textbook and take notes, keep this section focus question in mind: **How did the United States use its influence after the Cold War ended?**

► Use this chart to record key information from the section. Some information has been filled in to get you started.

Promoting Democracy and Peace	
Countries	**United States Uses Its Influence**
South Africa	• Applied ___sanctions___ in order to end_____
Philippines	• Sent _____ to freely elected government after the dictator __Ferdinand Marcos__ lost power
Northern Ireland	• Helped negotiate an agreement between_____
China	• Tried to _____ the government to reform after the brutal crackdown at _____
Cuba	• Banned trade to weaken leader _____

Arms Control	
Strategic Arms Limitation Treaty (SALT) Countries Involved: __U.S., Soviet Union__ Year:_____ What Was Agreed to:_____ _____	**SALT II** Countries Involved:_____ Year:_____ What Was Agreed to:_____ _____
Strategic Arms Reduction Treaty (START) Countries Involved:_____ Leaders:_____ Year:_____ What Was Agreed to:_____	**START II** Countries Involved:_____ Year:_____ Year Revised:_____ What Was Agreed to:_____

The Nuclear Threat Continues
• Four former Soviet states agreed to_____. • The United States sent aid to _____ or _____ weapons. • _____ and _____ tested nuclear weapons for the first time in 1998. • The United States is concerned about more countries obtaining nuclear weapons because _____.

Refer to this page to answer the Chapter 28 Focus Question on page 436.

Section 4

Conflict in the Middle East

Section 4 Focus Question

How have tensions in the Middle East posed concerns for the United States? To begin answering this question,

- Learn about the importance of the Middle East to the United States.
- Find out about the continuing conflict between Arabs and Israelis.
- Read about U.S. activity in the region.

Section 4 Summary

The Middle East is important as a site of major world religions and for its oil reserves. Conflicts between Arabs and Israelis who founded the state of Israel remain unresolved. The United States has been involved in negotiation and war in the region.

A Vital Region

The area first called the Middle East by Europeans includes Southwest Asia, Egypt, and Afghanistan. Its location has made it an important crossroads for Europe, Asia, and Africa. Judaism, Christianity, and Islam all arose in the Middle East, and conflict between members of these faiths has gone on for centuries. Today the region is important due to its oil, used for transportation and in industry. Oil production and price levels are set by the Arab nations that form the Organization of Petroleum Exporting Countries (OPEC).

The United States has a difficult role in the region. It has a strong relationship with Israel, but it has also tried to maintain relations with Arab nations that do not support Israel. ✓

Arab-Israeli Conflict

Many Jews began settling in Palestine in the late 1800s. They wanted to establish a Jewish state, putting them at odds with the Arabs who lived there. With the rise of Nazism and the Holocaust, thousands more Jews settled in Palestine. Arab nations opposed their formation of the state of Israel in 1948, and war began. With Israel's victory, hundreds of thousands of Palestinian Arabs lost their homes, living in refugee camps in neighboring Arab nations.

Other wars followed. Israel invaded Egypt in 1956, but left due to international pressure. In 1967 and 1973, Arab countries attacked Israel. However, Israel gained land in Egypt, Jordan, and Syria as a result of these wars, and Israelis settled in the newly acquired regions. Arabs called these lands "occupied territories."

Key Events

1979 Militants take 53 Americans hostage in Iran.

1987 United States and Soviet Union agree on an arms control treaty.

1991 United States leads the coalition against Iraq in the Persian Gulf War.

✓ Checkpoint

Give two reasons why OPEC is important.

_____

_____

Progress was made in 1978 when President Carter brought Egyptian leader Anwar el-Sadat and Israeli leader Menachim Begin to Camp David in Maryland. They signed the Camp David Accords, with Egypt recognizing Israel, and Israel returning the Sinai Peninsula to Egypt. However, the Palestinian Liberation Organization (PLO), led by **Yasir Arafat,** declared that Israel could not exist, and that there should be a Palestinian state run by Palestinians.

Other countries worked for peace between Israelis and Palestinians. When President Clinton hosted leaders from Israel and the PLO in 1993, they signed a peace agreement that gave Palestinians limited self-rule in the Gaza Strip and part of the West Bank. In return, Arafat agreed to renounce violence and recognize Israel. Yet extremists on both sides did not want to <u>comply</u> with this agreement. When Arab extremists committed suicide bombings in Israel, the Israeli military was called in. Israeli troops surrounded Arafat's compound, believing he supported the bombers. Over the years, some Israelis and Palestinians have kept working for peace. A year after Arafat died in 2004, a cease-fire was declared. In 2005, Israel withdrew all Jewish settlements from Gaza and several from the West Bank. ✔

Increasing Tensions

U.S. support for Israel has not been the only source of stress with Muslim nations. The revolutionaries who gained power in Iran were part of a new kind of Islam. These Islamists, including Iran's revolutionary leader Ayatollah **Ruholla Khomeini,** limited women's rights and rejected **westernization,** or the adoption of ideas, culture, and technology from Western regions such as the United States and Europe. Islamists did not want American forces in Saudi Arabia. In some instances, they attacked Americans and other Westerners.

Iraq, ruled by dictator **Saddam Hussein,** was another trouble spot. When Hussein invaded Kuwait in 1990, President George H. W. Bush worked with 28 other countries to make Iraq pull out of Kuwait. When Saddam Hussein refused, these countries launched an attack on Iraq, and the Persian Gulf War began. Within weeks, Hussein withdrew his forces from Kuwait. After-ward, the UN enforced sanctions against Iraq, but Hussein stayed in power. ✔

Check Your Progress

1. Why is the Middle East important to the United States?

_____

_____

2. How did President George H. W. Bush respond to Iraq's invasion of Kuwait?

_____

_____

Vocabulary Builder

The underlined word *comply* means "to follow or obey." Why do you think extremists did not want to follow the terms of the agreement?

_____

_____

✓ Checkpoint

State the position taken by Palestinian Arabs in opposing the creation of the state of Israel.

_____

_____

✓ Checkpoint

List reasons that Islamists pose a problem for the United States.

_____

_____

Question to Think About As you read Section 4 in your textbook and take notes, keep this section focus question in mind: **How have tensions in the Middle East posed concerns for the United States?**

▶ Use this chart to record key information from the section. Some information has been filled in to get you started.

The Middle East
• The Middle East is a European term for ___Southwest Asia___, and it also often includes __Egypt__ and _____. • Three major religions that began in the Middle East are _____, _____, and _____. • The Middle East is of vital interest today because of its _____.

Arab-Israeli Conflict
• Jews moved to Palestine to establish a ___Jewish state___. • In 1948, Jews formed _____. • After war with Israel, Palestinian Arabs became _____. • Wars in 1967 and 1973 resulted in Israel _____. • The Camp David Accords were an agreement between _____ and Israel. • The PLO under Yasir Arafat wanted _____. They led a mass protest known as the _____. • After meeting with Clinton and Israel's leader in 1993, Arafat agreed to _____ _____. Israel agreed to let Palestinians_____ _____. • After the agreement, some Arab extremists launched _____ in Israel. Israel responded by _____. • A year after Arafat died in 2004, a _____ was announced.

Islamist Extremism
• In Iran, many people opposed the ___Shah of Iran___, who was an ally of the United States. • Revolutionaries in Iran banned_____. • Followers of an extreme form of Islam are called _____. • These extremists resent the United States for the following reasons: _____ _____ _____ _____

The Persian Gulf War
• When Iraq invaded ___Kuwait___ in 1990, President George H. W. Bush responded quickly. • The American forces in the Persian Gulf War were led by _____ and _____. • After six weeks of war, Saddam Hussein _____. • The United Nations imposed _____ on Iraq.

Refer to this page to answer the Chapter 28 Focus Question on page 436.

Directions: Circle the letter of the correct answer.

1. Who of the following American Presidents helped to usher in the conservative movement in U.S. politics?

   A Jimmy Carter
   B Ronald Reagan

   C George H. W. Bush
   D Bill Clinton

2. The period of détente between the United States and the Soviet Union ended when

   A the Soviet Union invaded Afghanistan.
   B the United States boycotted the Moscow Olympics.
   C the Soviet Union allowed glasnost.
   D the United States and the Soviet Union agreed to the Strategic Arms Limitation Talks.

3. To what country did the United States apply sanctions to protest its policy of apartheid?

   A Cuba
   B Iraq

   C Soviet Union
   D South Africa

Directions: Follow the steps to answer this question:

How did U.S. foreign policy goals change under President George H. W. Bush and President Bill Clinton with the end of the Cold War?

Step 1: Recall information: Briefly list the major goals of U.S. foreign policy during the Cold War.

Cold War Goals
• • •

Step 2: List the major goals of U.S. foreign policy after the Cold War ended.

Bush's Foreign Policy Goals	Clinton's Foreign Policy Goals
• • •	• • •

Step 3: Draw conclusions: Complete the topic sentence that follows. Then write two or three more sentences that support your topic sentence.

After the Cold War ended, U.S. foreign policy goals _____

_____

_____

_____

Chapter 28 Notetaking Study Guide

Now you are ready to answer the chapter 28 Focus Question: **How did major national and international events affect the nation?**

▶ Complete the charts to help you answer this question. Use the notes that you took for each section.

National Events Change the Nation

President Jimmy Carter struggled with the economic problem of _____.
President Reagan made the following economic changes:
- _____
- _____
President George H. W. Bush faced an economic _____
President Bill Clinton made the following economic changes:
- _____
- _____
- _____

International Events Affect the Nation

President Reagan fought communism by _____,
_____, and _____.
The Soviet Union's economy was weakened when_____.
Some changes under Gorbachev included: _____,_____
_____, and _____.
The Cold War ended when _____.

Other Major World Events

In South Africa, the United States applied _____ to end _____.
In China, the United States responded to the crackdown at Tiananmen Square by

_____.
After the Cold War ended, the United States worried about the spread of

_____.
Two neighboring countries that tested nuclear weapons for the first time in 1998 were
_____ and _____.

Tensions in the Middle East

Palestinian Arabs were unhappy in 1948 when Jews formed _____.
The PLO was led by _____. The PLO wanted a _____
state run by _____.
In 1993, leaders from Israel and the PLO met with Clinton and made the following agreement:
Palestinians would get _____. In return, the PLO would
_____ _.
Islamists are __ _____.
The Persian Gulf War occurred after _____ invaded_____.

Refer to this page to answer the Unit 9 Focus Question on 451.

Challenges for a New Century
(1980–Present)

What You Will Learn

After deadly terrorist attacks in 2001, the United States began a global war against terrorism. Meanwhile, the nation faced many other challenges, including an increasingly global economy, environmental problems, and a changing population.

Chapter 29 Focus Question
As you read this chapter, keep this question in mind: **What challenges face the nation in the 21st century?**

Section 1

The Threat of Terrorism

Section 1 Focus Question
How did the war on terrorism affect American actions at home and abroad? To begin answering this question,
- Understand the pattern of terrorist strikes against Americans.
- Find out about the terrorist attack on September 11, 2001.
- Read about the war on terrorism.
- Learn about the presidential election of 2004.

Section 1 Summary

When the use of terrorism spread to the United States, the nation became involved in a global effort to combat this violence.

Terrorism on the World Stage
Terrorism is the use of violence, often against civilians, to force political or social change. Terrorists use bombings, hijackings, kidnappings, and other violent acts to create a climate of fear. Individuals and groups have carried out terrorist attacks in many nations, from Ireland to Israel. Middle Eastern extremists have used terrorist attacks to try to reduce Western influence in their lands.

The first terrorist attacks against Americans occurred abroad. In 1988, an explosion on an airplane over Scotland killed 270 people, including 189 Americans. Between 1996 and 2000, terrorists in Africa and the Middle East struck U.S. embassies and ships. In 1993, however, a truck bomb exploded under the World Trade Center in New York, killing six people and injuring more than 1,000. In 1995, another truck bomb exploded near a federal office building in Oklahoma City, killing 168 people. The terrorists in this second attack were two American men who resented the federal government. ✓

Key Events

1970	President Nixon forms the Environmental Protection Agency (EPA).
2001	Terrorists attack New York's World Trade Center and the Pentagon, killing thousands of people.
2003	Latinos, or Hispanics, become the largest ethnic minority in the United States.

✓ Checkpoint

Name one way the bombing in 1993 was different from previous terrorist attacks against Americans.

_____

_____

✓ **Checkpoint**

List two ways President Bush responded to the attacks of September 11, 2001.

_____

_____

Vocabulary Builder

To *perpetrate* is to "commit" or "carry out." Reread the bracketed paragraph. How might Bin Laden have helped perpetrate the 9/11 attacks?

_____

_____

✓ **Checkpoint**

Name the two countries the United States attacked in order to combat terrorism.

_____

_____

✓ **Checkpoint**

Why did President Bush send more troops to Iraq?

_____

_____

The Nation Is Attacked

On September 11, 2001, Arab terrorists hijacked four passenger jets departing from the East Coast. The terrorists crashed two of the planes into the World Trade Center in New York City. They crashed a third plane into the Pentagon in Arlington, Virginia, near Washington, D.C. The fourth jet crashed into a field in Pennsylvania when passengers fought the terrorists. The twin towers of the World Trade Center collapsed. Nearly 3,000 people were killed in New York, at the Pentagon, or on the airplanes. President Bush took steps to protect America. He made it a priority to promote **counterterrorism**, action taken against terrorists. In 2001, Bush signed the Patriot Act, which granted authorities sweeping powers to investigate and jail people suspected of having terrorist ties. Suspects could be held indefinitely without being charged or being allowed to consult a lawyer. ✓

The War on Terror

Osama Bin Laden was a wealthy Saudi Arabian who ran a worldwide terrorist network called al Qaeda (al KY duh). He was suspected of having played a role in helping to <u>perpetrate</u> the September 11 attacks. He took refuge in Afghanistan, protected by the ruling Taliban, a group of extremists. When the Taliban refused to give up Bin Laden, the United States attacked. The Taliban lost power, but Bin Laden escaped.

President Bush next targeted the Iraqi dictator Saddam Hussein as a threat. Bush accused Hussein of having ties with Bin Laden and developing weapons of mass destruction (WMDs), such as nuclear and chemical weapons. In March 2003, the United States led a coalition in an attack on Iraq. On May 1, Bush announced the end of major combat. However, rebuilding Iraq proved difficult, and fighting continued even after Hussein was captured in 2003 and executed in 2006. ✓

Frustration at Home and Abroad

President Bush won a second term in 2004. The nation's disagreement over the Iraq war made it hard for him to get things done. Americans grew frustrated as the war dragged on. In 2006, Democrats won control of Congress with the promise to "bring the troops home." But Iraqis were fighting each other for control of their country. President Bush decided to send 20,000 more troops, hoping to help end the violence. ✓

Check Your Progress

1. What is the difference between terrorism and counterterrorism?

   _____

   _____

2. Why was the war in Iraq frustrating for Americans?

   _____

   _____

Question to Think About As you read Section 1 in your textbook and take notes, keep this section focus question in mind: **How did the war on terrorism affect American actions at home and abroad?**

▶ Use these charts to record key information from the section. Some information has been filled in to get you started.

Terrorism on the World Stage		
When	**Where**	**Event**
1988	Scotland	explosion on airplane kills 270 people (189 Americans)
1993		
1995		

The Nation Is Attacked		
When	**Where**	**Event**
2001	New York City, near Washington, D.C.	Four passenger jets are hijacked by _____. Two of the jets _____. One crashes into _____. As a result, President Bush promotes counterterrorism, which is _____. He also signs the Patriot Act, which _____ _____.

The War on Terror

Afghanistan

Osama Bin Laden: leader of al Qaeda terrorist network
The Taliban:

_____

Iraq

Saddam Hussein: _____
American election in 2006: _____

_____

Civil strife in Iraq: _____
President Bush sends more troops: _____

_____

Refer to this page to answer the Chapter 29 Essential Question on page 450.

Key Events

1970	President Nixon forms the Environmental Protection Agency (EPA).
2001	Terrorists attack New York's World Trade Center and the Pentagon, killing thousands of people.
2003	Latinos, or Hispanics, become the largest ethnic minority in the United States.

Vocabulary Builder

The word *advocate* includes the Latin root *voc*, which means "voice." Use this fact and clues from the underlined sentence to write a definition of *advocate*.

_____

_____

✓ Checkpoint

List two different strategies for dealing with economic competition between countries.

_____

_____

✓ Checkpoint

What happened to the American economy in 2007?

_____

Section 2 Focus Question

How do economic and environmental issues link the United States and the world? To begin answering this question,

- Understand how globalization affects the U.S. economy.
- Read about the development of the environmental movement.
- Examine the energy supply.
- Learn about the issue of global warming.

Section 2 Summary

As economic ties between nations grew stronger, the United States faced growing economic and environmental challenges.

A World Linked by Trade

Globalization is the process of creating an international network. One sign of globalization is the fact that foreign trade currently accounts for about 25 percent of the American economy. Foreign goods are cheaper to produce and sell because workers in Latin America, Eastern Europe, and Asia are generally paid less than American workers. A **trade deficit** occurs when a country buys more from other nations than it sells to them. The U.S. trade deficit reached more than $725 billion in 2005. As a result, American companies have begun **outsourcing,** or having work done in other countries. This strategy allows companies to take advantage of cheap labor outside the United States. Critics of outsourcing say it hurts American workers.

Tariffs and free trade are two different strategies for dealing with foreign competition. People who support tariffs believe that raising tariffs on foreign goods will protect American profits and jobs. <u>Those who support **free trade** advocate the removal of trade barriers</u>. In 1994, President Clinton signed the North American Free Trade Agreement (NAFTA), which removed trade barriers between the United States, Mexico, and Canada. NAFTA and global trade regulators such as the World Trade Organization (WTO) have increased trade and generated jobs. However, opponents of free trade argue that it weakens workers' rights and harms the environment. ✓

Financial Meltdown

Late in 2007, the economy of the United States plunged into recession. Unemployment rose and consumer spending fell. The stock market dropped by nearly 40 percent, the largest downturn since the Great Depression. Mortgages and banks were at the heart of the problem. In 2008, Congress agreed to advance up to $750 billion to cash-strapped lenders by creating the Troubled Assets Relief Program, or TARP. In 2009, Congress enacted a massive aid package to stimulate the economy. Nearly $800 billion was set aside for cities, states, and private industries to help them recover. ✓

The Environment

The modern environmental movement began when biologist **Rachel Carson** published *Silent Spring* in 1962. The book led to laws restricting the use of DDT, a chemical pesticide that was killing birds and fish. Public alarm over threats to nature increased due to environmental disasters. In 1969, an oil spill polluted water off the coast of California. In response, the Nixon administration formed the Environmental Protection Agency (EPA). New legislation targeted auto emissions, lakes, and rivers for cleanup. Local governments started recycling programs.

Natural disasters also can harm the environment and the economy. In 2005, Hurricane Katrina tore into Louisiana, Mississippi, and Alabama. Economic losses are estimated to have been $100 billion, and many people lost their homes. ✓

The Energy Supply

The United States has less than 5 percent of the world's people but uses more than 25 percent of the world's energy supplies. In 1973, Arab members of OPEC supported an embargo that cut off Middle Eastern oil supplies to the United States. The price of oil quadrupled. But the need for foreign oil continued to be a problem. In the early 2000s, more Americans turned to smaller cars or to cars that ran on both gasoline and electricity.

People began to look for alternative sources of energy. Coal supplies are plentiful, but burning coal produces air pollution. Also, fossil fuels, such as petroleum and coal, take thousands of years to form. **Renewable resources** are energy resources that are more easily restored by nature. Water, solar, and wind power can be turned into electricity. However, they also have limitations. These resources are not always available and do not always deliver consistent energy. Nuclear power plants can provide near-limitless energy, but they are costly and produce radioactive waste. ✓

The Question of Global Warming

Global warming is a worldwide rise in temperatures. Many scientists blame the current trend of global warming on gases such as carbon dioxide emitted by cars, factories, and homes. The United States signed the Kyoto Protocol in 1997 to reduce carbon dioxide emissions. President Bush rejected this protocol in 2001. ✓

Check Your Progress

1. Why did some American companies turn to outsourcing?

_____

_____

2. What were some responses to America's need for foreign oil?

_____

_____

✓ **Checkpoint**

List three areas of focus for the environmental movement.

_____

_____

_____

✓ **Checkpoint**

Name three renewable energy resources.

_____

_____

_____

✓ **Checkpoint**

Name the source that many scientists believe is responsible for the increase in global temperatures.

_____

_____

Question to Think About As you read Section 2 in your textbook and take notes, keep this section focus question in mind: **How do economic and environmental issues link the United States and the world?**

▶ Use these charts to record key information from the section. Some information has been filled in to get you started.

A World Linked by Trade		
Term	**Definition**	**Why It Is Important**
globalization	creating an international network	
trade deficit		
outsourcing		

Financial Meltdown
A recession started in _____. Congress created the _____. To stimulate the economy, Congress set aside _____.

The Environment		
Early Awareness	**Environmental Actions**	**Critics of the Movement**
In __1962__, Rachel Carson's book _Silent Spring_ criticized _____.	The Nixon administration formed the _____. Legislation targeted ____ _____ _____.	Some critics argue that _____ _____.

The Energy Supply	
Cause	**Effects**
The need for oil	In 1973, OPEC _____. In the 2000s, more people bought _____. Car makers introduced _____. Alternative energy sources were explored, including _____, _____, _____, _____, and _____.

The Question of Global Warming
Global warming is _____. Environmentalists argue that _____. Critics of this theory argue that _____.

Refer to this page to answer the Chapter 29 Essential Question on page 450.

Section 3
Science and Technology

Section 3 Focus Question
How have science and technology transformed modern society?
To begin answering this question,
- Learn how computers led to an information revolution throughout the world.
- Read about important advances in medical science.

Section 3 Summary

The emergence and improvement of computer technology as well as advances in medical science have contributed to many important changes in American life.

The Computer Age
The computer has revolutionized daily life in America, making it possible to store, analyze, and share vast amounts of information in a flash. Before the 1970s, most <u>computing</u> was done by machines called mainframes. They were very large, expensive, and used mostly by governments, universities, and big business. The invention of transistors, or circuits on tiny silicon chips, made smaller computers possible. In 1977, Apple introduced the first computer for home use. International Business Machines (IBM) marketed its own personal computer four years later. During the 1970s, Bill Gates developed software to help ordinary people run computers. He cofounded Microsoft, today one of the world's most successful businesses. By 1990, Americans were buying more than 9 million computers every year.

In 1969, the U.S. Department of Defense began to link its computers with those in several American universities. This electronic network formed the basis for the Internet. The Internet helped to create an information revolution. The World Wide Web was first proposed in 1989 by British scientist Tim Berners-Lee. By 2008, nearly three-quarters of all Americans used the Internet to search for information and to communicate. **E-commerce,** or buying and selling online, grew rapidly as companies used the Internet to advertise and conduct business. The Internet also made it possible for people to post their own opinions, pictures, and videos online.

Not all of the changes caused by technology have been positive. Privacy can be threatened by "hackers" who tap into computers, contributing to a new crime known as identity theft. The use of cellular phones, introduced in 1973, also threatened the privacy of bystanders who are forced to listen to other people's

Key Events

1970 President Nixon forms the Environmental Protection Agency (EPA).

2001 Terrorists attack New York's World Trade Center and the Pentagon, killing thousands of people.

2003 Latinos, or Hispanics, become the largest ethnic minority in the United States.

Vocabulary Builder

Suffixes change word forms. The noun *computer* and the verb *compute* share the same base word. The suffix *–ing* is added to the verb form to show a gerund, which names an action. Use your knowledge of words to define *computing*.

_____

_____

_____

_____

_____

✓ Checkpoint

Name two recently developed tools that help doctors diagnose and treat illnesses.

_____

_____

conversations. Many Americans favor restrictions on cell phone use in public places and when driving, because cell phone use has been blamed for many auto accidents. ✓

Medical Advances

Technology has helped doctors to detect and treat many medical problems. A **laser** is a powerful beam of focused light. Lasers have become critical tools for surgeons because they are more flexible than scalpels and can be focused on very small areas. Doctors use lasers to perform delicate eye and skin surgery. Magnetic resonance imaging (MRI) provides an accurate view of internal organs and helps doctors identify injuries or illnesses and reduce the need for surgery.

Since Acquired Immune Deficiency Syndrome (AIDS) first appeared in the 1980s, the AIDS epidemic has killed millions of people in the United States and worldwide. In some African countries, over 20 percent of the population is infected with the virus that causes AIDS. New drugs have extended the lives of many AIDS sufferers, but they are too expensive for most people in developing countries. In 2003, President Bush promised a $15 billion program to distribute these medicines worldwide.

Cloning is the process of making a genetic double of a plant or an animal. This controversial scientific process made headlines in 1997 when a Scottish researcher cloned a sheep named Dolly. Scientists are also doing stem cell research, hoping to find cures for serious medical conditions. However, using stem cells from human embryos has been controversial. In 2006, President Bush vetoed a bill allowing the use of federal money for such research. ✓

Check Your Progress

1. Explain what is meant by the phrase "information revolution."

_____

_____

_____

2. How has AIDS affected the global population?

_____

_____

_____

Section 3 Notetaking Study Guide

Question to Think About As you read Section 3 in your textbook and take notes, keep this section focus question in mind: **How have science and technology transformed modern society?**

► Use these charts to record key information from the section. Some information has been filled in to get you started.

The Computer Age	
Computer Technology	• Before the __1970s__ , computers were very _____ and _____. • When the _____ was developed, computers became smaller. • The first home computer was introduced by _____ in _____.
The Internet	• This technology was developed to link computers in the Department of _____ and computers in _____. • _____ proposed the World Wide Web in 1989. • By 2008, _____ of all Americans used the Internet. • E-commerce is _____.
Privacy Issues	• Hackers can_____. • Identity theft is_____. • Many Americans favor restricting the use of cell phones in _____.

Medical Advances		
New Tools	**AIDS**	**Other Research**
• Lasers are _____ _____ _____. • Doctors use them to _____ _____ _____. • MRI stands for _____ _____ _____. • MRIs are used to_____ _____ _____.	• The first AIDS cases appeared in _____ . • AIDS has killed _____ _____ worldwide. • AIDS sufferers in Africa often go without medication because _____ _____ _____.	• Cloning is _____ _____ _____. • Dolly was _____ _____ _____. • Another type of medical research uses _____ _____.

Refer to this page to answer the Chapter 29 Essential Question on page 450.

Key Events

1970	President Nixon forms the Environmental Protection Agency (EPA).
2001	Terrorists attack New York's World Trade Center and the Pentagon, killing thousands of people.
2003	Latinos, or Hispanics, become the largest ethnic minority in the United States.

Key Events

1970	President Nixon forms the Environmental Protection Agency (EPA).
2001	Terrorists attack New York's World Trade Center and the Pentagon, killing thousands of people.
2003	Latinos, or Hispanics, become the largest ethnic minority in the United States.

Vocabulary Builder

Which two of the following words are synonyms for the underlined word *incentive*?

motivation   regulation
admiration   disadvantage
hardship   encouragement

_____

_____

✓ Checkpoint

List four countries from which refugees fled after 1965.

_____

_____

_____

_____

Section 4 Focus Question

How have new immigration and population patterns increased diversity? To begin answering this question,
- Understand immigration patterns after 1965.
- Learn about key shifts in the U.S. population.
- Find out how opportunities have expanded for African Americans, women, and Native Americans.
- Identify challenges faced by young Americans.

Section 4 Summary

The American population has changed as immigration trends shifted and diversity has grown. The average age of the American people has increased.

Immigration Affects Society

Immigration to the United States is at its highest rate since the early 1900s. Some immigrants are attracted to the United States by the incentive of economic opportunities. Others are **refugees**, people who flee war or persecution in their own countries.

The largest source of immigration is Latin America. Refugees fled dictators in Cuba and Chile and civil wars in El Salvador and Guatemala. Poverty drove people from Mexico, Central America, and the Caribbean. In 2003, Latinos, or people of Latin American origin, became the largest minority in the United States. Miami, Florida, became the first major U.S. city with a Latino majority. Asian immigration has also grown.

Undocumented workers are laborers who enter the country without legal permission. The Immigration Reform and Control Act of 1986 imposed penalties on employers who hired undocumented workers. The attacks of September 11, 2001, raised new concerns about immigration. Federal officials began to monitor immigrants and foreign-born college students and professors. In 2004, President Bush proposed allowing more **guest workers,** or temporary immigrant workers, to enter the country. Congress did not pass such a law, however. ✓

A Society Transformed

American society is changing. Birthrates have been declining, and people have been living longer due to improved medical care. As a result, the percentage of older Americans is growing. In 2006, about 12.5 percent of the population was 65 or older. Older Americans vote in larger percentages than younger people, giving them political strength. The aging population has raised concerns about health care and Social Security. Many people worry that the number of people collecting benefits from Social Security will rise faster than the number of people paying taxes to fund it.

The population has also shifted. Many people have moved from the Northeast and Midwest to the South and Southwest, areas called the Sun Belt. States in these areas now have more seats in Congress.

In today's economy, people with more education earn more than those with less schooling. Getting that education is more expensive, though. The cost of college tripled from 1986 to 2006.

Families now come in many shapes and sizes. Single women now head many families. In 2007, over 18 million children were being raised by a single parent. These families are more likely to be poor and have more difficulty affording health care than two-parent families. ✓

Americans Face Challenges

More African Americans were earning college degrees and entering the middle class than in the past. Some problems persisted for this group, though. Unemployment and poverty rates remained high among African Americans. Latinos have also made many economic and political gains. They also suffer from high unemployment and poverty rates. Women have also expanded their roles in the workplace and in government, but women lag behind men in earnings. Native Americans have seen some gains, with new businesses arising on reservations. They also have high rates of unemployment and poverty, however.

Health care remains a concern. Heart disease kills more Americans than any other cause. Diabetes and obesity are on the rise. Health professionals urge Americans to eat properly and get regular exercise to control their weight. The rising cost of health care is another worry. In 2008, nearly 46 million Americans had no health insurance.

The Changing Face of Politics

The election of 2008 produced changes in Washington. Barack Obama won the nomination of Democrats for the presidency over former First Lady and U.S. Senator Hillary Clinton. He was the first African American selected by a major party.

Obama promised hope for the future and a less divisive style of politics. Republicans nominated longtime Arizona senator John McCain. He stressed his experience in foreign policy and supported the war in Iraq. Obama, on the other hand, vowed to "bring the troops home."

Nearly 150 years after the end of slavery, Obama won the election to become the nation's first African American President. His win also helped Democrats enlarge their majorities in the House and Senate. ✓

Check Your Progress

1. How are undocumented workers and guest workers different?

_____

2. Why has the average age of the American population changed?

_____

✓ **Checkpoint**

Name three ways in which the U.S. population has changed.

_____

_____

_____

✓ **Checkpoint**

Why was it significant that Obama won the 2008 election?

_____

_____

Question to Think About As you read Section 4 in your textbook and take notes, keep this section focus question in mind: **How have new immigration and population patterns increased diversity?**

▶ Use these charts to record key information from the section. Some information has been filled in to get you started.

Changing Immigration Patterns	
Sources of Immigration	**Immigration Policies**
• Most immigrants seek_____ _____ in America. • _____ flee war or persecution. • The largest source of immigration was _____.	• In 1986, an act imposed penalties on _____. • New worries about immigration were raised by _____. • In 2004, President Bush proposed <u>allowing more guest workers</u>.

A Changing Population			
Older Population	**Population Center**	**Education**	**Changing Family**
The percentage of older Americans has increased because _____ _____ _____. Challenges: _____ _____	People have moved from _____ _____ to _____ _____. This region is called _____.	More years of education leads to _____ _____. The cost of a college education _____.	_____ head more families than in the past. These families are poorer and have less access to _____.

Challenges		
Expanding Opportunities	**Health Care**	**Politics**
Groups making gains: _____ _____ Groups with high unemploy-ment and poverty: _____ _____	Two major illnesses: _____ Advice to fight obesity: _____ _____ Additional problem: _____	Debate over Iraq war: _____ _____ Changes in politics: _____ _____ _____

Refer to this page to answer the Chapter 29 Essential Question on page 450.

Chapter 29 Assessment

Directions: Circle the letter of the correct answer.

1. What was the goal of the Patriot Act?
   - **A** to place tariffs on foreign goods
   - **B** to help authorities investigate terrorists
   - **C** to reduce the trade deficit
   - **D** to encourage immigration

2. What is the result when a country buys more from foreign countries than it sells to them?
   - **A** free trade
   - **B** globalization
   - **C** tariffs
   - **D** a trade deficit

3. Why do AIDS sufferers in developing nations receive few medicines?
   - **A** The medicines are ineffective.
   - **B** The medicines are expensive.
   - **C** The medicines are unethical.
   - **D** The medicines are illegal.

4. What is the largest minority in the United States today?
   - **A** Latinos
   - **B** Asian Americans
   - **C** Native Americans
   - **D** African Americans

Directions: Follow the steps to answer this question:

How might the United States be different in 25 years if current patterns of change continue?

Step 1: Recall information: Describe three patterns of change that you have read about. You might consider the threat of terrorism, the economy, technology, or the population.

Three Important Changes
•
•
•

Step 2: Now choose two changes from your list and predict how they might continue in the next 25 years.

How Two Changes Could Continue
•
•

Step 3: Complete the topic sentence that follows. Then write two or three more sentences that support your topic sentence.

If current patterns continue, in 25 years the United States will _____

_____

_____

_____

Chapter 29 Notetaking Study Guide

Now you are ready to answer the Chapter 29 Essential Question: **What challenges face the nation in the 21st century?**

► Complete the following chart to help you answer this question. Use the notes that you took for each section.

The Threat of Terrorism	
On September 11, 2001, _____ _____ _____.	In response to these attacks, the United States _____ _____.

Economy and the Environment	
Trade Deficits	Trade deficits occur when _____. Outsourcing is _____.
Free Trade	Free trade is _____.
Environmental Movement	This movement has called attention to problems such as _____ _____.

Science and Technology	
Computer Technology	**Medical Science**
The information revolution began when _____. The Internet helps Americans _____ _____.	Medical science has developed new tools, such as _____ and _____, but also faces new challenges such as the _____ epidemic.

A Changing Society	
Immigration	Immigration increased from regions such as _____. As a result, _____ have become America's largest minority.
Aging Population	Declining birthrates and longer life spans have led to _____ _____.
Population Shift	The population has moved from _____ to _____.
Politics	It is changing because _____.

Refer to this page to answer the Unit 9 Essential Question on page 451.

Unit 9 Pulling It Together Activity

Chapter 26 The African American civil rights movement gained momentum after World War II, with organized protests, court decisions, and elected leaders all creating changes. Other groups, such as women and Mexican Americans, also worked for gains.

Chapter 27 To prevent the spread of communism, the United States got deeply involved in Vietnam, and America was sharply divided about the war. When U.S. troops withdrew, Communists took over. Under Nixon, the Watergate affair brought more turmoil.

Chapter 28 Reagan's presidency helped to advance the conservative movement. The Cold War ended when the Soviet Union dissolved, and the United States became the world's only superpower. Conflicts in the Middle East and Islamic extremists presented challenges.

Chapter 29 After terrorists attacked on September 11, 2001, the United States led a war against terrorism throughout the world. Other challenges facing the United States include the global economy and environmental issues.

Think Like a Historian

Read the Unit 9 Essential Question: **How did the United States strive to strengthen democracy at home and to foster democracy abroad?**

▶ Use the organizers on this page and the next to collect information to answer this question.

What are some examples of strengthening democracy at home? Some of them are listed in this organizer. Review your section and chapter notes. Then complete the organizer.

Examples of the United States Striving to Strengthen Democracy at Home

Legislative Action	Court Decisions	Reform Movements
• Civil Rights Act of 1964	• Brown v. Board of Education of Topeka	• African American civil rights movement
•	•	•
•	•	•
•	•	•

Look at the second part of the Unit Essential Question. It asks how the United States strove to foster democracy abroad. The organizer below gives you a part of the answer. Review your section and chapter notes. Then fill in the rest of the organizer.

Examples of the United States Striving to Foster Democracy Abroad

Economic Action
Sanctions:

- economic boycott of South Africa to protest apartheid
-
-

Military Action

- Vietnam—tried to stop the spread of communism
-
-
-

Diplomatic Action
Arms control treaties:

- Strategic Arms Limitation Treaty (SALT)
-
-
-

Peace talks:

-
-
-
-
-